Programming Logic and Design

Stark State College

Joyce Farrell

CENGAGE
Learning·

Australia • Brazil • Japan • Korea • Mexico • Singapore • Spain • United Kingdom • United States

CENGAGE
Learning·

Programming Logic and Design: Stark State College, 8th Edition

Programming Logic and Design, Comprehensive, 8th Edition
Joyce Farrell

For product information and technology assistance, contact us at
Cengage Learning Customer & Sales Support, 1-800-354-9706

For permission to use material from this text or product,
submit all requests online at **cengage.com/permissions**
Further permissions questions can be emailed to
permissionrequest@cengage.com

This book contains select works from existing Cengage Learning resources and
was produced by Cengage Learning Custom Solutions for collegiate use. As such,
those adopting and/or contributing to this work are responsible for editorial
content accuracy, continuity and completeness.

Compilation © 2016 Cengage Learning

ISBN: 978-1-337-32339-0

Cengage Learning
20 Channel Center Street
Boston, MA 02210
USA

Cengage Learning is a leading provider of customized learning solutions with
office locations around the globe, including Singapore, the United Kingdom,
Australia, Mexico, Brazil, and Japan. Locate your local office at:
www.international.cengage.com/region.

Cengage Learning products are represented in Canada by Nelson Education, Ltd.

For your lifelong learning solutions, visit **www.cengage.com/custom.**

Visit our corporate website at **www.cengage.com.**

Brief Contents

Contents

Preface

Programming Logic and Design, Comprehensive, Eighth Edition provides the beginning programmer with a guide to developing structured program logic. This textbook assumes no programming language experience. The writing is nontechnical and emphasizes good programming practices. The examples are business examples; they do not assume mathematical background beyond high school business math. Additionally, the examples illustrate one or two major points; they do not contain so many features that students become lost following irrelevant and extraneous details.

The examples in this book have been created to provide students with a sound background in logic, no matter what programming languages they eventually use to write programs. This book can be used in a stand-alone logic course that students take as a prerequisite to a programming course, or as a companion book to an introductory programming text using any programming language.

Organization and Coverage

Programming Logic and Design, Comprehensive, Eighth Edition introduces students to programming concepts and enforces good style and logical thinking. General programming concepts are introduced in Chapter 1. Chapter 2 discusses using data and introduces two important concepts: modularization and creating high-quality programs. It is important to emphasize these topics early so that students start thinking in a modular way and concentrate on making their programs efficient, robust, easy to read, and easy to maintain.

Chapter 3 covers the key concepts of structure, including what structure is, how to recognize it, and most importantly, the advantages to writing structured programs. This chapter's content is unique among programming texts. The early overview of structure presented here gives students a solid foundation in thinking in a structured way.

Chapters 4, 5, and 6 explore the intricacies of decision making, looping, and array manipulation. Chapter 7 provides details of file handling so students can create programs that process a significant amount of data.

In Chapters 8 and 9, students learn more advanced techniques in array manipulation and modularization. Chapters 10 and 11 provide a thorough yet accessible introduction to concepts and terminology used in object-oriented programming. Students learn about classes, objects, instance and static class members, constructors, destructors, inheritance, and the advantages of object-oriented thinking.

Chapter 12 explores additional object-oriented programming issues: event-driven GUI programming, multithreading, and animation. Chapter 13 discusses system design issues and details the features of the Unified Modeling Language. Chapter 14 is a thorough introduction to important database concepts that business programmers should understand.

Four appendices instruct students in working with numbering systems, large unstructured programs, print charts, and post-test loops and case structures.

Programming Logic and Design combines text explanation with flowcharts and pseudocode examples to provide students with alternative means of expressing structured logic. Numerous detailed, full-program exercises at the end of each chapter illustrate the concepts explained within the chapter, and reinforce understanding and retention of the material presented.

Programming Logic and Design distinguishes itself from other programming logic books in the following ways:

- It is written and designed to be non-language specific. The logic used in this book can be applied to any programming language.

- The examples are everyday business examples; no special knowledge of mathematics, accounting, or other disciplines is assumed.

- The concept of structure is covered earlier than in many other texts. Students are exposed to structure naturally, so they will automatically create properly designed programs.

- Text explanation is interspersed with both flowcharts and pseudocode so students can become comfortable with these logic development tools and understand their interrelationship. Screen shots of running programs also are included, providing students with a clear and concrete image of the programs' execution.

- Complex programs are built through the use of complete business examples. Students see how an application is constructed from start to finish instead of studying only segments of programs.

Features

This text focuses on helping students become better programmers and understand the big picture in program development through a variety of key features. In addition to chapter Objectives, Summaries, and Key Terms, these useful features will help students regardless of their learning style.

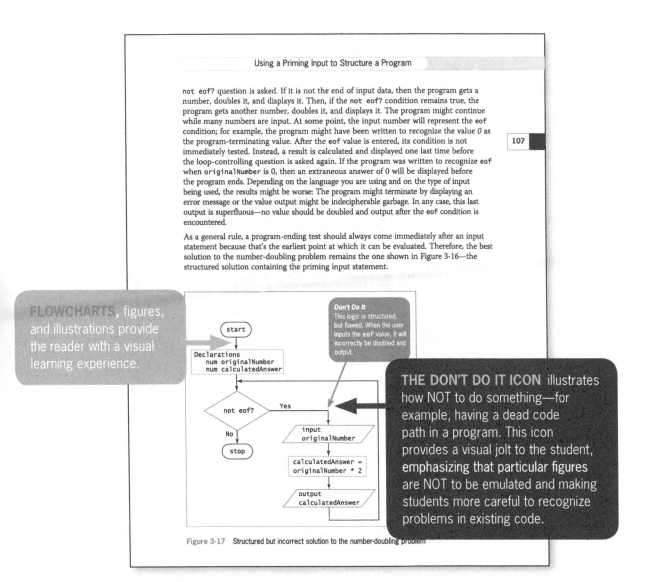

not eof? question is asked. If it is not the end of input data, then the program gets a number, doubles it, and displays it. Then, if the not eof? condition remains true, the program gets another number, doubles it, and displays it. The program might continue while many numbers are input. At some point, the input number will represent the eof condition; for example, the program might have been written to recognize the value 0 as the program-terminating value. After the eof value is entered, its condition is not immediately tested. Instead, a result is calculated and displayed one last time before the loop-controlling question is asked again. If the program was written to recognize eof when originalNumber is 0, then an extraneous answer of 0 will be displayed before the program ends. Depending on the language you are using and on the type of input being used, the results might be worse: The program might terminate by displaying an error message or the value output might be indecipherable garbage. In any case, this last output is superfluous—no value should be doubled and output after the eof condition is encountered.

As a general rule, a program-ending test should always come immediately after an input statement because that's the earliest point at which it can be evaluated. Therefore, the best solution to the number-doubling problem remains the one shown in Figure 3-16—the structured solution containing the priming input statement.

FLOWCHARTS, figures, and illustrations provide the reader with a visual learning experience.

Don't Do It
This logic is structured, but flawed. When the user inputs the eof value, it will incorrectly be doubled and output.

THE DON'T DO IT ICON illustrates how NOT to do something—for example, having a dead code path in a program. This icon provides a visual jolt to the student, emphasizing that particular figures are NOT to be emulated and making students more careful to recognize problems in existing code.

```
start

Declarations
   num originalNumber
   num calculatedAnswer

not eof?     Yes
No                input
stop              originalNumber

                  calculatedAnswer =
                  originalNumber * 2

                  output
                  calculatedAnswer
```

Figure 3-17   Structured but incorrect solution to the number-doubling problem

TWO TRUTHS & A LIE mini quizzes appear after each chapter section, with answers provided. The quiz contains three statements based on the preceding section of text—two statements are true and one is false. Answers give immediate feedback without "giving away" answers to the multiple-choice questions and programming problems later in the chapter. Students also have the option to take these quizzes electronically through the enhanced CourseMate site.

VIDEO LESSONS help explain important chapter concepts. Videos are part of the text's enhanced CourseMate site.

Structuring and Modularizing Unstructured Logic

One advantage to modularizing the steps needed to catch the dog and start the water is that the main program becomes shorter and easier to understand. Another advantage is that if this process needs to be modified, the changes can be made in just one location. For example, if you decided it was necessary to test the water temperature each time you turned on the water, you would add those instructions only once in the modularized version. In the original version in Figure 3-22, you would have to add those instructions in three places, causing more work and increasing the chance for errors.

117

No matter how complicated, any set of steps can always be reduced to combinations of the three basic sequence, selection, and loop structures. These structures can be nested and stacked in an infinite number of ways to describe the logic of any process and to create the logic for every computer program written in the past, present, or future.

 For convenience, many programming languages allow two variations of the three basic structures. The case structure is a variation of the selection structure and the do loop is a variation of the while loop. You can learn about these two structures in Appendix D. Even though these extra structures can be used in most programming languages, all logical problems can be solved without them.

 Watch the video *Structuring Unstructured Logic*.

TWO TRUTHS & A LIE

Structuring and Modularizing Unstructur

1. When you encounter a question in a logical diagram, be ending.

2. In a structured loop, the logic returns to the loop-co loop body executes.

3. If a flowchart or pseudocode contains a question to varies, you can eliminate the question.

NOTES provide additional information— for example, another location in the book that expands on a topic, or a common error to watch out for.

 red.

uld start. However, any type of structure might end before

1. When you encounter a question in a logical diagram, either

Assessment

PROGRAMMING EXERCISES provide opportunities to practice concepts. These exercises increase in difficulty and allow students to explore logical programming concepts. Each exercise can be completed using flowcharts, pseudocode, or both. In addition, instructors can assign the exercises as programming problems to be coded and executed in a particular programming language.

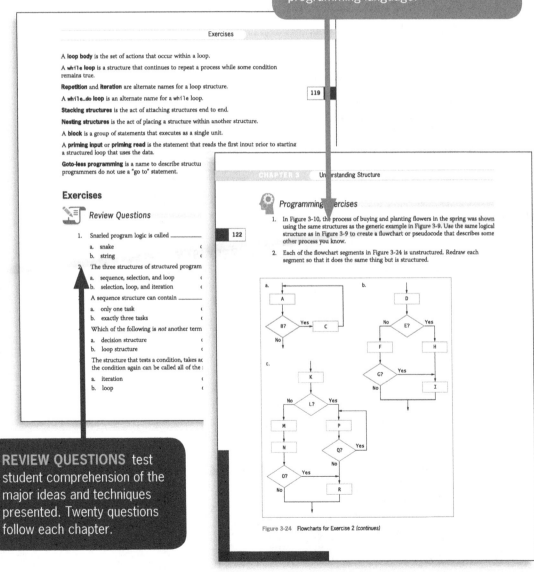

Exercises

A **loop body** is the set of actions that occur within a loop.

A **while loop** is a structure that continues to repeat a process while some condition remains true.

Repetition and **iteration** are alternate names for a loop structure.

A **while_do loop** is an alternate name for a while loop.

Stacking structures is the act of attaching structures end to end.

Nesting structures is the act of placing a structure within another structure.

A **block** is a group of statements that executes as a single unit.

A **priming input** or **priming read** is the statement that reads the first input prior to starting a structured loop that uses the data.

Goto-less programming is a name to describe structu programmers do not use a "go to" statement.

119

Exercises

Review Questions

1. Snarled program logic is called _____
   a. snake
   b. string

2. The three structures of structured program
   a. sequence, selection, and loop
   b. selection, loop, and iteration

   A sequence structure can contain _____
   a. only one task
   b. exactly three tasks

   Which of the following is *not* another term
   a. decision structure
   b. loop structure

   The structure that tests a condition, takes ac the condition again can be called all of the
   a. iteration
   b. loop

122

CHAPTER 3 Understanding Structure

Programming Exercises

1. In Figure 3-10, the process of buying and planting flowers in the spring was shown using the same structures as the generic example in Figure 3-9. Use the same logical structure as in Figure 3-9 to create a flowchart or pseudocode that describes some other process you know.

2. Each of the flowchart segments in Figure 3-24 is unstructured. Redraw each segment so that it does the same thing but is structured.

Figure 3-24 Flowcharts for Exercise 2 (continues)

REVIEW QUESTIONS test student comprehension of the major ideas and techniques presented. Twenty questions follow each chapter.

PERFORMING MAINTENANCE exercises ask students to modify working logic based on new requested specifications. This activity mirrors real-world tasks that students are likely to encounter in their first programming jobs.

ESSAY QUESTIONS present personal and ethical issues that programmers must consider. These questions can be used for written assignments or as a starting point for classroom discussion.

...escribing how to do a

...escribing how to

10. Draw a structured flowchart or write structured pseudocode describing how to wrap a present. Include at least two decisions and two loops.

11. Draw a structured flowchart or write structured pseudocode describing the steps to prepare your favorite dish. Include at least two decisions and two loops.

Performing Maintenance

1. A file named MAINTENANCE03-01.txt is included with your downloadable student files. Assume that this program is a working program in your organization and that it needs modifications as described in the comments (lines that begin with two slashes) at the beginning of the file. Your job is to alter the program to meet the new specifications.

Find the Bugs

1. Your downloadable files for Chapter 3 include DEBU... and DE...G03-03.txt. Each file starts with some com... Comments are lines that begin with two slashes (//). F... contains pseudocode that has one or more bugs you...

2. Your downloadable files for Chapter 3 include a file containing a flowchart with syntax and/or logical error... then find and correct all the bugs.

Understanding Structure

Game Zone

1. Choose a simple children's game and describe its log... or pseudocode. For example, you might try to expla... Chairs; Duck, Duck, Goose; the card game War; or... Meenie, Minie, Moe.

2. Choose a television game show such as *Wheel of Fo...* its rules using a structured flowchart or pseudocode...

3. Choose a sport such as baseball or football and des... play period (such as an at-bat in baseball or a posse... structured flowchart or pseudocode.

Up for Discussion

1. Find more information about one of the following people and explain why he or she is important to structured programming: Edsger Dijkstra, Corrado Bohm, Giuseppe Jacopini, and Grace Hopper.

2. Computer programs can contain structures within structures and stacked structures, creating very large programs. Computers also can perform millions of arithmetic calculations in an hour. How can we possibly know the results are correct?

3. Develop a checklist of rules you can use to help you determine whether a flowchart or pseudocode segment is structured.

GAME ZONE EXERCISES are included at the end of each chapter. Students can create games as an additional entertaining way to understand key programming concepts.

DEBUGGING EXERCISES are included with each chapter because examining programs critically and closely is a crucial programming skill. Students can download these exercises at *www.cengagebrain.com* and through the CourseMate available for this text. These files are also available to instructors at *sso.cengage.com*.

Other Features of the Text

This edition of the text includes many features to help students become better programmers and understand the big picture in program development.

- **Clear explanations**. The language and explanations in this book have been refined over eight editions, providing the clearest possible explanations of difficult concepts.

- **Emphasis on structure**. More than its competitors, this book emphasizes structure. Chapter 3 provides an early picture of the major concepts of structured programming.

- **Emphasis on modularity**. From the second chapter, students are encouraged to write code in concise, easily manageable, and reusable modules. Instructors have found that modularization should be encouraged early to instill good habits and a clearer understanding of structure.

- **Objectives**. Each chapter begins with a list of objectives so the student knows the topics that will be presented in the chapter. In addition to providing a quick reference to topics covered, this feature provides a useful study aid.

- **Chapter summaries**. Following each chapter is a summary that recaps the programming concepts and techniques covered in the chapter.

- **Key terms**. Each chapter lists key terms and their definitions; the list appears in the order the terms are encountered in the chapter. A glossary at the end of the book lists all the key terms in alphabetical order, along with working definitions.

CourseMate

The more you study, the better the results. Make the most of your study time by accessing everything you need to succeed in one place. Read your textbook, review flashcards, watch videos, and take practice quizzes online. CourseMate goes beyond the book to deliver what you need! Learn more at *www.cengage.com/coursemate*.

The *Programming Logic and Design* CourseMate includes:

- **Video Lessons**. Designed and narrated by the author, videos in each chapter explain and enrich important concepts.

- **Two Truths & A Lie**, **Debugging Exercises**, and **Performing Maintenance**. Complete popular exercises from the text online.

- **An interactive eBook**. Highlighting and note-taking, flashcards, quizzing, study games, and more.

Instructors may add CourseMate to the textbook package, or students may purchase CourseMate directly at *www.cengagebrain.com*.

Instructor Resources

The following teaching tools are available to the instructor for download through our Instructor Companion Site at *sso.cengage.com*.

- **Electronic Instructor's Manual**. The Instructor's Manual follows the text chapter by chapter to assist in planning and organizing an effective, engaging course. The manual includes learning objectives, chapter overviews, lecture notes, ideas for classroom activities, and abundant additional resources. A sample course syllabus is also available.

- **PowerPoint Presentations**. This text provides PowerPoint slides to accompany each chapter. Slides are included to guide classroom presentation, to make available to students for chapter review, or to print as classroom handouts.

- **Solutions**. Solutions to review questions and exercises are provided to assist with grading.

- **Test Bank®**. Cengage Learning Testing Powered by Cognero is a flexible, online system that allows you to:

  - author, edit, and manage test bank content from multiple Cengage Learning solutions

  - create multiple test versions in an instant

  - deliver tests from your LMS, your classroom, or anywhere you want

Additional Options

- **Visual Logic™ software**. Visual Logic is a simple but powerful tool for teaching programming logic and design without traditional high-level programming language syntax. Visual Logic also interprets and executes flowcharts, providing students with immediate and accurate feedback.

- **PAL (Programs to Accompany) Guides**. Together with *Programming Logic and Design*, these brief books, or PAL Guides, provide an excellent opportunity to learn the fundamentals of programming while gaining exposure to a programming language. PAL guides are available for C++, Java, and Visual Basic; please contact your sales rep for more information on how to add the PAL guides to your course.

Acknowledgments

I would like to thank all of the people who helped to make this book a reality, especially Dan Seiter, Development Editor; Alyssa Pratt, Senior Content Developer; Jim Gish, Senior Product Manager; and Jennifer Feltri-George, Content Project Manager. I am grateful to be able to work with so many fine people who are dedicated to producing quality instructional materials.

I am indebted to the many reviewers who provided helpful and insightful comments during the development of this book, including Gail Gehrig, Florida State College at Jacksonville; Yvonne Leonard, Coastal Carolina Community College; and Meri Winchester, McHenry County College.

Thanks, too, to my husband, Geoff, and our daughters, Andrea and Audrey, for their support. This book, as were all its previous editions, is dedicated to them.

–Joyce Farrell

An Overview of Computers and Programming

Understanding Computer Systems

CHAPTER 1

An Overview
of Computers
and Programming

In this chapter, you will learn about:

◎ Computer systems

◎ Simple program logic

◎ The steps involved in the program development cycle

◎ Pseudocode statements and flowchart symbols

◎ Using a sentinel value to end a program

◎ Programming and user environments

◎ The evolution of programming models

Understanding Computer Systems

A **computer system** is a combination of all the components required to process and store data using a computer. Every computer system is composed of multiple pieces of hardware and software.

- **Hardware** is the equipment, or the physical devices, associated with a computer. For example, keyboards, mice, speakers, and printers are all hardware. The devices are manufactured differently for computers of varying sizes—for example, large mainframes, laptops, and very small devices embedded into products such as telephones, cars, and thermostats. However, the types of operations performed by different-sized computers are very similar. When you think of a computer, you often think of its physical components first, but for a computer to be useful, it needs more than devices; a computer needs to be given instructions. Just as your stereo equipment does not do much until you provide music, computer hardware needs instructions that control how and when data items are input, how they are processed, and the form in which they are output or stored.

- **Software** is computer instructions that tell the hardware what to do. Software is **programs**, which are instruction sets written by programmers. You can buy prewritten programs that are stored on a disk or that you download from the Web. For example, businesses use word-processing and accounting programs, and casual computer users enjoy programs that play music and games. Alternatively, you can write your own programs. When you write software instructions, you are **programming**. This book focuses on the programming process.

Software can be classified into two broad types:

- **Application software** comprises all the programs you apply to a task, such as word-processing programs, spreadsheets, payroll and inventory programs, and games. When you hear people say they have "downloaded an **app** onto a mobile device," they are simply using an abbreviation of *application*.

- **System software** comprises the programs that you use to manage your computer, including operating systems such as Windows, Linux, or UNIX for larger computers and Google Android and Apple iOS for smartphones.

This book focuses on the logic used to write application software programs, although many of the concepts apply to both types of software.

Together, computer hardware and software accomplish three major operations in most programs:

- **Input**—Data items enter the computer system and are placed in memory, where they can be processed. Hardware devices that perform input operations include keyboards and mice. **Data items** include all the text, numbers, and other raw material that are entered into and processed by a computer. In business, many of the data items used are facts and figures about such entities as products, customers, and personnel. However, data can also include items such as images, sounds, and a user's mouse or finger-swiping movements.

- **Processing**—Processing data items may involve organizing or sorting them, checking them for accuracy, or performing calculations with them. The hardware component that performs these types of tasks is the **central processing unit**, or **CPU**. Some devices, such as tablets and smartphones, usually contain multiple processors. Writing programs that efficiently use several CPUs requires special techniques.

- **Output**—After data items have been processed, the resulting information usually is sent to a printer, monitor, or some other output device so people can view, interpret, and use the results. Programming professionals often use the term *data* for input items, but use the term **information** for data that has been processed and output. Sometimes you place output on **storage devices**, such as your hard drive, flash media, or a cloud-based device. (The **cloud** refers to devices at remote locations accessed through the Internet.) People cannot read data directly from these storage devices, but the devices hold information for later retrieval. When you send output to a storage device, sometimes it is used later as input for another program.

You write computer instructions in a computer **programming language** such as Visual Basic, C#, C++, or Java. Just as some people speak English and others speak Japanese, programmers write programs in different languages. Some programmers work exclusively in one language, whereas others know several and use the one that is best suited to the task at hand.

The instructions you write using a programming language are called **program code**; when you write instructions, you are **coding the program**.

Every programming language has rules governing its word usage and punctuation. These rules are called the language's **syntax**. Mistakes in a language's usage are **syntax errors**. If you ask, "How the geet too store do I?" in English, most people can figure out what you probably mean, even though you have not used proper English syntax—you have mixed up the word order, misspelled a word, and used an incorrect word. However, computers are not nearly as smart as most people; in this case, you might as well have asked the computer, "Xpu mxv ort dod nmcad bf B?" Unless the syntax is perfect, the computer cannot interpret the programming language instruction at all.

When you write a program, you usually type its instructions using a keyboard. When you type program instructions, they are stored in **computer memory**, which is a computer's temporary, internal storage. **Random access memory**, or **RAM**, is a form of internal, volatile memory. Programs that are currently running and data items that are currently being used are stored in RAM for quick access. Internal storage is **volatile**—its contents are lost when the computer is turned off or loses power. Usually, you want to be able to retrieve and perhaps modify the stored instructions later, so you also store them on a permanent storage device, such as a disk. Permanent storage devices are **nonvolatile**—that is, their contents are persistent and are retained even when power is lost. If you have had a power loss while working on a computer, but were able to recover your work when power was restored, it's not because the work was still in RAM. Your system has been configured to automatically save your work at regular intervals on a nonvolatile storage device—often your hard drive.

After a computer program is typed using programming language statements and stored in memory, it must be translated to **machine language** that represents the millions of on/off circuits within the computer. Your programming language statements are called **source code**, and the translated machine language statements are **object code**.

Each programming language uses a piece of software, called a **compiler** or an **interpreter**, to translate your source code into machine language. Machine language is also called **binary**

4

language, and is represented as a series of 0s and 1s. The compiler or interpreter that translates your code tells you if any programming language component has been used incorrectly. Syntax errors are relatively easy to locate and correct because your compiler or interpreter highlights them. If you write a computer program using a language such as C++ but spell one of its words incorrectly or reverse the proper order of two words, the software lets you know that it found a mistake by displaying an error message as soon as you try to translate the program.

Although there are differences in how compilers and interpreters work, their basic function is the same—to translate your programming statements into code the computer can use. When you use a compiler, an entire program is translated before it can execute; when you use an interpreter, each instruction is translated just prior to execution. Usually, you do not choose which type of translation to use—it depends on the programming language. However, there are some languages for which both compilers and interpreters are available.

After a program's source code is successfully translated to machine language, the computer can carry out the program instructions. When instructions are carried out, a program **runs**, or **executes**. In a typical program, some input will be accepted, some processing will occur, and results will be output.

Besides the popular, comprehensive programming languages such as Java and C++, many programmers use **scripting languages** (also called **scripting programming languages** or **script languages**) such as Python, Lua, Perl, and PHP. Scripts written in these languages usually can be typed directly from a keyboard and are stored as text rather than as binary executable files. Scripting language programs are interpreted line by line each time the program executes, instead of being stored in a compiled (binary) form. Still, with all programming languages, each instruction must be translated to machine language before it can execute.

TWO TRUTHS & A LIE

Understanding Computer Systems

In each Two Truths and a Lie section, two of the numbered statements are true, and one is false. Identify the false statement and explain why it is false.

1. Hardware is the equipment, or the devices, associated with a computer. Software is computer instructions.

2. The grammar rules of a computer programming language are its syntax.

3. You write programs using machine language, and translation software converts the statements to a programming language.

The false statement is #3. You write programs using a programming language such as Visual Basic or Java, and a translation program (called a compiler or interpreter) converts the statements to machine language, which is 0s and 1s.

Understanding Simple Program Logic

A program with syntax errors cannot be fully translated and cannot execute. A program with no syntax errors is translatable and can execute, but it still might contain **logical errors** and produce incorrect output as a result. For a program to work properly, you must develop correct **logic**; that is, you must write program instructions in a specific sequence, you must not leave any instructions out, and you must not add extraneous instructions.

Suppose you instruct someone to make a cake as follows:

```
Get a bowl
Stir
Add two eggs
Add a gallon of gasoline
Bake at 350 degrees for 45 minutes
Add three cups of flour
```

Don't Do It
Don't bake a cake like this!

 The dangerous cake-baking instructions are shown with a Don't Do It icon. You will see this icon when the book contains an unrecommended programming practice that is used as an example of what *not* to do.

Even though the cake-baking instructions use English language syntax correctly, the instructions are out of sequence, some are missing, and some instructions belong to procedures other than baking a cake. If you follow these instructions, you will not make an edible cake, and you may end up with a disaster. Many logical errors are more difficult to locate than syntax errors—it is easier for you to determine whether *eggs* is spelled incorrectly in a recipe than it is for you to tell if there are too many eggs or if they are added too soon.

Just as baking directions can be provided in Mandarin, Urdu, or Spanish, program logic can be expressed correctly in any number of programming languages. Because this book is not concerned with a specific language, the programming examples could have been written in Visual Basic, C++, or Java. For convenience, this book uses instructions written in English!

 After you learn French, you automatically know, or can easily figure out, many Spanish words. Similarly, after you learn one programming language, it is much easier to understand several other languages.

Most simple computer programs include steps that perform input, processing, and output. Suppose you want to write a computer program to double any number you provide. You can write the program in a programming language such as Visual Basic or Java, but if you were to write it using English-like statements, it would look like this:

```
input myNumber
set myAnswer = myNumber * 2
output myAnswer
```

The number-doubling process includes three instructions:

- The instruction to input myNumber is an example of an input operation. When the computer interprets this instruction, it knows to look to an input device to obtain a number. When you work in a specific programming language, you write instructions that tell the computer which device to access for input. For example, when a user enters a number as data for a program, the user might click on the number with a mouse, type it from a keyboard, or speak it into a microphone. Logically, however, it doesn't matter which hardware device is used, as long as the computer knows to accept a number. When the number is retrieved from an input device, it is placed in the computer's memory in a variable named myNumber. A **variable** is a named memory location whose value can vary—for example, the value of myNumber might be 3 when the program is used for the first time and 45 when it is used the next time. In this book, variable names will not contain embedded spaces; for example, the book will use myNumber instead of my Number.

 From a logical perspective, when you input, process, or output a value, the hardware device is irrelevant. The same is true in your daily life. If you follow the instruction "Get eggs for the cake," it does not really matter if you purchase them from a store or harvest them from your own chickens—you get the eggs either way. There might be different practical considerations to getting the eggs, just as there are for getting data from a large database as opposed to getting data from an inexperienced user working at home on a laptop computer. For now, this book is only concerned with the logic of operations, not the minor details.

 A college classroom is similar to a named variable in that its name (perhaps 204 Adams Building) can hold different contents at different times. For example, your Logic class might meet there on Monday night, and a math class might meet there on Tuesday morning.

- The instruction set myAnswer = myNumber * 2 is an example of a processing operation. In most programming languages, an asterisk is used to indicate multiplication, so this instruction means "Change the value of the memory location myAnswer to equal the value at the memory location myNumber times two." Mathematical operations are not the only kind of processing operations, but they are very typical. As with input operations, the type of hardware used for processing is irrelevant—after you write a program, it can be used on computers of different brand names, sizes, and speeds.

- In the number-doubling program, the output myAnswer instruction is an example of an output operation. Within a particular program, this statement could cause the output to appear on the monitor (which might be a flat-panel plasma screen or a smartphone display), or the output could go to a printer (which could be laser or ink-jet), or the output could be written to a disk or DVD. The logic of the output process is the same no matter what hardware device you use. When this instruction executes, the value stored in memory at the location named myAnswer is sent to an output device. (The output value also remains in computer memory until something else is stored at the same memory location or power is lost.)

 Watch the video *A Simple Program.*

Computer memory consists of millions of numbered locations where data can be stored. The memory location of **myNumber** has a specific numeric address, but when you write programs, you seldom need to be concerned with the value of the memory address; instead, you use the easy-to-remember name you created. Computer programmers often refer to memory addresses using hexadecimal notation, or base 16. Using this system, they might use a value like 42FF01A to refer to a memory address. Despite the use of letters, such an address is still a hexadecimal number. Appendix A contains information on this numbering system.

TWO TRUTHS & A LIE

Understanding Simple Program Logic

1. A program with syntax errors can execute but might produce incorrect results.

2. Although the syntax of programming languages differs, the same program logic can be expressed in different languages.

3. Most simple computer programs include steps that perform input, processing, and output.

The false statement is #1. A program with syntax errors cannot execute; a program with no syntax errors can execute, but might produce incorrect results.

Understanding the Program Development Cycle

A programmer's job involves writing instructions (such as those in the doubling program in the preceding section), but a professional programmer usually does not just sit down at a computer keyboard and start typing. Figure 1-1 illustrates the **program development cycle**, which can be broken down into at least seven steps:

1. Understand the problem.
2. Plan the logic.
3. Code the program.
4. Use software (a compiler or interpreter) to translate the program into machine language.
5. Test the program.
6. Put the program into production.
7. Maintain the program.

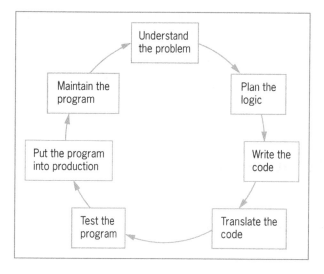

Figure 1-1   The program development cycle
© 2015 Cengage Learning

Understanding the Problem

Professional computer programmers write programs to satisfy the needs of others, called **users** or **end users**. Examples of end users include a Human Resources department that needs a printed list of all employees, a Billing department that wants a list of clients who are 30 or more days overdue on their payments, and an Order department that needs a Web site to provide buyers with an online shopping cart. Because programmers are providing a service to these users, programmers must first understand what the users want. When a program runs, you usually think of the logic as a cycle of input-processing-output operations, but when you plan a program, you think of the output first. After you understand what the desired result is, you can plan the input and processing steps to achieve it.

Suppose the director of Human Resources says to a programmer, "Our department needs a list of all employees who have been here over five years, because we want to invite them to a special thank-you dinner." On the surface, this seems like a simple request. An experienced programmer, however, will know that the request is incomplete. For example, you might not know the answers to the following questions about which employees to include:

- Does the director want a list of full-time employees only, or a list of full- and part-time employees together?

- Does she want to include people who have worked for the company on a month-to-month contractual basis over the past five years, or only regular, permanent employees?

- Do the listed employees need to have worked for the organization for five years as of today, as of the date of the dinner, or as of some other cutoff date?

- What about an employee who worked three years, took a two-year leave of absence, and has been back for three years?

The programmer cannot make any of these decisions; the user (in this case, the Human Resources director) must address these questions.

More decisions still might be required. For example:

- What data should be included for each listed employee? Should the list contain both first and last names? Social Security numbers? Phone numbers? Addresses?

- Should the list be in alphabetical order? Employee ID number order? Length-of-service order? Some other order?

- Should the employees be grouped by any criteria, such as department number or years of service?

Several pieces of documentation are often provided to help the programmer understand the problem. **Documentation** consists of all the supporting paperwork for a program; it might include items such as original requests for the program from users, sample output, and descriptions of the data items available for input.

Understanding the problem might be even more difficult if you are writing an app that you hope to market for mobile devices. Business developers are usually approached by a user with a need, but successful developers of mobile apps often try to identify needs that users aren't even aware of yet. For example, no one knew they wanted to play *Angry Birds* or leave messages on Facebook before those applications were developed. Mobile app developers also must consider a wider variety of user skills than programmers who develop applications that are used internally in a corporation. Mobile app developers must make sure their programs work with a range of screen sizes and hardware specifications because software competition is intense and the hardware changes quickly.

Fully understanding the problem may be one of the most difficult aspects of programming. On any job, the description of what the user needs may be vague—worse yet, users may not really know what they want, and users who think they know frequently change their minds after seeing sample output. A good programmer is often part counselor, part detective!

 Watch the video *The Program Development Cycle, Part 1*.

Planning the Logic

The heart of the programming process lies in planning the program's logic. During this phase of the process, the programmer plans the steps of the program, deciding what steps to include and how to order them. You can plan the solution to a problem in many ways. The two most common planning tools are flowcharts and pseudocode. Both tools involve writing the steps of the program in English, much as you would plan a trip on paper before getting into the car or plan a party theme before shopping for food and favors.

You may hear programmers refer to planning a program as "developing an algorithm." An **algorithm** is the sequence of steps or rules you follow to solve a problem.

9

In addition to flowcharts and pseudocode, programmers use a variety of other tools to help in program development. One such tool is an **IPO chart**, which delineates input, processing, and output tasks. Some object-oriented programmers also use **TOE charts**, which list tasks, objects, and events. In the comprehensive version of this book, you can learn about *storyboards* and the *UML*, which are frequently used in interactive, object-oriented applications.

The programmer shouldn't worry about the syntax of any particular language during the planning stage, but should focus on figuring out what sequence of events will lead from the available input to the desired output. Planning the logic includes thinking carefully about all the possible data values a program might encounter and how you want the program to handle each scenario. The process of walking through a program's logic on paper before you actually write the program is called **desk-checking**. You will learn more about planning the logic throughout this book; in fact, the book focuses on this crucial step almost exclusively.

Coding the Program

After the logic is developed, only then can the programmer write the source code for a program. Hundreds of programming languages are available. Programmers choose particular languages because some have built-in capabilities that make them more efficient than others at handling certain types of operations. Despite their differences, programming languages are quite alike in their basic capabilities—each can handle input operations, arithmetic processing, output operations, and other standard functions. The logic developed to solve a programming problem can be executed using any number of languages. Only after choosing a language must the programmer be concerned with proper punctuation and the correct spelling of commands—in other words, using the correct *syntax*.

Some experienced programmers can successfully combine logic planning and program coding in one step. This may work for planning and writing a very simple program, just as you can plan and write a postcard to a friend using one step. A good term paper or a Hollywood screenplay, however, needs planning before writing—and so do most programs.

Which step is harder: planning the logic or coding the program? Right now, it may seem to you that writing in a programming language is a very difficult task, considering all the spelling and syntax rules you must learn. However, the planning step is actually more difficult. Which is more difficult: thinking up the twists and turns to the plot of a best-selling mystery novel, or writing a translation of an existing novel from English to Spanish? And who do you think gets paid more, the writer who creates the plot or the translator? (Try asking friends to name any famous translator!)

Using Software to Translate the Program into Machine Language

Even though there are many programming languages, each computer knows only one language—its machine language, which consists of 1s and 0s. Computers understand machine language because they are made up of thousands of tiny electrical switches, each of which can be set in either the on or off state, which is represented by a 1 or 0, respectively.

Languages like Java or Visual Basic are available for programmers because someone has written a translator program (a compiler or interpreter) that changes the programmer's English-like **high-level programming language** into the **low-level machine language** that the computer understands. When you learn the syntax of a programming language, the commands work on any machine on which the language software has been installed. However, your commands then are translated to machine language, which differs in various computer makes and models.

If you write a programming statement incorrectly (for example, by misspelling a word, using a word that doesn't exist in the language, or using "illegal" grammar), the translator program doesn't know how to proceed and issues an error message identifying a syntax error. Although making errors is never desirable, syntax errors are not a programmer's deepest concern, because the compiler or interpreter catches every syntax error and displays a message that notifies you of the problem. The computer will not execute a program that contains even one syntax error.

Typically, a programmer develops logic, writes the code, and compiles the program, receiving a list of syntax errors. The programmer then corrects the syntax errors and compiles the program again. Correcting the first set of errors frequently reveals new errors that originally were not apparent to the compiler. For example, if you could use an English compiler and submit the sentence *The dg chase the cat*, the compiler at first might point out only one syntax error. The second word, *dg*, is illegal because it is not part of the English language. Only after you corrected the word to *dog* would the compiler find another syntax error on the third word, *chase*, because it is the wrong verb form for the subject *dog*. This doesn't mean *chase* is necessarily the wrong word. Maybe *dog* is wrong; perhaps the subject should be *dogs*, in which case *chase* is right. Compilers don't always know exactly what you mean, nor do they know what the proper correction should be, but they do know when something is wrong with your syntax.

 Watch the video *The Program Development Cycle, Part 2.*

Programmers often compile their code one section at a time. It is far less overwhelming and easier to understand errors that are discovered in 20 lines of code at a time than to try to correct mistakes after 2,000 lines of code have been written. When writing a program, a programmer might need to recompile the code several times. An executable program is created only when the code is free of syntax errors. After a program has been translated into machine language, the machine language program is saved and can be run any number of times without repeating the translation step. You only need to retranslate your code if you make changes to your source code statements. Figure 1-2 shows a diagram of this entire process.

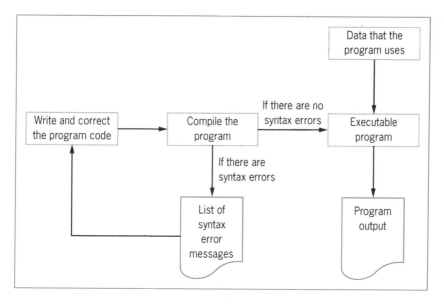

Figure 1-2   Creating an executable program
© 2015 Cengage Learning

Testing the Program

A program that is free of syntax errors is not necessarily free of logical errors. A logical error results when you use a syntactically correct statement but use the wrong one for the current context. For example, the English sentence *The dog chases the cat*, although syntactically perfect, is not logically correct If the dog chases a ball or the cat is the aggressor.

Once a program is free of syntax errors, the programmer can test it—that is, execute it with some sample data to see whether the results are logically correct. Recall the number-doubling program:

```
input myNumber
set myAnswer = myNumber * 2
output myAnswer
```

If you execute the program, provide the value 2 as input to the program, and the answer 4 is displayed, you have executed one successful test run of the program.

However, if the answer 40 is displayed, maybe the program contains a logical error. Maybe the second line of code was mistyped with an extra zero, so that the program reads:

```
input myNumber
set myAnswer = myNumber * 20
output myAnswer
```

Don't Do It
The programmer typed 20 instead of 2.

Placing 20 instead of 2 in the multiplication statement caused a logical error. Notice that nothing is syntactically wrong with this second program—it is just as reasonable to multiply a number by 20 as by 2—but if the programmer intends only to double myNumber, then a logical error has occurred.

The process of finding and correcting program errors is called **debugging**. You debug a program by testing it using many sets of data. For example, if you write the program to double a number, then enter 2 and get an output value of 4, that doesn't necessarily mean you have a correct program. Perhaps you have typed this program by mistake:

```
input myNumber
set myAnswer = myNumber + 2
output myAnswer
```

Don't Do It
The programmer typed
"+" instead of "*".

An input of 2 results in an answer of 4, but that doesn't mean your program doubles numbers—it actually only adds 2 to them. If you test your program with additional data and get the wrong answer—for example, if you enter 7 and get an answer of 9—you know there is a problem with your code.

Selecting test data is somewhat of an art in itself, and it should be done carefully. If the Human Resources department wants a list of the names of five-year employees, it would be a mistake to test the program with a small sample file of only long-term employees. If no newer employees are part of the data being used for testing, you do not really know if the program would have eliminated them from the five-year list. Many companies do not know that their software has a problem until an unusual circumstance occurs—for example, the first time an employee has more than nine dependents, the first time a customer orders more than 999 items at a time, or when the Internet runs out of allocated IP addresses, a problem known as *IPV4 exhaustion*.

Putting the Program into Production

Once the program is thoroughly tested and debugged, it is ready for the organization to use. Putting the program into production might mean simply running the program once, if it was written to satisfy a user's request for a special list. However, the process might take months if the program will be run on a regular basis, or if it is one of a large system of programs being developed. Perhaps data-entry people must be trained to prepare the input for the new program, users must be trained to understand the output, or existing data in the company must be changed to an entirely new format to accommodate this program. **Conversion**, the entire set of actions an organization must take to switch over to using a new program or set of programs, can sometimes take months or years to accomplish.

Maintaining the Program

After programs are put into production, making necessary changes is called **maintenance**. Maintenance can be required for many reasons: for example, because new tax rates are legislated, the format of an input file is altered, or the end user requires additional information not included in the original output specifications. Frequently, your first programming job will require maintaining previously written programs. When you maintain the programs others have written, you will appreciate the effort the original programmer put into writing clear code, using reasonable variable names, and documenting his or her work. When you make changes to existing programs, you repeat the development cycle. That is, you must understand the changes, then plan, code, translate, and test them before putting them into production. If a substantial number of program changes are required, the original program might be retired, and the program development cycle might be started for a new program.

14

 Watch the video *The Program Development Cycle, Part 3.*

TWO TRUTHS & A LIE

Understanding the Program Development Cycle

1. Understanding the problem that must be solved can be one of the most difficult aspects of programming.

2. The two most commonly used logic-planning tools are flowcharts and pseudocode.

3. Flowcharting a program is a very different process if you use an older programming language instead of a newer one.

The false statement is #3. Despite their differences, programming languages are quite alike in their basic capabilities—each can handle input operations, arithmetic processing, output operations, and other standard functions. The logic developed to solve a programming problem can be executed using any number of languages.

Using Pseudocode Statements and Flowchart Symbols

When programmers plan the logic for a solution to a programming problem, they often use one of two tools: pseudocode (pronounced *sue-doe-code*) or flowcharts.

- **Pseudocode** is an English-like representation of the logical steps it takes to solve a problem. *Pseudo* is a prefix that means *false*, and to *code* a program means to put it in a programming language; therefore, *pseudocode* simply means *false code*, or sentences that appear to have been written in a computer programming language but do not necessarily follow all the syntax rules of any specific language.

- A **flowchart** is a pictorial representation of the same thing.

Writing Pseudocode

You have already seen examples of statements that represent pseudocode earlier in this chapter, and there is nothing mysterious about them. The following five statements constitute a pseudocode representation of a number-doubling problem:

```
start
   input myNumber
   set myAnswer = myNumber * 2
   output myAnswer
stop
```

Using pseudocode involves writing down all the steps you will use in a program. Usually, programmers preface their pseudocode with a beginning statement like start and end it with a terminating statement like stop. The statements between start and stop look like English and are indented slightly so that start and stop stand out. Most programmers do not bother with punctuation such as periods at the end of pseudocode statements, although it would not be wrong to use them if you prefer that style. Similarly, there is no need to capitalize the first word in a statement, although you might choose to do so.

Pseudocode is fairly flexible because it is a planning tool, and not the final product. Therefore, for example, you might prefer any of the following:

- Instead of start and stop, some pseudocode developers would use other terms such as begin and end.

- Instead of writing input myNumber, some developers would write get myNumber or read myNumber.

- Instead of writing set myAnswer = myNumber * 2, some developers would write calculate myAnswer = myNumber times 2 or compute myAnswer as myNumber doubled.

- Instead of writing output myAnswer, many pseudocode developers would write display myAnswer, print myAnswer, or write myAnswer.

The point is, the pseudocode statements are instructions to retrieve an original number from an input device and store it in memory where it can be used in a calculation, and then to get the calculated answer from memory and send it to an output device so a person can see it. When you eventually convert your pseudocode to a specific programming language, you do not have such flexibility because specific syntax will be required. For example, if you use the C# programming language and write the statement to output the answer to the monitor, you will code the following:

```
Console.Write(myAnswer);
```

The exact use of words, capitalization, and punctuation are important in the C# statement, but not in the pseudocode statement. Quick Reference 1-1 summarizes the pseudocode standards used in this book. (Note that the Quick Reference mentions modules; you will learn about modules in Chapter 2. Additional pseudocode style features will be discussed as topics are introduced throughout this book.)

QUICK REFERENCE 1-1 Pseudocode Standards

Programs begin with start and end with stop; these two words are always aligned.

Whenever a module name is used, it is followed by a set of parentheses.

Modules begin with the module name and end with return. The module name and return are always aligned.

Each program statement performs one action—for example, input, processing, or output.

Program statements are indented a few spaces more than start or the module name.

Each program statement appears on a single line if possible. When this is not possible, continuation lines are indented.

Program statements begin with lowercase letters.

No punctuation is used to end statements.

As you learn to create pseudocode and flowchart statements, you will develop a sense for how much detail to include. The statements represent the main steps that must be accomplished without including minute points. The concept is similar to writing an essay outline in which each statement of the outline represents a paragraph.

Drawing Flowcharts

Some professional programmers prefer writing pseudocode to drawing flowcharts, because using pseudocode is more similar to writing the final statements in the programming language. Others prefer drawing flowcharts to represent the logical flow, because flowcharts allow programmers to visualize more easily how the program statements will connect. Especially for beginning programmers, flowcharts are an excellent tool that helps them to visualize how the statements in a program are interrelated.

You can draw a flowchart by hand or use software, such as Microsoft Word and Microsoft PowerPoint, that contains flowcharting tools. You can use several other software programs, such as Visio and Visual Logic, specifically to create flowcharts.

When you create a flowchart, you draw geometric shapes that contain the individual statements and that are connected with arrows. You use a parallelogram to represent an **input symbol**, which indicates an input operation. You write an input statement in English inside the parallelogram, as shown in Figure 1-3.

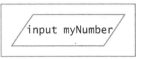

Figure 1-3   Input symbol
© 2015 Cengage Learning

Arithmetic operation statements are examples of processing. In a flowchart, you use a rectangle as the **processing symbol** that contains a processing statement, as shown in Figure 1-4.

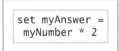

Figure 1-4   Processing symbol
© 2015 Cengage Learning

To represent an output statement, you use the same symbol as for input statements—the **output symbol** is a parallelogram, as shown in Figure 1-5. Because the parallelogram is used for both input and output, it is often called the **input/output symbol** or **I/O symbol**.

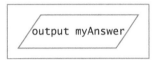

Figure 1-5   Output symbol
© 2015 Cengage Learning

Some software programs that use flowcharts (such as Visual Logic) use a left-slanting parallelogram to represent output. As long as the flowchart creator and the flowchart reader are communicating, the actual shape used is irrelevant. This book will follow the most standard convention of using the right-slanting parallelogram for both input and output.

To show the correct sequence of these statements, you use arrows, or **flowlines**, to connect the steps. Whenever possible, most of a flowchart should read from top to bottom or from left to right on a page. That's the way we read English, so when flowcharts follow this convention, they are easier for us to understand.

To be complete, a flowchart should include two more elements: **terminal symbols**, or start/stop symbols, at each end. Often, you place a word like start or begin in the first terminal symbol and a word like end or stop in the other. The standard terminal symbol is shaped like a racetrack; many programmers refer to this shape as a lozenge, because it resembles the shape of the medication you might use to soothe a sore throat. Figure 1-6 shows a complete flowchart for the program that doubles a number, and the pseudocode for the same problem. You can see from the figure that the flowchart and pseudocode statements are the same—only the presentation format differs.

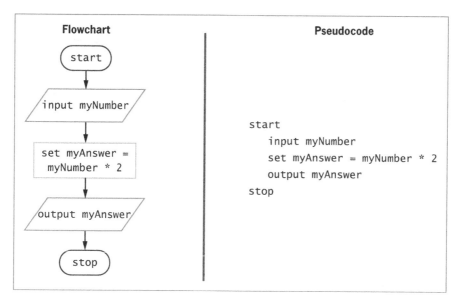

Figure 1-6   Flowchart and pseudocode of program that doubles a number
© 2015 Cengage Learning

Programmers seldom create both pseudocode and a flowchart for the same problem. You usually use one or the other. In a large program, you might even prefer to write pseudocode for some parts and to draw a flowchart for others.

When you tell a friend how to get to your house, you might write a series of instructions or you might draw a map. Pseudocode is similar to written, step-by-step instructions; a flowchart, like a map, is a visual representation of the same thing. Quick Reference 1 2 summarizes the flowchart symbols used in this book.

QUICK REFERENCE 1-2 Flowchart Symbols

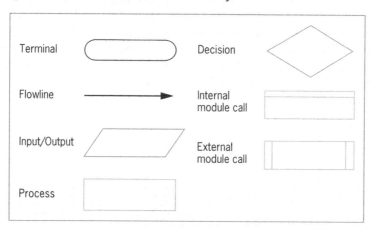

Repeating Instructions

After the flowchart or pseudocode has been developed, the programmer only needs to: (1) buy a computer, (2) buy a language compiler, (3) learn a programming language, (4) code the program, (5) attempt to compile it, (6) fix the syntax errors, (7) compile it again, (8) test it with several sets of data, and (9) put it into production.

"Whoa!" you are probably saying to yourself. "This is simply not worth it! All that work to create a flowchart or pseudocode, and *then* all those other steps? For five dollars, I can buy a pocket calculator that will double any number for me instantly!" You are absolutely right. If this were a real computer program, and all it did was double the value of a number, it would not be worth the effort. Writing a computer program would be worthwhile only if you had many numbers (let's say 10,000) to double in a limited amount of time—let's say the next two minutes.

Unfortunately, the program represented in Figure 1-6 does not double 10,000 numbers; it doubles only one. You could execute the program 10,000 times, of course, but that would require you to sit at the computer and run the program over and over again. You would be better off with a program that could process 10,000 numbers, one after the other.

One solution is to write the program shown in Figure 1-7 and execute the same steps 10,000 times. Of course, writing this program would be very time consuming; you might as well buy the calculator.

```
start
   input myNumber
   set myAnswer = myNumber * 2
   output myAnswer
   input myNumber
   set myAnswer = myNumber * 2
   output myAnswer
   input myNumber                    Don't Do It
   set myAnswer = myNumber * 2       You would never want to
   output myAnswer                   write such a repetitious
   ...and so on for 9,997 more times list of instructions.
```

Figure 1-7   Inefficient pseudocode for program that doubles 10,000 numbers
© 2015 Cengage Learning

A better solution is to have the computer execute the same set of three instructions over and over again, as shown in Figure 1-8. The repetition of a series of steps is called a **loop**. With this approach, the computer gets a number, doubles it, displays the answer, and then starts again with the first instruction. The same spot in memory, called myNumber, is reused for the second number and for any subsequent numbers. The spot in memory named myAnswer is reused each time to store the result of the multiplication operation. However, the logic illustrated in the flowchart in Figure 1-8 contains a major problem—the sequence of instructions never ends. This programming situation is known as an **infinite loop**—a repeating flow of logic with no end. You will learn one way to handle this problem later in this chapter; you will learn a superior way in Chapter 3.

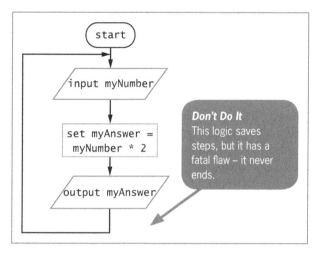

Figure 1-8   Flowchart of infinite number-doubling program
© 2015 Cengage Learning

TWO TRUTHS & A LIE

Using Pseudocode Statements and Flowchart Symbols

1. When you draw a flowchart, you use a parallelogram to represent an input operation.

2. When you draw a flowchart, you use a parallelogram to represent a processing operation.

3. When you draw a flowchart, you use a parallelogram to represent an output operation.

The false statement is #2. When you draw a flowchart, you use a rectangle to represent a processing operation.

Using a Sentinel Value to End a Program

The logic in the flowchart for doubling numbers, shown in Figure 1-8, has a major flaw—the program contains an infinite loop. If, for example, the input numbers are being entered at the keyboard, the program will keep accepting numbers and outputting their doubled values forever. Of course, the user could refuse to type any more numbers. But the program cannot progress any further while it is waiting for input; meanwhile, the program is occupying computer memory and tying up operating system resources. Refusing to enter any more numbers is not a practical solution. Another way to end the program is simply to turn off the computer. But again, that's neither the best solution nor an elegant way for the program to end.

A better way to end the program is to set a predetermined value for myNumber that means "Stop the program!" For example, the programmer and the user could agree that the user will never need to know the double of 0 (zero), so the user could enter a 0 to stop. The program could then test any incoming value contained in myNumber and, if it is a 0, stop the program. Testing a value is also called **making a decision**.

You represent a decision in a flowchart by drawing a **decision symbol**, which is shaped like a diamond. The diamond usually contains a question, the answer to which is one of two mutually exclusive options—often yes or no. All good computer questions have only two mutually exclusive answers, such as yes and no or true and false. For example, "What day of the year is your birthday?" is not a good computer question because there are 366 possible answers. However, "Is your birthday June 24?" is a good computer question because the answer is always either yes or no.

The question to stop the doubling program should be "Is the value of myNumber just entered equal to 0?" or "myNumber = 0?" for short. The complete flowchart will now look like the one shown in Figure 1-9.

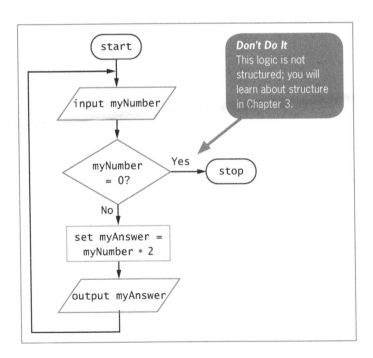

Figure 1-9 Flowchart of number-doubling program with sentinel value of 0
© 2015 Cengage Learning

One drawback to using 0 to stop a program, of course, is that it won't work if the user does need to find the double of 0. In that case, some other data-entry value that the user never will need, such as 999 or –1, could be selected to signal that the program should end. A preselected value that stops the execution of a program is often called a **dummy value** because it does not represent real data, but just a signal to stop. Sometimes, such a value is called a **sentinel value** because it represents an entry or exit point, like a sentinel who guards a fortress.

Not all programs rely on user data entry from a keyboard; many read data from an input device, such as a disk. When organizations store data on a disk or other storage device, they do not commonly use a dummy value to signal the end of the file. For one thing, an input record might have hundreds of fields, and if you store a dummy record in every file, you are wasting a large quantity of storage on "nondata." Additionally, it is often difficult to choose sentinel values for fields in a company's data files. Any balanceDue, even a zero or a negative number, can be a legitimate value, and any customerName, even "ZZ", could be someone's name. Fortunately, programming languages can recognize the end of data in a file automatically, through a code that is stored at the end of the data. Many programming languages use the term **eof** (for *end of file*) to refer to this marker that automatically acts as a sentinel. This book, therefore, uses **eof** to indicate the end of data whenever using a dummy value is impractical or inconvenient. In the flowchart shown in Figure 1-10, the **eof** question is shaded.

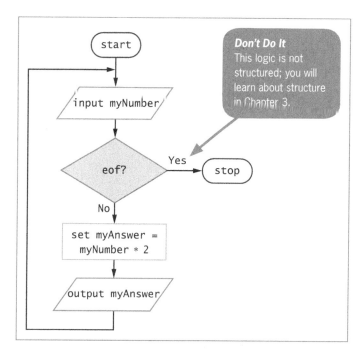

Figure 1-10   Flowchart using **eof**
© 2015 Cengage Learning

TWO TRUTHS & A LIE

Using a Sentinel Value to End a Program

1. A program that contains an infinite loop is one that never ends.

2. A preselected value that stops the execution of a program is often called a dummy value or a sentinel value.

3. Many programming languages use the term fe (for *file end*) to refer to a marker that automatically acts as a sentinel.

The false statement is #3. The term eof (for *end of file*) is the common term for a file sentinel.

Understanding Programming and User Environments

Many approaches can be used to write and execute a computer program. When you plan a program's logic, you can use a flowchart, pseudocode, or a combination of the two. When you code the program, you can type statements into a variety of text editors. When your program executes, it might accept input from a keyboard, mouse, microphone, or any other input device, and when you provide a program's output, you might use text, images, or sound. This section describes the most common environments you will encounter as a new programmer.

Understanding Programming Environments

When you plan the logic for a computer program, you can use paper and pencil to create a flowchart, or you might use software that allows you to manipulate flowchart shapes. If you choose to write pseudocode, you can do so by hand or by using a word-processing program. To enter the program into a computer so you can translate and execute it, you usually use a keyboard to type program statements into an editor. You can type a program into one of the following:

- A plain text editor
- A text editor that is part of an integrated development environment

A **text editor** is a program that you use to create simple text files. It is similar to a word processor, but without as many features. You can use a text editor such as Notepad that is included with Microsoft Windows. Figure 1-11 shows a C# program in Notepad that accepts a number and doubles it. An advantage to using a simple text editor to type and save a program is that the completed program does not require much disk space for storage. For example, the file shown in Figure 1-11 occupies only 314 bytes of storage.

24

```
NumberDoublingProgram.cs - Notepad
File  Edit  Format  View  Help
using System;
public class NumberDoublingProgram
{
    public static void Main()
    {
        int myNumber;
        int myAnswer;
        Console.Write("Please enter a number >> ");
        myNumber = Convert.ToInt32(Console.ReadLine());
        myAnswer = myNumber * 2;
        Console.WriteLine(myAnswer);
    }
}
```

This line contains a prompt that tells the user what to enter. You will learn more about prompts in Chapter 2.

Figure 1-11   A C# number-doubling program in Notepad

You can use the editor of an **integrated development environment** (**IDE**) to enter your program. An IDE is a software package that provides an editor, compiler, and other programming tools. For example, Figure 1-12 shows a C# program in the **Microsoft Visual Studio IDE**, an environment that contains tools useful for creating programs in Visual Basic, C++, and C#.

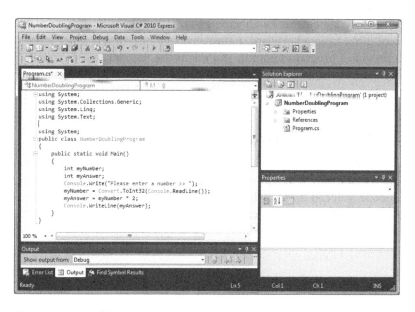

Figure 1-12   A C# number-doubling program in Visual Studio

Using an IDE is helpful to programmers because usually it provides features similar to those you find in many word processors. In particular, an IDE's editor commonly includes such features as the following:

- It uses different colors to display various language components, making elements like data types easier to identify.

- It highlights syntax errors visually for you.

- It employs automatic statement completion; when you start to type a statement, the IDE suggests a likely completion, which you can accept with a keystroke.

- It provides tools that allow you to step through a program's execution one statement at a time so you can more easily follow the program's logic and determine the source of any errors.

When you use the IDE to create and save a program, you occupy much more disk space than when using a plain text editor. For example, the program in Figure 1-12 occupies more than 49,000 bytes of disk space.

Although various programming environments might look different and offer different features, the process of using them is very similar. When you plan the logic for a program using pseudocode or a flowchart, it does not matter which programming environment you will use to write your code, and when you write the code in a programming language, it does not matter which environment you use to write it.

Understanding User Environments

A user might execute a program you have written in any number of environments. For example, a user might execute the number-doubling program from a command line like the one shown in Figure 1-13. A **command line** is a location on your computer screen at which you type text entries to communicate with the computer's operating system. In the program in Figure 1-13, the user is asked for a number, and the results are displayed.

Figure 1-13   Executing a number-doubling program in a command-line environment

Many programs are not run at the command line in a text environment, but are run using a **graphical user interface**, or **GUI** (pronounced *gooey*), which allows users to interact with a program in a graphical environment. When running a GUI program, the user might type input into a text box or use a mouse or other pointing device to select options on the screen. Figure 1-14 shows a number-doubling program that performs exactly the same task as the one in Figure 1-13, but this program uses a GUI.

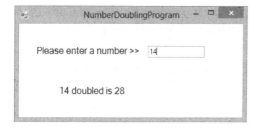

Figure 1-14   Executing a number-doubling program in a GUI environment

A command-line program and a GUI program might be written in the same programming language. (For example, the programs shown in Figures 1-13 and 1-14 were both written using C#.) However, no matter which environment is used to write or execute a program, the logical process is the same. The two programs in Figures 1-13 and 1-14 both accept input, perform multiplication, and perform output. In this book, you will not concentrate on which environment is used to type a program's statements, nor will you care about the type of environment the user will see. Instead, you will be concerned with the logic that applies to all programming situations.

TWO TRUTHS & A LIE

Understanding Programming and User Environments

1. You can type a program into an editor that is part of an integrated development environment, but using a plain text editor provides you with more programming help.

2. When a program runs from the command line, a user types text to provide input.

3. Although GUI and command-line environments look different, the logic of input, processing, and output apply to both program types.

The false statement is #1. An integrated development environment provides more programming help than a plain text editor.

Understanding the Evolution of Programming Models

People have been writing modern computer programs since the 1940s. The oldest programming languages required programmers to work with memory addresses and to memorize awkward codes associated with machine languages. Newer programming languages look much more like natural language and are easier to use, partly because they allow programmers to name variables instead of using unwieldy memory addresses. Also, newer programming languages allow programmers to create self-contained modules or program segments that can be pieced together in a variety of ways. The oldest computer programs were written in one piece, from start to finish, but modern programs are rarely written that way—they are created by teams of programmers, each developing reusable and connectable program procedures. Writing several small modules is easier than writing one large program, and most large tasks are easier when you break the work into units and get other workers to help with some of the units.

 Ada Byron Lovelace predicted the development of software in 1843; she is often regarded as the first programmer. The basis for most modern software was proposed by Alan Turing in 1935.

Currently, two major models or paradigms are used by programmers to develop programs and their procedures:

- **Procedural programming** focuses on the procedures that programmers create. That is, procedural programmers focus on the actions that are carried out—for example, getting input data for an employee and writing the calculations needed to produce a paycheck from the data. Procedural programmers would approach the job of producing a paycheck by breaking down the process into manageable subtasks.

- **Object-oriented programming** focuses on objects, or "things," and describes their features (also called attributes) and behaviors. For example, object-oriented programmers might design a payroll application by thinking about employees and paychecks, and by describing their attributes. Employees have names and Social Security numbers, and paychecks have names and check amounts. Then the programmers would think about the behaviors of employees and paychecks, such as employees getting raises and adding dependents and paychecks being calculated and output. Object-oriented programmers would then build applications from these entities.

With either approach, procedural or object oriented, you can produce a correct paycheck, and both models employ reusable program modules. The major difference lies in the focus the programmer takes during the earliest planning stages of a project. For now, this book focuses on procedural programming techniques. The skills you gain in programming procedurally—declaring variables, accepting input, making decisions, producing output, and so on—will serve you well whether you eventually write programs using a procedural approach, an object-oriented approach, or both. The programming language in which you write your source code might determine your approach. You can write a procedural program in any language that supports object orientation, but the opposite is not always true.

TWO TRUTHS & A LIE

Understanding the Evolution of Programming Models

1. The oldest computer programs were written in many separate modules.

2. Procedural programmers focus on actions that are carried out by a program.

3. Object-oriented programmers focus on a program's objects and their attributes and behaviors.

The false statement is #1. The oldest programs were written in a single piece; newer programs are divided into modules.

Chapter Summary

- Together, computer hardware (physical devices) and software (instructions) accomplish three major operations: input, processing, and output. You write computer instructions in a computer programming language that requires specific syntax; the instructions are translated into machine language by a compiler or interpreter. When both the syntax and logic of a program are correct, you can run, or execute, the program to produce the desired results.

- For a program to work properly, you must develop correct logic. Logical errors are much more difficult to locate than syntax errors.

- A programmer's job involves understanding the problem, planning the logic, coding the program, translating the program into machine language, testing the program, putting the program into production, and maintaining it.

- When programmers plan the logic for a solution to a programming problem, they often use flowcharts or pseudocode. When you draw a flowchart, you use parallelograms to represent input and output operations, and rectangles to represent processing. Programmers also use decisions to control repetition of instruction sets.

- To avoid creating an infinite loop when you repeat instructions, you can test for a sentinel value. You represent a decision in a flowchart by drawing a diamond-shaped symbol that contains a question, the answer to which is either yes or no.

- You can type a program into a plain text editor or one that is part of an integrated development environment. When a program's data values are entered from a keyboard, they can be entered at the command line in a text environment or in a GUI. Either way, the logic is similar.

- Procedural and object-oriented programmers approach problems differently. Procedural programmers concentrate on the actions performed with data. Object-oriented programmers focus on objects and their behaviors and attributes.

Key Terms

A **computer system** is a combination of all the components required to process and store data using a computer.

Hardware is the collection of physical devices that comprise a computer system.

Software consists of the programs that tell the computer what to do.

Programs are sets of instructions for a computer.

Programming is the act of developing and writing programs.

Application software comprises all the programs you apply to a task.

An **app** is a piece of application software; the term is frequently used for applications on mobile devices.

System software comprises the programs that you use to manage your computer.

Input describes the entry of data items into computer memory using hardware devices such as keyboards and mice.

Data items include all the text, numbers, and other information processed by a computer.

Processing data items may involve organizing them, checking them for accuracy, or performing mathematical operations on them.

The **central processing unit**, or **CPU**, is the computer hardware component that processes data.

Output describes the operation of retrieving information from memory and sending it to a device, such as a monitor or printer, so people can view, interpret, and work with the results.

Information is processed data.

Storage devices are types of hardware equipment, such as disks, that hold information for later retrieval.

The **cloud** refers to remote computers accessed through the Internet.

Programming languages, such as Visual Basic, C#, C++, or Java, are used to write programs.

Program code is the set of instructions a programmer writes in a programming language.

Coding the program is the act of writing programming language instructions.

The **syntax** of a language is its grammar rules.

A **syntax error** is an error in language or grammar.

Computer memory is the temporary, internal storage within a computer.

Random access memory (**RAM**) is temporary, internal computer storage.

Volatile describes storage whose contents are lost when power is lost.

Nonvolatile describes storage whose contents are retained when power is lost.

Machine language is a computer's on/off circuitry language.

Source code is the statements a programmer writes in a programming language.

Object code is translated machine language.

A **compiler** or **interpreter** translates a high-level language into machine language and indicates if you have used a programming language incorrectly.

Binary language is represented using a series of 0s and 1s.

To **run** or **execute** a program is to carry out its instructions.

Scripting languages (also called **scripting programming languages** or **script languages**) such as Python, Lua, Perl, and PHP are used to write programs that are typed directly from a keyboard. Scripting languages are stored as text rather than as binary executable files.

A **logical error** occurs when incorrect instructions are performed, or when instructions are performed in the wrong order.

The **logic** of a computer program is the complete sequence of instructions that lead to a problem's solution.

A **variable** is a named memory location whose value can vary.

The **program development cycle** consists of the steps that occur during a program's lifetime.

Users (or **end users**) are people who employ and benefit from computer programs.

Documentation consists of all the supporting paperwork for a program.

An **algorithm** is the sequence of steps necessary to solve any problem.

An **IPO chart** is a program development tool that delineates input, processing, and output tasks.

A **TOE chart** is a program development tool that lists tasks, objects, and events.

Desk-checking is the process of walking through a program solution on paper.

A **high-level programming language** supports English-like syntax.

A **low-level machine language** is made up of 1s and 0s and does not use easily interpreted variable names.

Debugging is the process of finding and correcting program errors.

Conversion is the entire set of actions an organization must take to switch over to using a new program or set of programs.

Maintenance consists of all the improvements and corrections made to a program after it is in production.

Pseudocode is an English-like representation of the logical steps it takes to solve a problem.

A **flowchart** is a pictorial representation of the logical steps it takes to solve a problem.

An **input symbol** indicates an input operation and is represented by a parallelogram in flowcharts.

A **processing symbol** indicates a processing operation and is represented by a rectangle in flowcharts.

An **output symbol** indicates an output operation and is represented by a parallelogram in flowcharts.

An **input/output symbol** or **I/O symbol** is represented by a parallelogram in flowcharts.

Flowlines, or arrows, connect the steps in a flowchart.

A **terminal symbol** indicates the beginning or end of a flowchart segment and is represented by a lozenge.

A **loop** is a repetition of a series of steps.

An **infinite loop** occurs when repeating logic cannot end.

Making a decision is the act of testing a value.

A **decision symbol** is shaped like a diamond and used to represent decisions in flowcharts.

A **dummy value** is a preselected value that stops the execution of a program.

A **sentinel value** is a preselected value that stops the execution of a program.

The term **eof** means *end of file.*

A **text editor** is a program that you use to create simple text files; it is similar to a word processor, but without as many features.

An **integrated development environment** (**IDE**) is a software package that provides an editor, compiler, and other programming tools.

Microsoft Visual Studio IDE is a software package that contains useful tools for creating programs in Visual Basic, C++, and C#.

A **command line** is a location on your computer screen at which you type text entries to communicate with the computer's operating system.

A **graphical user interface**, or **GUI** (pronounced *gooey*), allows users to interact with a program in a graphical environment.

Procedural programming is a programming model that focuses on the procedures that programmers create.

Object-oriented programming is a programming model that focuses on objects, or "things," and describes their features (also called attributes) and behaviors.

31

Exercises

 Review Questions

1. Computer programs also are known as _____.

   a. hardware   c. data
   b. software   d. information

2. The major computer operations include _____.

   a. hardware and software
   b. input, processing, and output
   c. sequence and looping
   d. spreadsheets, word processing, and data communications

3. Visual Basic, C++, and Java are all examples of computer _____.

    a. operating systems
    c. machine languages
    b. hardware
    d. programming languages

4. A programming language's rules are its _____.

    a. syntax
    c. format
    b. logic
    d. options

5. The most important task of a compiler or interpreter is to _____.

    a. create the rules for a programming language
    b. translate English statements into a language such as Java
    c. translate programming language statements into machine language
    d. execute machine language programs to perform useful tasks

6. Which of the following is temporary, internal storage?

    a. CPU
    c. keyboard
    b. hard disk
    d. memory

7. Which of the following pairs of steps in the programming process is in the correct order?

    a. code the program, plan the logic
    b. test the program, translate it into machine language
    c. put the program into production, understand the problem
    d. code the program, translate it into machine language

8. A programmer's most important task before planning the logic of a program is to _____.

    a. decide which programming language to use
    b. code the problem
    c. train the users of the program
    d. understand the problem

9. The two most commonly used tools for planning a program's logic are _____.

    a. flowcharts and pseudocode
    b. ASCII and EBCDIC
    c. Java and Visual Basic
    d. word processors and spreadsheets

10. Writing a program in a language such as C++ or Java is known as _____ the program.

    a. translating
    c. interpreting
    b. coding
    d. compiling

11. An English-like programming language such as Java or Visual Basic is a _____ programming language.

    a. machine-level
    c. high-level
    b. low-level
    d. binary-level

12. Which of the following is an example of a syntax error?

    a. producing output before accepting input
    b. subtracting when you meant to add
    c. misspelling a programming language word
    d. all of the above

13. Which of the following is an example of a logical error?

    a. performing arithmetic with a value before inputting it
    b. accepting two input values when a program requires only one
    c. dividing by 3 when you meant to divide by 30
    d. all of the above

14. The parallelogram is the flowchart symbol representing _____.

    a. input
    c. either a or b
    b. output
    d. none of the above

15. In a flowchart, a rectangle represents _____.

    a. input
    c. a question
    b. a sentinel
    d. processing

16. In flowcharts, the decision symbol is a _____.

    a. parallelogram
    c. lozenge
    b. rectangle
    d. diamond

17. The term *eof* represents _____.

    a. a standard input device
    b. a generic sentinel value
    c. a condition in which no more memory is available for storage
    d. the logical flow in a program

18. When you use an IDE instead of a simple text editor to develop a program, _____.

    a. the logic is more complicated
    c. the syntax is different
    b. the logic is simpler
    d. some help is provided

19. When you write a program that will run in a GUI environment as opposed to a command-line environment, _____.

    a. the logic is very different
    c. you do not need to plan the logic
    b. some syntax is different
    d. users are more confused

20.   As compared to procedural programming, with object-oriented programming, _____ .

   a.   the programmer's focus differs

   b.   you cannot use some languages, such as Java

   c.   you do not accept input

   d.   you do not code calculations; they are created automatically

 Programming Exercises

1.   Match the definition with the appropriate term.

1.	Computer system devices	a.	compiler
2.	Another word for *programs*	b.	syntax
3.	Language rules	c.	logic
4.	Order of instructions	d.	hardware
5.	Language translator	e.	software

2.   In your own words, describe the steps to writing a computer program.

3.   Match the term with the appropriate shape (see Figure 1-15).

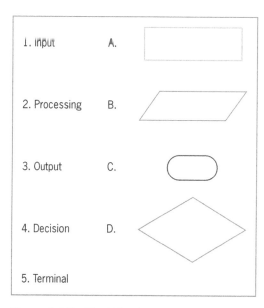

Figure 1-15   Identifying shapes
© 2015 Cengage Learning

4. Draw a flowchart or write pseudocode to represent the logic of a program that allows the user to enter a value. The program divides the value by 2 and outputs the result.

5. Draw a flowchart or write pseudocode to represent the logic of a program that allows the user to enter a value for one edge of a cube. The program calculates the surface area of one side of the cube, the surface area of the cube, and its volume. The program outputs all the results.

6. Draw a flowchart or write pseudocode to represent the logic of a program that allows the user to enter two values. The program outputs the product of the two values.

7. a. Draw a flowchart or write pseudocode to represent the logic of a program that allows the user to enter values for the width and length of a room's floor in feet. The program outputs the area of the floor in square feet.

   b. Modify the program that computes floor area to compute and output the number of 6-inch square tiles needed to tile the floor.

8. a. Draw a flowchart or write pseudocode to represent the logic of a program that allows the user to enter values for the width and length of a wall in feet. The program outputs the area of the wall in square feet.

   b. Modify the program that computes wall area to allow the user to enter the price of a gallon of paint. Assume that a gallon of paint covers 350 square feet of a wall. The program outputs the number of gallons needed and the cost of the job. (For this exercise, assume that you do not need to account for windows or doors, and that you can purchase partial gallons of paint.)

   c. Modify the program that computes paint cost to allow the user to enter the number of doorways that do not have to be painted. Assume that each doorway is 14 square feet. Output the number of gallons needed and the cost of the job.

9. Research current rates of monetary exchange. Draw a flowchart or write pseudocode to represent the logic of a program that allows the user to enter a number of dollars and convert it to Euros and Japanese yen.

10. Draw a flowchart or write pseudocode to represent the logic of a program that allows the user to enter values for a salesperson's base salary, total sales, and commission rate. The program computes and outputs the salesperson's pay by adding the base salary to the product of the total sales and commission rate.

11. A consignment shop accepts a product for sale and sets an initial price. Each month that the item doesn't sell, the price is reduced by 20 percent. When the item sells, the item's owner receives 60 percent of the sale price, and the shop gets 40 percent. Draw a flowchart or write pseudocode to represent the logic of a program that allows the user to enter an original product price. The output is the sale price, the owner's cut, and the shop's cut each month for the first three months the item is on sale.

12. A mobile phone app allows a user to press a button that starts a timer that counts seconds. When the user presses the button again, the timer stops. Draw a flowchart or write pseudocode that accepts the elapsed time in seconds and displays the value in minutes and seconds. For example, if the elapsed time was 130 seconds, the output would be 2 minutes and 10 seconds.

Performing Maintenance

1. In this chapter you learned that some of the tasks assigned to new programmers frequently involve maintenance—making changes to existing programs because of new requirements. A file named MAINTENANCE01-01.txt is included with your downloadable student files. Assume that this program is a working program in your organization and that it needs modifications as described in the comments (lines that begin with two slashes) at the beginning of the file. Your job is to alter the program to meet the new specifications.

Find the Bugs

Since the early days of computer programming, program errors have been called bugs. The term is often said to have originated from an actual moth that was discovered trapped in the circuitry of a computer at Harvard University in 1945. Actually, the term *bug* was in use prior to 1945 to mean trouble with any electrical apparatus; even during Thomas Edison's life, it meant an industrial defect. However, the term *debugging* is more closely associated with correcting program syntax and logic errors than with any other type of trouble.

1. Your downloadable files for Chapter 1 include DEBUG01-01.txt, DEBUG01-02.txt, and DEBUG01-03.txt. Each file starts with some comments (lines that begin with two slashes) that describe the program. Examine the pseudocode that follows the introductory comments, then find and correct all the bugs.

2. Your downloadable files for Chapter 1 include a file named DEBUG01-04.jpg that contains a flowchart with syntax and/or logical errors. Examine the flowchart and then find and correct all the bugs.

Game Zone

1. In 1952, A. S. Douglas wrote his University of Cambridge Ph.D. dissertation on human-computer interaction, and created the first graphical computer game—a version of Tic-Tac-Toe. The game was programmed on an EDSAC vacuum-tube mainframe computer. The first computer game is generally assumed to be *Spacewar!*,

developed in 1962 at MIT; the first commercially available video game was *Pong*, introduced by Atari in 1972. In 1980, Atari's *Asteroids* and *Lunar Lander* became the first video games to be registered with the U. S. Copyright Office. Throughout the 1980s, players spent hours with games that now seem very simple and unglamorous; do you recall playing *Adventure, Oregon Trail, Where in the World Is Carmen Sandiego?,* or *Myst?*

Today, commercial computer games are much more complex; they require many programmers, graphic artists, and testers to develop them, and large management and marketing staffs are needed to promote them. A game might cost many millions of dollars to develop and market, but a successful game might earn hundreds of millions of dollars. Obviously, with the brief introduction to programming you have had in this chapter, you cannot create a very sophisticated game. However, you can get started.

Mad Libs® is a children's game in which players provide a few words that are then incorporated into a silly story. The game helps children understand different parts of speech because they are asked to provide specific types of words. For example, you might ask a child for a noun, another noun, an adjective, and a past-tense verb. The child might reply with such answers as *table, book, silly,* and *studied*. The newly created Mad Lib might be:

Mary had a little *table*

Its *book* was *silly* as snow

And everywhere that Mary *studied*

The *table* was sure to go.

Create the logic for a Mad Lib program that accepts five words from input, then creates and displays a short story or nursery rhyme that uses them.

 ## Up for Discussion

1. Which is the better tool for learning programming—flowcharts or pseudocode? Cite any educational research you can find.

2. What is the image of the computer programmer in popular culture? Is the image different in books than in TV shows and movies? Would you like that image for yourself?

Elements of High-Quality Programs

In this chapter, you will learn about:

- ◎ Declaring and using variables and constants
- ◎ Performing arithmetic operations
- ◎ The advantages of modularization
- ◎ Modularizing a program
- ◎ Hierarchy charts
- ◎ Features of good program design

Declaring and Using Variables and Constants

As you learned in Chapter 1, data items include all the text, numbers, and other information that are processed by a computer. When you input data items into a computer, they are stored in variables in memory where they can be processed and converted to information that is output.

When you write programs, you work with data in three different forms: literals (or unnamed constants), variables, and named constants.

Understanding Unnamed, Literal Constants and their Data Types

All programming languages support two broad data types; **numeric** describes data that consists of numbers and **string** describes data that is nonnumeric. Most programming languages support several additional data types, including multiple types for numeric values that are very large or very small and for those that do and do not have fractional decimal digits. Languages such as C++, C#, Visual Basic, and Java distinguish between **integer** (whole number) numeric variables and **floating-point** (fractional) numeric variables that contain a decimal point. (Floating-point numbers are also called **real numbers**.) Thus, in some languages, the values 4 and 4.3 would be stored in different types of numeric variables. Additionally, many languages allow you to distinguish between smaller and larger values that occupy different numbers of bytes in memory. You will learn a little more about these specialized data types later in this chapter, and even more when you study a programming language, but this book uses the two broadest types: numeric and string.

When you use a specific numeric value, such as 43, within a program, you write it using the digits and no quotation marks. A specific numeric value is often called a **numeric constant** (or **literal numeric constant**) because it does not change—a 43 always has the value 43. When you store a numeric value in computer memory, additional characters such as dollar signs and commas are not input or stored. Those characters can be added to output for readability, but they are not part of the number.

A specific text value, or string of characters, such as "Amanda", is a **string constant** (or **literal string constant**). String constants, unlike numeric constants, appear within quotation marks in computer programs. String values are also called **alphanumeric values** because they can contain alphabetic characters as well as numbers and other characters. For example, "$3,215.99 U.S.", including the dollar sign, comma, periods, letters, and numbers, is a string. Although strings can contain numbers, numeric values cannot contain alphabetic characters. The numeric constant 43 and the string constant "Amanda" are examples of **unnamed constants**—they do not have identifiers like variables do.

Watch the video *Declaring Variables and Constants*.

Working with Variables

Variables are named memory locations whose contents can vary or differ over time. For example, in the number-doubling program in Figure 2-1, myNumber and myAnswer are variables. At any moment in time, a variable holds just one value. Sometimes, myNumber holds 2 and myAnswer holds 4; at other times, myNumber holds 6 and myAnswer holds 12. The ability of variables to change in value is what makes computers and programming worthwhile. Because one memory location can be used repeatedly with different values, you can write program instructions once and then use them for thousands of separate calculations. *One* set of payroll instructions at your company produces each employee paycheck, and *one* set of instructions at your electric company produces each household's bill.

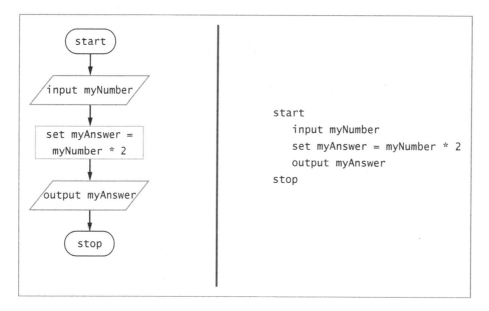

Figure 2-1   Flowchart and pseudocode for the number-doubling program
© 2015 Cengage Learning

In most programming languages, before you can use any variable, you must include a declaration for it. A **declaration** is a statement that provides a data type and an identifier for a variable. An **identifier** is a program component's name. A data item's **data type** is a classification that describes the following:

- What values can be held by the item

- How the item is stored in computer memory

- What operations can be performed on the item

As mentioned earlier, most programming languages support several data types, but in this book, only two data types will be used: num and string.

When you declare a variable, you provide both a data type and an identifier. Optionally, you can declare a starting value for any variable. Declaring a starting value is known as **initializing the variable**. For example, each of the following statements is a valid declaration. Two of the statements include initializations, and two do not:

```
num mySalary
num yourSalary = 14.55
string myName
string yourName = "Juanita"
```

Figure 2-2 shows the number-doubling program from Figure 2-1 with the added declarations shaded. Variables must be declared before they are used for the first time in a program. Some languages require all variables to be declared at the beginning of the program, others allow variables to be declared at the beginning of each module, and others allow variables to be declared anywhere at all as long as they are declared before their first use. This book will follow the convention of declaring all variables together.

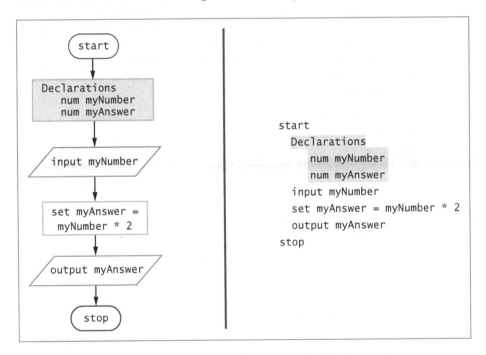

Figure 2-2   Flowchart and pseudocode of number-doubling program with variable declarations
© 2015 Cengage Learning

In many programming languages, if you declare a variable and do not initialize it, the variable contains an unknown value until it is assigned a value. A variable's unknown value commonly is called **garbage**. Although some languages use a default value for some variables (such as assigning 0 to any unassigned numeric variable), this book will assume that an unassigned variable holds garbage. In many languages it is illegal to use a garbage-holding variable in an arithmetic statement or to display it as output. Even if you work with a language that allows you to display garbage, it serves no purpose to do so and constitutes a logical error.

When you create a variable without assigning it an initial value (as with myNumber and myAnswer in Figure 2-2), your intention is to assign a value later—for example, by receiving one as input or placing the result of a calculation there.

Naming Variables

The number-doubling example in Figure 2-2 requires two variables: myNumber and myAnswer. Alternatively, these variables could be named userEntry and programSolution, or inputValue and twiceTheValue. As a programmer, you choose reasonable and descriptive names for your variables. The language translator (interpreter or compiler) then associates the names you choose with specific memory addresses.

Every computer programming language has its own set of rules for creating identifiers. Most languages allow letters and digits within identifiers. Some languages allow hyphens in variable names, such as hourly-wage, and some allow underscores, as in hourly_wage. Some languages allow dollar signs or other special characters in variable names (for example, hourly$); others allow foreign-alphabet characters, such as π or Ω. Each programming language has a few (perhaps 100 to 200) reserved **keywords** that are not allowed as variable names because they are part of the language's syntax. For example, the data type names in a language, such as num and string, would not be allowed as variable names. When you learn a programming language, you will learn its list of keywords.

Different languages put different limits on the length of variable names, although in general, the length of identifiers in newer languages is virtually unlimited. In the oldest computer languages, all variable names were written using all uppercase letters because the keypunch machines used at that time created only uppercase letters. In most modern languages, identifiers are case sensitive, so HoUrLyWaGe, hourlywage, and hourlyWage are three separate variable names. Programmers use multiple conventions for naming variables, often depending on the programming language or standards adopted by their employers. Quick Reference 2-1 describes commonly used variable naming conventions.

QUICK REFERENCE 2-1 Variable Naming Conventions

Convention for naming variables	Examples	Languages where commonly used
Camel casing is the convention in which the variable starts with a lowercase letter and any subsequent word begins with an uppercase letter. It is sometimes called **lower camel casing** to emphasize the difference from Pascal casing.	hourlyWage lastName	Java, C#

(continues)

(continues)

Convention for naming variables	Examples	Languages where commonly used
Pascal casing is a convention in which the first letter of a variable name is uppercase. It is sometimes called **upper camel casing** to distinguish it from lower camel casing.	`HourlyWage` `LastName`	Visual Basic
Hungarian notation is a form of camel casing in which a variable's data type is part of the identifier.	`numHourlyWage` `stringLastName`	C for Windows API programming
Snake casing is a convention in which parts of a variable name are separated by underscores.	`hourly_wage` `last_name`	C, C++, Python, Ruby
Mixed case with underscores is a variable naming convention similar to snake casing, but new words start with an uppercase letter.	`Hourly_Wage` `Last_Name`	Ada
Kebob case is sometimes used as the name for the style that uses dashes to separate parts of a variable name. The name derives from the fact that the words look like pieces of food on a skewer.	`hourly-wage` `last-name`	Lisp (with lowercase letters), COBOL (with uppercase letters)

43

Adopting a naming convention for variables and using it consistently will help make your programs easier to read and understand.

Even though every language has its own rules for naming variables, you should not concern yourself with the specific syntax of any particular computer language when designing the logic of a program. The logic, after all, works with any language. The variable names used throughout this book follow only three rules:

1. *Variable names must be one word.* The name can contain letters, digits, hyphens, or underscores. No language allows embedded spaces in variable names, and most do not allow punctuation such as periods, commas, or colons. This book uses only alphabetic letters, digits, and underscores in variable names. Therefore, r is a legal variable name, as are `rate` and `interestRate`. The variable name `interest rate` is not allowed because of the space.

2. *Variable names must start with a letter.* Some programming languages allow variable names to start with a nonalphabetic character such as an underscore. Almost all programming languages prohibit variable names that start with a digit. This book follows the most common convention of starting variable names with a letter.

When you write a program using an editor that is packaged with a compiler in an IDE, the compiler may display variable names in a different color from other program components. This visual aid helps your variable names stand out from words that are part of the programming language.

3. *Variable names should have some appropriate meaning.* This is not a formal rule of any programming language. When computing an interest rate in a program, the computer does not care if you call the variable g, u84, or fred. As long as the correct numeric result is placed in the variable, its actual name doesn't matter. However, it's much easier to follow the logic of a statement like `set interestEarned = initialInvestment * interestRate` than a statement like `set f = i * r` or `set someBanana = j89 * myFriendLinda`. When a program requires changes, which could be months or years after you write the original version, you and your fellow programmers will appreciate clear, descriptive variable names in place of cryptic identifiers. Later in this chapter, you will learn more about selecting good identifiers.

Notice that the flowchart in Figure 2-2 follows the preceding rules for variables: Both variable names, myNumber and myAnswer, are single words without embedded spaces, and they have appropriate meanings. Some programmers name variables after friends or create puns with them, but computer professionals consider such behavior unprofessional and amateurish.

Assigning Values to Variables

When you create a flowchart or pseudocode for a program that doubles numbers, you can include a statement such as the following:

```
set myAnswer = myNumber * 2
```

Such a statement is an **assignment statement**. This statement incorporates two actions. First, the computer calculates the arithmetic value of myNumber * 2. Second, the computed value is stored in the myAnswer memory location.

The equal sign is the **assignment operator**. The assignment operator is an example of a **binary operator**, meaning it requires two operands—one on each side. (An **operand** is simply a value used by an operator.) The assignment operator always operates from right to left, which means that it has **right-associativity** or **right-to-left associativity**. This means that the value of the expression to the right of the assignment operator is evaluated first, and then the result is assigned to the operand on the left. The operand to the right of an assignment operator must be a value—for example, a named or unnamed constant or an arithmetic expression. The operand to the left of an assignment operator must be a name that represents a memory address—the name of the location where the result will be stored.

For example, if you have declared two numeric variables named someNumber and someOtherNumber, then each of the following is a valid assignment statement:

```
set someNumber = 2
set someNumber = 3 + 7
set someOtherNumber = someNumber
set someOtherNumber = someNumber * 5
```

In each case, the expression to the right of the assignment operator is evaluated and stored at the location referenced on the left side. The result to the left of an assignment operator is called an **lvalue**. The *l* is for left. Lvalues are always memory address identifiers.

The following statements, however, are *not* valid:

```
set 2 + 4 = someNumber
set someOtherNumber * 10 = someNumber
set someNumber + someOtherNumber = 10
```

> **Don't Do It**
> The operand to the left of an assignment operator must represent a memory address.

In each of these cases, the value to the left of the assignment operator is not a memory address, so the statements are invalid.

When you write pseudocode or draw a flowchart, it might help you to use the word *set* in assignment statements, as shown in these examples, to emphasize that the left-side value is being set. However, in most programming languages, the word *set* is not used, and assignment statements take the following simpler form:

```
someNumber = 2
someOtherNumber = someNumber
```

Because the abbreviated form is how assignments appear in most languages, this convention is used for the rest of this book.

Understanding the Data Types of Variables

Computers handle string data differently from the way they handle numeric data. You may have experienced these differences if you have used application software such as spreadsheets or database programs. For example, in a spreadsheet, you cannot sum a column of words. Similarly, every programming language requires that you specify the correct type for each variable, and that you use each type appropriately.

- A **numeric variable** is one that can hold digits and have mathematical operations performed on it. In this book, all numeric variables can hold a decimal point and a sign indicating positive or negative; some programming languages provide specialized numeric types for these options. In the statement myAnswer = myNumber * 2, both myAnswer and myNumber are numeric variables; that is, their intended contents are numeric values, such as 6 and 3, 14.8 and 7.4, or −18 and −9.

- A **string variable** can hold text, such as letters of the alphabet, and other special characters, such as punctuation marks. If a working program contains the statement lastName = "Lincoln", then lastName is a string variable. A string variable also can hold digits either with or without other characters. For example, "235 Main Street" and "86" are both strings. A string like "86" is stored differently than the numeric value 86, and you cannot perform arithmetic with the string. Programmers frequently use strings to hold digits when they will never be used in arithmetic statements—for example, an account number or a zip code.

Type-safety is the feature of some programming languages that prevents assigning values of an incorrect data type. You can assign data to a variable only if it is the correct type. (Such languages are called *strongly typed*.) If you declare `taxRate` as a numeric variable and `inventoryItem` as a string, then the following statements are valid:

```
taxRate = 2.5
inventoryItem = "monitor"
```

The following are invalid because the type of data being assigned does not match the variable type:

```
taxRate = "2.5"
inventoryItem = 2.5
taxRate = inventoryItem
inventoryItem = taxRate
```

> **Don't Do It**
> If `taxRate` is numeric and `inventoryItem` is a string, then these assignments are invalid.

 Watch the video *Understanding Data Types*.

Declaring Named Constants

Besides variables, most programming languages allow you to create named constants. A **named constant** is similar to a variable, except it can be assigned a value only once. You use a named constant when you want to assign a useful name for a value that will never be changed during a program's execution. Using named constants makes your programs easier to understand by eliminating magic numbers. A **magic number** is an unnamed constant, like 0.06, whose purpose is not immediately apparent.

For example, if a program uses a sales tax rate of 6 percent, you might want to declare a named constant as follows.

```
num SALES_TAX_RATE = 0.06
```

After `SALES_TAX_RATE` is declared, the following statements have identical meaning:

```
taxAmount = price * 0.06
taxAmount = price * SALES_TAX_RATE
```

The way in which named constants are declared differs among programming languages. This book follows the convention of using all uppercase letters in constant identifiers, and using underscores to separate words for readability. Using these conventions makes named constants easier to recognize. In many languages a constant must be assigned its value when it is declared, but in some languages a constant can be assigned its value later. In both cases, however, a constant's value cannot be changed after the first assignment. This book follows the convention of initializing all constants when they are declared.

When you declare a named constant, program maintenance becomes easier. For example, if the value of the sales tax rate changes from 0.06 to 0.07 in the future, and you have declared a named constant `SALES_TAX_RATE`, you only need to change the value assigned to the named constant at the beginning of the program, then retranslate the program into machine language, and all references to `SALES_TAX_RATE` are automatically updated. If you used the unnamed literal 0.06 instead, you would have to search for every instance of the value and replace it with the new one. Additionally, if the literal 0.06 was used in other calculations within the program (for example, as a discount rate or price), you would have to carefully select which instances of the value to alter, and you would be likely to make a mistake.

 Sometimes, using unnamed literal constants is appropriate in a program, especially if their meaning is clear to most readers. For example, in a program that calculates half of a value by dividing by two, you might choose to use the unnamed literal 2 instead of incurring the extra time and memory costs of creating a named constant HALF and assigning 2 to it. Extra costs that result from adding variables or instructions to a program are known as **overhead**.

TWO TRUTHS & A LIE

Declaring and Using Variables and Constants

1. A variable's data type describes the kind of values the variable can hold and the types of operations that can be performed with it.

2. If name is a string variable, then the statement set name = "Ed" is valid.

3. The operand to the right of an assignment operator must be a name that represents a memory address.

The false statement is #3. The operand to the left of an assignment operator must be a name that represents a memory address—the name of the location where the result will be stored. The value to the right of an assignment operator might be a constant, arithmetic expression, or other value.

Performing Arithmetic Operations

Most programming languages use the following standard arithmetic operators:

+ (plus sign)—addition

− (minus sign)—subtraction

* (asterisk)—multiplication

/ (slash)—division

Many languages also support additional operators that calculate the remainder after division, raise a number to a power, manipulate individual bits stored within a value, and perform other operations.

Each of the standard arithmetic operators is a binary operator; that is, each requires an expression on both sides. For example, the following statement adds two test scores and assigns the sum to a variable named totalScore:

```
totalScore = test1 + test2
```

The following adds 10 to `totalScore` and stores the result in `totalScore`:

```
totalScore = totalScore + 10
```

In other words, this example increases the value of `totalScore`. This last example looks odd in algebra because it might appear that the value of `totalScore` and `totalScore` plus 10 are equivalent. You must remember that the equal sign is the assignment operator, and that the statement is actually taking the original value of `totalScore`, adding 10 to it, and assigning the result to the memory address on the left of the operator, which is `totalScore`.

In programming languages, you can combine arithmetic statements. When you do, every operator follows **rules of precedence** (also called the **order of operations**) that dictate the order in which operations in the same statement are carried out. The rules of precedence for the basic arithmetic statements are as follows:

- Expressions within parentheses are evaluated first. If there are multiple sets of parentheses, the expression within the innermost parentheses is evaluated first.

- Multiplication and division are evaluated next, from left to right.

- Addition and subtraction are evaluated next, from left to right.

The assignment operator has a very low precedence. Therefore, in a statement such as `d = e * f + g`, the operations on the right of the assignment operator are always performed before the final assignment to the variable on the left.

 When you learn a specific programming language, you will learn about all the operators that are used in that language. Many programming language books contain a table that specifies the relative precedence of every operator used in the language.

For example, consider the following two arithmetic statements:

```
firstAnswer = 2 + 3 * 4
secondAnswer = (2 + 3) * 4
```

After these statements execute, the value of `firstAnswer` is 14. According to the rules of precedence, multiplication is carried out before addition, so 3 is multiplied by 4, giving 12, and then 2 and 12 are added, and 14 is assigned to `firstAnswer`. The value of `secondAnswer`, however, is 20, because the parentheses force the contained addition operation to be performed first. The 2 and 3 are added, producing 5, and then 5 is multiplied by 4, producing 20.

Forgetting about the rules of arithmetic precedence, or forgetting to add parentheses when you need them, can cause logical errors that are difficult to find in programs. For example, the following statement might appear to average two test scores:

```
average = score1 + score2 / 2
```

However, it does not. Because division has a higher precedence than addition, the preceding statement takes half of `score2`, adds it to `score1`, and stores the result in `average`. The correct statement is:

```
average = (score1 + score2) / 2
```

You are free to add parentheses even when you don't need them to force a different order of operations; sometimes you use them just to make your intentions clearer. For example, the following statements operate identically:

```
totalPriceWithTax = price + price * TAX_RATE
totalPriceWithTax = price + (price * TAX_RATE)
```

In both cases, `price` is multiplied by `TAX_RATE` first, then it is added to `price`, and finally the result is stored in `totalPriceWithTax`. Because multiplication occurs before addition on the right side of the assignment operator, both statements are the same. However, if you feel that the statement with the parentheses makes your intentions clearer to someone reading your program, then you should use them.

All the arithmetic operators have **left-to-right associativity**. This means that operations with the same precedence take place from left to right. Consider the following statement:

```
answer = a + b + c * d / e - f
```

Multiplication and division have higher precedence than addition or subtraction, so the multiplication and division are carried out from left to right as follows:

c is multiplied by d, and the result is divided by e, giving a new result.

Therefore, the statement becomes:

```
answer = a + b + (temporary result just calculated) - f
```

Then, addition and subtraction are carried out from left to right as follows:

a and b are added, the temporary result is added, and then f is subtracted. The final result is then assigned to `answer`.

Another way to say this is that the following two statements are equivalent:

```
answer = a + b + c * d / e - f
answer = a + b + ((c * d) / e) - f
```

Quick Reference 2-2 summarizes the precedence and associativity of the five most frequently used operators.

QUICK REFERENCE 2-2 Precedence and Associativity of Five Common Operators

Operator symbol	Operator name	Precedence (compared to other operators in this table)	Associativity
=	Assignment	Lowest	Right-to-left
+	Addition	Medium	Left-to-right
−	Subtraction	Medium	Left-to-right
*	Multiplication	Highest	Left-to-right
/	Division	Highest	Left-to-right

Watch the video *Arithmetic Operator Precedence*.

The Integer Data Type

As mentioned earlier in this chapter, many modern programming languages allow programmers to make fine distinctions between numeric data types. In particular, many languages treat integer numeric values (whole numbers) and floating-point numeric values (numbers with decimal places) differently. In these languages, you can always assign an integer, such as 3, to a floating-point variable or named constant, and it will be converted to 3.0. However, you cannot assign a floating-point value (such as 3.0) directly to an integer variable, because the decimal position values will be lost, even when they are 0.

When you work with a language that makes distinctions between integer and floating-point values, you can combine the different types in arithmetic expressions. When you do, addition, subtraction, and multiplication work as expected. For example, the result of 2.3 + 5 is 7.3, and the result of 4.2 * 2 is 8.4. When you mix types, division works as expected as well. For example, the result of 9.3 / 3 is 3.1.

However, in many languages, dividing an integer by another integer is a special case. In languages such as Java, C++, and C#, dividing two integers results in an integer, and any fractional part of the result is lost. For example, in these languages, the result of 7 / 2 is 3, not 3.5 as you might expect. Programmers say that the decimal portion of the result is cut off, or *truncated*.

 When programming in a language that truncates the results of integer division, you must be particularly careful with numbers lower than 1. For example, if you write a program that halves a recipe, you might use an expression such as 1 / 2 * cupsSugar. No matter what the value of cupsSugar is, the result will always be 0 because 2 goes into 1 zero whole times.

Many programming languages also support a **remainder operator**, which is sometimes called the *modulo operator* or the *modulus operator*. When used with two integer operands, the remainder operator is the value that remains after division. For example, 24 Mod 10 is 4 because when 24 is divided by 10, 4 is the remainder. In Visual Basic, the remainder operator is the keyword Mod. In Java, C++, and C#, the operator is the percent sign (%).

The remainder operator can be useful in a variety of situations. For example, you can determine whether a number is even or odd by finding the remainder when the number is divided by 2. Any number that has a remainder of 0 is even, and any number with a remainder of 1 is odd.

Because the remainder operator differs among programming languages, and because the operation itself is handled differently when used with negative operands, the remainder operator will not be used in the rest of this language-independent book. Similarly, this book uses one data type, num, for all numeric values, and it is assumed that both integer and floating-point values can be stored in num variables and named constants.

TWO TRUTHS & A LIE

Performing Arithmetic Operations

1. Parentheses have higher precedence than any of the common arithmetic operators.

2. Operations in arithmetic statements occur from left to right in the order in which they appear.

3. The following adds 5 to a variable named points:

   ```
   points = points + 5
   ```

The false statement is #2. Operations of equal precedence in an arithmetic statement are carried out from left to right, but operations within parentheses are carried out first, multiplication and division are carried out next, and addition and subtraction take place last.

Understanding the Advantages of Modularization

Programmers seldom write programs as one long series of steps. Instead, they break down their programming problems into smaller units and tackle one cohesive task at a time. These smaller units are **modules**. Programmers also refer to them as **subroutines**, **procedures**, **functions**, or **methods**; the name usually reflects the programming language being used. For example, Visual Basic programmers use *procedure* (or *subprocedure*). C and C++ programmers call their modules *functions*, whereas C#, Java, and other object-oriented language programmers are more likely to use *method*. Programmers in COBOL, RPG, and BASIC (all older languages) are most likely to use *subroutine*.

You can learn about modules that receive and return data in Chapter 9 of the comprehensive version of this book.

A main program executes a module by calling it. To **call a module** is to use its name to invoke the module, causing it to execute. When the module's tasks are complete, control returns to the spot from which the module was called in the main program. When you access a module, the action is similar to putting a DVD player on pause. You abandon your primary action (watching a video), take care of some other task (for example, making a sandwich), and then return to the main task exactly where you left off.

The process of breaking down a large program into modules is **modularization**; computer scientists also call it **functional decomposition**. You are never required to modularize a large program to make it run on a computer, but there are at least three reasons for doing so:

- Modularization provides abstraction.

- Modularization helps multiple programmers to work on a problem.

- Modularization allows you to reuse work more easily.

Modularization Provides Abstraction

One reason that modularized programs are easier to understand is that they enable a programmer to see the "big picture." **Abstraction** is the process of paying attention to important properties while ignoring nonessential details. Abstraction is selective ignorance. Life would be tedious without abstraction. For example, you can create a list of things to accomplish today:

```
Do laundry
Call Aunt Nan
Start term paper
```

Without abstraction, the list of chores would begin:

```
Pick up laundry basket
Put laundry basket in car
Drive to Laundromat
Get out of car with basket
Walk into Laundromat
Set basket down
Find quarters for washing machine
... and so on.
```

You might list a dozen more steps before you finish the laundry and move on to the second chore on your original list. If you had to consider every small, low-level detail of every task in your day, you would probably never make it out of bed in the morning. Using a higher-level, more abstract list makes your day manageable. Abstraction makes complex tasks look simple.

 Abstract artists create paintings in which they see only the big picture—color and form—and ignore the details. Abstraction has a similar meaning among programmers.

Likewise, some level of abstraction occurs in every computer program. Fifty years ago, a programmer had to understand the low-level circuitry instructions the computer used. But now, newer high-level programming languages allow you to use English-like vocabulary in which one broad statement corresponds to dozens of machine instructions. No matter which high-level programming language you use, if you display a message on the monitor, you are never required to understand how a monitor works to create each pixel on the screen. You write an instruction like `output message` and the details of the hardware operations are handled for you by the operating system.

Modules provide another way to achieve abstraction. For example, a payroll program can call a module named `computeFederalWithholdingTax()`. When you call this module from your program, you use one statement; the module itself might contain dozens of statements. You can write the mathematical details of the module later, someone else can write them, or you can purchase them from an outside source. When you plan your main payroll program, your only concern is that a federal withholding tax will have to be calculated; you save the details for later.

Modularization Helps Multiple Programmers to Work on a Problem

When you divide any large task into modules, you gain the ability to more easily divide the task among various people. Rarely does a single programmer write a commercial program that you buy. Consider any word-processing, spreadsheet, or database program you have used. Each program has so many options, and responds to user selections in so many possible ways, that it would take years for a single programmer to write all the instructions. Professional software developers can write new programs in weeks or months, instead of years, by dividing large programs into modules and assigning each module to an individual programmer or team.

Modularization Allows You to Reuse Work

If a module is useful and well written, you may want to use it more than once within a program or in other programs. For example, a routine that verifies the validity of dates is useful in many programs written for a business. (For example, a month value is valid if it is not lower than 1 or higher than 12, a day value is valid if it is not lower than 1 or higher than 31 if the month is 1, and so on.) If a computerized personnel file contains each employee's birth date, hire date, last promotion date, and termination date, the date-validation module can be used four times with each employee record. Other programs in an organization can also use the module; these programs might ship customer orders, plan employees' birthday parties, or calculate when loan payments should be made. If you write the date-checking instructions so they are entangled with other statements in a program, they are difficult to isolate and reuse. On the other hand, if you place the instructions in a separate module, the unit is easy to use and portable to other applications. The feature of modular programs that allows individual modules to be used in a variety of applications is **reusability**.

You can find many real-world examples of reusability. When you build a house, you don't invent plumbing and heating systems; you incorporate systems with proven designs. This certainly reduces the time and effort it takes to build a house. The systems you choose are in service in other houses, so they have been tested under a variety of circumstances, increasing their reliability. **Reliability** is the feature of programs that assures you a module has been proven to function correctly. Reliable software saves time and money. If you create the functional components of your programs as stand-alone modules and test them in your current programs, much of the work will already be done when you use the modules in future applications.

TWO TRUTHS & A LIE

Understanding the Advantages of Modularization

1. Modularization eliminates abstraction, a feature that makes programs more confusing.

2. Modularization makes it easier for multiple programmers to work on a problem.

3. Modularization allows you to reuse work more easily.

The false statement is #1. Modularization enables abstraction, which allows you to see the big picture.

Modularizing a Program

Most programs consist of a **main program**, which contains the basic steps, or the **mainline logic**, of the program. The main program then accesses modules that provide more refined details.

When you create a module, you include the following:

- A header—The **module header** includes the module identifier and possibly other necessary identifying information.

- A body—The **module body** contains all the statements in the module.

- A `return` statement—The **module return statement** marks the end of the module and identifies the point at which control returns to the program or module that called the module. In most programming languages, if you do not include a `return` statement at the end of a module, the logic will still return. However, this book follows the convention of explicitly including a `return` statement with every module.

Naming a module is similar to naming a variable. The rules and conventions for naming modules are slightly different in every programming language, but in this text, module names follow the same general rules used for variable identifiers:

- Module names must start with a letter and cannot contain spaces.

- Module names should have some meaning.

Although it is not a requirement of any programming language, it frequently makes sense to use a verb as all or part of a module's name, because modules perform some action. Typical module names begin with action words such as get, calculate, and display. When you program in visual languages that use screen components such as buttons and text boxes, the module names frequently contain verbs representing user actions, such as click or drag.

Additionally, in this text, module names are followed by a set of parentheses. This will help you distinguish module names from variable names. This style corresponds to the way modules are named in many programming languages, such as Java, C++, and C#.

As you learn more about modules in specific programming languages, you will find that you sometimes place variable names within the parentheses that follow module names. Any variables enclosed in the parentheses contain information you want to send to the module. For now, the parentheses at the end of module names will be empty in this book.

When a main program wants to use a module, it calls the module. A module can call another module, and the called module can call another. The number of chained calls is limited only by the amount of memory available on your computer. In this book, the flowchart symbol used to call a module is a rectangle with a bar across the top. You place the name of the module you are calling inside the rectangle.

Some programmers use a rectangle with stripes down each side to represent a module in a flowchart, and this book uses that convention if a module is external to a program. For example, prewritten, built-in modules that generate random numbers, compute standard trigonometric functions, and sort values often are external to your programs. However, if the module is being created as part of the program, the book uses a rectangle with a single stripe across the top.

In a flowchart, you draw each module separately with its own sentinel symbols. The beginning sentinel contains the name of the module. This name must be identical to the name used in the calling program or module. The ending sentinel contains return, which indicates that when the module ends, the logical progression of statements will exit the module and return to the calling program or module. Similarly, in pseudocode, you start each module with its name and end with a return statement; the module name and return statements are vertically aligned and all the module statements are indented between them.

For example, consider the program in Figure 2-3, which does not contain any modules. It accepts a customer's name and balance due as input and produces a bill. At the top of the bill, the company's name and address are displayed on three lines, which are followed by the customer's name and balance due. To display the company name and address, you can simply include three output statements in the mainline logic of a program, as shown in Figure 2-3, or you can modularize the program by creating both the mainline logic and a displayAddressInfo() module, as shown in Figure 2-4.

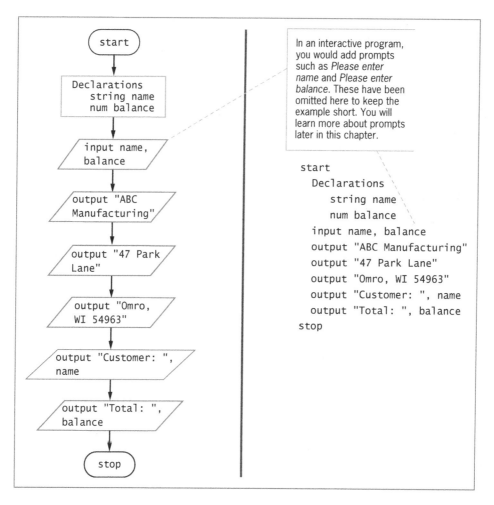

In an interactive program, you would add prompts such as *Please enter name* and *Please enter balance*. These have been omitted here to keep the example short. You will learn more about prompts later in this chapter.

```
start
   Declarations
      string name
      num balance
   input name, balance
   output "ABC Manufacturing"
   output "47 Park Lane"
   output "Omro, WI 54963"
   output "Customer: ", name
   output "Total: ", balance
stop
```

Figure 2-3   Program that produces a bill using only main program
© 2015 Cengage Learning

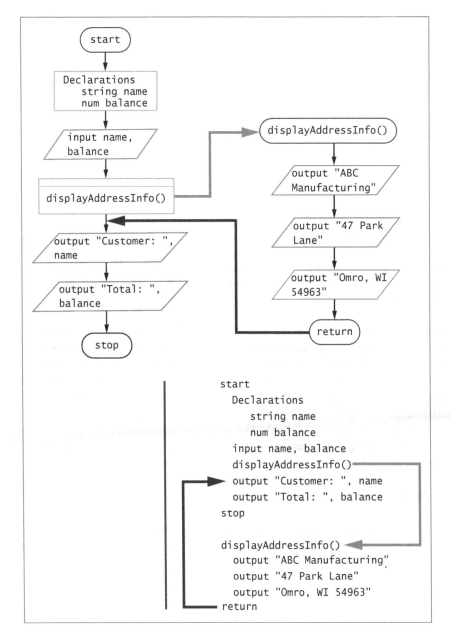

Figure 2-4 Program that produces a bill using main program that calls displayAddressInfo() module
© 2015 Cengage Learning

When the displayAddressInfo() module is called in Figure 2-4, logic transfers from the main program to the displayAddressInfo() module, as shown by the large red arrow in both the flowchart and the pseudocode. There, each module statement executes in turn before logical control is transferred back to the main program, where it continues with the statement that follows the module call, as shown by the large blue arrow. Programmers say the statements that are contained in a module have been **encapsulated**.

Neither of the programs in Figures 2-3 and 2-4 is superior to the other in terms of functionality; both perform exactly the same tasks in the same order. However, you may prefer the modularized version of the program for at least two reasons:

- First, the main program remains short and easy to follow because it contains just one statement to call the module, rather than three separate `output` statements to perform the work of the module.

- Second, a module is easy to reuse. After you create the address information module, you can use it in any application that needs the company's name and address. In other words, you do the work once, and then you can use the module many times.

A potential drawback to creating modules and moving between them is the overhead incurred. The computer keeps track of the correct memory address to which it should return after executing a module by recording the memory address in a location known as the **stack**. This process requires a small amount of computer time and resources. In most cases, the advantage to creating modules far outweighs the small amount of overhead required.

Determining when to modularize a program does not depend on a fixed set of rules; it requires experience and insight. Programmers do follow some guidelines when deciding how far to break down modules or how much to put in each of them. Some companies may have arbitrary rules, such as "a module's instructions should never take more than a page," or "a module should never have more than 30 statements," or "never have a module with only one statement." Rather than use such arbitrary rules, a better policy is to place together statements that contribute to one specific task. The more the statements contribute to the same job, the greater the **functional cohesion** of the module. A module that checks the validity of a date variable's value, or one that asks a user for a value and accepts it as input, is considered cohesive. A module that checks date validity, deducts insurance premiums, and computes federal withholding tax for an employee would be less cohesive.

Chapter 9 of the comprehensive version of this book provides more information on designing modules for high cohesion. It also explores the topic of *coupling*, which is a measure of how much modules depend on each other.

Watch the video *Modularizing a Program*.

Declaring Variables and Constants within Modules

You can place any statements within modules, including input, processing, and output statements. You also can include variable and constant declarations within modules. For example, you might decide to modify the billing program in Figure 2-4 so it looks like the one in Figure 2-5. In this version of the program, three named constants that hold the three lines of company data are declared within the displayAddressInfo() module. (See shading.)

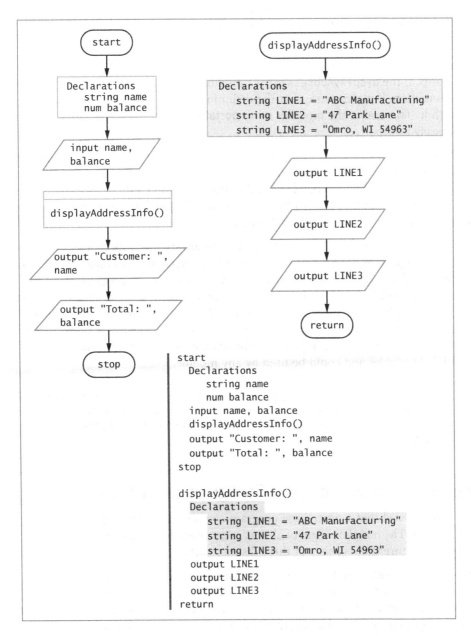

Figure 2-5   The billing program with constants declared within the module
© 2015 Cengage Learning

Variables and constants are usable only in the module in which they are declared. Programmers say the data items are **visible** or **in scope** only within the module in which they are declared. That means the program only recognizes them there. Programmers also say that variables and constants are **local** to the module in which they are declared. In other words, when the strings LINE1, LINE2, and LINE3 are declared in the displayAddressInfo() module in Figure 2-5, they are not recognized and cannot be used by the main module.

One of the motivations for creating modules is that separate modules are easily reusable in multiple programs. If the displayAddressInfo() module will be used by several programs within the organization, it makes sense that the definitions for its variables and constants must come with it. This makes the modules more **portable**; that is, they are self-contained units that are easily transported.

Besides local variables and constants, you can create global variables and constants. **Global** variables and constants are known to the entire program; they are said to be declared at the *program level*. That means they are visible to and usable in all the modules called by the program. The opposite is not true—variables and constants declared within a module are not usable elsewhere; they are visible only to that module.

In many modern programming languages, the main program itself is a module, so variables and constants declared there cannot be used elsewhere. To make the examples in this book easier to follow, variables and constants declared at the start of a main program will be considered global and usable in all modules. Until Chapter 9 in the comprehensive version, this book will use only global variables and constants so that you can concentrate on the main logic and not yet be concerned with the techniques necessary to make one module's data available to another. For example, in Figure 2-5, the main program variables name and balance are global variables and could be used by any module.

Many programmers do not approve of using global variables and constants. They are used here so you can more easily understand modularization before you learn the techniques of sending local variables from one module to another. Chapter 9 of the comprehensive version of this book will describe how you can make every variable local.

Understanding the Most Common Configuration for Mainline Logic

In Chapter 1, you learned that a procedural program contains procedures that follow one another in sequence. The mainline logic of almost every procedural computer program can follow a general structure that consists of three distinct parts:

1. **Housekeeping tasks** include any steps you must perform at the beginning of a program to get ready for the rest of the program. They can include tasks such as variable and constant declarations, displaying instructions to users, displaying report headings, opening any files the program requires, and inputting the first piece of data.

Inputting the first data item is always part of the housekeeping module. You will learn the theory behind this practice in Chapter 3. Chapter 7 covers file handling, including what it means to open and close a file.

2. **Detail loop tasks** do the core work of the program. When a program processes many records, detail loop tasks execute repeatedly for each set of input data until there are no more. For example, in a payroll program, the same set of calculations is executed repeatedly until a check has been produced for each employee.

3. **End-of-job tasks** are the steps you take at the end of the program to finish the application. You can call these finish-up or clean-up tasks. They might include displaying totals or other final messages and closing any open files.

Figure 2-6 shows the relationship of these three typical program parts. Notice how the housekeeping() and endOfJob() tasks are executed just once, but the detailLoop() tasks repeat as long as the eof condition has not been met. The flowchart uses a flowline to show how the detailLoop() module repeats; the pseudocode uses the words while and endwhile to contain statements that execute in a loop. You will learn more about the while and endwhile terms in subsequent chapters; for now, understand that they are a way of expressing repeated actions.

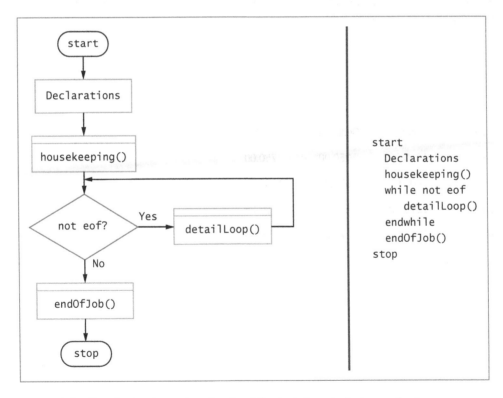

Figure 2-6 Flowchart and pseudocode of mainline logic for a typical procedural program
© 2015 Cengage Learning

Many everyday tasks follow the three-module format just described. For example, a candy factory opens in the morning, and the machines are started and filled with ingredients. These housekeeping tasks occur just once at the start of the day. Then, repeatedly during the day, candy is manufactured. This process might take many steps, each of which occurs many times. These are the steps in the detail loop. Then, at the end of the day, the machines are cleaned and shut down. These are the end-of-job tasks.

Not all programs take the format of the logic shown in Figure 2-6, but many do. Keep this general configuration in mind as you think about how you might organize many programs. For example, Figure 2-7 shows a sample payroll report for a small company. A user enters employee names until there are no more to enter, at which point the user enters *XXX*. As long as the entered name is not *XXX*, the user enters the employee's weekly gross pay. Deductions are computed as a flat 25 percent of the gross pay, and the statistics for each employee are output. The user enters another name, and as long as it is not *XXX*, the process continues. Examine the logic in Figure 2-8 to identify the components in the housekeeping, detail loop, and end-of-job tasks. You will learn more about the payroll report program in the next few chapters. For now, concentrate on the big picture of how a typical application works.

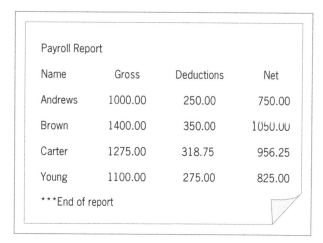

Figure 2-7   Sample payroll report
© 2015 Cengage Learning

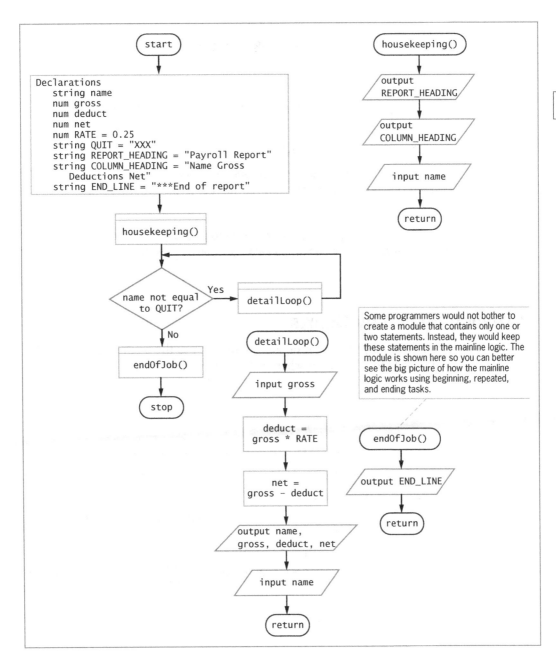

Figure 2-8 Logic for payroll report
© 2015 Cengage Learning

TWO TRUTHS & A LIE

Modularizing a Program

1. A calling program calls a module's name when it wants to use the module.

2. Whenever a main program calls a module, the logic transfers to the module; when the module ends, the program ends.

3. Housekeeping tasks include any steps you must perform just once at the beginning of a program to get ready for the rest of the program.

The false statement is #2. When a module ends, the logical flow transfers back to the main calling module and resumes where it left off.

Creating Hierarchy Charts

You may have seen hierarchy charts for organizations, such as the one in Figure 2-9. The chart shows who reports to whom, not when or how often they report.

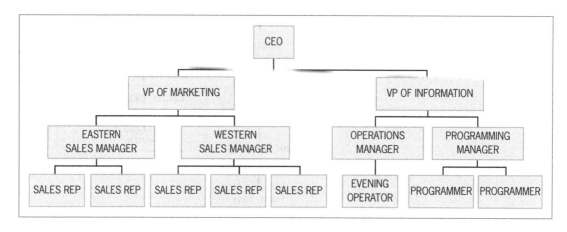

Figure 2-9   An organizational hierarchy chart
© 2015 Cengage Learning

When a program has several modules calling other modules, programmers often use a program **hierarchy chart** (sometimes called a *structure chart*) that operates in a similar manner to show the overall picture of how modules are related to one another. A hierarchy chart does not tell you what tasks are to be performed *within* a module, *when* the modules are called, *how* a module executes, or *why* they are called—that information is in the flowchart or pseudocode. A hierarchy chart tells you only *which* modules exist within a program and *which* modules call others. The hierarchy chart for the program in Figure 2-8 looks like Figure 2-10. It shows that the main module calls three others—housekeeping(), detailLoop(), and endOfJob().

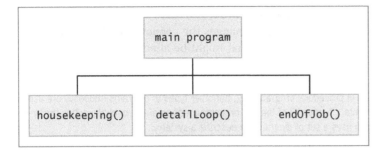

Figure 2-10   Hierarchy chart of payroll report program in Figure 2-8
© 2015 Cengage Learning

Figure 2-11 shows an example of a hierarchy chart for the billing program of a mail-order company. The hierarchy chart is for a more complicated program, but like the payroll report chart in Figure 2-10, it supplies module names and a general overview of the tasks to be performed, without specifying any details.

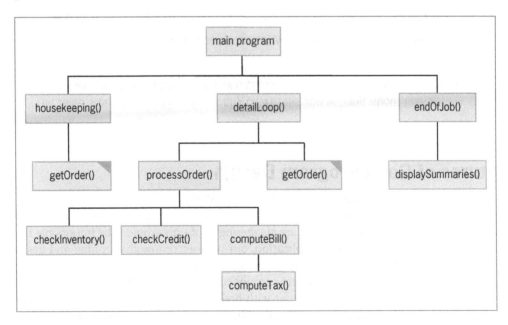

Figure 2-11   Billing program hierarchy chart
© 2015 Cengage Learning

Because program modules are reusable, a specific module may be called from several locations within a program. For example, in the billing program hierarchy chart in Figure 2-11, you can see that the getOrder() module is used twice. By convention, you blacken a corner of each box that represents a module used more than once. This action alerts readers that any change to this module could have consequences in multiple locations.

A hierarchy chart can be both a planning tool for developing the overall relationship of program modules before you write them and a documentation tool to help others see how modules are related after a program is written. For example, if a tax law changes, a programmer might be asked to rewrite the computeTax() module in the billing program diagrammed in Figure 2-11. As the programmer changes the computeTax() module, the hierarchy chart shows other dependent modules that might be affected. A hierarchy chart is useful for getting the big picture in a complex program.

 Hierarchy charts are used in procedural programming, but other types of diagrams frequently are used in object-oriented environments. Chapter 13 of the comprehensive edition of this book describes the Unified Modeling Language, which uses a set of diagrams to describe a system.

TWO TRUTHS & A LIE

Creating Hierarchy Charts

1. You can use a hierarchy chart to illustrate modules' relationships.

2. A hierarchy chart tells you what tasks are to be performed within a module.

3. A hierarchy chart tells you only which modules call other modules.

The false statement is #2. A hierarchy chart tells you nothing about tasks performed within a module; it only depicts how modules are related to each other.

Features of Good Program Design

As your programs become larger and more complicated, the need for good planning and design increases. Think of an application you use, such as a word processor or a spreadsheet. The number and variety of user options are staggering. Not only would it be impossible for a single programmer to write such an application, but without thorough planning and design, the components would never work together properly. Ideally, each program module you design needs to work well as a stand-alone component and as an element of larger systems. Just as a house with poor plumbing or a car with bad brakes is fatally flawed, a computer-based application can be highly functional only if each component is designed well. Walking through your program's logic on paper (called desk-checking, as you learned in Chapter 1) is an important step to achieving superior programs. Additionally, you can implement several design features while creating programs that are easier to write and maintain. To create good programs, you should do the following:

- Provide program comments where appropriate.

- Choose identifiers thoughtfully.

- Strive to design clear statements within your programs and modules.

- Write clear prompts and echo input.

- Continue to maintain good programming habits as you develop your programming skills.

Using Program Comments

When you write programs, you often might want to insert program comments. **Program comments** are written explanations that are not part of the program logic but that serve as documentation for readers of the program. In other words, they are nonexecuting statements that help readers understand programming statements. Readers might include users who help you test the program and other programmers who might have to modify your programs in the future. Even you, as the program's author, will appreciate comments when you make future modifications and forget why you constructed a statement in a certain way.

The syntax used to create program comments differs among programming languages. This book starts comments in pseudocode with two forward slashes. For example, Figure 2-12 contains comments that explain the origins and purposes of variables in a real estate program.

 Program comments are a type of **internal documentation**. This term distinguishes them from supporting documents outside the program, which are called **external documentation**. Appendix C discusses other types of documentation.

```
Declarations
    num sqFeet
        // sqFeet is an estimate provided by the seller of the property
    num pricePerFoot
        // pricePerFoot is determined by current market conditions
    num lotPremium
        // lotPremium depends on amenities such as whether lot is waterfront
```

Figure 2-12   Pseudocode that declares variables and includes comments
© 2015 Cengage Learning

In a flowchart, you can use an annotation symbol to hold information that expands on what is stored within another flowchart symbol. An **annotation symbol** is most often represented by a three-sided box that is connected to the step it references by a dashed line. Annotation symbols are used to hold comments or sometimes statements that are too long to fit neatly into a flowchart symbol. For example, Figure 2-13 shows how a programmer might use some annotation symbols in a flowchart for a payroll program.

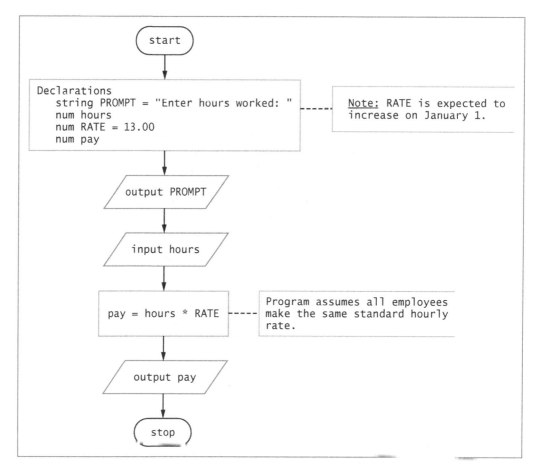

Figure 2-13   Flowchart that includes annotation symbols
© 2015 Cengage Learning

You probably will use comments in your coded programs more frequently than you use them in pseudocode or flowcharts. For one thing, flowcharts and pseudocode are more English-like than the code in some languages, so your statements might be less cryptic. Also, your comments will remain in the program as part of the program documentation, but your planning tools are likely to be discarded once the program goes into production.

Including program comments is not necessary to create a working program, but comments can help you to remember the purpose of variables or to explain complicated calculations, especially when you come back to a program months or years after writing it. Some students do not like to include comments in their programs because it takes time to type them and they aren't part of the "real" program, but the programs you write in the future probably will require some comments. When you acquire your first programming job and modify a program written by another programmer, you will appreciate well-placed comments that explain complicated sections of the code.

An additional responsibility regarding comments is that they must be kept current as a program is modified. Outdated comments can provide misleading information about a program's status.

Choosing Identifiers

The selection of good identifiers is an often-overlooked element in program design. When you write programs, you choose identifiers for variables, constants, and modules. You learned the rules for naming variables and modules earlier in this chapter: Each must be a single word with no embedded spaces and must start with a letter. Those simple rules provide a lot of leeway in naming program elements, but not all identifiers are equally good. Choosing good identifiers simplifies your programming job and makes it easier for others to understand your work.

Some general guidelines include the following:

- Although not required in any programming language, it usually makes sense to give a variable or constant a name that is a noun (or a combination of an adjective and noun) because it represents a thing. Similarly, it makes sense to give a module an identifier that is a verb, or a combined verb and noun, because a module takes action.

- Use meaningful names. Creating a data item named someData or a module named firstModule() makes a program cryptic. Not only will others find it hard to read your programs, but you will forget the purpose of these identifiers even within your own programs. All programmers occasionally use short, nondescriptive names such as x or temp in a quick program; however, in most cases, data and module names should be meaningful. Programmers refer to programs that contain meaningful names as **self-documenting**. This means that even without further documentation, the program code explains itself to readers.

- Use pronounceable names. A variable name like pzf is neither pronounceable nor meaningful. A name that looks meaningful when you write it might not be as meaningful when someone else reads it; for instance, preparead() might mean "Prepare ad" to you, but "Prep a read" to others. Look at your names critically to make sure they can be pronounced. Very standard abbreviations do not have to be pronounceable. For example, most businesspeople would interpret ssn as a Social Security number.

- Don't forget that not all programmers share your culture. An abbreviation whose meaning seems obvious to you might be cryptic to someone in a different part of the world, or even a different part of your country. For example, you might name a variable roi to hold a value for *return on investment*, but a French-speaking person might interpret the meaning as *king*.

- Be judicious in your use of abbreviations. You can save a few keystrokes when creating a module called getStat(), but is the module's purpose to find the state in which a city is located, input some statistics, or determine the status of some variables? Similarly, is a variable named fn meant to hold a first name, file number, or something else? Abbreviations can also confuse people in different lines of work: AKA might suggest a sorority (Alpha Kappa Alpha) to a college administrator, a registry (American Kennel Association) to a dog breeder, or an alias (also known as) to a police detective.

To save typing time when you develop a program, you can use a short name like `efn`. After the program operates correctly, you can use a text editor's Search and Replace feature to replace your coded name with a more meaningful name such as `employeeFirstName`. When working in an integrated development environment, you can use the technique known as *refactoring* to rename every instance of an identifier.

Many IDEs support an automatic statement-completion feature that saves typing time. After the first time you use a name like `employeeFirstName`, you need to type only the first few letters before the compiler editor offers a list of available names from which to choose. The list is constructed from all the names you have used that begin with the same characters.

- Usually, avoid digits in a name. A zero can be confused with the letter *O*, and the lowercase letter *l* is misread as the numeral 1. Of course, use your judgment: `budgetFor2014` probably will not be misinterpreted.

- Use the rules your language allows to separate words in long, multiword variable names. For example, if the programming language you use allows hyphens or underscores, then use a module name like `initialize-data()` or `initialize_data()`, which is easier to read than `initializedata()`. Another option is to use camel casing to create an identifier such as `initializeData()`. If you use a language that is case sensitive, it is legal but confusing to use variable names that differ only in case. For example, if a single program contains `empName`, `EmpName`, and `Empname`, confusion is sure to follow.

- Consider including a form of the verb *to be*, such as *is* or *are*, in names for variables that are intended to hold a status. For example, use `isFinished` as a string variable that holds a *Y* or *N* to indicate whether a file is exhausted. The shorter name `finished` is more likely to be confused with a module that executes when a program is done. (Many languages support a Boolean data type, which you assign to variables meant to hold only true or false. Using a form of *to be* in identifiers for Boolean variables is appropriate.)

- Many programmers follow the convention of naming constants using all uppercase letters, inserting underscores between words for readability. In this chapter you saw examples such as `SALES_TAX_RATE`.

- Organizations sometimes enforce different rules for programmers to follow when naming program components. It is your responsibility to find out the conventions used in your organization and to adhere to them.

Programmers sometimes create a **data dictionary**, which is a list of every variable name used in a program, along with its type, size, and description. When a data dictionary is created, it becomes part of the program documentation.

When you begin to write programs, the process of determining what variables, constants, and modules you need and what to name them all might seem overwhelming. The design process is crucial, however. When you acquire your first professional programming assignment, the design process might very well be completed already. Most likely, your first assignment will be to write or modify one small member module of a much larger application. The more the original programmers adhered to naming guidelines, the better the original design was, and the easier your job of modification will be.

Designing Clear Statements

In addition to using program comments and selecting good identifiers, you can use the following tactics to contribute to the clarity of the statements within your programs:

- Avoid confusing line breaks.

- Use temporary variables to clarify long statements.

Avoiding Confusing Line Breaks

Some older programming languages require that program statements be placed in specific columns. Most modern programming languages are free-form; you can arrange your lines of code any way you see fit. As in real life, with freedom comes responsibility; when you have flexibility in arranging your lines of code, you must take care to make sure your meaning is clear. With free-form code, programmers are allowed to place two or three statements on a line, or, conversely, to spread a single statement across multiple lines. Both make programs harder to read. All the pseudocode examples in this book use appropriate, clear spacing and line breaks.

Using Temporary Variables to Clarify Long Statements

When you need several mathematical operations to determine a result, consider using a series of temporary variables to hold intermediate results. A **temporary variable** (or **work variable**) is not used for input or output, but instead is just a working variable that you use during a program's execution. For example, Figure 2-14 shows two ways to calculate a value for a real estate salespersonCommission variable. Each example achieves the same result—the salesperson's commission is based on the square feet multiplied by the price per square foot, plus any premium for a lot with special features, such as a wooded or waterfront lot. However, the second example uses two temporary variables: basePropertyPrice and totalSalePrice. When the computation is broken down into less complicated, individual steps, it is easier to see how the total price is calculated. In calculations with even more computation steps, performing the arithmetic in stages would become increasingly helpful.

```
// Using a single statement to compute commission
salespersonCommission = (sqFeet * pricePerFoot + lotPremium) * commissionRate

// Using multiple statements to compute commission
basePropertyPrice = sqFeet * pricePerFoot
totalSalePrice = basePropertyPrice + lotPremium
salespersonCommission = totalSalePrice * commissionRate
```

Figure 2-14   Two ways of achieving the same salespersonCommission result

Programmers might say using temporary variables, like the second example in Figure 2-14, is *cheap*. When executing a lengthy arithmetic statement, even if you don't explicitly name temporary variables, the programming language compiler creates them behind the scenes (although without descriptive names), so declaring them yourself does not cost much in terms of program execution time.

Writing Clear Prompts and Echoing Input

When program input should be retrieved from a user, you almost always want to provide a prompt for the user. A **prompt** is a message that is displayed on a monitor to ask the user for a response and perhaps explain how that response should be formatted. Prompts are used both in command-line and GUI interactive programs.

For example, suppose a program asks a user to enter a catalog number for an item the user is ordering. The following prompt is not very helpful:

`Please enter a number.`

The following prompt is more helpful:

`Please enter a five-digit catalog order number.`

The following prompt is even more helpful:

`The five-digit catalog order number appears to the right of the item's picture in the catalog. Please enter it now.`

When program input comes from a stored file instead of a user, prompts are not needed. However, when a program expects a user response, prompts are valuable. For example, Figure 2-15 shows the flowchart and pseudocode for the beginning of the bill-producing program shown earlier in this chapter. If the input was coming from a data file, no prompt would be required, and the logic might look like the logic in Figure 2-15.

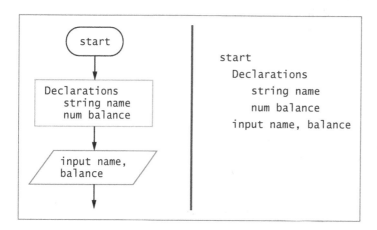

Figure 2-15   Beginning of a program that accepts a name and balance as input
© 2015 Cengage Learning

However, if the input was coming from a user, including prompts would be helpful. You could supply a single prompt such as *Please enter a customer's name and balance due*, but inserting more requests into a prompt generally makes it less likely that the user can remember to enter all the parts or enter them in the correct order. It is almost always best to include a separate prompt for each item to be entered. Figure 2-16 shows an example.

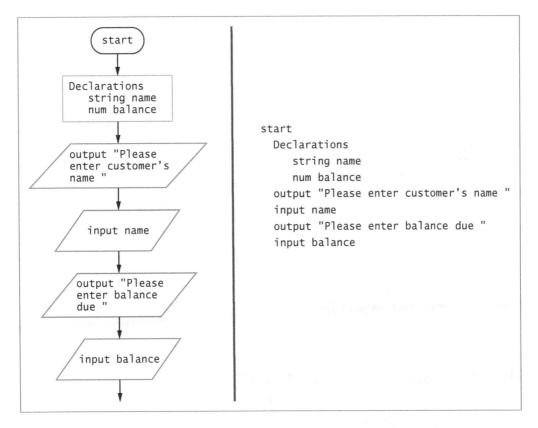

Figure 2-16 Beginning of a program that accepts a name and balance as input and uses a separate prompt for each item
© 2015 Cengage Learning

Users also find it helpful when you echo their input. **Echoing input** is the act of repeating input back to a user either in a subsequent prompt or in output. For example, Figure 2-17 shows how the second prompt in Figure 2-16 can be improved by echoing the user's first piece of input data in the second prompt. When a user runs the program that is started in Figure 2-17 and enters *Green* for the customer name, the second prompt will not be *Please enter balance due*. Instead, it will be *Please enter balance due for Green*. For example, if a clerk was about to enter the balance for the wrong customer, the mention of *Green* might be enough to alert the clerk to the potential error.

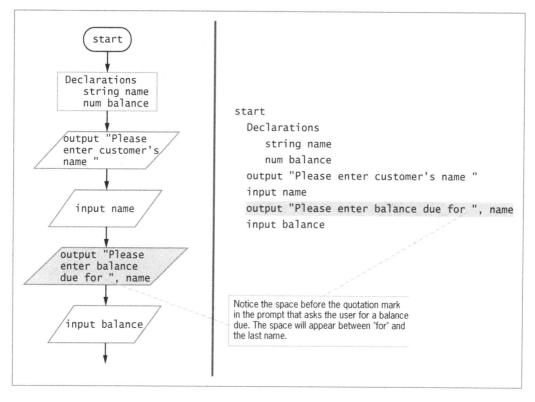

Figure 2-17   Beginning of a program that accepts a customer's name and uses it in the second prompt
© 2015 Cengage Learning

Maintaining Good Programming Habits

When you learn a programming language and begin to write lines of program code, it is easy to forget the principles you have learned in this text. Having some programming knowledge and a keyboard at your fingertips can lure you into typing lines of code before you think things through. But every program you write will be better if you plan before you code. Maintaining the habits of first drawing flowcharts or writing pseudocode, as you have learned here, will make your future programming projects go more smoothly. If you desk-check your program logic on paper before coding statements in a programming language, your programs will run correctly sooner. If you think carefully about the variable and module names you choose, and design program statements to be easy to read and use, your programs will be easier to develop and maintain.

TWO TRUTHS & A LIE

Features of Good Program Design

1. A program comment is a message that is displayed on a monitor to ask the user for a response and perhaps explain how that response should be formatted.

2. It usually makes sense to give each variable a name that contains a noun and to give each module a name that contains a verb.

3. Echoing input can help a user to confirm that a data item was entered correctly.

The false statement is #1. A program comment is a written explanation that is not part of the program logic but that serves as documentation for those reading the program. A prompt is a message that is displayed on a monitor to ask the user for a response and perhaps explain how that response should be formatted.

Chapter Summary

- Programs contain data in three different forms: literals (or unnamed constants), variables, and named constants. Each of these types of data can be numeric or string. Variables are named memory locations, the contents of which can vary. A variable declaration includes a data type and an identifier; optionally, it can include an initialization. Every computer programming language has its own set of rules for naming variables; however, all variable names must be written as one word without embedded spaces and should have appropriate meaning. A named constant is similar to a variable, except it can be assigned a value only once.

- Most programming languages use +, −, *, and / as the four standard arithmetic operators. Every operator follows rules of precedence that dictate the order in which operations in the same statement are carried out; multiplication and division always take precedence over addition and subtraction. The rules of precedence can be overridden using parentheses.

- Programmers break down programming problems into smaller, cohesive units called modules, subroutines, procedures, functions, or methods. To execute a module, you call it from another program or module. Any program can contain an unlimited number of modules, and each module can be called an unlimited number of times. Modularization provides abstraction, allows multiple programmers to work on a problem, and makes it easier for you to reuse work.

- When you create a module, you include a header, a body, and a `return` statement. A program or module calls a module's name to execute it. You can place any statements within modules, including declarations, which are local to the module. Global variables and constants are those that are known to the entire program. The mainline logic of almost every procedural computer program can follow a general structure that consists of three distinct parts: housekeeping tasks, detail loop tasks, and end-of-job tasks.

- A hierarchy chart illustrates modules and their relationships; it indicates which modules exist within a program and which modules call others.

- As programs become larger and more complicated, the need for good planning and design increases. You should use program comments where appropriate. Choose identifiers wisely, strive to design clear statements within your programs and modules, write clear prompts and echo input, and continue to maintain good programming habits as you develop your programming skills.

Key Terms

Numeric describes data that consists of numbers.

String describes data that is nonnumeric.

An **integer** is a whole number.

A **floating-point** number is a number with decimal places.

Real numbers are floating-point numbers.

A **numeric constant** (or **literal numeric constant**) is a specific numeric value.

A **string constant** (or **literal string constant**) is a specific group of characters enclosed within quotation marks.

Alphanumeric values can contain alphabetic characters, numbers, and punctuation.

An **unnamed constant** is a literal numeric or string value.

A **declaration** is a statement that provides a data type, an identifier, and, optionally, an initial value.

An **identifier** is a program component's name.

A data item's **data type** is a classification that describes what values can be assigned, how the item is stored, and what types of operations can be performed with the item.

Initializing a variable is the act of assigning its first value, often at the same time the variable is declared.

Garbage describes the unknown value stored in an unassigned variable.

Keywords comprise the limited word set that is reserved in a language.

Camel casing is a naming convention in which the initial letter is lowercase, multiple-word names are run together, and each new word within the name begins with an uppercase letter.

Lower camel casing is another name for the *camel casing* naming convention.

Pascal casing is a naming convention in which the initial letter is uppercase, multiple-word names are run together, and each new word within the name begins with an uppercase letter.

Upper camel casing is another name for the *Pascal casing* naming convention.

Hungarian notation is a naming convention in which a data type or other information is stored as part of a name.

Snake casing is a convention in which parts of a name are separated by underscores.

Mixed case with underscores is a naming convention similar to snake casing, but new words start with an uppercase letter.

Kebob case is sometimes used as the name for the style that uses dashes to separate parts of a name.

An **assignment statement** assigns a value from the right of an assignment operator to the variable or constant on the left of the assignment operator.

The **assignment operator** is the equal sign; it is used to assign a value to the variable or constant on its left.

A **binary operator** is an operator that requires two operands—one on each side.

An **operand** is a value used by an operator.

Right-associativity and **right-to-left associativity** describe operators that evaluate the expression to the right first.

An **lvalue** is the memory address identifier to the left of an assignment operator.

A **numeric variable** is one that can hold digits, have mathematical operations performed on it, and usually can hold a decimal point and a sign indicating positive or negative.

A **string variable** can hold text that includes letters, digits, and special characters such as punctuation marks.

Type-safety is the feature of some programming languages that prevents assigning values of an incorrect data type.

A **named constant** is similar to a variable, except that its value cannot change after the first assignment.

A **magic number** is an unnamed constant whose purpose is not immediately apparent.

Overhead describes the extra resources a task requires.

Rules of precedence dictate the order in which operations in the same statement are carried out.

The **order of operations** describes the rules of precedence.

Left-to-right associativity describes operators that evaluate the expression to the left first.

The **remainder operator** is an arithmetic operator used in some programming languages; when used with two integer operands, it results in the remainder after division.

Modules are small program units that you can use together to make a program. Programmers also refer to modules as **subroutines**, **procedures**, **functions**, or **methods**.

To **call a module** is to use the module's name to invoke it, causing it to execute.

Modularization is the process of breaking down a program into modules.

Functional decomposition is the act of reducing a large program into more manageable modules.

Abstraction is the process of paying attention to important properties while ignoring nonessential details.

Reusability is the feature of modular programs that allows individual modules to be used in a variety of applications.

Reliability is the feature of modular programs that assures you a module has been tested and proven to function correctly.

A **main program** runs from start to stop and calls other modules.

The **mainline logic** is the logic that appears in a program's main module; it calls other modules.

The **module header** includes the module identifier and possibly other necessary identifying information.

The **module body** contains all the statements in the module.

The **module return statement** marks the end of the module and identifies the point at which control returns to the program or module that called the module.

Encapsulation is the act of containing a task's instructions in a module.

A **stack** is a memory location in which the computer keeps track of the correct memory address to which it should return after executing a module.

The **functional cohesion** of a module is a measure of the degree to which all the module statements contribute to the same task.

Visible describes data items when a module can recognize them.

In scope describes data that is visible.

Local describes variables that are declared within the module that uses them.

A **portable** module is one that can more easily be reused in multiple programs.

Global describes variables that are known to an entire program.

Housekeeping tasks include steps you must perform at the beginning of a program to get ready for the rest of the program.

Detail loop tasks of a program include the steps that are repeated for each set of input data.

End-of-job tasks hold the steps you take at the end of the program to finish the application.

A **hierarchy chart** is a diagram that illustrates modules' relationships to each other.

Program comments are written explanations that are not part of the program logic but that serve as documentation for those reading the program.

Internal documentation is documentation within a coded program.

External documentation is documentation that is outside a coded program.

An **annotation symbol** contains information that expands on what appears in another flowchart symbol; it is most often represented by a three-sided box that is connected to the step it references by a dashed line.

Self-documenting programs are those that contain meaningful identifiers that describe their purpose.

A **data dictionary** is a list of every variable name used in a program, along with its type, size, and description.

A **temporary variable** (or **work variable**) is a variable that you use to hold intermediate results during a program's execution.

A **prompt** is a message that is displayed on a monitor to ask the user for a response and perhaps explain how that response should be formatted.

Echoing input is the act of repeating input back to a user either in a subsequent prompt or in output.

Exercises

 Review Questions

1. What does a declaration provide for a variable?

   a. a name   c. both of the above
   b. a data type   d. none of the above

2. A variable's data type describes all of the following *except* _____ .

   a. what values the variable can hold
   b. how the variable is stored in memory
   c. what operations can be performed with the variable
   d. the scope of the variable

3. The value stored in an uninitialized variable is _____.

    a. garbage   c. compost

    b. null   d. its identifier

4. The value 3 is a _____.

    a. numeric variable   c. string variable

    b. numeric constant   d. string constant

5. The assignment operator _____.

    a. is a binary operator   c. is most often represented by a colon

    b. has left-to-right associativity   d. two of the above

6. Which of the following is true about arithmetic precedence?

    a. Multiplication has a higher precedence than division.

    b. Operators with the lowest precedence always have left-to-right associativity.

    c. Division has higher precedence than subtraction.

    d. all of the above

7. Which of the following is a term used as a synonym for *module* in some programming languages?

    a. method   c. both of these

    b. procedure   d. none of these

8. Which of the following is a reason to use modularization?

    a. Modularization avoids abstraction.

    b. Modularization reduces overhead.

    c. Modularization allows you to more easily reuse your work.

    d. Modularization eliminates the need for syntax.

9. What is the name for the process of paying attention to important properties while ignoring nonessential details?

    a. abstraction   c. extinction

    b. extraction   d. modularization

10. Every module has all of the following *except* _____.

    a. a header   c. a body

    b. local variables   d. a return statement

11. Programmers say that one module can _____ another, meaning that the first module causes the second module to execute.

    a. declare   c. enact

    b. define   d. call

12. The more that a module's statements contribute to the same job, the greater the _____ of the module.

    a. structure   c. functional cohesion
    b. modularity   d. size

13. In most modern programming languages, a variable or constant that is declared in a module is _____ in that module.

    a. global   c. in scope
    b. invisible   d. undefined

14. Which of the following is *not* a typical housekeeping task?

    a. displaying instructions   c. opening files
    b. printing summaries   d. displaying report headings

15. Which module in a typical program will execute the most times?

    a. the housekeeping module   c. the end-of-job module
    b. the detail loop   d. It is different in every program.

16. A hierarchy chart tells you _____ .

    a. what tasks are to be performed within each program module
    b. when a module executes
    c. which routines call which other routines
    d. all of the above

17. What are nonexecuting statements that programmers place within code to explain program statements in English?

    a. comments   c. trivia
    b. pseudocode   d. user documentation

18. Program comments are _____ .

    a. required to create a runnable program
    b. a form of external documentation
    c. both of the above
    d. none of the above

19. Which of the following is valid advice for naming variables?

    a. To save typing, make most variable names one or two letters.
    b. To avoid conflict with names that others are using, use unusual or unpronounceable names.
    c. To make names easier to read, separate long names by using underscores or capitalization for each new word.
    d. To maintain your independence, shun the conventions of your organization.

20. A message that asks a user for input is a(n) _____.

    a. comment

    b. prompt

    c. echo

    d. declaration

 Programming Exercises

1. Explain why each of the following names does or does not seem like a good variable name to you.

    a. d

    b. dsctamt

    c. discountAmount

    d. discount Amount

    e. discount

    f. discountAmountForEachNewCustomer

    g. discountYear2015

    h. 2015Discountyear

2. If productCost and productPrice are numeric variables, and productName is a string variable, which of the following statements are valid assignments? If a statement is not valid, explain why not.

    a. productCost = 100

    b. productPrice = productCost

    c. productPrice = productName

    d. productPrice = "24.95"

    e. 15.67 = productCost

    f. productCost = $1,345.52

    g. productCost = productPrice - 10

    h. productName = "mouse pad"

    i. productCost + 20 = productPrice

    j. productName = 3-inch nails

    k. productName = 43

    l. productName = "44"

    m. "99" = productName

    n. productName = brush

o. `battery = productName`

p. `productPrice = productPrice`

q. `productName = productCost`

3. Assume that `income = 8` and `expense = 6`. What is the value of each of the following expressions?

a. `income + expense * 2`

b. `income + 4 - expense / 2`

c. `(income + expense) * 2`

d. `income - 3 * 2 + expense`

e. `4 * ((income - expense) + 2) + 10`

4. Draw a typical hierarchy chart for a program that produces a monthly bill for a cell phone customer. Try to think of at least 10 separate modules that might be included. For example, one module might calculate the charge for daytime phone minutes used.

5. a. Draw the hierarchy chart and then plan the logic for a program needed by the sales manager of The Henry Used Car Dealership. The program will determine the profit on any car sold. Input includes the sale price and actual purchase price for a car. The output is the profit, which is the sale price minus the purchase price. Use three modules. The main program declares global variables and calls housekeeping, detail, and end-of-job modules. The housekeeping module prompts for and accepts a sale price. The detail module prompts for and accepts the purchase price, computes the profit, and displays the result. The end-of-job module displays the message *Thanks for using this program.*

    b. Revise the profit-determining program so that it runs continuously for any number of cars. The detail loop executes continuously while the sale price is not 0; in addition to calculating the profit, it prompts the user for and gets the next sale price. The end-of-job module executes after 0 is entered for the sale price.

6. a. Draw the hierarchy chart and then plan the logic for a program that calculates a person's body mass index (BMI). BMI is a statistical measure that compares a person's weight and height. The program uses three modules. The first prompts a user for and accepts the user's height in inches. The second module accepts the user's weight in pounds and converts the user's height to meters and weight to kilograms. Then, it calculates BMI as weight in kilograms divided by height in meters squared, and displays the results. There are 2.54 centimeters in an inch, 100 centimeters in a meter, 453.59 grams in a pound, and 1,000 grams in a kilogram. Use named constants whenever you think they are appropriate. The last module displays the message *End of job.*

    b. Revise the BMI-determining program to execute continuously until the user enters 0 for the height in inches.

7. Draw the hierarchy chart and design the logic for a program that calculates service charges for Hazel's Housecleaning service. The program contains housekeeping, detail loop, and end-of-job modules. The main program declares any needed global variables and constants and calls the other modules. The housekeeping module displays a prompt for and accepts a customer's last name. While the user does not enter ZZZZ for the name, the detail loop accepts the number of bathrooms and the number of other rooms to be cleaned. The service charge is computed as $40 plus $15 for each bathroom and $10 for each of the other rooms. The detail loop also displays the service charge and then prompts the user for the next customer's name. The end-of-job module, which executes after the user enters the sentinel value for the name, displays a message that indicates the program is complete.

8. Draw the hierarchy chart and design the logic for a program that calculates the projected cost of an automobile trip. Assume that the user's car travels 20 miles per gallon of gas. Design a program that prompts the user for a number of miles driven and a current cost per gallon. The program computes and displays the cost of the trip as well as the cost if gas prices rise by 10 percent. The program accepts data continuously until 0 is entered for the number of miles. Use appropriate modules, including one that displays *End of program* when the program is finished.

9. a. Draw the hierarchy chart and design the logic for a program needed by the manager of the Stengel County softball team, who wants to compute slugging percentages for his players. A slugging percentage is the total bases earned with base hits divided by the player's number of at-bats. Design a program that prompts the user for a player jersey number, the number of bases earned, and the number of at-bats, and then displays all the data, including the calculated slugging average. The program accepts players continuously until 0 is entered for the jersey number. Use appropriate modules, including one that displays *End of job* after the sentinel is entered for the jersey number.

    b. Modify the slugging percentage program to also calculate a player's on-base percentage. An on-base percentage is calculated by adding a player's hits and walks, and then dividing by the sum of at-bats, walks, and sacrifice flies. Prompt the user for all the additional data needed, and display all the data for each player.

    c. Modify the softball program so that it also computes a gross production average (GPA) for each player. A GPA is calculated by multiplying a player's on-base percentage by 1.8, then adding the player's slugging percentage, and then dividing by four.

10. Draw the hierarchy chart and design the logic for a program for the River Falls Homes Construction Company. Design a program that prompts the user for a lot number in the River Falls subdivision and data about the home to be built there, including number of bedrooms, number of bathrooms, and the number of cars the garage holds. Output is the price of the home, which is a $50,000 base price plus $17,000 for each bedroom, $12,500 for each bathroom, and $6,000 for

each car the garage holds. The program accepts lot numbers continuously until 0 is entered. Use named constants where appropriate. Also, use appropriate modules, including one that displays *End of job* after the sentinel is entered for the lot number.

11. Draw the hierarchy chart and design the logic for a program for Arnie's Appliances. Design a program that prompts the user for a refrigerator model name and the interior height, width, and depth in inches. Calculate the refrigerator capacity in cubic feet by first multiplying the height, width, and depth to get cubic inches, and then dividing by 1728 (the number of cubic inches in a cubic foot). The program accepts model names continuously until "XXX" is entered. Use named constants where appropriate. Also use modules, including one that displays *End of job* after the sentinel is entered for the model name.

Performing Maintenance

1. A file named MAINTENANCE02-01.txt is included with your downloadable student files. Assume that this program is a working program in your organization and that it needs modifications as described in the comments (lines that begin with two slashes) at the beginning of the file. Your job is to alter the program to meet the new specifications.

Find the Bugs

1. Your downloadable files for Chapter 2 include DEBUG02-01.txt, DEBUG02-02.txt, and DEBUG02-03.txt. Each file starts with some comments that describe the problem. Comments are lines that begin with two slashes (//). Following the comments, each file contains pseudocode that has one or more bugs you must find and correct.

2. Your downloadable files for Chapter 2 include a file named DEBUG02-04.jpg that contains a flowchart with syntax and/or logical errors. Examine the flowchart and then find and correct all the bugs.

Game Zone

1. For games to hold your interest, they almost always include some random, unpredictable behavior. For example, a game in which you shoot asteroids loses some of its fun if the asteroids follow the same, predictable path each time you play. Therefore, generating random values is a key component in creating most interesting computer games. Many programming languages come with a built-in

module you can use to generate random numbers. The syntax varies in each language, but it is usually something like the following:

`myRandomNumber = random(10)`

In this statement, `myRandomNumber` is a numeric variable you have declared and the expression `random(10)` means "call a method that generates and returns a random number between 1 and 10." By convention, in a flowchart, you would place a statement like this in a processing symbol with two vertical stripes at the edges, as shown below.

```
myRandomNumber =
random(10)
```

Create a flowchart or pseudocode that shows the logic for a program that generates a random number, then asks the user to think of a number between 1 and 10. Then display the randomly generated number so the user can see whether his or her guess was accurate. (In future chapters, you will improve this game so that the user can enter a guess and the program can determine whether the user was correct.)

Up for Discussion

1. Many programming style guides are published on the Web. These guides suggest good identifiers, explain standard indentation rules, and identify style issues in specific programming languages. Find style guides for at least two languages (for example, C++, Java, Visual Basic, or C#) and list any differences you notice.

2. What advantages are there to requiring variables to have a data type?

3. As this chapter mentions, some programming languages require that named constants are assigned a value when they are declared; other languages allow a constant's value to be assigned later in a program. Which requirement do you think is better? Why?

4. Many products use Pascal casing or camel casing in their names—for example, *MasterCard*. Name as many more as you can.

5. Distance measurement is one situation in which using integer division and the remainder operator might be useful. For example, if the programming language supports it, you can divide a measurement of 123 inches by 12 to get 10 feet, and then use the remainder operator to discover that the measurement is 3 inches over 10 feet. Think of several other situations in which you might find a remainder operator useful.

6. Would you prefer to write a large program by yourself, or to work on a team in which each programmer produces one or more modules? Why?

7. Extreme programming is a system for rapidly developing software. One of its tenets is that all production code is written by two programmers sitting at one machine. Is this a good idea? Does working this way as a programmer appeal to you? Why or why not?

Understanding Structure

In this chapter, you will learn about:

◎ The disadvantages of unstructured spaghetti code

◎ The three basic structures—sequence, selection, and loop

◎ Using a priming input to structure a program

◎ The need for structure

◎ Recognizing structure

◎ Structuring and modularizing unstructured logic

The Disadvantages of Unstructured Spaghetti Code

Professional business applications usually get far more complicated than the examples you have seen so far in Chapters 1 and 2. Imagine the number of instructions in the computer programs that guide an airplane's flight or audit an income tax return. Even the program that produces your paycheck at work contains many, many instructions. Designing the logic for such a program can be a time-consuming task. When you add hundreds or thousands of instructions to a program, it is easy to create a complicated mess. The descriptive name for logically snarled program statements is **spaghetti code**, because the logic is as hard to follow as one noodle through a plate of spaghetti. Not only is spaghetti code confusing, the programs that contain it are prone to error, difficult to reuse, and hard to use as building blocks for larger applications. Programs that use spaghetti code logic are **unstructured programs**; that is, they do not follow the rules of structured logic that you will learn in this chapter. **Structured programs** *do* follow those rules, and eliminate the problems caused by spaghetti code.

For example, suppose that you start a job as a dog washer and that you receive the instructions shown in Figure 3-1. This flowchart is an example of unstructured spaghetti code. A computer program that is organized similarly might "work"—that is, it might produce correct results—but it would be difficult to read and maintain, and its logic would be hard to follow.

You might be able to follow the logic of the dog-washing process in Figure 3-1 for two reasons:

- You might already know how to wash a dog.

- The flowchart contains a limited number of steps.

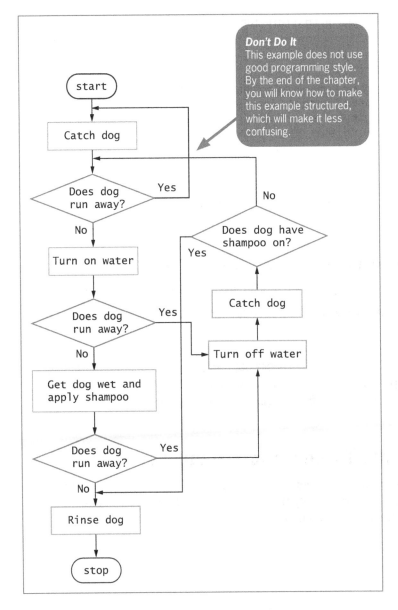

Figure 3-1 Spaghetti code logic for washing a dog
© 2015 Cengage Learning

However, imagine that you were not familiar with dog washing, or that the process was far more complicated. (For example, imagine you must wash 100 dogs concurrently while applying flea and tick medication, giving them haircuts, and researching their genealogy.)

Depicting more complicated logic in an unstructured way would be cumbersome. By the end of this chapter, you will understand how to make the unstructured process in Figure 3-1 clearer and less error-prone.

Software developers say that a program that contains spaghetti code has a shorter life than one with structured code. This means that programs developed using spaghetti code exist as production programs in an organization for less time. Such programs are so difficult to alter that when improvements are required, developers often find it easier to abandon the existing program and start from scratch. This takes extra time and costs more money.

TWO TRUTHS & A LIE

The Disadvantages of Unstructured Spaghetti Code

1. Spaghetti code is the descriptive name for logically snarled programs.

2. Programs written using spaghetti code cannot produce correct results.

3. Programs written using spaghetti code are more difficult to maintain than other programs.

The false statement is #2. Programs written using spaghetti code can produce correct results, but they are more difficult to understand and maintain than programs that use structured techniques.

Understanding the Three Basic Structures

In the mid-1960s, mathematicians proved that any program, no matter how complicated, can be constructed using one or more of only three structures. A **structure** is a basic unit of programming logic; each structure is one of the following:

- sequence

- selection

- loop

With these three structures alone, you can diagram any task, from doubling a number to performing brain surgery. You can diagram each structure with a specific configuration of flowchart symbols.

The Sequence Structure

The **sequence structure** is shown in Figure 3-2. It performs actions or tasks in order, one after the other. A sequence can contain any number of tasks, but there is no option to branch off and skip any of the tasks. Once you start a series of actions in a sequence, you must continue step by step until the sequence ends.

As an example, driving directions often are listed as a sequence. To tell a friend how to get to your house from school, you might provide the following sequence, in which one step follows the other and no steps can be skipped:

```
go north on First Avenue for 3 miles
turn left on Washington Boulevard
go west on Washington for 2 miles
stop at 634 Washington
```

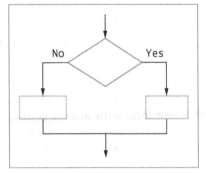

Figure 3-2　Sequence structure
© 2015 Cengage Learning

The Selection Structure

The **selection structure**, or **decision structure**, is shown in Figure 3-3. With this structure, one of two courses of action is taken based on the answer to a question. A flowchart that describes a selection structure begins with a decision symbol, and the branches of the decision must join at the bottom of the structure. Pseudocode that describes a selection structure starts with if. Pseudocode uses the **end-structure statement** endif to clearly show where the structure ends.

Some people call the selection structure an **if-then-else** because it fits the following statement:

```
if someCondition is true then
    do oneProcess
else
    do theOtherProcess
endif
```

Figure 3-3　Selection structure
© 2015 Cengage Learning

For example, you might provide part of the directions to your house as follows:

```
if traffic is backed up on Washington Boulevard then
    continue for 1 block on First Avenue and turn left on Adams Lane
else
    turn left on Washington Boulevard
endif
```

Similarly, a payroll program might include a statement such as:

```
if hoursWorked is more than 40 then
    calculate regularPay and overtimePay
else
    calculate regularPay
endif
```

These if-else examples can also be called **dual-alternative ifs** (or **dual-alternative selections**) because they contain two alternatives—the action taken when the tested condition is true and the action taken when it is false. Note that it is perfectly correct for one branch of the selection to be a "do nothing" branch. In each of the following examples, an action is taken only when the tested condition is true:

```
if it is raining then
    take an umbrella
endif
```

```
if employee participates in the dental plan then
    deduct $40 from employee gross pay
endif
```

The previous examples without else clauses are **single-alternative ifs** (or **single-alternative selections**); a diagram of their structure is shown in Figure 3-4. In these cases, you do not take any special action if it is not raining or if the employee does not belong to the dental plan. The branch in which no action is taken is called the **null case** or **null branch**.

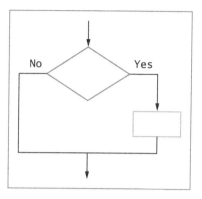

Figure 3-4   Single-alternative selection structure
© 2015 Cengage Learning

The Loop Structure

The **loop structure** is shown in Figure 3-5. A loop continues to repeat actions while a condition remains true. The action or actions that occur within the loop are the **loop body**. In the most common type of loop, a condition is evaluated; if the answer is true, you execute the loop body and evaluate the condition again. If the condition is still true, you execute the loop body again and then reevaluate the condition. This continues until the condition becomes false, and then you exit the loop structure. Programmers call this structure a **while loop**; pseudocode that describes this type of loop starts with

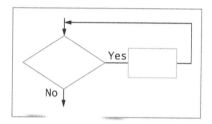

Figure 3-5   Loop structure
© 2015 Cengage Learning

while and ends with the end-structure statement endwhile. A flowchart that describes the while loop structure always begins with a decision symbol that has a branch that returns to a spot prior to the decision. You may hear programmers refer to looping as **repetition** or **iteration**.

 The while loop tests a condition before executing the loop body even once. Another type of structured loop tests a condition after the first loop body execution. You will learn more about this alternate type of loop in Chapter 4 and in Appendix D. For the rest of this chapter, assume that all loops are while loops that ask the controlling question before the loop body ever executes. All logical problems can be solved using only the three structures—sequence, selection, and while loop.

Some programmers call a while loop a **while...do loop**, because it fits the following statement:

```
while testCondition continues to be true do
    someProcess
endwhile
```

When you provide directions to your house, part of the directions might be:

```
while the address of the house you are passing remains below 634
    travel forward to the next house
    look at the address on the house
endwhile
```

You encounter examples of looping every day, as in each of the following:

```
while you continue to be hungry
    take another bite of food
    determine whether you still feel hungry
endwhile
```

```
while unread pages remain in the reading assignment
    read another unread page
    determine whether there are more pages to read
endwhile
```

Combining Structures

All logic problems can be solved using only these three structures—sequence, selection, and loop. The structures can be combined in an infinite number of ways. For example, you can have a sequence of tasks followed by a selection, or a loop followed by a sequence. Attaching structures end to end is called **stacking structures**. For example, Figure 3-6 shows a structured flowchart achieved by stacking structures, and shows pseudocode that follows the flowchart logic.

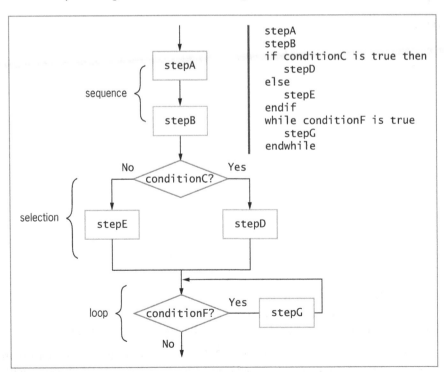

```
stepA
stepB
if conditionC is true then
    stepD
else
    stepE
endif
while conditionF is true
    stepG
endwhile
```

Figure 3-6   Structured flowchart and pseudocode with three stacked structures

Whether you are drawing a flowchart or writing pseudocode, you can use any opposite, mutually exclusive words to represent decision outcomes—for example, *Yes* and *No* or *true* and *false*. This book follows the convention of using *Yes* and *No* in flowchart diagrams and *true* and *false* in pseudocode.

The pseudocode in Figure 3-6 shows a sequence, followed by a selection, followed by a loop. First stepA and stepB execute in sequence. Then a selection structure starts with the test of conditionC. The instruction that follows the if clause (stepD) executes when its tested condition (conditionC) is true, the instruction that follows else (stepE) executes when the tested condition is false, and any instructions that follow endif execute in either case. In other words, statements beyond the endif statement are "outside" the selection structure. Similarly, the endwhile statement shows where the loop structure ends. In Figure 3-6, while conditionF continues to be true, stepG continues to execute. If any statements followed the endwhile statement, they would be outside of, and not a part of, the loop.

Besides stacking structures, you can replace any individual steps in a structured flowchart diagram or pseudocode with additional structures. This means that any sequence, selection, or loop can contain other sequence, selection, or loop structures. For example, you can have a sequence of three tasks on one branch of a selection, as shown in Figure 3-7. Placing a structure within another structure is called **nesting structures**.

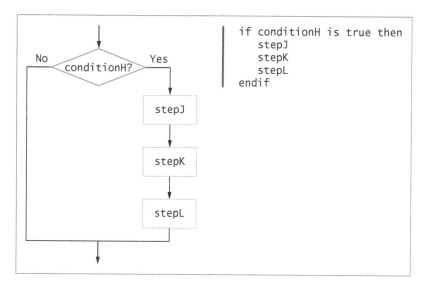

Figure 3-7 Flowchart and pseudocode showing nested structures—a sequence nested within a selection
© 2015 Cengage Learning

In the pseudocode for the logic shown in Figure 3-7, the indentation shows that all three statements (stepJ, stepK, and stepL) must execute if conditionH is true. These three statements constitute a **block**, or a group of statements that executes as a single unit.

In place of one of the steps in the sequence in Figure 3-7, you can insert another structure. In Figure 3-8, the process named stepK has been replaced with a loop structure that begins with a test of the condition named conditionM.

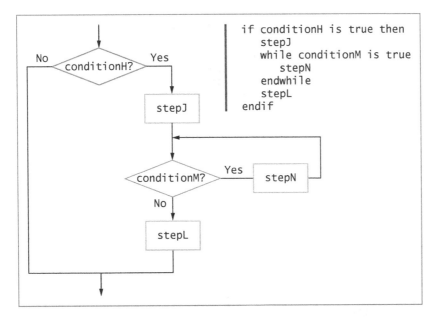

```
if conditionH is true then
    stepJ
    while conditionM is true
        stepN
    endwhile
    stepL
endif
```

Figure 3-8 Flowchart and pseudocode showing nested structures—a loop nested within a sequence, nested within a selection
© 2015 Cengage Learning

In the pseudocode shown in Figure 3-8, notice that if and endif are vertically aligned. This shows that they are "on the same level." Similarly, stepJ, while, endwhile, and stepL are aligned, and they are evenly indented. In the flowchart in Figure 3-8, you could draw a vertical line through the symbols containing stepJ, the entry and exit points of the while loop, and stepL. The flowchart and the pseudocode represent exactly the same logic.

When you nest structures, the statements that start and end a structure are always on the same level and are always in pairs. Structures cannot overlap. For example, if you have an if structure that contains a while structure, then the endwhile statement will come before the endif. On the other hand, if you have a while that contains an if, then the endif statement will come before the endwhile.

There is no limit to the number of levels you can create when you nest and stack structures. For example, Figure 3-9 shows logic that has been made more complicated by replacing stepN with a selection. The structure that performs stepP or stepQ based on the outcome of conditionO is nested within the loop that is controlled by conditionM. In the pseudocode in Figure 3-9, notice how the if, else, and endif that describe the condition selection are aligned with each other and within the while structure that is controlled by conditionM. As before, the indentation used in the pseudocode reflects the logic laid out graphically in the flowchart.

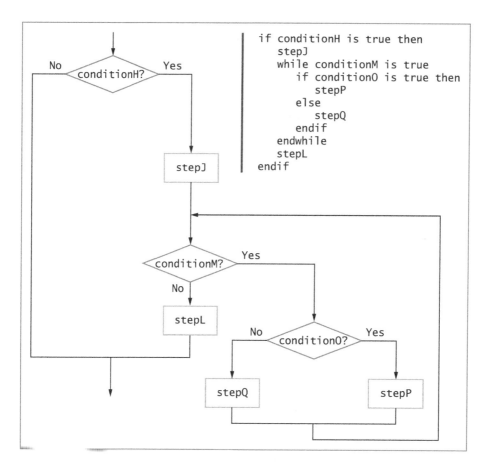

```
if conditionH is true then
    stepJ
    while conditionM is true
        if conditionO is true then
            stepP
        else
            stepQ
        endif
    endwhile
    stepL
endif
```

Figure 3-9 Flowchart and pseudocode for a selection within a loop within a sequence within a selection
© 2015 Cengage Learning

Many of the preceding examples are generic so that you can focus on the relationships of the symbols without worrying what they do. Keep in mind that generic instructions like stepA and generic conditions like conditionC can stand for anything. For example, Figure 3-10 shows the process of buying and planting flowers outdoors in the spring after the danger of frost is over. The flowchart and pseudocode structures are identical to those in Figure 3-9. In the exercises at the end of this chapter, you will be asked to develop more scenarios that fit the same pattern.

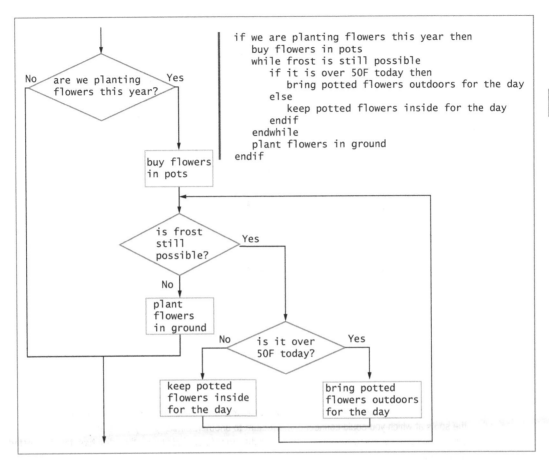

```
if we are planting flowers this year then
    buy flowers in pots
    while frost is still possible
        if it is over 50F today then
            bring potted flowers outdoors for the day
        else
            keep potted flowers inside for the day
        endif
    endwhile
    plant flowers in ground
endif
```

Figure 3-10 The process of buying and planting flowers in the spring
© 2015 Cengage Learning

The possible combinations of logical structures are endless, but each segment of a structured program is a sequence, a selection, or a loop. The three structures are shown together in Quick Reference 3-1. Notice that each structure has one entry point and one exit point. One structure can attach to another only at one of these points.

QUICK REFERENCE 3-1 The Three Structures

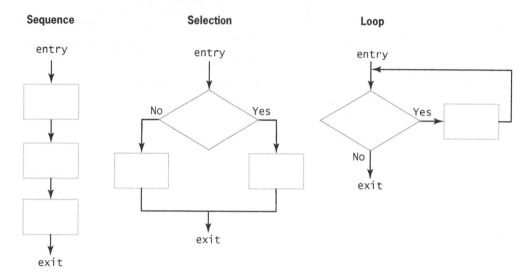

Sequence   Selection   Loop

Try to imagine physically picking up any of the three structures using the entry and exit "handles." These are the spots at which you could connect one structure to another. Similarly, any complete structure, from its entry point to its exit point, can be inserted within the process symbol of any other structure, forming nested structures.

In summary, a structured program has the following characteristics:

- A structured program includes only combinations of the three basic structures— sequence, selection, and loop. Any structured program might contain one, two, or all three types of structures.

- Each of the structures has a single entry point and a single exit point.

- Structures can be stacked or connected to one another only at their entry or exit points.

- Any structure can be nested within another structure.

A structured program is never required to contain examples of all three structures. For example, many simple programs contain only a sequence of several tasks that execute from start to finish without any needed selections or loops. As another example, a program might display a series of numbers, looping to do so, but never making any decisions about the numbers.

Watch the video *Understanding Structure*.

TWO TRUTHS & A LIE

Understanding the Three Basic Structures

1. Each structure in structured programming is a sequence, selection, or loop.

2. All logic problems can be solved using only three structures—sequence, selection, and loop.

3. The three structures cannot be combined in a single program.

The false statement is #3. The three structures can be stacked or nested in an infinite number of ways.

Using a Priming Input to Structure a Program

Recall the number-doubling program discussed in Chapter 2; Figure 3-11 shows a similar program. The program accepts a number as input and checks for the end-of-data condition. If the condition is not met, then the number is doubled, the answer is displayed, and the next number is input.

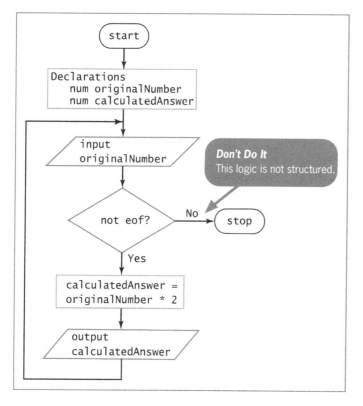

Figure 3-11   Unstructured flowchart of a number-doubling program
© 2015 Cengage Learning

 Recall from Chapter 1 that this book uses **eof** to represent a generic end-of-data condition when the exact tested parameters are not important to the discussion. In this example, the test is for **not eof** because processing will continue while the end of the data has not been reached.

Is the program represented by Figure 3-11 structured? At first, it might be hard to tell. The three allowed structures were illustrated in Quick Reference 3-1, and the flowchart in Figure 3-11 does not look exactly like any of those three shapes. However, because you may stack and nest structures while retaining overall structure, it might be difficult to determine whether a flowchart as a whole is structured. It is easiest to analyze the flowchart in Figure 3-11 one step at a time. The beginning of the flowchart looks like Figure 3-12. Is this portion of the flowchart structured? Yes, it is a sequence of two tasks—making declarations and inputting a value.

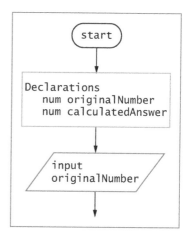

Figure 3-12   Beginning of a number-doubling flowchart
© 2015 Cengage Learning

Adding the next piece of the flowchart looks like Figure 3-13. After a value is input for `originalNumber`, the `not eof?` condition is tested. The sequence is finished; either a selection or a loop is starting. You might not know which one, but you do know that with a sequence, each task or step must follow without any opportunity to branch off. So, which type of structure starts with the question in Figure 3-13? Is it a selection or a loop?

Selection and loop structures both start with a question, but they differ as follows:

- In a selection structure, the logic branches in one of two directions after the question, and then the flow comes back together; the question is not asked a second time within the selection structure.

- In a loop, each time the answer to the question results in the execution of the loop body, the flow of logic returns to the question that started the loop. When the body of a loop executes, the question that controls the loop is always asked again.

Figure 3-13 Number-doubling flowchart continued
© 2015 Cengage Learning

If the end-of-data condition is not met in the number-doubling problem in the original Figure 3-11, then the result is calculated and output, a new number is obtained, and the logic returns to the question that tests for the end of the file. In other words, while the answer to the `not eof?` question continues to be *Yes*, a body of two statements continues to execute. Therefore, the `not eof?` question starts a structure that is more likely to be a loop than a selection.

The number-doubling problem *does* contain a loop, but it is not a structured loop. In a structured `while` loop, the rules are:

1. You ask a question.

2. If the answer indicates you should execute the loop body, then you do so.

3. After you execute the loop body, then you must go right back to ask the question again—you can't go anywhere else!

The flowchart in Figure 3-11 asks a question. If the answer is *Yes* (that is, while `not eof?` is true), then the program performs two tasks in the loop body: It does the arithmetic and it displays the results. Doing two things is acceptable because two tasks with no possible branching constitute a sequence, and it is fine to nest one structure within another structure. However, when the sequence ends, the logic does not flow right back to the loop-controlling question. Instead, it goes *above* the question to get another number. For the loop in Figure 3-11 to be a structured loop, the logic must return to the `not eof?` question when the embedded sequence ends.

The flowchart in Figure 3-14 shows the program with the flow of logic returning to the `not eof?` question immediately after the nested two-step sequence. Figure 3-14 shows

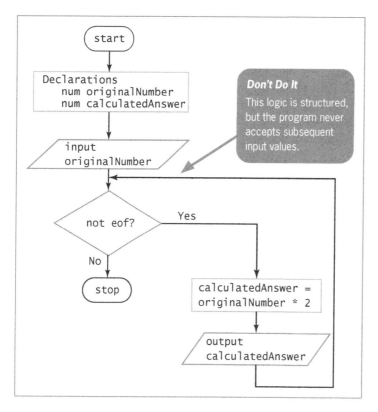

Figure 3-14   Structured, but nonfunctional, flowchart of number-doubling problem
© 2015 Cengage Learning

a structured flowchart, but it has one major flaw—the flowchart does not do the job of continuously doubling different numbers.

Follow the flowchart through a typical program run, assuming the eof condition is an input value of 0. Suppose that when the program starts, the user enters 9 for the value of originalNumber. That is not eof, so the number is multiplied by 2, and 18 is displayed as the value of calculatedAnswer. Then the question not eof? is asked again. The not eof? condition must still be true because a new value representing the sentinel (ending) value has not been entered and cannot be entered. The logic never returns to the input originalNumber task, so the value of originalNumber never changes. Therefore, 9 doubles again and the answer 18 is displayed again. The not eof? result is still true, so the same steps are repeated. This goes on *forever*, with the answer 18 being calculated and output repeatedly. The program logic shown in Figure 3-14 is structured, but it does not work as intended. Conversely, the program in Figure 3-15 works, but it is not structured because after the tasks execute within a structured loop, the flow of logic must return directly to the loop-controlling question. In Figure 3-15, the logic does not return to this question; instead, it goes "too high" outside the loop to repeat the input originalNumber task.

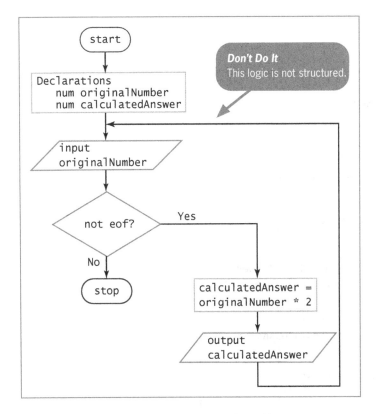

Figure 3-15 Functional but unstructured flowchart
© 2015 Cengage Learning

How can the number-doubling problem be both structured and work as intended? Often, for a program to be structured, you must add something extra. In this case, it is a priming input step. A **priming input** or **priming read** is an added statement that gets the first input value in a program. For example, if a program will receive 100 data values as input, you input the first value in a statement that is separate from the other 99. You must do this to keep the program structured.

Consider the solution in Figure 3-16; it is structured *and* it does what it is supposed to do. It contains a shaded, additional `input originalNumber` statement. The program logic contains a sequence and a loop. The loop contains another sequence.

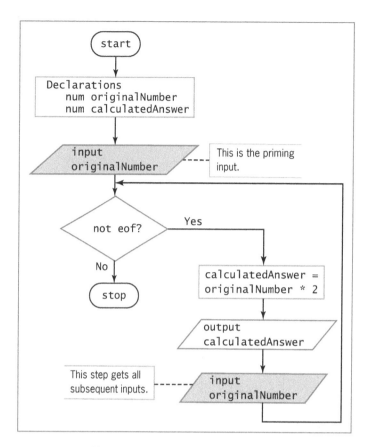

Figure 3-16   Functional, structured flowchart for the number doubling problem
© 2015 Cengage Learning

The additional `input originalNumber` step shown in Figure 3-16 is typical in structured programs. The first of the two input steps is the priming input. The term *priming* comes from the fact that the input is first, or *primary* (it gets the process going, as in "priming the pump"). The purpose of the priming input step is to control the upcoming loop that begins with the `not eof?` question. The last element within the structured loop gets the next, and all subsequent, input values. This is also typical in structured loops—the last step executed within the loop body alters the condition tested in the question that begins the loop, which in this case is the `not eof?` question.

 In Chapter 2, you learned that the group of preliminary tasks that sets the stage for the main work of a program is called the housekeeping section. The priming input is an example of a housekeeping task.

Figure 3-17 shows another way you might attempt to draw the logic for the number-doubling program. At first glance, the figure might seem to show an acceptable solution to the problem—it is structured, it contains a sequence followed by a single loop with a sequence of three steps nested within it, and it appears to eliminate the need for the priming input statement. When the program starts, the declarations are made and the not eof? question is asked. If it is not the end of input data, then the program gets a number, doubles it, and displays it. Then, if the not eof? condition remains true, the program gets another number, doubles it, and displays it. The program might continue while many numbers are input. At some point, the input number will represent the eof condition; for example, the program might have been written to recognize the value *0* as the program-terminating value. After the eof value is entered, its condition is not immediately tested. Instead, a result is calculated and displayed one last time before the loop-controlling question is asked again. If the program was written to recognize eof when originalNumber is 0, then an extraneous answer of 0 will be displayed before the program ends. Depending on the language you are using and on the type of input being used, the results might be worse: The program might terminate by displaying an error message or the value output might be indecipherable garbage. In any case, this last output is superfluous—no value should be doubled and output after the eof condition is encountered.

As a general rule, a program-ending test should always come immediately after an input statement because that's the earliest point at which it can be evaluated. Therefore, the best solution to the number-doubling problem remains the one shown in Figure 3-16—the structured solution containing the priming input statement.

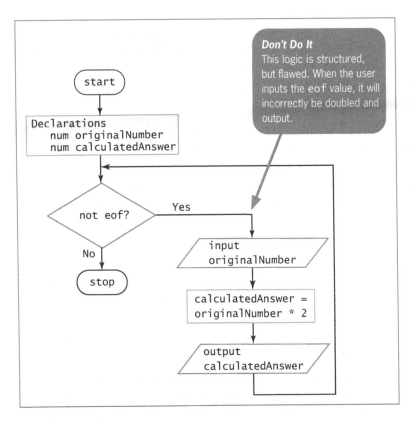

Figure 3-17 Structured but incorrect solution to the number-doubling problem
© 2015 Cengage Learning

TWO TRUTHS & A LIE

Using a Priming Input to Structure a Program

1. A priming input is the statement that repeatedly gets all the data that is input in a program.

2. A structured program might contain more instructions than an unstructured one.

3. A program can be structured yet still be incorrect.

The false statement is #1. A priming input gets the first input.

Understanding the Reasons for Structure

At this point, you may very well be saying, "I liked the original number-doubling program back in Figure 3-11 just fine. I could follow it. Also, the first program had one less step in it, so it was less work. Who cares if a program is structured?"

Until you have some programming experience, it is difficult to appreciate the reasons for using only the three structures—sequence, selection, and loop. However, staying with these three structures is better for the following reasons:

- *Clarity*—The number-doubling program is small. As programs get bigger, they get more confusing if they are not structured.

- *Professionalism*—All other programmers (and programming teachers you might encounter) expect your programs to be structured. It is the way things are done professionally.

- *Efficiency*—Most newer computer languages support structure and use syntax that lets you deal efficiently with sequence, selection, and looping. Older languages, such as assembly languages, COBOL, and RPG, were developed before the principles of structured programming were discovered. However, even programs that use those older languages can be written in a structured form. Newer languages such as C#, C++, and Java enforce structure by their syntax.

 In older languages, you could leave a selection or loop before it was complete by using a "go to" statement. The statement allowed the logic to "go to" any other part of the program whether it was within the same structure or not. Structured programming is sometimes called **goto-less programming**.

- *Maintenance*—You and other programmers will find it easier to modify and maintain structured programs as changes are required in the future.

- *Modularity*—Structured programs can be easily broken down into modules that can be assigned to any number of programmers. The routines are then pieced back together like modular furniture at each routine's single entry or exit point. Additionally, a module often can be used in multiple programs, saving development time in the new project.

TWO TRUTHS & A LIE

Understanding the Reasons for Structure

1. Structured programs are clearer than unstructured programs.

2. You and other programmers will find it easier to modify and maintain structured programs as changes are required in the future.

3. Structured programs are not easily divided into parts, making them less prone to error.

The false statement is #3. Structured programs can be easily broken down into modules that can be assigned to any number of programmers.

Recognizing Structure

When you are beginning to learn about structured program design, it is difficult to detect whether a flowchart of a program's logic is structured. For example, is the flowchart segment in Figure 3-18 structured?

Yes, it is. It has a sequence and a selection structure.

Is the flowchart segment in Figure 3-19 structured?

Yes, it is. It has a loop and a selection within the loop.

Is the flowchart segment in the upper-left corner of Figure 3-20 structured?

No, it is not built from the three basic structures. One way to straighten out an unstructured flowchart segment is to use the "spaghetti bowl" method; that is, picture the flowchart as a bowl of spaghetti that you must untangle. Imagine you can grab one piece of pasta at the top of the bowl and start pulling. As you "pull" each symbol out of the tangled mess, you can untangle the separate paths until the entire segment is structured.

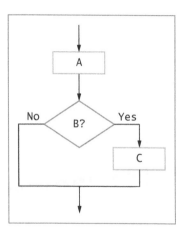

Figure 3-18 Example 1
© 2015 Cengage Learning

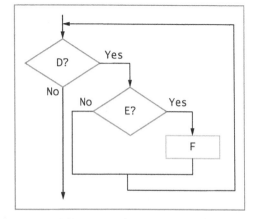

Figure 3-19 Example 2
© 2015 Cengage Learning

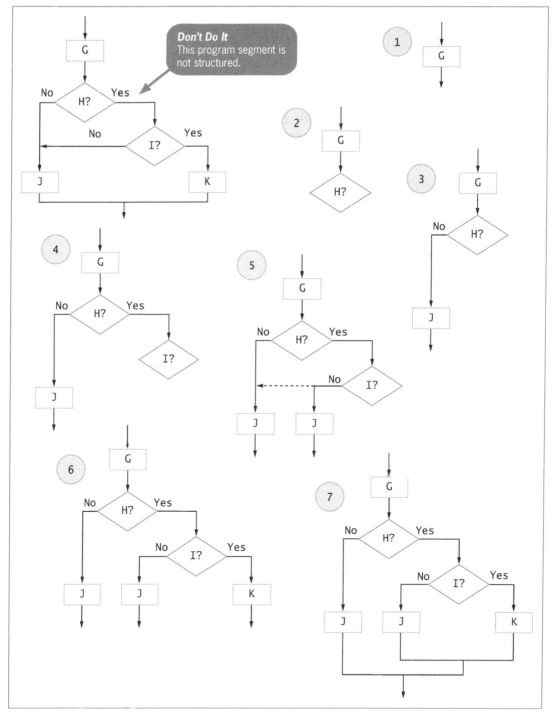

Figure 3-20 Example 3 and process to structure it
© 2015 Cengage Learning

Look at the diagram in the upper-left corner of Figure 3-20. If you could start pulling the arrow at the top, you would encounter a box labeled G. (See Figure 3-20, Step 1.) A single process like G is part of an acceptable structure—it constitutes at least the beginning of a sequence structure.

Imagine that you continue pulling symbols from the tangled segment. The next item in the flowchart is a question that tests a condition labeled H, as you can see in Figure 3-20, Step 2. At this point, you know the sequence that started with G has ended. Sequences never have questions in them, so the sequence is finished; either a selection or a loop is beginning with question H. A loop must return to the loop-controlling question at some later point. You can see from the original logic that whether the answer to H is *Yes* or *No*, the logic never returns to H. Therefore, H begins a selection structure, not a loop structure.

To continue detangling the logic, you would pull up on the flowline that emerges from the left side (the *No* side) of Question H. You encounter J, as shown in Step 3 of Figure 3-20. When you continue beyond J, you reach the end of the flowchart.

Now you can turn your attention to the *Yes* side (the right side) of the condition tested in H. When you pull up on the right side, you encounter Question I. (See Step 4 of Figure 3-20.)

In the original version of the flowchart in Figure 3-20, follow the line on the left side of Question I. The line emerging from the left side of selection I is attached to J, which is outside the selection structure. You might say the I-controlled selection is becoming entangled with the H-controlled selection, so you must untangle the structures by repeating the step that is causing the tangle. (In this example, you repeat Step J to untangle it from the other usage of J.) Continue pulling on the flowline that emerges from J until you reach the end of the program segment, as shown in Step 5 of Figure 3-20.

Now pull on the right side of Question I. Process K pops up, as shown in Step 6 of Figure 3-20; then you reach the end.

At this point, the untangled flowchart has three loose ends. The loose ends of Question I can be brought together to form a selection structure; then the loose ends of Question H can be brought together to form another selection structure. The result is the flowchart shown in Step 7 of Figure 3-20. The entire flowchart segment is structured—it has a sequence followed by a selection inside a selection.

 If you want to try structuring a more difficult example of an unstructured program, see Appendix B.

TWO TRUTHS & A LIE

Recognizing Structure

1. Some processes cannot be expressed in a structured format.

2. An unstructured flowchart can achieve correct outcomes.

3. Any unstructured flowchart can be "detangled" to become structured.

The false statement is #1. Any set of instructions can be expressed in a structured format.

Structuring and Modularizing Unstructured Logic

Recall the dog-washing process illustrated in Figure 3-1 at the beginning of this chapter. When you look at it now, you should recognize it as an unstructured process. Can this process be reconfigured to perform precisely the same tasks in a structured way? Of course!

Figure 3-21 demonstrates how you might approach structuring the dog-washing logic. Part 1 of the figure shows the beginning of the process. The first step, *Catch dog*, is a simple sequence. This step is followed by a question. When a question is encountered, the sequence is over, and either a loop or a selection starts. In this case, after the dog runs away, you must catch the dog and determine whether he runs away again, so a loop begins. To create a structured loop like the ones you have seen earlier in this chapter, you can repeat the *Catch dog* process and return immediately to the *Does dog run away?* question.

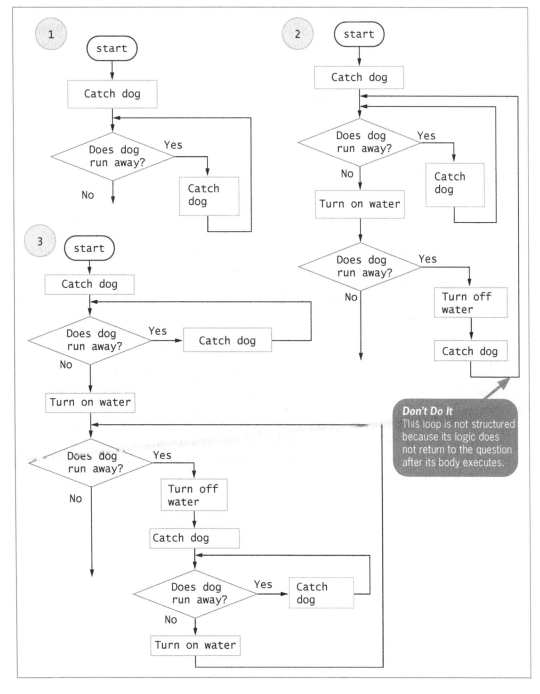

Figure 3-21   Steps to structure the dog-washing process
© 2015 Cengage Learning

In the original flowchart in Figure 3-1, you turn on the water when the dog does not run away. This step is a simple sequence, so it can correctly be added after the loop. When the water is turned on, the original logic checks whether the dog runs away after this new development. This starts a loop. In the original flowchart, the lines cross, creating a tangle, so you repeat as many steps as necessary to detangle the lines. After you turn off the water and catch the dog, you encounter the question *Does dog have shampoo on?* Because the logic has not yet reached the shampooing step, there is no need to ask this question; the answer at this point always will be *No*. When one of the logical paths emerging from a question can never be traveled, you can eliminate the question. Part 2 of Figure 3-21 shows that if the dog runs away after you turn on the water, but before you've gotten the dog wet and shampooed him, you must turn the water off, catch the dog, and return to the question that asks whether the dog runs away.

The logic in Part 2 of Figure 3-21 is not structured because the second loop that begins with the question *Does dog run away?* does not immediately return to the loop-controlling question after its body executes. So, to make the loop structured, you can repeat the actions that occur before returning to the loop-controlling question. The flowchart segment in Part 3 of Figure 3-21 is structured; it contains a sequence, a loop, a sequence, and a final, larger loop. This last loop contains its own sequence, loop, and sequence.

After the dog is caught and the water is on, you wet and shampoo the dog. Then, according to the original flowchart in Figure 3-1, you once again check to see whether the dog has run away. If he has, you turn off the water and catch the dog. From this location in the logic, the answer to the *Does dog have shampoo on?* question will always be *Yes*; as before, there is no need to ask a question when there is only one possible answer. So, if the dog runs away, the last loop executes. You turn off the water, continue to catch the dog as he repeatedly escapes, and turn the water on. When the dog is caught at last, you rinse the dog and end the program. Figure 3-22 shows both the complete flowchart and pseudocode.

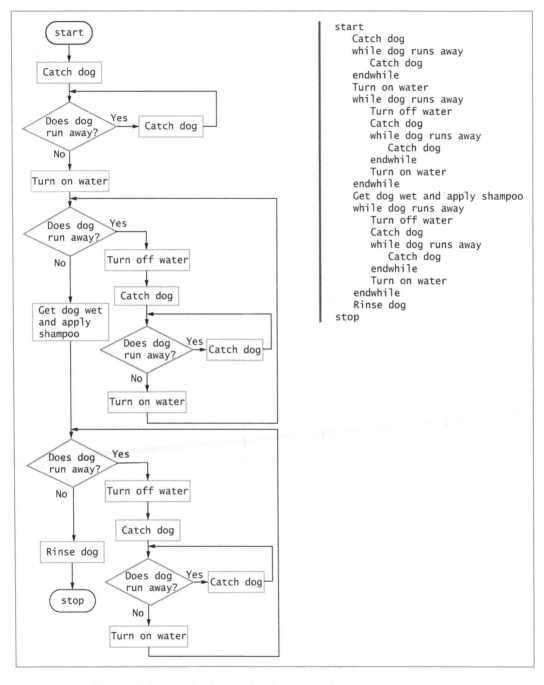

```
start
    Catch dog
    while dog runs away
        Catch dog
    endwhile
    Turn on water
    while dog runs away
        Turn off water
        Catch dog
        while dog runs away
            Catch dog
        endwhile
        Turn on water
    endwhile
    Get dog wet and apply shampoo
    while dog runs away
        Turn off water
        Catch dog
        while dog runs away
            Catch dog
        endwhile
        Turn on water
    endwhile
    Rinse dog
stop
```

Figure 3-22   Structured dog-washing flowchart and pseudocode
© 2015 Cengage Learning

The flowchart in Figure 3-22 is complete and is structured. It contains alternating sequence and loop structures.

Figure 3-22 includes three places where the sequence-loop-sequence of catching the dog and turning on the water are repeated. If you wanted to, you could modularize the duplicate sections so that their instruction sets are written once and contained in a separate module. Figure 3-23 shows a modularized version of the program; the three module calls are shaded.

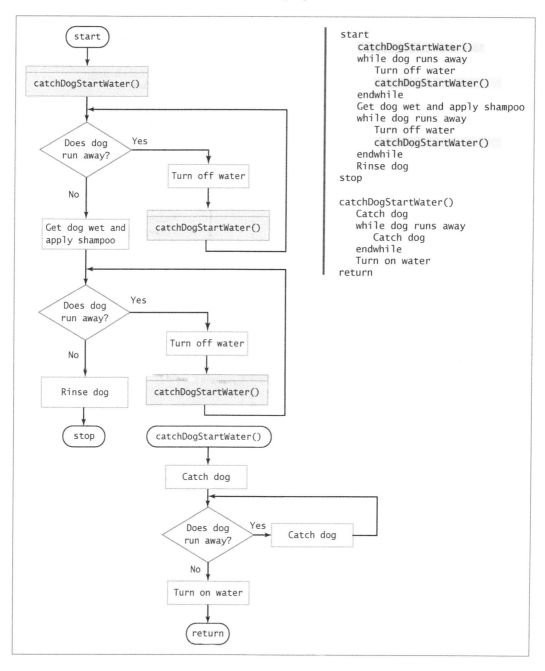

```
start
    catchDogStartWater()
    while dog runs away
        Turn off water
        catchDogStartWater()
    endwhile
    Get dog wet and apply shampoo
    while dog runs away
        Turn off water
        catchDogStartWater()
    endwhile
    Rinse dog
stop

catchDogStartWater()
    Catch dog
    while dog runs away
        Catch dog
    endwhile
    Turn on water
return
```

Figure 3-23 Modularized version of the dog-washing program
© 2015 Cengage Learning

One advantage to modularizing the steps needed to catch the dog and start the water is that the main program becomes shorter and easier to understand. Another advantage is that if this process needs to be modified, the changes can be made in just one location. For example, if you decided it was necessary to test the water temperature each time you turned on the water, you would add those instructions only once in the modularized version. In the original version in Figure 3-22, you would have to add those instructions in three places, causing more work and increasing the chance for errors.

No matter how complicated, any set of steps can always be reduced to combinations of the three basic sequence, selection, and loop structures. These structures can be nested and stacked in an infinite number of ways to describe the logic of any process and to create the logic for every computer program written in the past, present, or future.

For convenience, many programming languages allow two variations of the three basic structures. The `case` structure is a variation of the selection structure and the `do` loop is a variation of the `while` loop. You can learn about these two structures in Appendix D. Even though these extra structures can be used in most programming languages, all logical problems can be solved without them.

Watch the video *Structuring Unstructured Logic*.

TWO TRUTHS & A LIE

Structuring and Modularizing Unstructured Logic

1. When you encounter a question in a logical diagram, a sequence should be ending.

2. In a structured loop, the logic returns to the loop-controlling question after the loop body executes.

3. If a flowchart or pseudocode contains a question to which the answer never varies, you can eliminate the question.

The false statement is #1. When you encounter a question in a logical diagram, either a selection or a loop should start. However, any type of structure might end before the question is encountered.

Chapter Summary

- Spaghetti code is the descriptive name for unstructured program statements that do not follow the rules of structured logic.

- Clearer programs can be constructed using only three basic structures: sequence, selection, and loop. These three structures can be combined in an infinite number of ways by stacking and nesting them. Each structure has a single entry point and a single exit point; one structure can attach to another only at one of these points.

- A priming input is the statement that gets the first input value prior to starting a structured loop. Usually, the last step within the loop body gets the next and all subsequent input values.

- Programmers use structured techniques to promote clarity, professionalism, efficiency, and modularity.

- One way to order an unstructured flowchart segment is to imagine it as a bowl of spaghetti that you must untangle.

- Any set of logical steps can be rewritten to conform to the three structures: sequence, selection, and loop.

Key Terms

Spaghetti code is snarled, unstructured program logic.

Unstructured programs are programs that do *not* follow the rules of structured logic.

Structured programs are programs that do follow the rules of structured logic.

A **structure** is a basic unit of programming logic; each structure is a sequence, selection, or loop.

A **sequence structure** contains series of steps executed in order. A sequence can contain any number of tasks, but there is no option to branch off, skipping any of the tasks.

A **selection structure** or **decision structure** contains a question, and, depending on the answer, takes one of two courses of action before continuing with the next task.

An **end-structure statement** designates the end of a pseudocode structure.

An **if-then-else** is another name for a dual-alternative selection structure.

Dual-alternative ifs (or **dual-alternative selections**) define one action to be taken when the tested condition is true and another action to be taken when it is false.

Single-alternative ifs (or **single-alternative selections**) take action on just one branch of the decision.

The **null case** or **null branch** is the branch of a decision in which no action is taken.

A **loop structure** continues to repeat actions while a test condition remains true.

A **loop body** is the set of actions that occur within a loop.

A `while` **loop** is a structure that continues to repeat a process while some condition remains true.

Repetition and **iteration** are alternate names for a loop structure.

A `while...do` **loop** is an alternate name for a `while` loop.

Stacking structures is the act of attaching structures end to end.

Nesting structures is the act of placing a structure within another structure.

A **block** is a group of statements that executes as a single unit.

A **priming input** or **priming read** is the statement that reads the first input prior to starting a structured loop that uses the data.

Goto-less programming is a name to describe structured programming, because structured programmers do not use a "go to" statement.

Exercises

 Review Questions

1. Snarled program logic is called _____ code.

   a. snake   c. spaghetti
   b. string   d. gnarly

2. The three structures of structured programming are _____ .

   a. sequence, selection, and loop   c. sequence, order, and process
   b. selection, loop, and iteration   d. if, else, and then

3. A sequence structure can contain _____ .

   a. only one task   c. no more than three tasks
   b. exactly three tasks   d. any number of tasks

4. Which of the following is *not* another term for a selection structure?

   a. decision structure   c. dual-alternative `if` structure
   b. loop structure   d. `if-then-else` structure

5. The structure that tests a condition, takes action if the result is true, and then tests the condition again can be called all of the following except a(n) _____ .

   a. iteration   c. repetition
   b. loop   d. `if-then-else`

6. Placing a structure within another structure is called _____ the structures.

   a. stacking   c. building
   b. untangling   d. nesting

7. Attaching structures end to end is called _____ .

   a. stacking   c. building
   b. untangling   d. nesting

8. When an action is required if a condition is true, but no action is needed if it is false, you use a _____ .

   a. sequence   c. dual-alternative selection
   b. loop   d. single-alternative selection

9. To take action as long as a condition remains true, you use a _____ .

   a. sequence   c. dual-alternative selection
   b. loop   d. single-alternative selection

10. When you must perform one action when a condition is true and a different one when it is false, you use a _____ .

    a. sequence   c. dual-alternative selection
    b. loop   d. single-alternative selection

11. Which of the following attributes do all three basic structures share?

    a. Their flowcharts all contain exactly three processing symbols.
    b. They all have one entry and one exit point.
    c. They all contain a decision.
    d. They all begin with a process.

12. Which is true of stacking structures?

    a. Two incidences of the same structure cannot be stacked adjacently.
    b. When you stack structures, you cannot nest them in the same program.
    c. Each structure has only one point where it can be stacked on top of another.
    d. When you stack structures, the top structure must be a sequence.

13. When you input data in a loop within a program, the input statement that precedes the loop _____ .

    a. is the only part of the program allowed to be unstructured
    b. cannot result in eof
    c. is called a priming input
    d. executes hundreds or even thousands of times in most business programs

14. A group of statements that executes as a unit is a _____.

   a. block   c. chunk
   b. family   d. cohort

15. Which of the following is acceptable in a structured program?

   a. placing a sequence within the true branch of a dual-alternative decision
   b. placing a decision within a loop
   c. placing a loop within one of the steps in a sequence
   d. All of these are acceptable.

16. In a selection structure, the structure-controlling question is _____.

   a. asked once at the beginning of the structure
   b. asked once at the end of the structure
   c. asked repeatedly until it is false
   d. asked repeatedly until it is true

17. When a loop executes, the structure-controlling question is _____.

   a. asked exactly once
   b. never asked more than once
   c. asked either before or after the loop body executes
   d. asked only if it is true, and not asked if it is false

18. Which of the following is *not* a reason for enforcing structure rules in computer programs?

   a. Structured programs are clearer to understand than unstructured ones.
   b. Other professional programmers will expect programs to be structured.
   c. Structured programs usually are shorter than unstructured ones.
   d. Structured programs can be broken down into modules easily.

19. Which of the following is *not* a benefit of modularizing programs?

   a. Modular programs are easier to read and understand than nonmodular ones.
   b. If you use modules, you can ignore the rules of structure.
   c. Modular components are reusable in other programs.
   d. Multiple programmers can work on different modules at the same time.

20. Which of the following is true of structured logic?

   a. You can use structured logic with newer programming languages, such as Java and C#, but not with older ones.
   b. Any task can be described using some combination of the three structures: sequence, selection, and loop.
   c. Structured programs require that you break the code into easy-to-handle modules that each contain no more than five actions.
   d. All of these are true.

Programming Exercises

1. In Figure 3-10, the process of buying and planting flowers in the spring was shown using the same structures as the generic example in Figure 3-9. Use the same logical structure as in Figure 3-9 to create a flowchart or pseudocode that describes some other process you know.

2. Each of the flowchart segments in Figure 3-24 is unstructured. Redraw each segment so that it does the same thing but is structured.

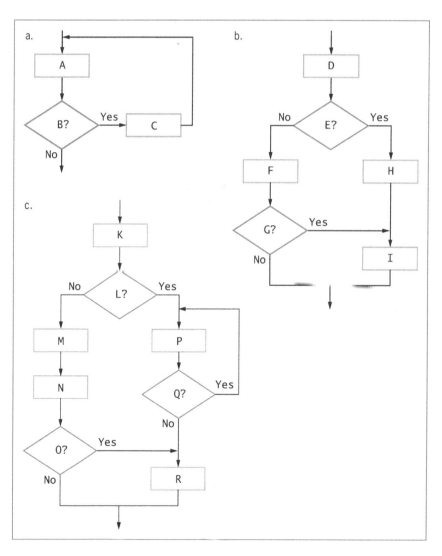

Figure 3-24   Flowcharts for Exercise 2 *(continues)*
© 2015 Cengage Learning

(continued)

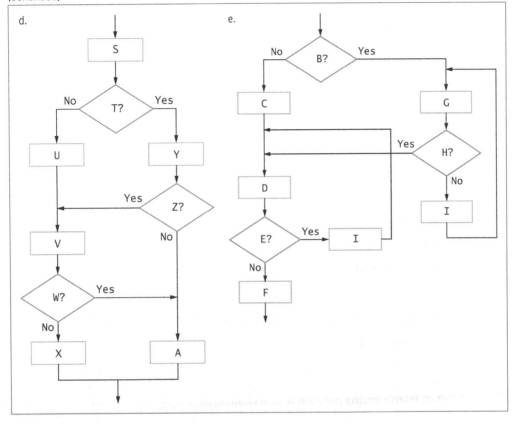

Figure 3-24 Flowcharts for Exercise 2
© 2015 Cengage Learning

3. Write pseudocode for each example (a through e) in Exercise 2, making sure your pseudocode is structured and accomplishes the same tasks as the flowchart segment.

4. Assume that you have created a mechanical arm that can hold a pen. The arm can perform the following tasks:

- Lower the pen to a piece of paper.

- Raise the pen from the paper.

- Move the pen 1 inch along a straight line. (If the pen is lowered, this action draws a 1-inch line from left to right; if the pen is raised, this action just repositions the pen 1 inch to the right.)

- Turn 90 degrees to the right.

- Draw a circle that is 1 inch in diameter.

Draw a structured flowchart or write structured pseudocode describing the logic that would cause the arm to draw or write the following. Have a fellow student act as the mechanical arm and carry out your instructions. Don't reveal the desired outcome to your partner until the exercise is complete.

a. a 1-inch square

b. a 2-inch by 1-inch rectangle

c. a string of three beads

d. a short word (for example, *cat*)

e. a four-digit number

5. Assume that you have created a mechanical robot that can perform the following tasks:

- Stand up.

- Sit down.

- Turn left 90 degrees.

- Turn right 90 degrees.

- Take a step.

Additionally, the robot can determine the answer to one test condition:

- Am I touching something?

a. Place two chairs 20 feet apart, directly facing each other. Draw a structured flowchart or write pseudocode describing the logic that would allow the robot to start from a sitting position in one chair, cross the room, and end up sitting in the other chair. Have a fellow student act as the robot and carry out your instructions.

b. Draw a structured flowchart or write pseudocode describing the logic that would allow the robot to start from a sitting position in one chair, stand up and circle the chair, cross the room, circle the other chair, return to the first chair, and sit. Have a fellow student act as the robot and carry out your instructions.

6. Draw a structured flowchart or write pseudocode that describes the process of guessing a number between 1 and 100. After each guess, the player is told that the guess is too high or too low. The process continues until the player guesses the correct number. Pick a number and have a fellow student try to guess it by following your instructions.

7. Looking up a word in a dictionary can be a complicated process. For example, assume that you want to look up *logic*. You might open the dictionary to a random page and see *juice*. You know this word comes alphabetically before *logic*, so you flip forward and see *lamb*. That is still not far enough, so you flip forward and see *monkey*. You have gone too far, so you flip back, and so on. Draw a structured flowchart or write pseudocode that describes the process of looking up a word in a dictionary. Pick a word at random and have a fellow student attempt to carry out your instructions.

8. Draw a structured flowchart or write structured pseudocode describing how to do a load of laundry. Include at least two decisions and two loops.

9. Draw a structured flowchart or write structured pseudocode describing how to study for an exam. Include at least two decisions and two loops.

10. Draw a structured flowchart or write structured pseudocode describing how to wrap a present. Include at least two decisions and two loops.

11. Draw a structured flowchart or write structured pseudocode describing the steps to prepare your favorite dish. Include at least two decisions and two loops.

 ## Performing Maintenance

1. A file named MAINTENANCE03-01.txt is included with your downloadable student files. Assume that this program is a working program in your organization and that it needs modifications as described in the comments (lines that begin with two slashes) at the beginning of the file. Your job is to alter the program to meet the new specifications.

 ## Find the Bugs

1. Your downloadable files for Chapter 3 include DEBUG03-01.txt, DEBUG03-02.txt, and DEBUG03-03.txt. Each file starts with some comments that describe the problem. Comments are lines that begin with two slashes (//). Following the comments, each file contains pseudocode that has one or more bugs you must find and correct.

2. Your downloadable files for Chapter 3 include a file named DEBUG03-04.jpg that contains a flowchart with syntax and/or logical errors. Examine the flowchart and then find and correct all the bugs.

 ## Game Zone

1. Choose a simple children's game and describe its logic, using a structured flowchart or pseudocode. For example, you might try to explain Rock, Paper, Scissors; Musical Chairs; Duck, Duck, Goose; the card game War; or the elimination game Eenie, Meenie, Minie, Moe.

2. Choose a television game show such as *Wheel of Fortune* or *Jeopardy!* and describe its rules using a structured flowchart or pseudocode.

3. Choose a sport such as baseball or football and describe the actions in one limited play period (such as an at-bat in baseball or a possession in football) using a structured flowchart or pseudocode.

Up for Discussion

1. Find more information about one of the following people and explain why he or she is important to structured programming: Edsger Dijkstra, Corrado Bohm, Giuseppe Jacopini, and Grace Hopper.

2. Computer programs can contain structures within structures and stacked structures, creating very large programs. Computers also can perform millions of arithmetic calculations in an hour. How can we possibly know the results are correct?

3. Develop a checklist of rules you can use to help you determine whether a flowchart or pseudocode segment is structured.

Making Decisions

In this chapter, you will learn about:

◎ Boolean expressions and the selection structure

◎ The relational comparison operators

◎ AND logic

◎ OR logic

◎ NOT logic

◎ Making selections within ranges

◎ Precedence when combining AND and OR operators

Boolean Expressions and the Selection Structure

The reason people frequently think computers are smart lies in the ability of computer programs to make decisions. A medical diagnosis program that can decide if your symptoms fit various disease profiles seems quite intelligent, as does a program that can offer different potential driving routes based on your destination.

Every decision a computer program makes involves evaluating a **Boolean expression**—an expression whose value can be only true or false. True/false evaluation is natural from a computer's standpoint, because computer circuitry consists of two-state on-off switches, often represented by 1 or 0. Every computer decision yields a true-or-false, yes-or-no, 1-or-0 result. A Boolean expression is used to control every selection structure. The selection structure is not new to you—it's one of the three basic structures you learned about in Chapter 3. See Figures 4-1 and 4-2.

 Mathematician George Boole (1815–1864) approached logic more simply than his predecessors did, by expressing logical selections with common algebraic symbols. He is considered the founder of mathematical logic, and Boolean (true/false) expressions are named for him.

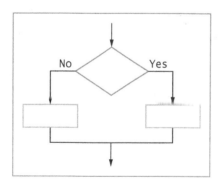

Figure 4-1   The dual-alternative selection structure
© 2015 Cengage Learning

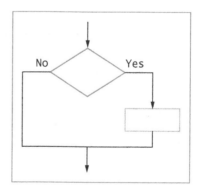

Figure 4-2   The single-alternative selection structure
© 2015 Cengage Learning

In Chapter 3 you learned that the structure in Figure 4-1 is a dual-alternative selection because an action is associated with each of two possible outcomes: Depending on the answer to the question in the decision symbol, the logical flow proceeds either to the left branch of the structure or to the right. The choices are mutually exclusive; that is, the logic can flow to only one of the two alternatives, never to both. This form of the selection structure is an if-then-else selection.

This book follows the convention that the two logical paths emerging from a dual-alternative selection are drawn to the right and left of a diamond in a flowchart. Some programmers draw one of the flowlines emerging from the bottom of the diamond. The exact format of the diagram is not as important as the idea that one logical path flows into a selection, and two possible outcomes emerge. Your flowcharts will be easier for readers to follow if you are consistent when you draw selections. For example, if the **Yes** branch flows to the right for one selection, it should flow to the right for all subsequent selections in the same flowchart.

The flowchart segment in Figure 4-2 represents a single-alternative selection in which action is required for only one outcome of the question. This form of the selection structure is called an **if-then** selection, because no alternative or else action is necessary.

Quick Reference 4-1 shows the pseudocode standards used to construct if statements in this book.

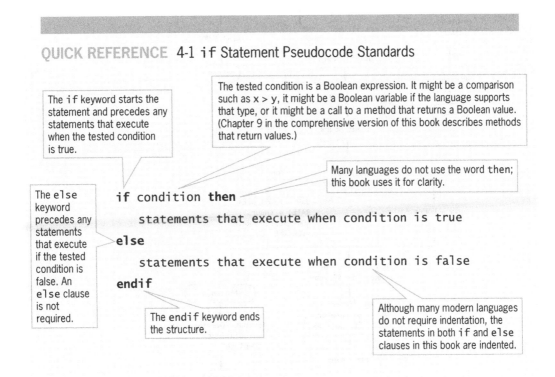

QUICK REFERENCE 4-1 if Statement Pseudocode Standards

Figure 4-3 shows the flowchart and pseudocode for an interactive program that computes pay for employees. The program displays the weekly pay for each employee at the same hourly rate ($10.00) and assumes that there are no payroll deductions. The mainline logic calls housekeeping(), detailLoop(), and finish() modules. The detailLoop() module contains a typical dual-alternative selection that determines whether an employee has worked more than a standard workweek (40 hours), and pays one and one-half times the employee's usual hourly rate for hours worked in excess of 40 per week.

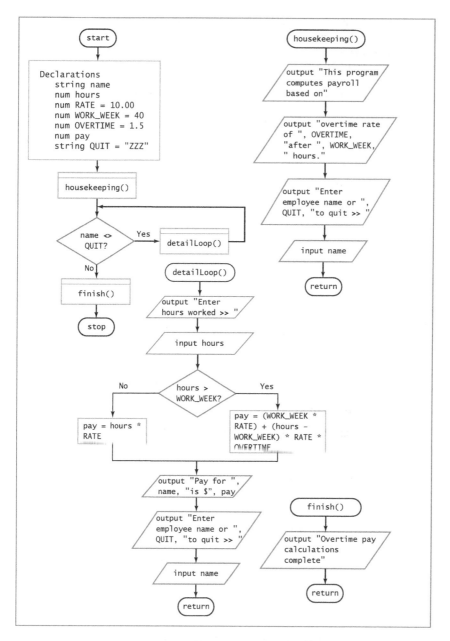

Figure 4-3   Flowchart and pseudocode for overtime payroll program *(continues)*

(continued)

```
start
    Declarations
        string name
        num hours
        num RATE = 10.00
        num WORK_WEEK = 40
        num OVERTIME = 1.5
        num pay
        string QUIT = "ZZZ"
    housekeeping()
    while name <> QUIT
        detailLoop()
    endwhile
    finish()
stop

housekeeping()
    output "This program computes payroll based on"
    output "overtime rate of ", OVERTIME, "after ", WORK_WEEK, " hours."
    output "Enter employee name or ", QUIT, "to quit >> "
    input name
return

detailLoop()
    output "Enter hours worked >> "
    input hours
    if hours > WORK_WEEK then
        pay = (WORK_WEEK * RATE) + (hours - WORK_WEEK) * RATE * OVERTIME
    else
        pay = hours * RATE
    endif
    output "Pay for ", name, "is $", pay
    output "Enter employee name or ", QUIT, "to quit >> "
    input name
return

finish()
    output "Overtime pay calculations complete"
return
```

Figure 4-3   Flowchart and pseudocode for overtime payroll program
© 2015 Cengage Learning

Throughout this book, many examples are presented in both flowchart and pseudocode form. When you analyze a solution, you might find it easier to concentrate on just one of the two design tools at first. When you understand how the program works using one design tool (for example, the flowchart), you can confirm that the solution is identical using the other tool.

In the detailLoop() module of the program in Figure 4-3, the decision contains two clauses:

- The **if-then clause** is the part of the decision that holds the action or actions that execute when the tested condition in the decision is true. In this example, the clause holds the longer overtime calculation.

- The **else clause** of the decision is the part that executes only when the tested condition in the decision is false. In this example, the clause contains the shorter calculation.

Figure 4-4 shows a sample execution of the program in a command-line environment. Data values are entered for three employees. The first two employees do not work more than 40 hours, so their pay is displayed simply as hours times 10.00. The third employee, however, has worked one hour of overtime, and so makes $15 for the last hour instead of $10.

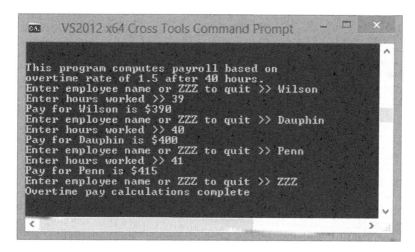

Figure 4-4   Sample execution of the overtime payroll program in Figure 4-3

Many modern programming languages support Boolean data types. Instead of holding numbers or words, each Boolean variable can hold only one of two values—true or false.

Watch the video *Boolean Expressions and Decisions.*

TWO TRUTHS & A LIE

Boolean Expressions and the Selection Structure

1. The if-then clause is the part of a decision that executes when a tested condition in a decision is true.

2. The else clause is the part of a decision that executes when a tested condition in a decision is true.

3. A Boolean expression is one whose value is true or false.

The false statement is #2. The else clause is the part of a decision that executes when a tested condition in a decision is false.

Using Relational Comparison Operators

Quick Reference 4-2 describes the six **relational comparison operators** supported by all modern programming languages. Each of these operators is binary—that is, like the arithmetic operators you learned about in Chapter 2, each relational comparison operator in Quick Reference 4-2 requires two operands. Each expression that uses one of these operators evaluates to true or false. Notice that some operators are formed using two characters with no space between them.

Both operands in a comparison expression must be the same data type; that is, you can compare numeric values to other numeric values, and text strings to other strings. Some programming languages allow exceptions; for example, you can compare a character to a number using the character's numeric code value. Appendix A contains more information on coding systems. In this book, only operands of the same data type will be compared.

In any Boolean expression, the two values compared can be either variables or constants. For example, the Boolean expression currentTotal = 100 compares a variable, currentTotal, to a numeric constant, 100. Depending on the value of currentTotal, the expression is true or false. In the expression currentTotal = previousTotal, both values are variables, and the result is also true or false depending on the values stored in each of the two variables. Although it's legal, you would never use expressions in which you compare two constants—for example, 20 = 20 or 30 = 40. Such expressions are **trivial expressions** because each will always evaluate to the same result: true for 20 = 20 and false for 30 = 40.

QUICK REFERENCE 4-2 Relational Comparison Operators

Operator	Name	Discussion
=	Equivalency operator	Evaluates as true when its operands are equivalent. Because the assignment operator in many languages is the equal sign, those languages often use a double equal sign (==) as the equivalency operator to avoid confusion with the assignment operator.
>	Greater-than operator	Evaluates as true when the left operand is greater than the right operand.
<	Less-than operator	Evaluates as true when the left operand is less than the right operand.
>=	Greater-than-or-equal-to operator	Evaluates as true when the left operand is greater than or equivalent to the right operand.
<=	Less-than-or-equal-to operator	Evaluates as true when the left operand is less than or equivalent to the right operand.
<>	Not-equal-to operator	Evaluates as true when its operands are not equivalent. Some languages use an exclamation point followed by an equal sign (!=) as the not-equal-to operator. In a flowchart or pseudocode, you might prefer to use the algebraic not-equal-to symbol ($\neq$) or to spell out the words "not equal to."

Some languages require special operations to compare strings, but this book will assume that the standard comparison operators work correctly with strings based on their alphabetic values. For example, the comparison "black" < "blue" would be evaluated as true because "black" precedes "blue" alphabetically. Usually, string variables are not considered to be equal unless they are identical, including the spacing and whether they appear in uppercase or lowercase. For example, "black pen" is not equal to "blackpen", "BLACK PEN", or "Black Pen".

Any decision can be made using combinations of just three types of comparisons: equal, greater than, and less than. You never need the three additional comparisons (greater than or equal, less than or equal, or not equal), but using them often makes decisions more convenient. For example, assume that you need to issue a 10 percent discount to any customer whose age is 65 or greater, and charge full price to other customers. You can use the greater-than-or-equal-to symbol to write the logic as follows:

```
if customerAge >= 65 then
    discount = 0.10
else
    discount = 0
endif
```

As an alternative, or if the >= operator did not exist, you could express the same
logic by writing:

```
if customerAge < 65 then
    discount = 0
else
    discount = 0.10
endif
```

In any decision for which a >= b is true, then a < b is false. Conversely, if a >= b is false, then
a < b is true. By rephrasing the question and swapping the actions taken based on the
outcome, you can make the same decision in multiple ways. The clearest route is often to ask
a question so the positive or true outcome results in the action that was your motivation for
making the test. When your company policy is to "provide a discount for those who are 65
and older," the phrase *greater than or equal to 65* comes to mind, so it is the most natural to
use. Conversely, if your policy is to "provide no discount for those under 65," then it is more
natural to use the *less than 65* syntax. Either way, the same people receive a discount.

Comparing two amounts to decide if they are *not* equal to each other is the most confusing of
all the comparisons. Using *not equal to* in decisions involves thinking in double negatives,
which can make you prone to introducing logical errors into your programs. For example,
consider the flowchart segment in Figure 4-5.

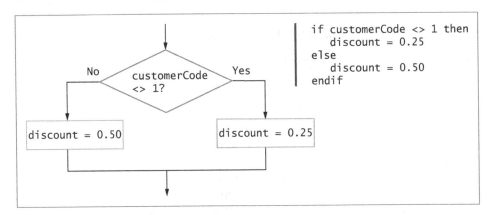

Figure 4-5 Using a negative comparison
© 2015 Cengage Learning

In Figure 4-5, if the value of customerCode *is* equal to 1, the logical flow follows the false branch
of the selection. If customerCode <> 1 is true, the discount is 0.25; if customerCode <> 1 is not
true, it means the customerCode *is* 1, and the discount is 0.50. Even reading the phrase "if
customerCode is not equal to 1 is not true" is awkward.

Figure 4-6 shows the same decision, this time asked using positive logic. Making the decision based on what `customerCode` *is* is clearer than trying to determine what `customerCode` is *not*.

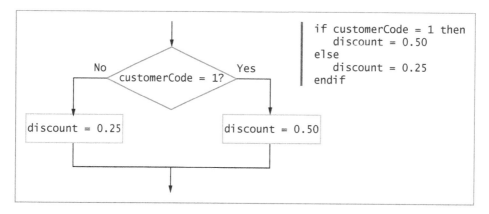

```
if customerCode = 1 then
    discount = 0.50
else
    discount = 0.25
endif
```

Figure 4-6   Using the positive equivalent of the negative comparison in Figure 4-5
© 2015 Cengage Learning

 Although negative comparisons can be awkward to use, your meaning is sometimes clearest when using them. Frequently, this occurs when you use an `if` without an `else`, taking action only when some comparison is false. An example would be:

```
if customerZipCode <> LOCAL_ZIP_CODE then
    total = total + deliveryCharge
endif
```

Avoiding a Common Error with Relational Operators

A common error that occurs when programming with relational operators is using the wrong one and missing the boundary or limit required for a selection. If you use the > symbol to make a selection when you should have used >=, all the cases that are equal will go unselected. Unfortunately, people who request programs do not always speak as precisely as a computer. If, for example, your boss says, "Write a program that selects all employees over 65," does she mean to include employees who are 65 or not? In other words, is the comparison `age > 65` or `age >= 65`? Although the phrase *over 65* indicates *greater than 65*, people do not always say what they mean, and the best course of action is to double-check the intended meaning with the person who requested the program—for example, the end user, your supervisor, or your instructor. Similar phrases that can cause misunderstandings are *no more than, at least,* and *not under.*

TWO TRUTHS & A LIE

Using Relational Comparison Operators

1. Usually, you can compare only values that are of the same data type.

2. A Boolean expression is defined as one that decides whether two values are equal.

3. In any Boolean expression, the two values compared can be either variables or constants.

The false statement is #2. Although deciding whether two values are equal is a Boolean expression, so is deciding whether one is greater than or less than another. A Boolean expression is one that results in a true or false value.

Understanding *AND* Logic

Often, you need to evaluate more than one expression to determine whether an action should take place. When you ask multiple questions before an outcome is determined, you create a **compound condition**. For example, suppose you work for a cell phone company that charges customers as follows:

- The basic monthly service bill is $30.

- An additional $20 is billed to customers who make more than 100 calls that last for a total of more than 500 minutes.

The logic needed for this billing program includes an **AND decision**—a decision that tests a condition with two parts that must both evaluate to true for an action to take place. In this case, both a minimum number of calls must be made *and* a minimum number of minutes must be used before the customer is charged the premium amount. A decision that uses an AND condition can be constructed using a **nested decision,** or a **nested if**—that is, a decision within the if-then or else clause of another decision. You first learned about nesting structures in Chapter 3. You can always stack and nest any of the three basic structures. A series of nested if statements is also called a **cascading if statement**. The flowchart and pseudocode for the program that determines the charges for customers is shown in Figure 4-7.

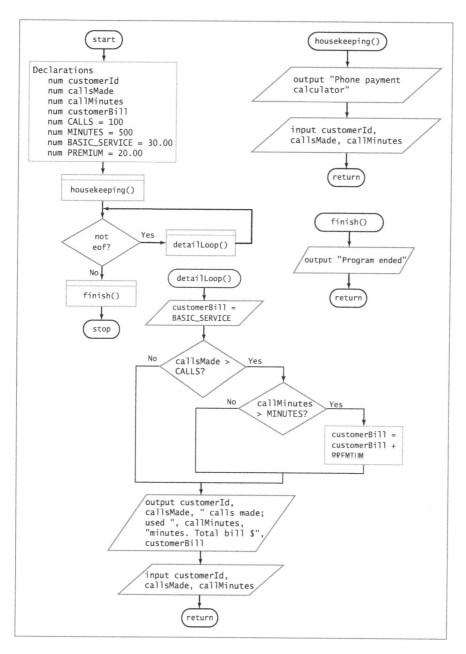

Figure 4-7   Flowchart and pseudocode for cell phone billing program *(continues)*

(continued)

```
start
    Declarations
        num customerId
        num callsMade
        num callMinutes
        num customerBill
        num CALLS = 100
        num MINUTES = 500
        num BASIC_SERVICE = 30.00
        num PREMIUM = 20.00
    housekeeping()
    while not eof
        detailLoop()
    endwhile
    finish()
stop

housekeeping()
    output "Phone payment calculator"
    input customerId, callsMade, callMinutes
return

detailLoop()
    customerBill = BASIC_SERVICE
    if callsMade > CALLS then
        if callMinutes > MINUTES then
            customerBill = customerBill + PREMIUM
        endif
    endif
    output customerId, callsMade, " calls made; used ",
        callMinutes, " minutes. Total bill $", customerBill
    input customerId, callsMade, callMinutes
return

finish()
    output "Program ended"
return
```

Figure 4-7   Flowchart and pseudocode for cell phone billing program
© 2015 Cengage Learning

The logic for the cell phone billing program assumes that the customer data is retrieved from a file. This eliminates the need for prompts and keeps the program shorter so you can concentrate on the decision-making process. If this were an interactive program, you would use a prompt before each input statement. Chapter 7 covers file processing and explains a few additional steps you can take when working with files.

In Figure 4-7, the appropriate variables and constants are declared, and then the housekeeping() module displays an introductory heading and gets the first set of input data. After control returns to the mainline logic, the **eof** condition is tested, and if data entry is not complete, the `detailLoop()` module executes. In the `detailLoop()` module, the customer's bill is set to the standard fee, and then the nested decision executes. In the nested `if` structure in Figure 4-7, the expression `callsMade > CALLS` is evaluated first. If this expression is true, only then is the second Boolean expression (`callMinutes > MINUTES`) evaluated. If that expression is also true, then the $20 premium is added to the customer's bill. If either of the tested conditions is false, the customer's bill value is never altered, retaining the initially assigned `BASIC_SERVICE` value of $30.

 Most languages allow you to use a variation of the selection structure called the *case structure* when you must nest a series of decisions about a single variable or expression. Appendix D contains information about the case structure.

Nesting *AND* Decisions for Efficiency

When you nest two decisions, you must choose which of the decisions to make first. Logically, either expression in an AND decision can be evaluated first. However, you often can improve your program's performance by correctly choosing which of two selections to make first.

For example, Figure 4-8 shows two ways to design the nested decision structure that assigns a premium to customers' bills if they make more than 100 cell phone calls and use more than 500 minutes in a billing period. The program can ask about calls made first, eliminate customers who have not made more than the minimum, and then ask about the minutes used only for customers who pass (that is, are evaluated as true on) the minimum calls test. Or, the program could ask about the minutes first, eliminate those who do not qualify, and then ask about the number of calls only for customers who pass the minutes test. Either way, only customers who exceed both limits must pay the premium. Does it make a difference which question is asked first? As far as the result goes, no. Either way, the same customers pay the premium—those who qualify on the basis of both criteria. As far as program efficiency goes, however, it *might* make a difference which question is asked first.

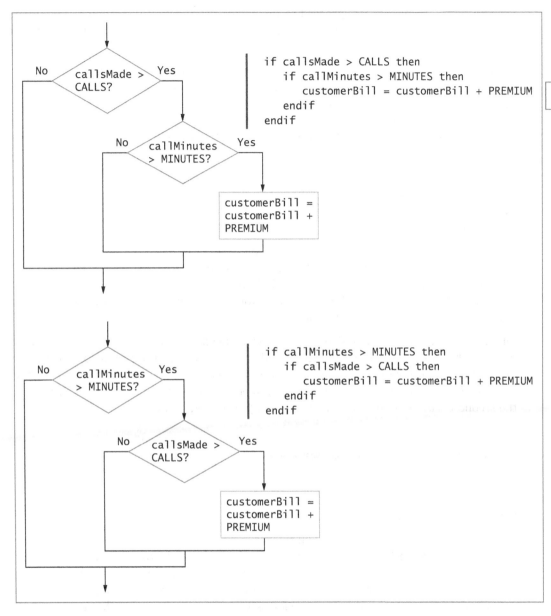

Figure 4-8 Two ways to produce cell phone bills using identical criteria
© 2015 Cengage Learning

Assume that you know that out of 1000 cell phone customers, about 90 percent, or 900, make more than 100 calls in a billing period. Assume that you also know that only about half the 1000 customers, or 500, use more than 500 minutes of call time.

If you use the logic shown first in Figure 4-8, and you need to produce 1000 phone bills, the first question, `callsMade > CALLS`, will execute 1000 times. For approximately 90 percent of the customers, or 900 of them, the answer is true, so 100 customers are eliminated from the premium assignment, and 900 proceed to the next question about the minutes used. Only about half the customers use more than 500 minutes, so 450 of the 900 pay the premium, and it takes 1900 decisions to identify them.

Using the alternate logic shown second in Figure 4-8, the first question, `callMinutes > MINUTES`, will also be asked 1000 times—once for each customer. Because only about half the customers use the high number of minutes, only 500 will pass this test and proceed to the question for number of calls made. Then, about 90 percent of the 500, or 450 customers, will pass the second test and be billed the premium amount. In this case, it takes 1500 decisions to identify the 450 premium-paying customers.

Whether you use the first or second decision order in Figure 4-8, the same 450 customers who satisfy both criteria pay the premium. The difference is that when you ask about the number of calls first, the program must make 400 more decisions than when you ask about the minutes used first.

The 400-decision difference between the first and second arrangement in Figure 4-8 doesn't take much time on most computers. But it does take *some* time, and if a corporation has hundreds of thousands of customers instead of only 1000, or if many such decisions have to be made within a program, performance (execution time) can be significantly improved by making decisions in the more efficient order.

Often when you must make nested decisions, you have no idea which event is more likely to occur; in that case, you can legitimately ask either question first. However, if you do know the probabilities of the conditions, or can make a reasonable guess, the general rule is: *In an AND decision, first ask the question that is less likely to be true.* This eliminates as many instances of the second decision as possible, which speeds up processing time.

 Watch the video *Writing Efficient Nested Selections*.

Using the AND Operator

Most programming languages allow you to ask two or more questions in a single comparison by using a **conditional AND operator**, or more simply, an **AND operator** that joins decisions in a single expression. For example, if you want to bill an extra amount to cell phone customers who make more than 100 calls that total more than 500 minutes in a billing period, you can use nested decisions, as shown in the previous section, or you can include both decisions in a single expression by writing the following question:

```
callsMade > CALLS AND callMinutes > MINUTES
```

When you use one or more AND operators to combine two or more Boolean expressions, each Boolean expression must be true for the entire expression to be evaluated as true. For example, if you ask, "Are you a native-born U.S. citizen and are you at least 35 years old?", the answer to both parts of the question must be *yes* before the response can be a single, summarizing *yes*. If either part of the expression is false, then the entire expression is false.

The conditional **AND** operator in Java, C++, and C# consists of two ampersands, with no spaces between them (&&). In Visual Basic, you use the keyword **And**.

One tool that can help you understand the AND operator is a truth table. **Truth tables** are diagrams used in mathematics and logic to help describe the truth of an entire expression based on the truth of its parts. Quick Reference 4-3 contains a truth table that lists all the possibilities with an AND operator. As the table shows, for any two expressions x and y, the expression x AND y is true only if both x and y are individually true. If either x or y alone is false, or if both are false, then the expression x AND y is false.

QUICK REFERENCE 4-3 Truth Table for the AND Operator

x?	y?	x AND y?
True	True	True
True	False	False
False	True	False
False	False	False

If the programming language you use allows an AND operator, you must realize that the question you place first (to the left of the AND operator) is the one that will be asked first, and cases that are eliminated based on the first question will not proceed to the second question. In other words, each part of an expression that uses an AND operator is evaluated only as far as necessary to determine whether the entire expression is true or false. This feature is called **short-circuit evaluation**. The computer can ask only one question at a time; even when your pseudocode looks like the first example in Figure 4-9, the computer will execute the logic shown in the second example. Even when you use an AND operator, the computer makes decisions one at a time, and makes them in the order you ask them. As you can see in the truth table, if the first question in an AND expression evaluates to false, then the entire expression is false. In that case, there is no point in evaluating the second Boolean expression. In other words, evaluating an AND expression is interrupted as soon as part of it is determined to be false.

You are never required to use the AND operator because using nested if statements can always achieve the same result. However, using the AND operator often makes your code more concise, less error-prone, and easier to understand.

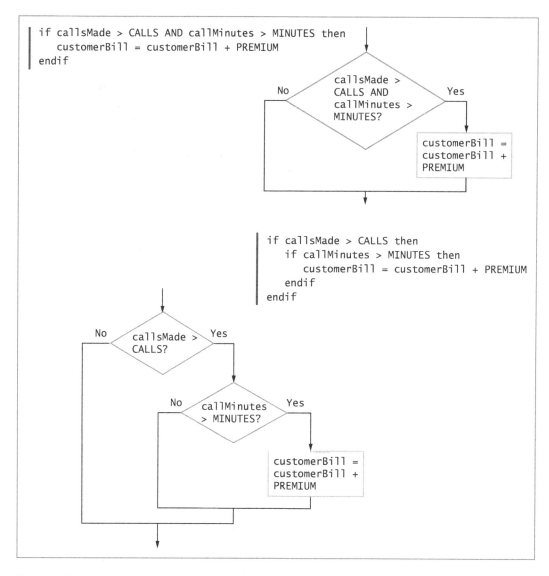

Figure 4-9   Using an AND operator and the logic behind it
© 2015 Cengage Learning

There can be confusion between the terms *conditional operator* and *logical operator*. *Conditional operator* is most often used when short-circuit evaluation is in effect, but you will sometimes hear programmers use the two terms interchangeably. To complicate matters, some programmers call the operators *conditional logical operators*.

Avoiding Common Errors in an *AND* Selection
Make Sure Decisions that Should Be Nested are Nested

When you need to satisfy two or more criteria to initiate an event in a program, you must make sure that the second decision is made entirely within the first decision. For example, if a program's objective is to add a $20 premium to the bill of cell phone customers who exceed 100 calls and 500 minutes in a billing period, then the program segment shown in Figure 4-10 contains three different types of logic errors.

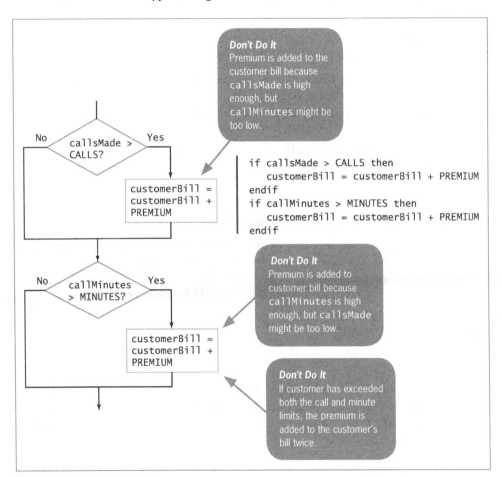

Don't Do It
Premium is added to the customer bill because `callsMade` is high enough, but `callMinutes` might be too low.

```
if callsMade > CALLS then
    customerBill = customerBill + PREMIUM
endif
if callMinutes > MINUTES then
    customerBill = customerBill + PREMIUM
endif
```

Don't Do It
Premium is added to customer bill because `callMinutes` is high enough, but `callsMade` might be too low.

Don't Do It
If customer has exceeded both the call and minute limits, the premium is added to the customer's bill twice.

Figure 4-10 Incorrect logic to add a $20 premium to the bills of cell phone customers who meet two criteria
© 2015 Cengage Learning

The logic in Figure 4-10 shows that if a customer makes too many calls, $20 is added to his bill. This customer should not necessarily be billed extra because the customer's minutes might be low. In addition, in Figure 4-10, a customer who has made few calls is not eliminated from the second decision. Instead, all customers are subjected to the minutes question, and some are assigned the premium even though they might have made only a few calls. Additionally, any customer who passes both tests because his calls and minutes are both high has the premium added to his bill twice. The decisions in Figure 4-10 are stacked when they should be nested, so the logic they represent is *not* correct for this problem.

Make Sure that Boolean Expressions are Complete

When you use the AND operator in most languages, you must provide a complete Boolean expression on each side of the operator. In other words, callMinutes > 100 AND callMinutes < 200 would be a valid expression to find callMinutes between 100 and 200. However, callMinutes > 100 AND < 200 would not be valid because the less-than sign and 200 that follow the AND operator do not constitute a complete Boolean expression.

For clarity, you can enclose each Boolean expression in a compound expression in its own set of parentheses. This makes it easier for you to see that each of the AND operator's operands is a complete Boolean expression. Use this format if it is clearer to you. For example, you might write the following:

```
if (callMinutes > MINUTES) AND (callsMade > CALLS) then
    customerBill = customerBill + PREMIUM
endif
```

Make Sure that Expressions are not Inadvertently Trivial

When you use the AND operator, it is easy to inadvertently create trivial expressions that are always true or always false. For example, suppose that you want to display a message if a cell phone customer makes no calls and if the customer makes more than 2000 calls. You might be tempted to write the following expression, but it would be incorrect:

```
if callsMade = 0 AND callsMade > 2000 then
    output "Irregular usage"
endif
```

Don't Do It
This AND expression is always false.

This if statement never results in a displayed message because both parts of the AND expression can never be true at the same time. For example, if the value of callsMade is over 2000, its value is not 0, and if callsMade is 0, it is not over 2000. The programmer intended to use the following code:

```
if callsMade = 0 then
    output "Irregular usage"
else
    if callsMade > 2000 then
        output "Irregular usage"
    endif
endif
```

Alternately, the programmer might use an OR operator, as you will see in the next section.

TWO TRUTHS & A LIE

Understanding *AND* Logic

1. When you nest selection structures because the resulting action requires that two conditions be true, either decision logically can be made first and the results will be the same.

2. When two selections are required for an action to take place, you often can improve your program's performance by appropriately choosing which selection to make first.

3. To improve efficiency in a nested selection in which two conditions must be true for some action to occur, you should first ask the question that is more likely to be true.

The false statement is #3. For efficiency in a nested selection, you should first ask the question that is less likely to be true.

Understanding *OR* Logic

Sometimes you want to take action when one *or* the other of two conditions is true. This is called an **OR decision** because either one condition *or* some other condition must be met in order for some action to take place. If someone asks, "Are you free for dinner Friday or Saturday?," only one of the two conditions has to be true for the answer to the whole question to be *yes*; only if the answers to both halves of the question are false is the value of the entire expression false.

For example, suppose the cell phone company has established a new fee schedule as follows:

*   The basic monthly service bill is $30.

*   An additional $20 is billed to customers who make more than 100 calls or send more than 200 text messages.

Figure 4-11 shows the altered `detailLoop()` module of the billing program that accomplishes this objective. Assume that new declarations have been made for the `textsSent` variable and a TEXTS constant that has been assigned the value 200.

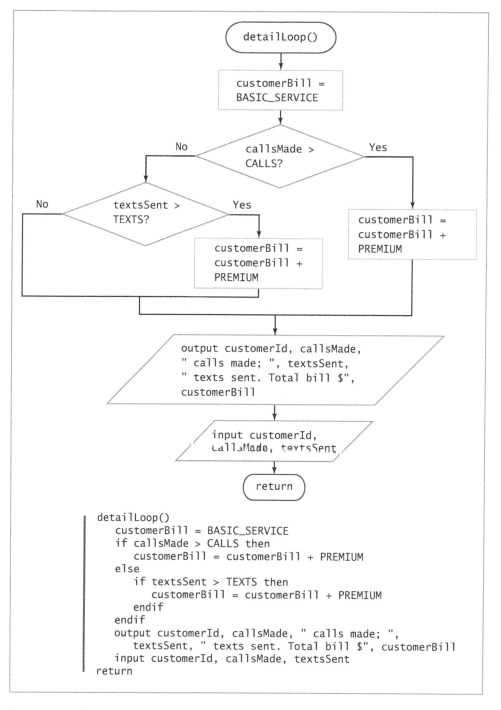

```
detailLoop()
    customerBill = BASIC_SERVICE
    if callsMade > CALLS then
        customerBill = customerBill + PREMIUM
    else
        if textsSent > TEXTS then
            customerBill = customerBill + PREMIUM
        endif
    endif
    output customerId, callsMade, " calls made; ",
        textsSent, " texts sent. Total bill $", customerBill
    input customerId, callsMade, textsSent
return
```

Figure 4-11   Flowchart and pseudocode for cell phone billing program in which a customer must meet one or both of two criteria to be billed a premium

The `detailLoop()` in the program in Figure 4-11 tests the expression `callsMade > CALLS`, and if the result is true, the premium amount is added to the customer's bill. Because making many calls is enough for the customer to incur the premium, there is no need for further questioning. If the customer has not made more than 100 calls, only then does the program need to ask whether `textsSent > TEXTS` is true. If the customer did not make over 100 calls, but did send more than 200 text messages, then the premium amount is added to the customer's bill.

Writing *OR* Selections for Efficiency

As with an AND condition, when you use an OR condition, you can choose to ask either question first. For example, you can add an extra $20 to the bills of customers who meet one or the other of two criteria using the logic in either part of Figure 4-12.

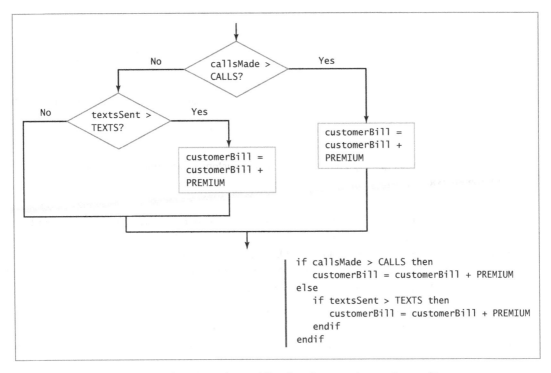

Figure 4-12   Two ways to assign a premium to bills of customers who meet one of two criteria *(continues)*

(continued)

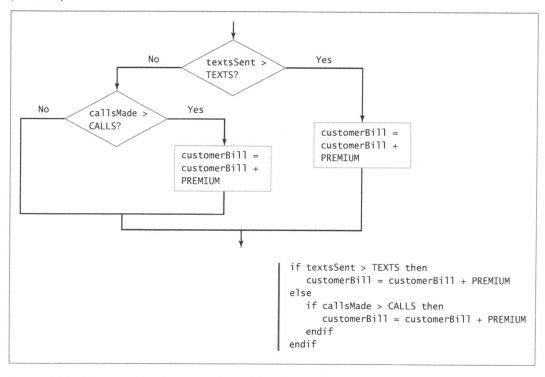

```
if textsSent > TEXTS then
    customerBill = customerBill + PREMIUM
else
    if callsMade > CALLS then
        customerBill = customerBill + PREMIUM
    endif
endif
```

Figure 4-12   Two ways to assign a premium to bills of customers who meet one of two criteria
© 2015 Cengage Learning

You might have guessed that one of these solutions is superior to the other when you have some background information about the relative likelihood of each tested condition. For example, let's say you know that out of 1000 cell phone customers, about 90 percent, or 900, make more than 100 calls in a billing period. Suppose that you also know that only about half of the 1000 customers, or 500, send more than 200 text messages.

When you use the logic shown in the first half of Figure 4-12, you first ask about the calls made. For 900 customers the answer is true, and you add the premium to their bills. Only about 100 sets of customer data continue to the next question regarding the text messages, where about 50 percent of the 100, or 50, are billed the extra amount. In the end, you have made 1100 decisions to correctly add premium amounts for 950 customers.

If you use the OR logic in the second half of Figure 4-12, you ask about text messages first—1000 times, once each for 1000 customers. The result is true for 50 percent, or 500 customers, whose bill is increased. For the other 500 customers, you ask about the number of calls made. For 90 percent of the 500, the result is true, so premiums are added for 450 additional people. In the end, the same 950 customers are billed an extra $20—but this approach requires executing 1500 decisions, 400 more decisions than when using the first decision logic.

The general rule is: *In an OR decision, first ask the question that is more likely to be true.* This approach eliminates as many executions of the second decision as possible, and the time it takes to process all the data is decreased. As with the AND situation, in an OR situation, it is more efficient to eliminate as many extra decisions as possible.

Using the OR Operator

If you need to take action when either one or the other of two conditions is met, you can use two separate, nested selection structures, as in the previous examples. However, most programming languages allow you to make two or more decisions in a single comparison by using a **conditional OR operator** (or simply the **OR operator**). For example, you can ask the following question:

```
callsMade > CALLS OR textsSent > TEXTS
```

When you use the logical OR operator, only one of the listed conditions must be met for the resulting action to take place. Quick Reference 4-4 contains the truth table for the OR operator. As you can see in the table, the entire expression x OR y is false only when x and y each are false individually.

QUICK REFERENCE 4-4 Truth Table for the OR Operator

x?	y?	x OR y?
True	True	True
True	False	True
False	True	True
False	False	False

If the programming language you use supports the OR operator, you still must realize that the comparison you place first is the expression that will be evaluated first, and cases that pass the test of the first comparison will not proceed to the second comparison. As with the AND operator, this feature is called short-circuiting. The computer can ask only one question at a time; even when you write code as shown at the top of Figure 4-13, the computer will execute the logic shown at the bottom.

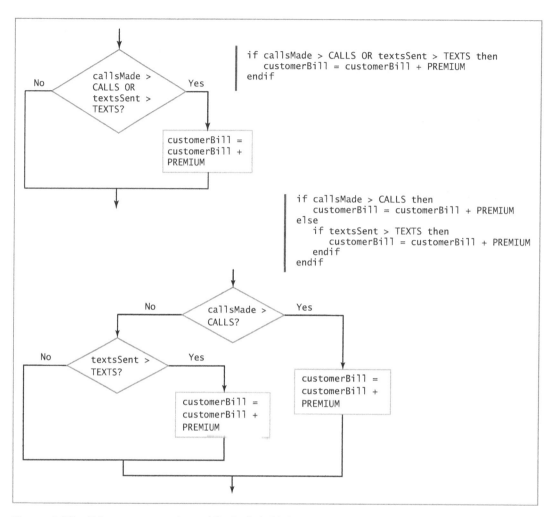

Figure 4-13   Using an OR operator and the logic behind it
© 2015 Cengage Learning

 C#, C++, C, and Java use two pipe symbols (||) as the logical OR operator. In Visual Basic, the keyword used for the operator is Or.

Avoiding Common Errors in an *OR* Selection
Make Sure that Boolean Expressions are Complete

As with the AND operator, most programming languages require a complete Boolean expression on each side of the OR operator. For example, if you wanted to display a message when customers make either 0 calls or more than 2000 calls, the expression callsMade = 0 OR callsMade > 2000 is appropriate but callsMade = 0 OR > 2000 is not, because the expression to the right of the OR operator is not a complete Boolean expression.

Also, as with the AND operator, you can enclose each simple comparison within parentheses for clarity if you want, as in the following statement:

```
if (callsMade = 0) OR (callsMade > 2000) then
    output "Irregular usage"
endif
```

Make Sure that Selections are Structured

You might have noticed that the assignment statement customerBill = customerBill + PREMIUM appears twice in the decision-making processes in Figures 4-12 and 4-13. When you create a flowchart, the temptation is to draw the logic to look like Figure 4-14. Logically, you might argue that the flowchart in Figure 4-14 is correct because the correct customers are billed the extra $20. However, this flowchart is not structured. The second question is not a self-contained structure with one entry and exit point; instead, the flowline breaks out of the inner selection structure to join the Yes side of the outer selection structure.

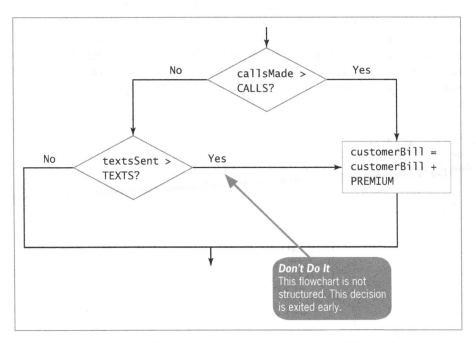

Figure 4-14 Unstructured flowchart for determining customer cell phone bill
© 2015 Cengage Learning

Make Sure that You Use OR Selections When They are Required

The OR selection has additional potential for errors due to the differences in the way people and computers use language. When your boss wants to add an extra amount to the bills of customers who make more than 100 calls *or* send more than 200 texts, she is likely to say, "Add $20 to the bill of anyone who makes more than 100 calls and to anyone who sends more than 200 texts." Her request contains the word *and* between two types of people—those who made many calls and those who sent many texts—placing the emphasis on the people.

However, each decision you make is about the added $20 for a single customer who has met one criterion *or* the other *or* both. In other words, the OR condition is between each customer's attributes, and not between different customers. Instead of the manager's previous statement, it would be clearer if she said, "Add $20 to the bill of anyone who has made more than 100 calls or has sent more than 200 texts," but you can't count on people to speak like computers. As a programmer, you have the job of clarifying what really is being requested. Often, a casual request for A *and* B logically means a request for A *or* B.

Make Sure that Expressions are not Inadvertently Trivial

The way we use English can cause another type of error when you are required to find whether a value falls between two other values. For example, a movie theater manager might say, "Provide a discount to patrons who are under 13 years old and to those who are over 64 years old; otherwise, charge the full price." Because the manager has used the word *and* in the request, you might be tempted to create the decision shown in Figure 4-15; however, this logic will not provide a discounted price for any movie patron. You must remember that every time the decision is made in Figure 4-15, it is made for a single movie patron. If `patronAge` contains a value lower than 13, then it cannot possibly contain a value over 64. Similarly, if `patronAge` contains a value over 64, there is no way it can contain a lesser value. Therefore, no value could be stored in `patronAge` for which both parts of the AND condition could be true—and the price will never be set to the discounted price for any patron. In other words, the decision made in Figure 4-15 is trivial. Figure 4-16 shows the correct logic.

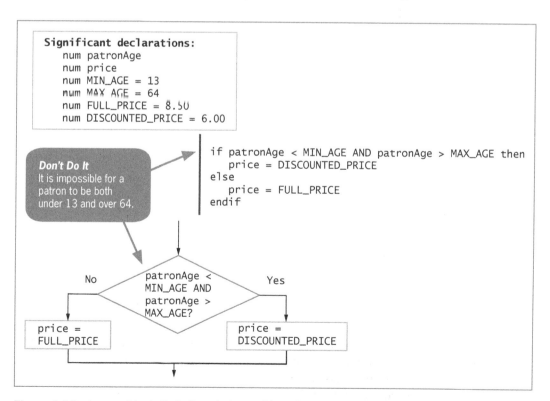

Figure 4-15   Incorrect logic that attempts to provide a discount for young and old movie patrons
© 2015 Cengage Learning

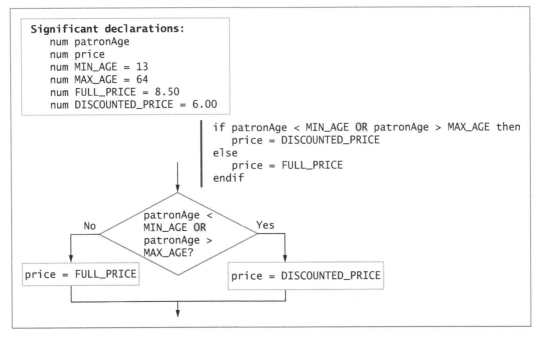

Significant declarations:
```
num patronAge
num price
num MIN_AGE = 13
num MAX_AGE = 64
num FULL_PRICE = 8.50
num DISCOUNTED_PRICE = 6.00
```

```
if patronAge < MIN_AGE OR patronAge > MAX_AGE then
    price = DISCOUNTED_PRICE
else
    price = FULL_PRICE
endif
```

Figure 4-16 Correct logic that provides a discount for young and old movie patrons
© 2015 Cengage Learning

A similar error can occur in your logic if the theater manager says something like, "Don't give a discount—that is, do charge full price—if a patron is over 12 or under 65." Because the word *or* appears in the request, you might plan your logic to resemble Figure 4-17. No patron ever receives a discount, because every patron is either over 12 or under 65. Remember, in an OR decision, only one of the conditions needs to be true for the entire expression to be evaluated as true. So, for example, because a patron who is 10 is under 65, the full price is charged, and because a patron who is 70 is over 12, the full price also is charged. Figure 4-18 shows the correct logic for this decision.

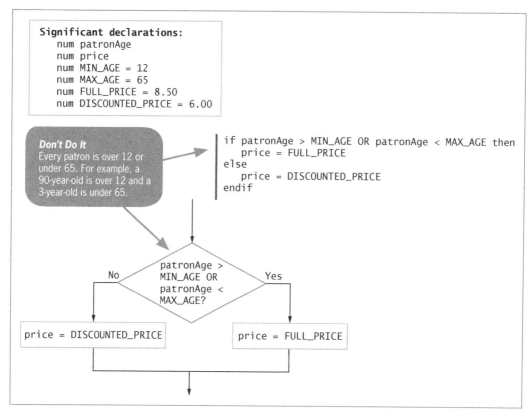

Figure 4-17   Incorrect logic that attempts to charge full price for patrons whose age is over 12 and under 65
© 2015 Cengage Learning

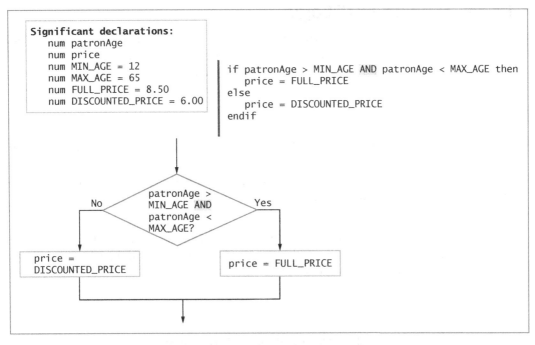

Figure 4-18   Correct logic that charges full price for patrons whose age is over 12 and under 65
© 2015 Cengage Learning

 Watch the video *Looking in Depth at AND and OR Decisions*.

TWO TRUTHS & A LIE

Understanding *OR* Logic

1. In an OR selection, two or more conditions must be met in order for an event to take place.

2. When you use an OR selection, you can choose to ask either question first and still achieve a usable program.

3. The general rule is: In an OR decision, first ask the question that is more likely to be true.

The false statement is #1. In an OR selection, only one of two conditions must be met in order for an event to take place.

Understanding *NOT* Logic

Besides AND and OR operators, most languages support a NOT operator. You use the **logical NOT operator** to reverse the meaning of a Boolean expression. For example, the following statement outputs *Can register to vote* when age is greater than or equal to 18:

```
if NOT (age < 18) then
    output "Can register to vote"
endif
```

This example uses parentheses around the expression age < 18 to show that the NOT operator applies to the entire Boolean expression age < 18. Without the parentheses, some languages might try to evaluate the expression NOT age before testing the less-than comparison. Depending on the programming language, the result would either be incorrect or the statement would not execute at all.

Quick Reference 4-5 contains the truth table for the NOT operator. As you can see, any expression that would be true without the operator becomes false with it, and any expression that would be false without the operator becomes true with it.

QUICK REFERENCE 4-5 Truth Table for the NOT Operator

x?	NOT x?
True	False
False	True

You have already learned that arithmetic operators such as + and −, and relational operators such as > and <, are binary operators that require two operands. Unlike those operators, the NOT operator is a **unary operator**, meaning it takes only one operand—that is, you do not use it between two expressions, but you use it in front of a single expression.

As when using the binary not-equal-to comparison operator, using the unary NOT operator can create confusing statements because negative logic is difficult to follow. For example, if your intention is not to allow voter registration for those under 18, then either of the following two statements will accomplish your goal, but the second one is easier to understand:

```
if NOT (age < 18) then
    output "Can register to vote"
endif

if age >= 18 then
    output "Can register to vote"
endif
```

Avoiding a Common Error in a *NOT* Expression

Because thinking with negatives is hard, you need to be careful not to create trivial expressions when using NOT logic. For example, suppose your boss tells you to display a message for all employees except those in Departments 1 and 2. You might write the following incorrect code:

```
if NOT employeeDept = 1 OR NOT employeeDept = 2 then
    output "Employee is not in Department 1 or 2"
endif
```

Don't Do It
This logic does not eliminate employees in Departments 1 and 2.

Suppose that an employee is in Department 1, and therefore no message should be displayed. The expression `employeeDept = 1` is evaluated as false, so `NOT employeeDept = 1` is true. Because the `OR` operator's left operand is true, the entire Boolean expression is true, and the message is incorrectly displayed. The correct decision follows:

```
if NOT (employeeDept = 1 OR employeeDept = 2) then
    output "Employee is not in Department 1 or 2"
endif
```

In C++, Java, and C#, the exclamation point is the symbol used for the NOT operator. In those languages, the exclamation point can be used in front of an expression or combined with other comparison operators. For example, the expression *a not equal to b* can be written as `!(a = b)` or as `a != b`. In Visual Basic, the operator is the keyword `Not`.

TWO TRUTHS & A LIE

Understanding *NOT* Logic

1. The value of `x <> 0` is the same as the value of `NOT (x = 0)`.

2. The value of `x > y` is the same as the value of `NOT (x < y)`.

3. The value of `x = y OR x > 5` is the same as the value of `x = y OR NOT (x <= 5)`.

The false statement is #2. The value of NOT (x < y) is not the value of x > y because the first expression is false and the second one is true when x and y are equal. The value of x > y is the same as the value of NOT (x => y).

Making Selections within Ranges

You often need to take action when a variable falls within a range of values. For example, suppose your company provides various customer discounts based on the number of items ordered, as shown in Figure 4-19.

Items Ordered	Discount Rate (%)
0 to 10	0
11 to 24	10
25 to 50	15
51 or more	20

Figure 4-19   Discount rates based on items ordered

© 2015 Cengage Learning

When you write the program that determines a discount rate based on the number of items, you could make hundreds of decisions, evaluating itemQuantity = 1, itemQuantity = 2, and so on. However, it is more convenient to find the correct discount rate by using a range check.

When you use a **range check**, you compare a variable to a series of values that mark the limiting ends of ranges. To perform a range check, make comparisons using either the lowest or highest value in each range of values. For example, to find each discount rate listed in Figure 4-19, you can use one of the following techniques:

- Make comparisons using the low ends of the ranges.

  - You can ask: Is itemQuantity less than 11? If not, is it less than 25? If not, is it less than 51? (If it's possible the value is negative, you would also check for a value less than 0 and take appropriate action if it is.)

  - You can ask: Is itemQuantity greater than or equal to 51? If not, is it greater than or equal to 25? If not, is it greater than or equal to 11? (If it's possible the value is negative, you would also check for a value greater than or equal to 0 and take appropriate action if it is not.)

- Make comparisons using the high ends of the ranges.

  - You can ask: Is itemQuantity greater than 50? If not, is it greater than 24? If not, is it greater than 10? (If there is a maximum allowed value for itemQuantity, you would also check for a value greater than that limit and take appropriate action if it is.)

  - You can ask: Is itemQuantity less than or equal to 10? If not, is it less than or equal to 24? If not, is it less than or equal to 50? (If there is a maximum allowed value for itemQuantity, you would also check for a value less than or equal to that limit and take appropriate action if it is not.)

Figure 4-20 shows the flowchart and pseudocode that represent the logic for a program that determines the correct discount for each order quantity. In the decision-making process, itemsOrdered is compared to the high end of the lowest-range group (RANGE1). If itemsOrdered is less than or equal to that value, then you know the correct discount, DISCOUNT1; if not, you continue checking. If itemsOrdered is less than or equal to the high end of the next range (RANGE2), then the customer's discount is DISCOUNT2; if not, you continue checking, and the customer's discount eventually is set to DISCOUNT3 or DISCOUNT4. In the pseudocode in Figure 4-20, notice how each associated if, else, and endif aligns vertically.

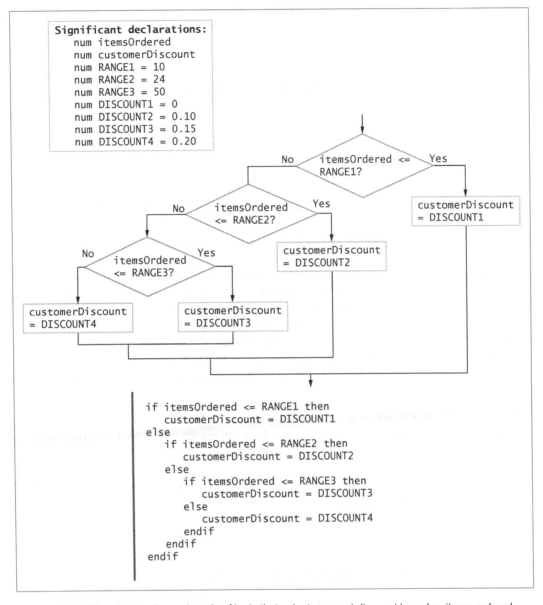

Significant declarations:
```
num itemsOrdered
num customerDiscount
num RANGE1 = 10
num RANGE2 = 24
num RANGE3 = 50
num DISCOUNT1 = 0
num DISCOUNT2 = 0.10
num DISCOUNT3 = 0.15
num DISCOUNT4 = 0.20
```

```
if itemsOrdered <= RANGE1 then
    customerDiscount = DISCOUNT1
else
    if itemsOrdered <= RANGE2 then
        customerDiscount = DISCOUNT2
    else
        if itemsOrdered <= RANGE3 then
            customerDiscount = DISCOUNT3
        else
            customerDiscount = DISCOUNT4
        endif
    endif
endif
```

Figure 4-20   Flowchart and pseudocode of logic that selects correct discount based on items ordered
© 2015 Cengage Learning

In computer memory, a percent sign (%) is not stored with a numeric value that represents a percentage. Instead, the mathematical equivalent is stored. For example, 15% is stored as 0.15. You can store a percent value as a string, as in "15%", but then you cannot perform arithmetic with it.

For example, consider an order for 30 items. The expression itemsOrdered <= RANGE1 evaluates as false, so the else clause of the decision executes. There, itemsOrdered <= RANGE2 also evaluates to false, so its else clause executes. The expression itemsOrdered <=

RANGE3 is true, so `customerDiscount` becomes `DISCOUNT3`, which is 0.15. Walk through the logic with other values for `itemsOrdered` and verify for yourself that the correct discount is applied each time.

Avoiding Common Errors When Using Range Checks

To create well-written programs that include range checks, you should be careful to eliminate dead paths and to avoid testing the same range limit multiple times.

Eliminate Dead Paths

When new programmers perform range checks, they are prone to including logic that has too many decisions, entailing more work than is necessary.

Figure 4-21 shows a program segment that contains a range check in which the programmer has asked one question too many—the shaded question in the figure. If you know that `itemsOrdered` is not less than or equal to RANGE1, not less than or equal to RANGE2, and not less than or equal to RANGE3, then `itemsOrdered` must be greater than RANGE3. The comparison to RANGE3 is trivial, so asking whether `itemsOrdered` is greater than RANGE3 is a waste of time; no customer order can ever travel the logical path on the far left of the flowchart. You might say such a path is a **dead** or **unreachable path**, and that the statements written there constitute dead or unreachable code. Although a program that contains such logic will execute and assign the correct discount to customers who order more than 50 items, providing such a path is inefficient.

In Figure 4-21, it is easier to see the useless path in the flowchart than in the pseudocode representation of the same logic. However, when you use an `if` without an `else`, you are doing nothing when the question's answer is false.

Sometimes there are good reasons to ask people questions for which you already know the answers. For example, a good trial lawyer seldom asks a question in court if the answer will be a surprise. With computer logic, however, such questions are an inefficient waste of time.

Avoid Testing the Same Range Limit Multiple Times

Another error that programmers make when writing the logic to perform a range check also involves asking unnecessary questions. Figure 4-22 shows an inefficient range selection that asks two unneeded questions. In the figure, if `itemsOrdered` is less than or equal to RANGE1, `customerDiscount` is set to DISCOUNT1. If `itemsOrdered` is not less than or equal to RANGE1, then it must be greater than RANGE1, so the next decision (shaded in the figure) is unnecessary. The computer logic will never execute the shaded decision unless `itemsOrdered` is already greater than RANGE1—that is, unless the logic follows the false branch of the first selection. If you use the logic in Figure 4-22, you are wasting computer time with a trivial decision that tests a range limit that has already been tested. The same logic applies to the

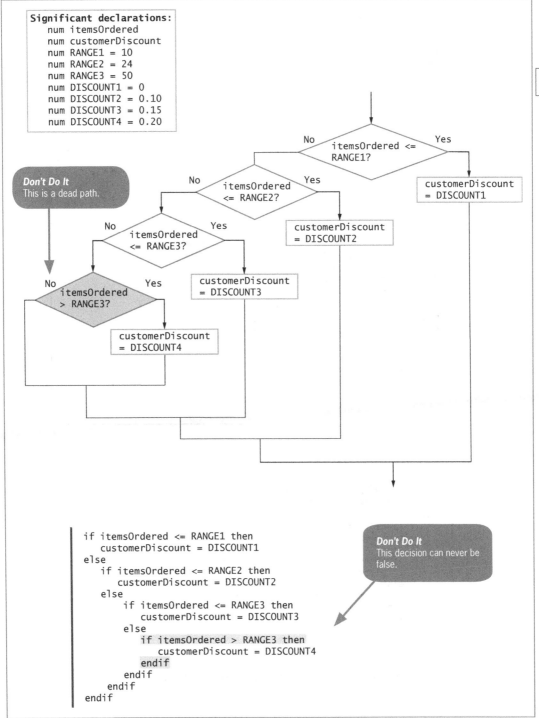

Significant declarations:
```
num itemsOrdered
num customerDiscount
num RANGE1 = 10
num RANGE2 = 24
num RANGE3 = 50
num DISCOUNT1 = 0
num DISCOUNT2 = 0.10
num DISCOUNT3 = 0.15
num DISCOUNT4 = 0.20
```

Don't Do It
This is a dead path.

Don't Do It
This decision can never be false.

```
if itemsOrdered <= RANGE1 then
   customerDiscount = DISCOUNT1
else
   if itemsOrdered <= RANGE2 then
      customerDiscount = DISCOUNT2
   else
      if itemsOrdered <= RANGE3 then
         customerDiscount = DISCOUNT3
      else
         if itemsOrdered > RANGE3 then
            customerDiscount = DISCOUNT4
         endif
      endif
   endif
endif
```

Figure 4-21   Inefficient range selection including unreachable path
© 2015 Cengage Learning

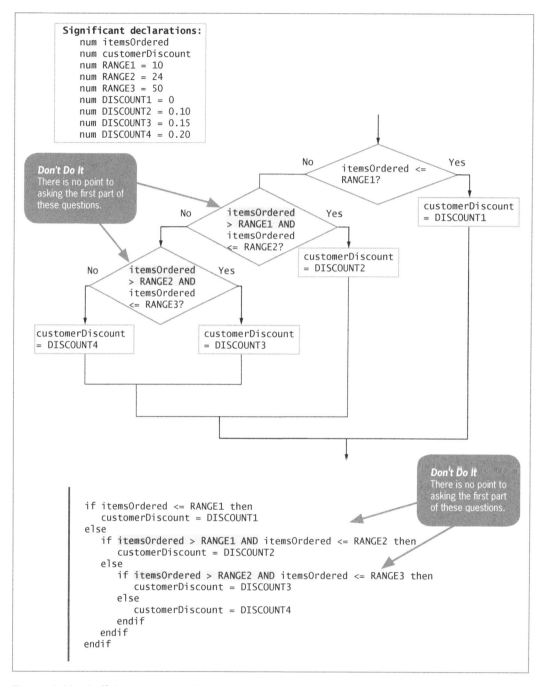

Significant declarations:
```
num itemsOrdered
num customerDiscount
num RANGE1 = 10
num RANGE2 = 24
num RANGE3 = 50
num DISCOUNT1 = 0
num DISCOUNT2 = 0.10
num DISCOUNT3 = 0.15
num DISCOUNT4 = 0.20
```

Don't Do It
There is no point to asking the first part of these questions.

itemsOrdered <= RANGE1?

No / Yes

customerDiscount = DISCOUNT1

itemsOrdered > RANGE1 AND itemsOrdered <= RANGE2?

No / Yes

customerDiscount = DISCOUNT2

itemsOrdered > RANGE2 AND itemsOrdered <= RANGE3?

No / Yes

customerDiscount = DISCOUNT4

customerDiscount = DISCOUNT3

Don't Do It
There is no point to asking the first part of these questions.

```
if itemsOrdered <= RANGE1 then
   customerDiscount = DISCOUNT1
else
   if itemsOrdered > RANGE1 AND itemsOrdered <= RANGE2 then
      customerDiscount = DISCOUNT2
   else
      if itemsOrdered > RANGE2 AND itemsOrdered <= RANGE3 then
         customerDiscount = DISCOUNT3
      else
         customerDiscount = DISCOUNT4
      endif
   endif
endif
```

Figure 4-22 Inefficient range selection including unnecessary questions
© 2015 Cengage Learning

second shaded decision in Figure 4-22. Beginning programmers sometimes justify their use of unnecessary questions as "just making really sure." Such caution is unnecessary when writing computer logic.

TWO TRUTHS & A LIE

Making Selections within Ranges

1. When you perform a range check, you compare a variable to every value in a series of ranges.

2. You can perform a range check by making comparisons using the lowest value in each range of values you are using.

3. You can perform a range check by making comparisons using the highest value in each range of values you are using.

The false statement is #1. When you use a range check, you compare a variable to a series of values that represent the ends of ranges. Depending on your logic, you can use either the high or low end of each range.

Understanding Precedence When Combining AND and OR Operators

Most programming languages allow you to combine as many AND and OR operators in an expression as you need. For example, assume that you need to achieve a score of at least 75 on each of three tests to pass a course. You can declare a constant MIN_SCORE equal to 75 and test the multiple conditions with a statement like the following:

```
if score1 >= MIN_SCORE AND score2 >= MIN_SCORE AND score3 >= MIN_SCORE then
   classGrade = "Pass"
else
   classGrade = "Fail"
endif
```

On the other hand, if you need to pass only one of three tests to pass a course, then the logic is as follows:

```
if score1 >= MIN_SCORE OR score2 >= MIN_SCORE OR score3 >= MIN_SCORE then
   classGrade = "Pass"
else
   classGrade = "Fail"
endif
```

The logic becomes more complicated when you combine AND and OR operators within the same statement. When you do, the AND operators take precedence, meaning the Boolean values of the AND expressions are evaluated first.

In Chapter 2 you learned that in arithmetic statements, multiplication and division have precedence over addition and subtraction. You also learned that precedence is sometimes referred to as *order of operations*.

For example, consider a program that determines whether a movie theater patron can purchase a discounted ticket. Assume that discounts are allowed for children and senior citizens who attend G-rated movies. The following code looks reasonable, but it produces incorrect results because the expression that contains the AND operator (see shading) evaluates before the one that contains the OR operator.

```
if age <= 12 OR age >= 65 AND rating = "G" then
    output "Discount applies"
endif
```

Don't Do It
The shaded AND expression evaluates first, which is not the intention.

For example, assume that a movie patron is 10 years old and the movie rating is R. The patron should not receive a discount (or be allowed to see the movie!). However, within the if statement, the part of the expression that contains the AND operator, age >= 65 AND rating = "G", is evaluated first. For a 10-year-old and an R-rated movie, the question is false (on both counts), so the entire if statement becomes the equivalent of the following:

```
if age <= 12 OR aFalseExpression then
    output "Discount applies"
endif
```

Because the patron is 10, age <= 12 is true, so the original if statement becomes the equivalent of:

```
if aTrueExpression OR aFalseExpression then
    output "Discount applies"
endif
```

The combination true OR false evaluates as true. Therefore, the string "Discount applies" is output when it should not be.

Many programming languages allow you to use parentheses to correct the logic and force the OR expression to be evaluated first, as shown in the following pseudocode:

```
if (age <= 12 OR age >= 65) AND rating = "G" then
    output "Discount applies"
endif
```

With the added parentheses, if the patron's age is 12 or under OR the age is 65 or over, the expression is evaluated as:

```
if aTrueExpression AND rating = "G" then
    output "Discount applies"
endif
```

In this statement, when the age value qualifies a patron for a discount, then the rating value must also be acceptable before the discount applies. This was the original intention.

You can use the following techniques to avoid confusion when mixing AND and OR operators:

- You can use parentheses to override the default precedence (order of operations).

- You can use parentheses for clarity even though they do not change what the order of operations would be without them. For example, if a customer should be between 12 and 19 or have a school ID to receive a high school discount, you can use the expression (age > 12 AND age < 19) OR validId = "Yes", even though the evaluation would be the same without the parentheses.

- You can use nested if statements instead of using AND and OR operators. With the flowchart and pseudocode shown in Figure 4-23, it is clear which movie patrons receive the discount. In the flowchart, you can see that the OR is nested entirely within the *Yes* branch of the rating = "G" decision. Similarly, in the pseudocode in Figure 4-23, you can see by the alignment that if the rating is not G, the logic proceeds directly to the last endif statement, bypassing any checking of age at all.

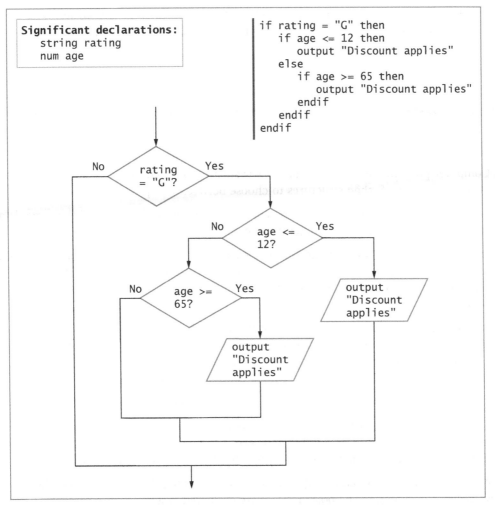

```
Significant declarations:
   string rating
   num age
```

```
if rating = "G" then
    if age <= 12 then
        output "Discount applies"
    else
        if age >= 65 then
            output "Discount applies"
        endif
    endif
endif
```

Figure 4-23   Nested decisions that determine movie patron discount
© 2015 Cengage Learning

TWO TRUTHS & A LIE

Understanding Precedence When Combining AND and OR Operators

1. Most programming languages allow you to combine as many AND and OR operators in an expression as you need.

2. When you combine AND and OR operators, the OR operators take precedence, meaning their Boolean values are evaluated first.

3. You always can avoid the confusion of mixing AND and OR decisions by nesting if statements instead of using AND and OR operators.

The false statement is #2. When you combine AND and OR operators, the AND operators take precedence, meaning the Boolean values of their expressions are evaluated first.

Chapter Summary

- Computer program decisions are made by evaluating Boolean expressions. You can use if-then-else or if-then structures to choose between two possible outcomes.

- You can use relational comparison operators to compare two operands of the same data type. The standard relational comparison operators are =, >, <, >=, <=, and <>.

- In an AND decision, two conditions must be true for a resulting action to take place. An AND decision requires a nested decision or the use of an AND operator. In an AND decision, the most efficient approach is to start by asking the question that is less likely to be true.

- In an OR decision, at least one of two conditions must be true for a resulting action to take place. In an OR decision, the most efficient approach is to start by asking the question that is more likely to be true. Most programming languages allow you to ask two or more questions in a single comparison by using a conditional OR operator.

- The logical NOT operator reverses the meaning of a Boolean expression.

- To perform a range check, make comparisons with either the lowest or highest value in each range of comparison values. Common errors that occur when programmers perform range checks include asking unnecessary and previously answered questions.

- When you combine AND and OR operators in an expression, the AND operators take precedence, meaning their Boolean values are evaluated first.

Key Terms

A **Boolean expression** is one that represents only one of two states, usually expressed as true or false.

An **if-then** decision structure contains a tested Boolean expression and an action that is taken only when the expression is true.

An **if-then clause** of a decision holds the statements that execute when the tested Boolean expression is true.

The **else clause** of a decision holds the statements that execute only when the tested Boolean expression is false.

Relational comparison operators are the symbols that express Boolean comparisons. Examples include =, >, <, >=, <=, and <>.

A **trivial expression** is one that always evaluates to the same value.

A **compound condition** is constructed when you need to ask multiple questions before determining an outcome.

An **AND decision** contains two or more decisions; all conditions must be true for an action to take place.

A **nested decision**, or a **nested if**, is a decision within either the if-then or else clause of another decision.

A **cascading if statement** is a series of nested if statements.

A **conditional AND operator** (or, more simply, an **AND operator**) is a symbol that you use to combine conditions when they all must be true for an action to occur.

Truth tables are diagrams used in mathematics and logic to help describe the truth of an entire expression based on the truth of its parts.

Short-circuit evaluation is a logical feature in which expressions in each part of a larger expression are evaluated only as far as necessary to determine the final outcome.

An **OR decision** contains two or more decisions; if at least one condition is met, the resulting action takes place.

A **conditional OR operator** (or, more simply, an **OR operator**) is a symbol that you use to combine conditions when at least one of them must be true for an action to occur.

The **logical NOT operator** is a symbol that reverses the meaning of a Boolean expression.

A **unary operator** is one that uses only one operand.

A **range check** determines where a variable falls arithmetically when compared to a series of values that mark limiting ends.

A **dead** or **unreachable path** is a logical path that can never be traveled.

Exercises

 Review Questions

1. A _____ expression has one of two values: true or false.

   a. Georgian   c. Barbarian

   b. Boolean   d. Selective

2. In a selection, the `else` clause executes _____.

   a. when the tested condition is true

   b. when the tested condition is false

   c. always

   d. only after the `if` clause executes

3. The greater-than operator evaluates as true when _____.

   a. the left operand is greater than the right operand

   b. the right operand is greater than the left operand

   c. the right operand is equal to the left operand

   d. Both b and c are true.

4. A trivial Boolean expression is one that _____.

   a. is not important   c. is always false

   b. is complicated   d. always has the same value

5. If `x <= y` is true, then _____.

   a. `x = y` is true   c. `x > y` is false

   b. `y <= x` is true   d. `x >= y` is false

6. If `j <> k` is true, then _____.

   a. `j = k` is true   c. `j < k` might be true

   b. `j > k` might be true   d. Both b and c are true.

7. In an AND condition, the most efficient technique is to first ask the question that _____.

   a. mixes constants and variables

   b. uses a less-than or less-than-or-equal-to operator

   c. is least likely to be true

   d. uses a named constant

8. If `m` is true and `n` is false, then _____.

   a. `m AND n` is true   c. `m OR n` is false

   b. `m AND n` is false   d. If `m` is true, then `n` must be true.

9. If p is true and q is false, then _____.

    a. `p OR q is true`   c. `p AND q is true`

    b. `p OR q is false`   d. `p is greater than q`

10. Which of the lettered choices is equivalent to the following decision?

```
if x > 10 then
   if y > 10 then
      output "X"
   endif
endif
```

    a. `if x > 10 OR y > 10 then output "X" endif`

    b. `if x > 10 AND x > y then output "X" endif`

    c. `if y > x then output "X" endif`

    d. `if x > 10 AND y > 10 then output "X" endif`

11. If `conditionA` is 30 percent likely to be true and `conditionB` is 10 percent likely to be true, then it is most efficient to test `conditionA` first _____.

    a. in an OR decision   c. in any decision

    b. in an AND decision   d. never

12. Which of the following is a poorly written, trivial Boolean expression?

    a. `a > b AND b > c`   c. `e < f AND g < 100 AND g <> 5`

    b. `d = 10 OR d > 20`   d. `h < 10 AND h = 4`

13. Which of the following is a trivial Boolean expression?

    a. `k < b AND k > b`   c. `n > 12 OR p > 12`

    b. `m = 10 OR m = 20`   d. `q > 10 AND q < 19`

14. Which of the following is a trivial Boolean expression?

    a. `r < b AND f > b`   c. `f > 12 OR f < 19`

    b. `r = 10 OR r < 0`   d. `r > f AND f < b`

15. In the following pseudocode, what percentage raise will an employee in Department 8 receive?

```
if department < 5 then
   raise = SMALL_RAISE
else
   if department < 14 then
      raise = MEDIUM_RAISE
   else
      if department < 9 then
         raise = BIG_RAISE
      endif
   endif
endif
```

a. SMALL_RAISE

b. MEDIUM_RAISE

c. BIG_RAISE

d. impossible to tell

16. In the following pseudocode, what percentage raise will an employee in Department 10 receive?

```
if department < 2 then
   raise = SMALL_RAISE
else
   if department < 6 then
      raise = MEDIUM_RAISE
   else
      if department < 10 then
         raise = BIG_RAISE
      endif
   endif
endif
```

a. SMALL_RAISE

b. MEDIUM_RAISE

c. BIG_RAISE

d. impossible to tell

17. When you use a range check, you compare a variable to the _____ value in the range.

a. lowest   c. highest

b. middle   d. lowest or highest

18. If sales = 100, rate = 0.10, and expenses = 50, which of the following expressions is true?

a. sales >= expenses AND rate < 1

b. sales < 200 OR expenses < 100

c. expenses = rate OR sales = rate

d. two of the above

19. If a is true, b is true, and c is false, which of the following expressions is true?

a. a OR b AND c   c. a AND b OR c

b. a AND b AND c   d. two of the above

20. If d is true, e is false, and f is false, which of the following expressions is true?

a. e OR f AND d   c. d OR e AND f

b. f AND d OR e   d. two of the above

Programming Exercises

1. Assume that the following variables contain the values shown:

   numberBig = 300   numberMedium = 100   numberSmall = 5

   wordBig = "Elephant"   wordMedium = "Horse"   wordSmall = "bug"

   For each of the following Boolean expressions, decide whether the statement is true, false, or illegal.

   a. numberBig = numberSmall

   b. numberBig > numberSmall

   c. numberMedium < numberSmall

   d. numberBig = wordBig

   e. numberBig = "Big"

   f. wordMedium = "Medium"

   g. wordBig = "Elephant"

   h. numberMedium <= numberBig / 3

   i. numberBig >= 200

   j. numberBig >= numberMedium + numberSmall

   k. numberBig > numberMedium AND numberBig < numberSmall

   l. numberBig = 100 OR numberBig > numberSmall

   m. numberBig < 10 OR numberSmall > 10

   n. numberBig = 30 AND numberMedium = 100 OR numberSmall = 100

2. Design a flowchart or pseudocode for a program that accepts two numbers from a user and displays one of the following messages: *First is larger, Second is larger, Numbers are equal.*

3. Design a flowchart or pseudocode for a program that accepts three numbers from a user and displays a message if the sum of any two numbers equals the third.

4. Mortimer Life Insurance Company wants several lists of salesperson data. Design a flowchart or pseudocode for the following:

   a. A program that accepts one salesperson's ID number and number of policies sold in the last month, and displays the data only if the salesperson is a high performer—a person who sells more than 25 policies in the month.

   b. A program that accepts salesperson data continuously until a sentinel value is entered and displays a list of high performers.

   c. A program that accepts salesperson data continuously until a sentinel value is entered and displays a list of salespeople who sold between 5 and 10 policies in the month.

5. ShoppingBay is an online auction service that requires several reports. Data for each auctioned item includes an ID number, item description, length of auction in days, and minimum required bid. Design a flowchart or pseudocode for the following:

    a. A program that accepts data for one auctioned item. Display data for an auction only if the minimum required bid is over $100.00.

    b. A program that continuously accepts auction item data until a sentinel value is entered and displays all data for auctions in which the minimum required bid is over $100.00.

    c. A program that continuously accepts auction item data and displays data for every auction in which there are no bids yet (in other words, the minimum bid is $0.00) and the length of the auction is one day or less.

    d. A program that continuously accepts auction data and displays data for every auction in which the length is between 7 and 30 days inclusive.

    e. A program that prompts the user for a maximum required bid, and then continuously accepts auction data and displays data for every auction in which the minimum bid is less than or equal to the amount entered by the user.

6. The Dash Cell Phone Company charges customers a basic rate of $5 per month to send text messages. Additional rates are as follows:

    •   The first 60 messages per month, regardless of message length, are included in the basic bill.

    •   An additional five cents is charged for each text message after the 60th message, up to 180 messages.

    •   An additional 10 cents is charged for each text message after the 180th message.

    •   Federal, state, and local taxes add a total of 12 percent to each bill.

    Design a flowchart or pseudocode for the following:

    a. A program that accepts the following data about one customer's messages: area code (three digits), phone number (seven digits), and number of text messages sent. Display all the data, including the month-end bill both before and after taxes are added.

    b. A program that continuously accepts data about text messages until a sentinel value is entered, and displays all the details.

    c. A program that continuously accepts data about text messages until a sentinel value is entered, and displays details only about customers who send more than 100 text messages.

    d. A program that continuously accepts data about text messages until a sentinel value is entered, and displays details only about customers whose total bill with taxes is over $20.

    e. A program that prompts the user for a three-digit area code from which to select bills. Then the program continuously accepts text message data until a sentinel value is entered, and displays data only for messages sent from the specified area code.

7. The Drive-Rite Insurance Company provides automobile insurance policies for drivers. Design a flowchart or pseudocode for the following:

    a. A program that accepts insurance policy data, including a policy number, customer last name, customer first name, age, premium due date (month, day, and year), and number of driver accidents in the last three years. If an entered policy number is not between 1000 and 9999 inclusive, set the policy number to 0. If the month is not between 1 and 12 inclusive, or the day is not correct for the month (for example, not between 1 and 31 for January or 1 and 29 for February), set the month, day, and year to 0. Display the policy data after any revisions have been made.

    b. A program that continuously accepts policy holders' data until a sentinel value has been entered, and displays the data for any policy holder over 35 years old.

    c. A program that continuously accepts policy holders' data until a sentinel value has been entered, and displays the data for any policy holder who is at least 21 years old.

    d. A program that continuously accepts policy holders' data and displays the data for any policy holder no more than 30 years old.

    e. A program that continuously accepts policy holders' data and displays the data for any policy holder whose premium is due no later than March 15 any year.

    f. A program that continuously accepts policy holders' data and displays the data for any policy holder whose premium is due up to and including January 1, 2016.

    g. A program that continuously accepts policy holders' data and displays the data for any policy holder whose premium is due by April 27, 2015.

    h. A program that continuously accepts policy holders' data and displays the data for anyone who has a policy number between 1000 and 4000 inclusive, whose policy comes due in April or May of any year, and who has had fewer than three accidents.

8. The Barking Lot is a dog day care center. Design a flowchart or pseudocode for the following:

    a. A program that accepts data for an ID number of a dog's owner, and the name, breed, age, and weight of the dog. Display a bill containing all the input data as well as the weekly day care fee, which is $55 for dogs under 15 pounds, $75 for dogs from 15 to 30 pounds inclusive, $105 for dogs from 31 to 80 pounds inclusive, and $125 for dogs over 80 pounds.

    b. A program that continuously accepts dogs' data until a sentinel value is entered, and displays billing data for each dog.

    c. A program that continuously accepts dogs' data until a sentinel value is entered, and displays billing data for dog owners who owe more than $100.

    d. A program that continuously accepts dogs' data until a sentinel value is entered, and displays billing data for dogs who weigh less than 20 pounds or more than 100 pounds.

9. Mark Daniels is a carpenter who creates personalized house signs. He wants an application to compute the price of any sign a customer orders, based on the following factors:

- The minimum charge for all signs is $30.

- If the sign is made of oak, add $15. No charge is added for pine.

- The first six letters or numbers are included in the minimum charge; there is a $3 charge for each additional character.

- Black or white characters are included in the minimum charge; there is an additional $12 charge for gold-leaf lettering.

Design a flowchart or pseudocode for the following:

a. A program that accepts data for an order number, customer name, wood type, number of characters, and color of characters. Display all the entered data and the final price for the sign.

b. A program that continuously accepts sign order data and displays all the relevant information for oak signs with five white letters.

c. A program that continuously accepts sign order data and displays all the relevant information for pine signs with gold-leaf lettering and more than 10 characters.

10. Black Dot Printing is attempting to organize carpools to save energy. Each input record contains an employee's name and town of residence. Ten percent of the company's employees live in Wonder Lake; 30 percent live in the adjacent town of Woodstock. Black Dot wants to encourage employees who live in either town to drive to work together. Design a flowchart or pseudocode for the following:

a. A program that accepts an employee's data and displays it with a message that indicates whether the employee is a candidate for the carpool (because he lives in one of the two cities).

b. A program that continuously accepts employee data until a sentinel value is entered, and displays a list of all employees who are carpool candidates. Make sure the decision-making process is as efficient as possible.

c. A program that continuously accepts employee data until a sentinel value is entered, and displays a list of all employees who are ineligible to carpool because they do not live in either Wonder Lake or Woodstock. Make sure the decision-making process is as efficient as possible.

11. Amanda Cho, a supervisor in a retail clothing store, wants to acknowledge high-achieving salespeople. Design a flowchart or pseudocode for the following:

a. A program that continuously accepts each salesperson's first and last names, the number of shifts worked in a month, number of transactions completed this month, and the dollar value of those transactions. Display each salesperson's name with a productivity score, which is computed by first dividing dollars by transactions and dividing the result by shifts worked. Display three asterisks after the productivity score if it is 50 or higher.

b. A program that accepts each salesperson's data and displays the name and a bonus amount. The bonuses will be distributed as follows:

- If the productivity score is 30 or less, the bonus is $25.

- If the productivity score is 31 or more and less than 80, the bonus is $50.

- If the productivity score is 80 or more and less than 200, the bonus is $100.

- If the productivity score is 200 or higher, the bonus is $200.

c. Modify Exercise 11b to reflect the following new fact, and have the program execute as efficiently as possible:

- Sixty percent of employees have a productivity score greater than 200.

Performing Maintenance

1. A file named MAINTENANCE04-01.jpg is included with your downloadable student files. Assume that this program is a working program in your organization and that it needs modifications as described in the comments (lines that begin with two slashes) at the beginning of the file. Your job is to alter the program to meet the new specifications.

Find the Bugs

1. Your downloadable files for Chapter 4 include DEBUG04-01.txt, DEBUG04-02.txt, and DEBUG04-03.txt. Each file starts with some comments that describe the problem. Comments are lines that begin with two slashes (//). Following the comments, each file contains pseudocode that has one or more bugs you must find and correct.

2. Your downloadable files for Chapter 4 include a file named DEBUG04-04.jpg that contains a flowchart with syntax and/or logical errors. Examine the flowchart and then find and correct all the bugs.

Game Zone

1. In Chapter 2, you learned that many programming languages allow you to generate a random number between 1 and a limiting value named limit by using a statement similar to randomNumber = random(limit). Create the logic for a guessing game in which the application generates a random number and the player

tries to guess it. Display a message indicating whether the player's guess was correct, too high, or too low. (After you finish Chapter 5, you will be able to modify the application so that the user can continue to guess until the correct answer is entered.)

2. Create a lottery game application. Generate three random numbers, each between 0 and 9. Allow the user to guess three numbers. Compare each of the user's guesses to the three random numbers and display a message that includes the user's guess, the randomly determined three digits, and the amount of money the user has won, as shown in Figure 4-24.

Matching Numbers	Award ($)
Any one matching	10
Two matching	100
Three matching, not in order	1000
Three matching in exact order	1,000,000
No matches	0

Figure 4-24   Awards for matching numbers in lottery game

Make certain that your application accommodates repeating digits. For example, if a user guesses 1, 2, and 3, and the randomly generated digits are 1, 1, and 1, do not give the user credit for three correct guesses—just one.

 Up for Discussion

1. Computer programs can be used to make decisions about your insurability as well as the rates you will be charged for health and life insurance policies. For example, certain preexisting conditions may raise your insurance premiums considerably. Is it ethical for insurance companies to access your health records and then make insurance decisions about you? Explain your answer.

2. Job applications are sometimes screened by software that makes decisions about a candidate's suitability based on keywords in the applications. Is such screening fair to applicants? Explain your answer.

3. Medical facilities often have more patients waiting for organ transplants than there are available organs. Suppose you have been asked to write a computer program that selects which candidates should receive an available organ. What data would you want on file to be able to use in your program, and what decisions would you make based on the data? What data do you think others might use that you would choose not to use?

Looping

In this chapter, you will learn about:

◎ The advantages of looping

◎ Using a loop control variable

◎ Nested loops

◎ Avoiding common loop mistakes

◎ Using a `for` loop

◎ Common loop applications

◎ The similarities and differences between selections and loops

Understanding the Advantages of Looping

Although making decisions is what makes computers seem intelligent, looping makes computer programming both efficient and worthwhile. When you use a loop, one set of instructions can operate on multiple, separate sets of data. Using fewer instructions results in less time required for design and coding, fewer errors, and shorter compile time.

Recall the loop structure that you learned about in Chapter 3; it looks like Figure 5-1. As long as a Boolean expression remains true, the body of a while loop executes.

Quick Reference 5-1 shows the pseudocode standards this book uses for the while statement.

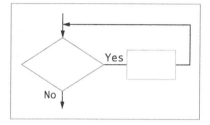

Figure 5-1   The loop structure
© 2015 Cengage Learning

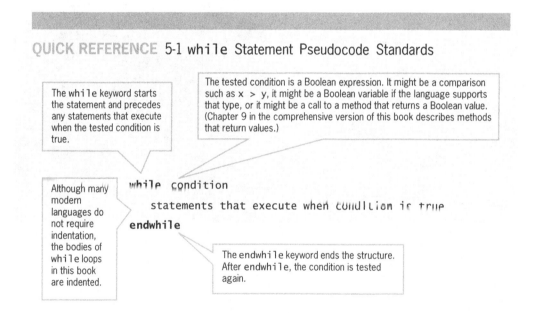

QUICK REFERENCE 5-1 while Statement Pseudocode Standards

The while keyword starts the statement and precedes any statements that execute when the tested condition is true.

The tested condition is a Boolean expression. It might be a comparison such as x > y, it might be a Boolean variable if the language supports that type, or it might be a call to a method that returns a Boolean value. (Chapter 9 in the comprehensive version of this book describes methods that return values.)

Although many modern languages do not require indentation, the bodies of while loops in this book are indented.

```
while condition
     statements that execute when condition is true
endwhile
```

The endwhile keyword ends the structure. After endwhile, the condition is tested again.

You have already learned that many programs use a loop to control repetitive tasks. For example, Figure 5-2 shows the basic structure of many business programs. After some housekeeping tasks are completed, the detail loop repeats once for every data record that must be processed.

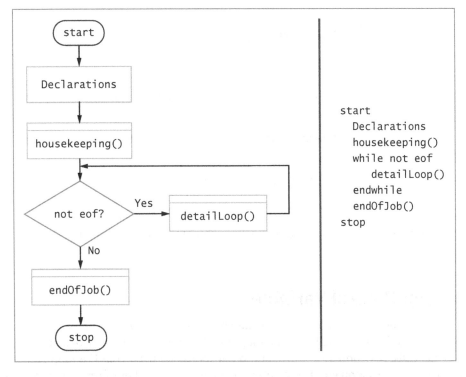

Figure 5-2 The mainline logic common to many business programs
© 2015 Cengage Learning

For example, Figure 5-2 might represent the mainline logic of a typical payroll program. The first employee's data would be entered in the housekeeping() module, and while the eof condition is not met, the detailLoop() module would perform such tasks as determining regular and overtime pay and deducting taxes, insurance premiums, charitable contributions, union dues, and other items. Then, after the employee's paycheck is output, the next employee's data would be entered, and the detailLoop() module would repeat. The advantage to having a computer produce payroll checks is that the calculation instructions need to be written only once and can be repeated indefinitely.

 Watch the video *A Quick Introduction to Loops.*

Using a Loop Control Variable

You can use a while loop to execute a body of statements continuously as long as some condition continues to be true. The body of a loop might contain any number of statements, including module calls, selection structures, and other loops. To make a while loop end correctly, you can declare a **loop control variable** to manage the number of repetitions a loop performs. Three separate actions should occur using a loop control variable:

• The loop control variable is initialized before entering the loop.

• The loop control variable's value is tested, and if the result is true, the loop body is entered.

• The loop control variable is altered within the body of the loop so that the tested condition that follows while eventually is false.

If you omit any of these actions or perform them incorrectly, you run the risk of creating an infinite loop. Once your logic enters the body of a structured loop, the entire loop body must execute. Your program can leave a structured loop only at the comparison that tests the loop control variable. Commonly, you can control a loop's repetitions in one of two ways:

• Use a counter to create a definite, counter-controlled loop.

• Use a sentinel value to create an indefinite loop.

Using a Definite Loop with a Counter

Figure 5-3 shows a loop that displays *Hello* four times. The variable count is the loop control variable. This loop is a **definite loop** because it executes a definite, predetermined number of times—in this case, four. The loop is a **counted loop**, or **counter-controlled loop**, because the program keeps track of the number of loop repetitions by counting them.

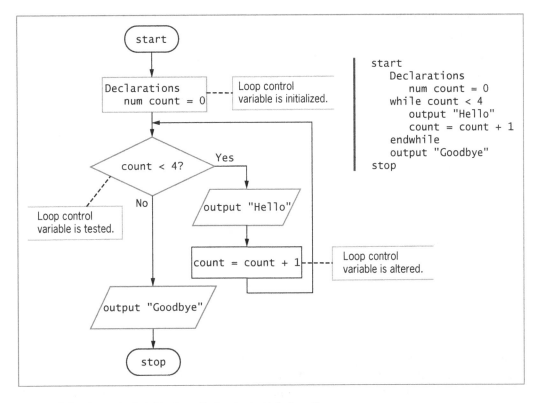

```
start
    Declarations
        num count = 0
    while count < 4
        output "Hello"
        count = count + 1
    endwhile
    output "Goodbye"
stop
```

Figure 5-3 A counted while loop that outputs *Hello* four times
© 2015 Cengage Learning

The loop in Figure 5-3 executes as follows:

- The loop control variable, count, is initialized to 0.

- The while expression compares count to 4.

- The value of count is less than 4, and so the loop body executes. The loop body shown in Figure 5-3 consists of two statements that display *Hello* and then add 1 to count.

- The next time the condition count < 4 is evaluated, the value of count is 1, which is still less than 4, so the loop body executes again. *Hello* is displayed a second time and count is incremented to 2, *Hello* is displayed a third time and count becomes 3, then *Hello* is displayed a fourth time and count becomes 4. Now when the expression count < 4? evaluates, it is false, so the loop ends.

Within a loop's body, you can change the value of the loop control variable in a number of ways. For example:

- You might simply assign a new value to the loop control variable.

- You might retrieve a new value from an input device.

- You might **increment**, or increase, the loop control variable, as in the logic in Figure 5-3.

- You might reduce, or **decrement**, the loop control variable. For example, the loop in Figure 5-3 could be rewritten so that count is initialized to 4, and reduced by 1 on each pass through the loop. The loop would then continue while count remains greater than 0.

The terms *increment* and *decrement* usually refer to small changes; often the value used to increase or decrease the loop control variable is 1. However, loops are also controlled by adding or subtracting values other than 1. For example, to display company profits at five-year intervals for the next 50 years, you would want to add 5 to a loop control variable during each iteration.

Because you frequently need to increment a variable, many programming languages contain a shortcut operator for incrementing. For example, in C++, C#, and Java, the expression ++value is a shortcut for the expression value = value + 1. You will learn about these shortcut operators when you study a programming language that uses them.

Watch the video *Looping*.

The looping logic shown in Figure 5-3 uses a counter. A **counter** is any numeric variable that counts the number of times an event has occurred. In everyday life, people usually count things starting with 1. Many programmers prefer starting their counted loops with a variable containing 0 for two reasons:

- In many computer applications, numbering starts with 0 because of the 0-and-1 nature of computer circuitry.

- When you learn about arrays in Chapter 6, you will discover that array manipulation naturally lends itself to 0-based loops.

Using an Indefinite Loop with a Sentinel Value

Often, the value of a loop control variable is not altered by arithmetic, but instead is altered by user input. For example, perhaps you want to keep performing some task while the user indicates a desire to continue. In that case, you do not know when you write the program whether the loop will be executed two times, 200 times, or at all. This type of loop is an **indefinite loop**.

Consider an interactive program that displays *Hello* repeatedly as long as the user wants to continue. The loop is indefinite because each time the program executes, the loop might be performed a different number of times. The program appears in Figure 5-4.

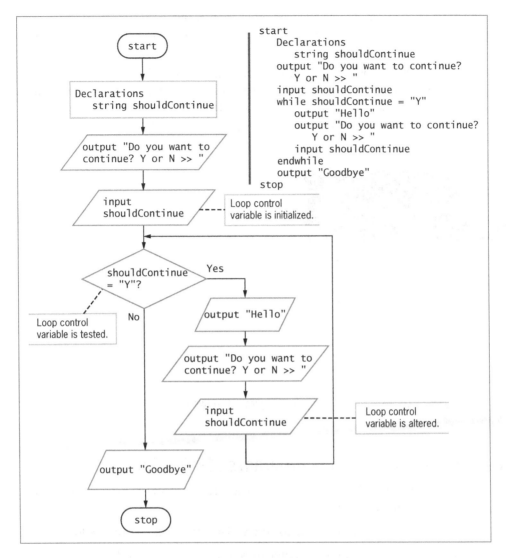

Figure 5-4 An indefinite while loop that displays *Hello* as long as the user wants to continue
© 2015 Cengage Learning

In the program in Figure 5-4, the loop control variable is shouldContinue. The program executes as follows:

- The first input shouldContinue statement in the application in Figure 5-4 is a priming input statement. In this statement, the loop control variable is initialized by the user's first response.

- The while expression compares the loop control variable to the sentinel value *Y*.

- If the user has entered *Y*, then *Hello* is output and the user is asked whether the program should continue. In this step, the value of shouldContinue might change.

- At any point, if the user enters any value other than *Y*, the loop ends. In most programming languages, simple comparisons are case sensitive, so any entry other than *Y*, including *y*, will end the loop.

Figure 5-5 shows how the program might look when it is executed at the command line and in a GUI environment. The screens in Figure 5-5 show programs that perform exactly the same tasks using different environments. In each environment, the user can continue choosing to see *Hello* messages, or can choose to quit the program and display *Goodbye*.

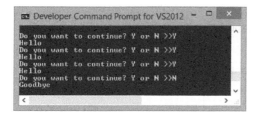

Figure 5-5   Typical executions of the program in Figure 5-4 in two environments
© 2015 Cengage Learning

Understanding the Loop in a Program's Mainline Logic

The flowchart and pseudocode segments in Figure 5-4 contain three steps that should occur in every properly functioning loop:

1. You must provide a starting value for the variable that will control the loop.

2. You must test the loop control variable to determine whether the loop body executes.

3. Within the loop, you must alter the loop control variable.

In Chapter 2 you learned that the mainline logic of many business programs follows a standard outline that consists of housekeeping tasks, a loop that repeats, and finishing tasks. The three crucial steps that occur in any loop also occur in standard mainline logic. Figure 5-6 shows the flowchart for the mainline logic of the payroll program that you saw in Figure 2-8. Figure 5-6 points out the three loop-controlling steps. In this case, the three steps—initializing, testing, and altering the loop control variable—are in different modules. However, the steps all occur in the correct places, showing that the mainline logic uses a standard and correct loop.

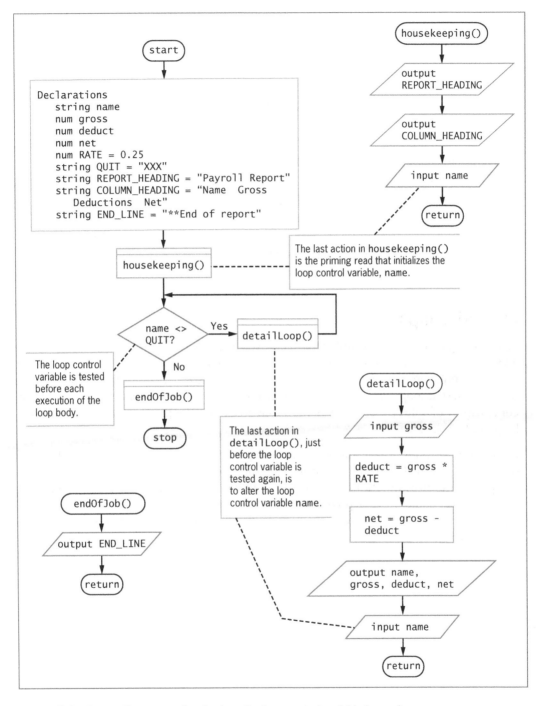

Figure 5-6 A payroll program showing how the loop control variable is used
© 2015 Cengage Learning

TWO TRUTHS & A LIE

Using a Loop Control Variable

1. To make a while loop execute correctly, a loop control variable must be set to 0 before entering the loop.

2. To make a while loop execute correctly, a loop control variable should be tested before entering the loop body.

3. To make a while loop execute correctly, the body of the loop must take some action that alters the value of the loop control variable.

The false statement is #1. A loop control variable must be initialized, but not necessarily to 0.

Nested Loops

Program logic gets more complicated when you must use loops within loops, or **nested loops**. When one loop appears inside another, the loop that contains the other loop is called the **outer loop**, and the loop that is contained is called the **inner loop**. You need to create nested loops when the values of two or more variables repeat to produce every combination of values. Usually, when you create nested loops, each loop has its own loop control variable.

For example, suppose you want to write a program that produces quiz answer sheets like the ones shown in Figure 5-7. Each answer sheet has a unique heading followed by five parts with three questions in each part, and you want a fill-in-the-blank line for each question. You could write a program that uses 63 separate output statements to produce three sheets (each sheet contains 21 printed lines), but it is more efficient to use nested loops.

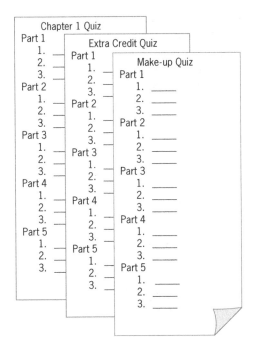

Figure 5-7 Quiz answer sheets
© 2015 Cengage Learning

Figure 5-8 shows the logic for the program that produces answer sheets. Three loop control variables are declared for the program:

- quizName controls the detailLoop() module that is called from the mainline logic.

- partCounter controls the outer loop within the detailLoop() module; it keeps track of the answer sheet parts.

- questionCounter controls the inner loop in the detailLoop() module; it keeps track of the questions and answer lines within each part section on each answer sheet.

Five named constants are also declared. Three of these constants (QUIT, PARTS, and QUESTIONS) hold the sentinel values for each of the three loops in the program. The other two constants hold the text that will be output (the word *Part* that precedes each part number, and the period-space-underscore combination that forms a fill-in line for each question).

When the program starts, the housekeeping() module executes and the user enters the name to be output at the top of the first quiz. If the user enters the QUIT value, the program ends immediately, but if the user enters anything else, such as *Make-up Quiz*, then the detailLoop() module executes.

In the detailLoop() the quiz name is output at the top of the answer sheet. Then partCounter is initialized to 1. The partCounter variable is the loop control variable for the outer loop in this module. The outer loop continues while partCounter is less than or equal to PARTS. The last statement in the outer loop adds 1 to partCounter. In other words, the outer loop will execute when partCounter is 1, 2, 3, 4, and 5.

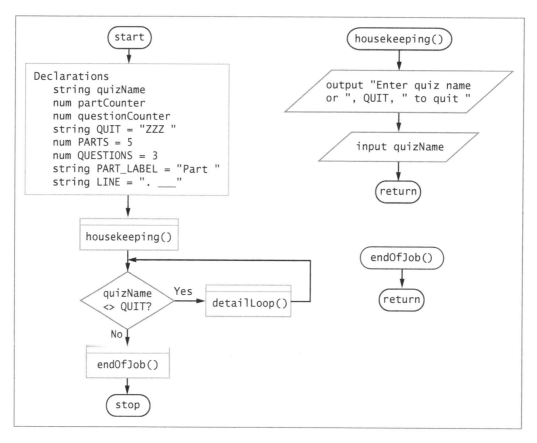

Figure 5-8 Flowchart and pseudocode for AnswerSheet program *(continues)*

(continued)

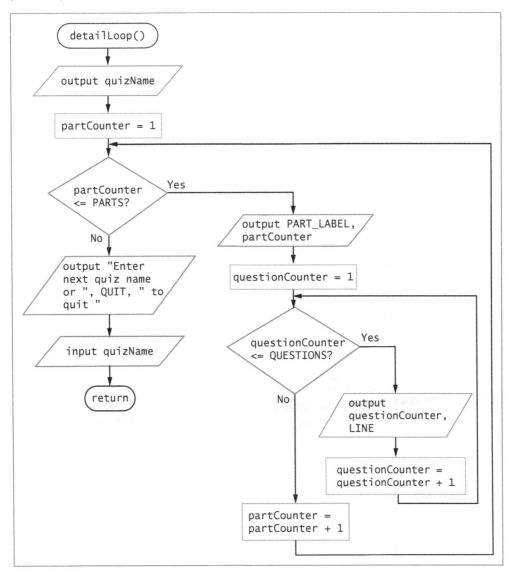

Figure 5-8   Flowchart and pseudocode for AnswerSheet program *(continues)*

(continued)

```
start
   Declarations
      string quizName
      num partCounter
      num questionCounter
      string QUIT = "ZZZ "
      num PARTS = 5
      num QUESTIONS = 3
      string PART_LABEL = "Part "
      string LINE = ". _____ "
   housekeeping()
   while quizName <> QUIT
      detailLoop()
   endwhile
   endOfJob()
stop

housekeeping()
   output "Enter quiz name or ", QUIT, " to quit "
   input quizName
return

detailLoop()
   output quizName
   partCounter = 1
   while partCounter <= PARTS
      output PART_LABEL, partCounter
      questionCounter = 1
      while questionCounter <= QUESTIONS
         output questionCounter, LINE
         questionCounter = questionCounter + 1
      endwhile
      partCounter = partCounter + 1
   endwhile
   output "Enter next quiz name or ", QUIT, " to quit "
   input quizName
return

endOfJob()
return
```

Figure 5-8   Flowchart and pseudocode for `AnswerSheet` program
© 2015 Cengage Learning

In Figure 5-8, some output (the user prompt) would be sent to one output device, such as a monitor. Other output (the quiz sheet) would be sent to another output device, such as a printer. The statements needed to send output to separate devices differ among languages. The statements to set up the printer would be included in the `housekeeping()` module, and the statements to disengage the printer would be included in the currently empty `endOfJob()` module. Chapter 7 provides more details about sending output to separate files.

In the outer loop in the `detailLoop()` module in Figure 5-8, the word *Part* and the current `partCounter` value are output. Then the following steps execute:

- The loop control variable for the inner loop is initialized by setting `questionCounter` to 1.

- The loop control variable questionCounter is evaluated. While questionCounter does not exceed QUESTIONS, the loop body executes: The value of questionCounter is output, followed by a period and a fill-in-the-blank line.

- At the end of the loop body, the loop control variable is altered by adding 1 to questionCounter and the questionCounter comparison is made again.

In other words, when partCounter is 1, the part heading is output and underscore lines are output for questions 1, 2, and 3. Then partCounter becomes 2, the part heading is output, and underscore lines are created for another set of questions 1, 2, and 3. Then partCounter becomes 3, 4, and 5 in turn, and three underscore lines numbered 1, 2, and 3 are created for each part. In all, 15 underscore answer lines are created for each quiz.

In the program in Figure 5-8, it is important that questionCounter is reset to 1 within the outer loop, just before entering the inner loop. If this step was omitted, Part 1 would contain questions 1, 2, and 3, but subsequent parts would be empty because questionCounter would never again be less than or equal to QUESTIONS.

Studying the answer sheet program reveals several facts about nested loops:

- Nested loops never overlap. An inner loop is always completely contained within an outer loop.

- An inner loop goes through all of its iterations each time its outer loop goes through just one iteration.

- The total number of iterations executed by a nested loop is the number of inner loop iterations times the number of outer loop iterations.

 Watch the video *Nested Loops*.

TWO TRUTHS & A LIE

Nested Loops

1. When one loop is nested inside another, the loop that contains the other loop is called the outer loop.

2. You need to create nested loops when the values of two or more variables repeat to produce every combination of values.

3. The number of times a loop executes always depends on a constant.

The false statement is #3. The number of times a loop executes might depend on a constant, but it might also depend on a value that varies.

Avoiding Common Loop Mistakes

Programmers make the following common mistakes with loops:

- Failing to initialize the loop control variable
- Neglecting to alter the loop control variable
- Using the wrong type of comparison when testing the loop control variable
- Including statements inside the loop body that belong outside the loop

The following sections explain these common mistakes in more detail.

Mistake: Failing to Initialize the Loop Control Variable

Failing to initialize a loop's control variable is a mistake. For example, consider the program in Figure 5-9. It prompts the user for a name, and while the value of name continues not to be the sentinel value ZZZ, the program outputs a greeting that uses the name and asks for the next name. This program works correctly.

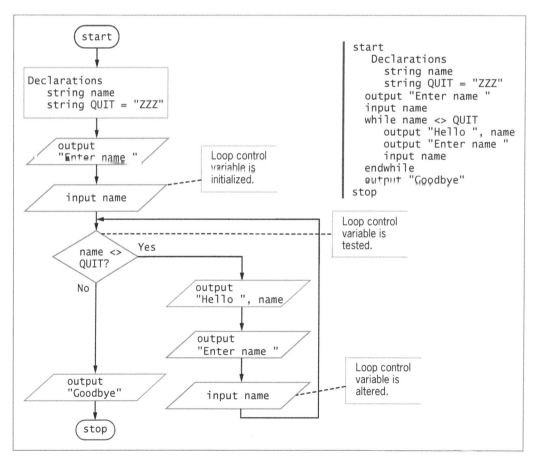

Figure 5-9 Correct logic for greeting program
© 2015 Cengage Learning

Figure 5-10 shows an incorrect program in which the loop control variable is not assigned a starting value. If the **name** variable is not set to a starting value, then when the **eof** condition is tested, there is no way to predict whether it will be true. If the user does not enter a value for **name**, the garbage value originally held by that variable might or might not be *ZZZ*. So, one of two scenarios follows:

● Most likely, the uninitialized value of **name** is not *ZZZ*, so the first greeting output will include garbage—for example, *Hello 12BGr5.*

● By a remote chance, the uninitialized value of **name** *is ZZZ*, so the program ends immediately before the user can enter any names.

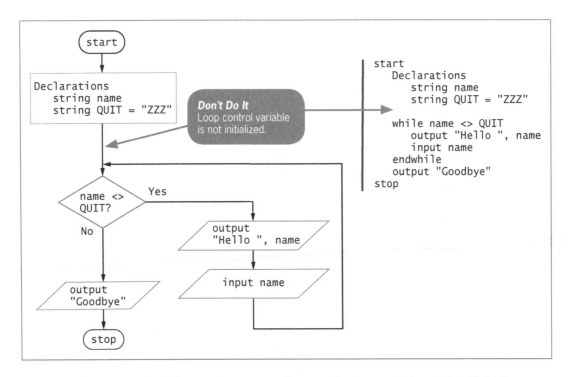

Figure 5-10 Incorrect logic for greeting program because the loop control variable initialization is missing
© 2015 Cengage Learning

Mistake: Neglecting to Alter the Loop Control Variable

Different sorts of errors will occur if you fail to alter a loop control variable within the loop. For example, in the program in Figure 5-9 that accepts and displays names, you create such an error if you don't accept names within the loop. Figure 5-11 shows the resulting incorrect logic.

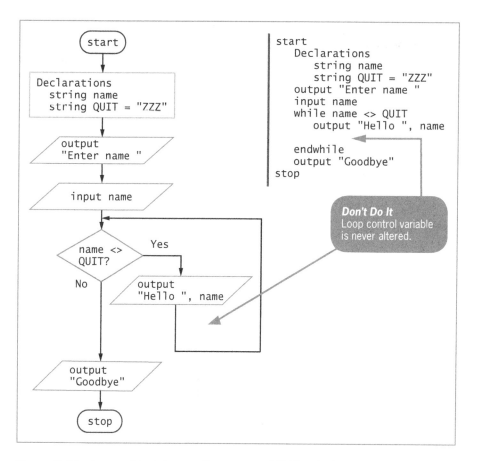

start
    Declarations
        string name
        string QUIT = "ZZZ"
    output "Enter name "
    input name
    while name <> QUIT
        output "Hello ", name

    endwhile
    output "Goodbye"
stop

Don't Do It
Loop control variable
is never altered.

Figure 5-11   Incorrect logic for greeting program because the loop control variable is not altered
© 2015 Cengage Learning

If you remove the input name instruction from the end of the loop in the program, no name is ever entered after the first one. For example, assume that when the program starts, the user enters *Fred*. The name will be compared to the sentinel value, and the loop will be entered. After a greeting is output for Fred, no new name is entered, so when the logic returns to the loop-controlling question, the name will still not be *ZZZ*, and greetings for Fred will continue to be output infinitely. Under normal conditions, you never want to create a loop that cannot terminate.

Mistake: Using the Wrong Type of Comparison When Testing the Loop Control Variable

Programmers must be careful to use the correct type of comparison in the statement that controls a loop. A comparison is correct only when the appropriate operands and operator are used. For example, although only one keystroke differs between the original greeting program in Figure 5-9 and the one in Figure 5-12, the original program correctly produces named greetings and the second one does not.

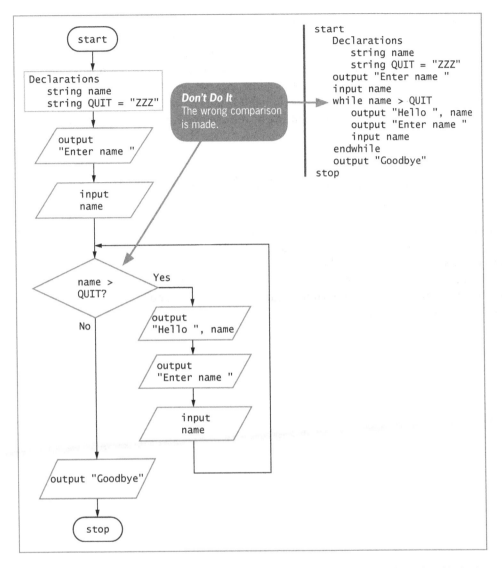

Figure 5-12 Incorrect logic for greeting program because the wrong test is made with the loop control variable
© 2015 Cengage Learning

In Figure 5-12, a greater-than comparison (>) is made instead of a not-equal-to (<>) comparison. Suppose that when the program executes, the user enters *Fred* as the first name. In most programming languages, when the comparison between *Fred* and *ZZZ* is made, the values are compared alphabetically. *Fred* is not greater than *ZZZ*, so the loop is never entered, and the program ends.

Using the wrong type of comparison in a loop can have serious effects. For example, in a counted loop, if you use <= instead of < to compare a counter to a sentinel value, the program will perform one loop execution too many. If the loop only displays greetings, the error might not be critical, but if such an error occurred in a loan company application, each customer might be charged a month's additional interest. If the error occurred in an airline's application, it might overbook a flight. If the error occurred in a pharmacy's drug-dispensing application, each patient might receive one extra (and possibly harmful) unit of medication.

Mistake: Including Statements Inside the Loop Body that Belong Outside the Loop

Suppose that you write a program for a store manager who wants to discount every item he sells by 30 percent. The manager wants 100 new price label stickers for each item. The user enters a price, the new discounted price is calculated, 100 stickers are printed, and the next price is entered. Figure 5-13 shows a program that performs the job inefficiently because the same value, newPrice, is calculated 100 separate times for each price that is entered.

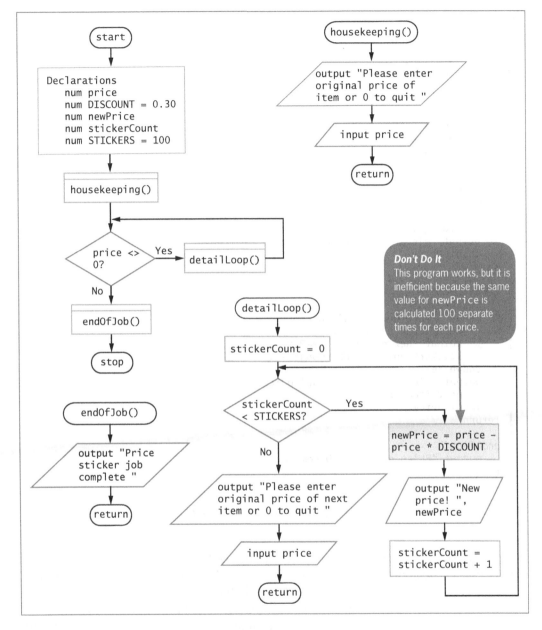

Figure 5-13 Inefficient way to produce 100 discount price stickers for differently priced items *(continues)*

(continued)

```
start
   Declarations
      num price
      num DISCOUNT = 0.30
      num newPrice
      num stickerCount
      num STICKERS = 100
   housekeeping()
   while price <> 0
      detailLoop()
   endwhile
   endOfJob()
stop

housekeeping()
   output "Please enter original price of item or 0 to quit "
   input price
return

detailLoop()
   stickerCount = 0
   while stickerCount < STICKERS
      newPrice = price - price * DISCOUNT
      output "New price! ", newPrice
      stickerCount = stickerCount + 1
   endwhile
   output "Please enter original price of
      next item or 0 to quit "
   input price
return

endOfJob()
   output "Price sticker job complete"
return
```

> **Don't Do It**
> This program works, but it is inefficient because the same value for newPrice is calculated 100 separate times for each price.

Figure 5-13   Inefficient way to produce 100 discount price stickers for differently priced items
© 2015 Cengage Learning

Figure 5-14 shows the same program, in which the newPrice value that is output on the sticker is calculated only once per new price; the calculation has been moved to a better location. The programs in Figures 5-13 and 5-14 do the same thing, but the second program does it more efficiently. As you become more proficient at programming, you will recognize many opportunities to perform the same tasks in alternate, more elegant, and more efficient ways.

 When you describe people or events as elegant, you mean they possess a refined gracefulness. Similarly, programmers use the term *elegant* to describe programs that are well designed and easy to understand and maintain.

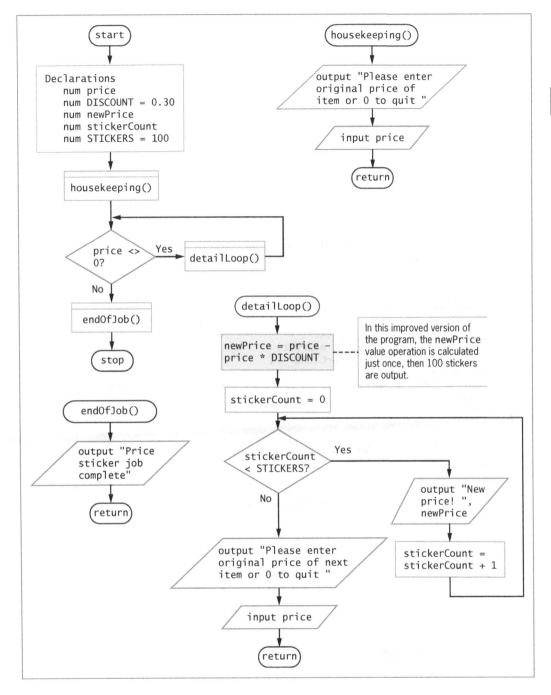

Figure 5-14 Improved discount sticker-making program *(continues)*

(continued)

```
start
   Declarations
      num price
      num DISCOUNT = 0.30
      num newPrice
      num stickerCount
      num STICKERS = 100
   housekeeping()
   while price <> 0
      detailLoop()
   endwhile
   endOfJob()
stop

housekeeping()
   output "Please enter original price of item or 0 to quit "
   input price
return

detailLoop()
   newPrice = price - price * DISCOUNT ----
   stickerCount = 0
   while stickerCount < STICKERS
      output "New price! ", newPrice
      stickerCount = stickerCount + 1
   endwhile
   output "Please enter original price of next item or 0 to quit "
   input price
return

endOfJob()
   output "Price sticker job complete"
return
```

In this improved version of the program, the newPrice value operation is calculated just once, then 100 stickers are output.

Figure 5-14   Improved discount sticker-making program
© 2015 Cengage Learning

TWO TRUTHS & A LIE

Avoiding Common Loop Mistakes

1. In a loop, neglecting to initialize the loop control variable is a mistake.
2. In a loop, neglecting to alter the loop control variable is a mistake.
3. In a loop, comparing the loop control variable using >= or <= is a mistake.

The false statement is #3. Many loops are created correctly using <= or >=.

Using a for Loop

Every high-level programming language contains a while statement that you can use to code any loop, including both indefinite and definite loops. In addition to the while statement, most computer languages support a for statement. You usually use the **for statement**, or **for loop**, with definite loops—those that will loop a specific number of times—when you know exactly how many times the loop will repeat. The for statement provides you with three actions in one compact statement. In a for statement, a loop control variable is:

- Initialized

- Tested

- Altered

Quick Reference 5-2 shows pseudocode standards for a for statement.

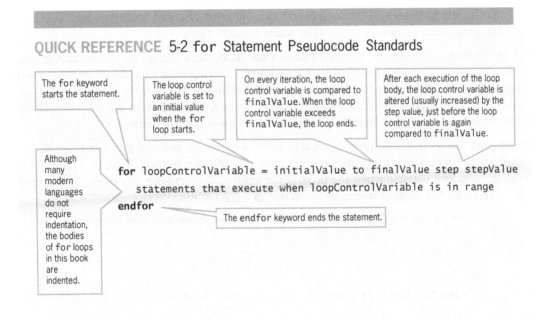

QUICK REFERENCE 5-2 for Statement Pseudocode Standards

The for keyword starts the statement.

The loop control variable is set to an initial value when the for loop starts.

On every iteration, the loop control variable is compared to finalValue. When the loop control variable exceeds finalValue, the loop ends.

After each execution of the loop body, the loop control variable is altered (usually increased) by the step value, just before the loop control variable is again compared to finalValue.

Although many modern languages do not require indentation, the bodies of for loops in this book are indented.

```
for loopControlVariable = initialValue to finalValue step stepValue
    statements that execute when loopControlVariable is in range
endfor
```

The endfor keyword ends the statement.

The amount by which a for loop control variable changes is often called a **step value**. The step value can be any number and can be either positive or negative; that is, it can increment or decrement.

A for loop can express the same logic as a while statement, but in a more compact form. You never are required to use a for statement for any loop; a while loop can always be used instead. For example, to display *Hello* four times, you can write either of the sets of statements in Figure 5-15.

```
count = 0                          for count = 0 to 3 step 1
while count <= 3                       output "Hello"
    output "Hello"                 endfor
    count = count + 1
endwhile
```

Figure 5-15   Comparable while and for statements that each output *Hello* four times
© 2015 Cengage Learning

The code segments in Figure 5-15 each accomplish the same tasks:

- The variable count is initialized to 0.

- The count variable is compared to the limit value 3; while count is less than or equal to 3, the loop body executes.

- As the last statement in the loop execution, the value of count increases by 1. After the increase, the comparison to the limit value is made again.

A while loop can always be used instead of a for loop, but when a loop's execution is based on a loop control variable progressing from a known starting value to a known ending value in equal steps, the for loop provides a convenient shorthand. It is easy for others to read, and because the loop control variable's initialization, testing, and alteration are all performed in one location, you are less likely to leave out one of these crucial elements.

Although for loops are commonly used to control execution of a block of statements a fixed number of times, the programmer doesn't need to know the starting, final, or step value for the loop control variable when the program is written. For example, any of the values might be entered by the user, or might be the result of a calculation.

The for loop is particularly useful when processing arrays. You will learn about arrays in Chapter 6.

In Java, C++, and C#, a for loop that displays 21 values (0 through 20) might look similar to the following:

```
for(count = 0; count <= 20; count++)
{
    output count;
}
```

The three actions (initializing, evaluating, and altering the loop control variable) are separated by semicolons within a set of parentheses that follow the keyword for. The expression count++ increases count by 1. In each of the three languages, the block of statements that depends on the loop sits between a pair of curly braces, so the endfor keyword is not used. None of the three languages uses the keyword output, but all of them end output statements with a semicolon.

Both the `while` loop and the `for` loop are examples of pretest loops. In a **pretest loop**, the loop control variable is tested before each iteration. That means the loop body might never execute because the question controlling the loop might be false the first time it is asked. Most languages allow you to use a variation of the looping structure known as a **posttest loop**, which tests the loop control variable after each iteration. In a posttest loop, the loop body executes at least one time because the loop control variable is not tested until after one iteration. Appendix D contains more information about posttest loops.

203

Some books and flowchart programs use a symbol that looks like a hexagon to represent a `for` loop in a flowchart. However, no special symbols are needed to express a `for` loop's logic. A `for` loop is simply a code shortcut, so this book uses standard flowchart symbols to represent initializing the loop control variable, testing it, and altering it.

TWO TRUTHS & A LIE

Using a `for` Loop

1. The `for` statement provides you with three actions in one compact statement: initializing, testing, and altering a loop control variable.

2. A `for` statement body always executes at least one time.

3. In most programming languages, you can provide a `for` loop with any step value.

The false statement is #2. A `for` statement body might not execute depending on the initial value of the loop control variable.

Common Loop Applications

Although every computer program is different, many techniques are common to a variety of applications. Loops, for example, are frequently used to accumulate totals and to validate data.

Using a Loop to Accumulate Totals

Business reports often include totals. The supervisor who requests a list of employees in the company dental plan is often as interested in the number of participating employees as in who they are. When you receive your telephone bill each month, you usually check the total as well as charges for the individual calls.

Assume that a real estate broker wants to see a list of all properties sold in the last month as well as the total value for all the properties. A program might accept sales data that includes the street address of each property sold and its selling price. The data records might be entered by a clerk as each sale is made, and stored in a file until the end of the month; then they can be used in a monthly report. Figure 5-16 shows an example of such a report.

```
MONTH-END SALES REPORT

Address            Price

287 Acorn St       150,000
12 Maple Ave       310,000
8723 Marie Ln       65,500
222 Acorn St       127,000
29 Bahama Way      450,000

Total            1,102,500
```

Figure 5-16   Month-end real estate sales report
© 2015 Cengage Learning

To create the sales report, you must output the address and price for each property sold and add its value to an accumulator. An **accumulator** is a variable that you use to gather or accumulate values, and is very similar to a counter that you use to count loop iterations. However, usually you add just one to a counter, whereas you add some other value to an accumulator. If the real estate broker wants to know how many listings the company holds, you *count* them. When the broker wants to know the total real estate value, you *accumulate* it.

To accumulate total real estate prices, you declare a numeric variable such as `accumPrice` and initialize it to 0. As you get data for each real estate transaction, you output it and add its value to the accumulator `accumPrice`, as shown shaded in Figure 5-17.

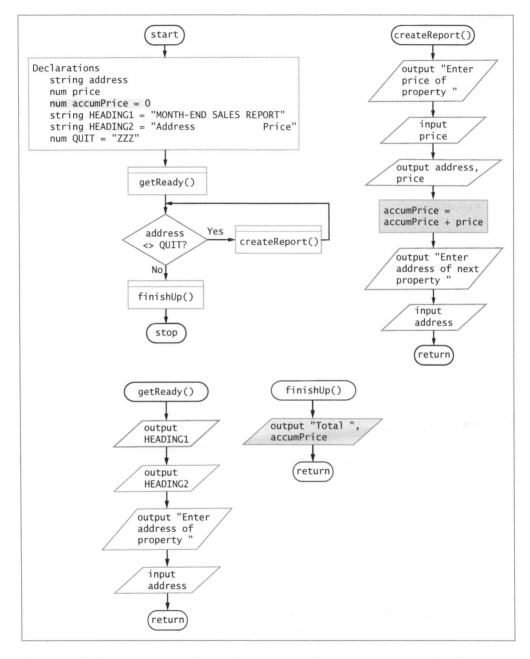

Figure 5-17   Flowchart and pseudocode for real estate sales report program *(continues)*

(continued)

```
start
   Declarations
      string address
      num price
      num accumPrice = 0
      string HEADING1 = "MONTH-END SALES REPORT"
      string HEADING2 = "Address                Price"
      num QUIT = "ZZZ"
   getReady()
   while address <> QUIT
      createReport()
   endwhile
   finishUp()
stop

getReady()
   output HEADING1
   output HEADING2
   output "Enter address of property "
   input address
return

createReport()
   output "Enter price of property "
   input price
   output address, price
   accumPrice = accumPrice + price
   output "Enter address of next property "
   input address
return

finishUp()
   output "Total ", accumPrice
return
```

Figure 5-17   Flowchart and pseudocode for real estate sales report program
© 2015 Cengage Learning

Some programming languages assign 0 to a variable you fail to initialize explicitly, but many do not. When you try to add a value to an uninitialized variable, most languages will issue an error message; worse, some languages, such as C and C++, will let you incorrectly start with an accumulator that holds garbage. All of the examples in this book assign the value 0 to each accumulator before using it.

In earlier program examples in this chapter, the modules were named `housekeeping()`, `detailLoop()`, and `endOfJob()`. In the program in Figure 5-17, they are named `getReady()`, `createReport()`, and `finishUp()`. You can assign modules any names that make sense to you, as long as you are consistent with the names within a program.

After the program in Figure 5-17 gets and displays the last real estate transaction, the user enters the sentinel value and loop execution ends. At that point, the accumulator will hold the grand total of all the real estate values. The program displays the word *Total* and the accumulated value `accumPrice`. Then the program ends.

Figure 5-17 highlights the three actions you usually must take with accumulators:

- Accumulators are initialized to 0.

- Accumulators are altered, usually once for every data set processed, and most often are altered through addition.

- At the end of processing, accumulators are output.

After outputting the value of `accumPrice`, new programmers often want to reset it to 0. Their argument is that they are "cleaning up after themselves." Although you can take this step without harming the execution of the program, it serves no useful purpose. You cannot set `accumPrice` to 0 in anticipation of having it ready for the next program, or even for the next time you execute the same program. Variables exist only during an execution of the program, and even if a future application happens to contain a variable named `accumPrice`, the variable will not necessarily occupy the same memory location as this one. Even if you run the same application a second time, the variables might occupy physical memory locations different from those during the first run. At the beginning of any module, it is the programmer's responsibility to initialize all variables that must start with a specific value. There is no benefit to changing a variable's value when it will never be used again during the current execution.

Some business reports are **summary reports**—they contain only totals with no data for individual records. In the example in Figure 5-17, suppose that the broker did not care about details of individual sales, but only about the total for all transactions. You could create a summary report by omitting the step that outputs `address` and `price` from the `createReport()` module. Then you could simply output `accumPrice` at the end of the program.

Using a Loop to Validate Data

When you ask a user to enter data into a computer program, you have no assurance that the data will be accurate. Incorrect user entries are by far the most common source of computer errors. The programs you write will be improved if you employ **defensive programming**, which means trying to prepare for all possible errors before they occur. Loops are frequently used to **validate data**—that is, to make sure it is meaningful and useful. For example, validation might ensure that a value is the correct data type or that it falls within an acceptable range.

Suppose that part of a program you are writing asks a user to enter a number that represents his or her birth month. If the user types a number lower than 1 or greater than 12, you must take some sort of action. For example:

- You could display an error message and stop the program.

- You could choose to assign a default value for the month (for example, 1) before proceeding.

- You could reprompt the user for valid input.

If you choose this last course of action, you could then take at least two approaches. You could use a selection, and if the month is invalid, you could ask the user to reenter a number, as shown in Figure 5-18.

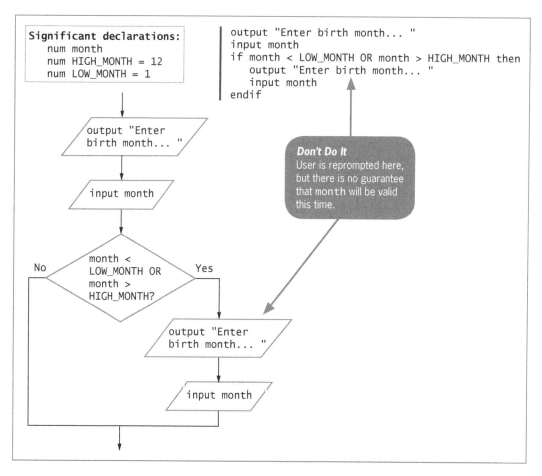

Significant declarations:
```
num month
num HIGH_MONTH = 12
num LOW_MONTH = 1
```

```
output "Enter birth month... "
input month
if month < LOW_MONTH OR month > HIGH_MONTH then
    output "Enter birth month... "
    input month
endif
```

output "Enter birth month... "

input month

month < LOW_MONTH OR month > HIGH_MONTH?   No   Yes

Don't Do It
User is reprompted here, but there is no guarantee that month will be valid this time.

output "Enter birth month... "

input month

Figure 5-18   Reprompting a user once after an invalid month is entered
© 2015 Cengage Learning

The problem with the logic in Figure 5-18 is that the comparisons of month to LOW_MONTH and HIGH_MONTH are made only once, and the user still might not enter valid data on the second attempt. Of course, you could add a third decision, but you still couldn't control what the user enters.

The superior solution is to use a loop to continuously prompt a user for a month until the user enters it correctly. Figure 5-19 shows this approach.

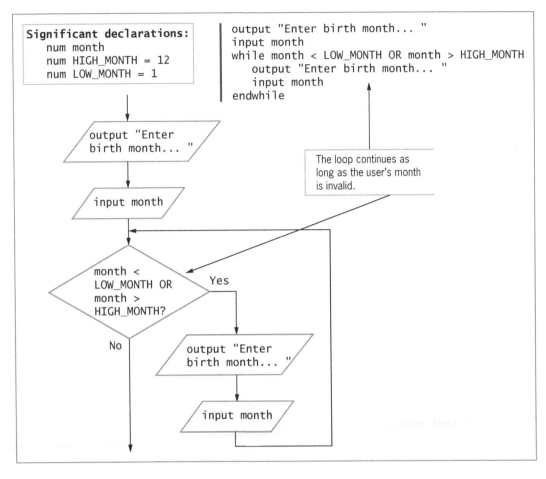

```
Significant declarations:
    num month
    num HIGH_MONTH = 12
    num LOW_MONTH = 1
```

```
output "Enter birth month... "
input month
while month < LOW_MONTH OR month > HIGH_MONTH
    output "Enter birth month... "
    input month
endwhile
```

output "Enter birth month... "

input month

The loop continues as long as the user's month is invalid.

month < LOW_MONTH OR month > HIGH_MONTH?

Yes

No

output "Enter birth month... "

input month

Figure 5-19 Reprompting a user continuously after an invalid month is entered
© 2015 Cengage Learning

Most languages provide a built-in way to check whether an entered value is numeric. When you rely on user input, you frequently accept each piece of input data as a string and then attempt to convert it to a number. The procedure for accomplishing numeric checks varies slightly in different programming languages.

Of course, data validation doesn't prevent all errors; just because a data item is valid does not mean that it is correct. For example, a program can determine that 5 is a valid birth month, but not that your birthday actually falls in month 5. Programmers employ the acronym **GIGO** for *garbage in, garbage out*. It means that if your input is incorrect, your output is worthless.

Limiting a Reprompting Loop

Reprompting a user is a good way to try to ensure valid data, but it can be frustrating to a user if it continues indefinitely. For example, suppose the user must enter a valid birth month, but has used another application in which January was month 0, and keeps entering 0 no matter how many times you repeat the prompt. One helpful addition to the program would be to use the limiting values as part of the prompt. In other words, instead of the statement output "Enter birth month… ", the following statement might be more useful:

```
output "Enter birth month between ", LOW_MONTH, ", and " HIGH_MONTH, " ... "
```

The user would see *Enter birth month between 1 and 12* …. Still, the user might not understand the prompt or not read it carefully, and might continue to enter unacceptable values, so you might want to employ the tactic used in Figure 5-20, in which the program maintains a count of the number of reprompts. In this example, a constant named ATTEMPTS is set to 3. While a count of the user's attempts at correct data entry remains below this limit, and the user enters invalid data, the user continues to be reprompted. If the user exceeds the limited number of allowed attempts, the loop ends.

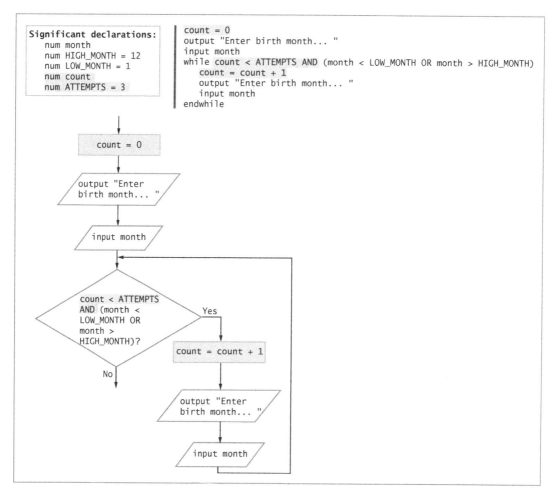

Figure 5-20   Limiting user reprompts
© 2015 Cengage Learning

The action that follows the loop in Figure 5-20 depends on the application. If count equals ATTEMPTS after the data-entry loop ends, you might want to force the invalid data to a default value. **Forcing** a data item means you override incorrect data by setting the variable to a specific, predetermined value. For example, you might decide that if a month value does not fall between 1 and 12, you will force the month to 0 or to the current month. In a different application, you might just choose to end the program. Ending a program prematurely can frustrate users, and can result in lost revenue for a company. For example, if it is difficult to complete a transaction on a company's Web site, users might give up and not do business with the organization. In an interactive, Web-based program, if a user is having trouble providing valid data, you might choose to have a customer service representative start a chat session with the user to offer help.

Validating a Data Type

The data you use within computer programs is varied. It stands to reason that validating data requires a variety of methods. For example, some programming languages allow you to check data items to make sure they are the correct data type. Although this technique varies from language to language, you can often make a statement like the one shown in Figure 5-21. In this program segment, isNumeric() represents a call to a module; it is used to check whether the entered employee salary falls within the category of numeric data. You check to ensure that a value is numeric for many reasons—an important one is that only numeric values can be used correctly in arithmetic statements. A module such as isNumeric() is most often provided with the language translator you use to write your programs. Such a module operates as a black box; in other words, you can use the module's results without understanding its internal statements.

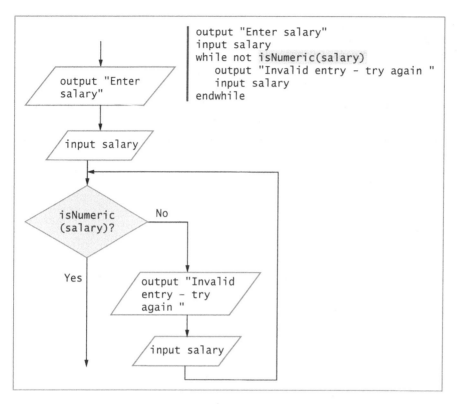

```
output "Enter salary"
input salary
while not isNumeric(salary)
    output "Invalid entry - try again "
    input salary
endwhile
```

Figure 5-21   Checking data for correct type
© 2015 Cengage Learning

Besides allowing you to check whether a value is numeric, some languages contain methods such as isChar(), which checks whether a value is a character data type; isWhitespace(), which checks whether a value is a nonprinting (whitespace) character, such as a space or tab; and isUpper(), which checks whether a value is a capital letter.

In many languages, you accept all user data as a string of characters, and then use built-in methods to attempt to convert the characters to the correct data type for your application. When the conversion methods succeed, you have useful data. When the conversion methods fail because the user has entered the wrong data type, you can take appropriate action, such as issuing an error message, reprompting the user, or forcing the data to a default value.

Validating Reasonableness and Consistency of Data

Data items can be the correct type and within range, but still be incorrect. You have experienced this problem yourself if anyone has ever misspelled your name or overbilled you. The data might have been the correct type—for example, alphabetic letters were used in your name—but the name itself was incorrect. Many data items cannot be checked for reasonableness; for example, the names *Catherine*, *Katherine*, and *Kathryn* are equally reasonable, but only one spelling is correct for a particular woman.

However, many data items can be checked for reasonableness. If you make a purchase on May 3, 2015, then the payment cannot possibly be due prior to that date. Perhaps within your organization, you cannot make more than $20.00 per hour if you work in Department 12. If your zip code is 90201, your state of residence cannot be New York. If your store's cash on hand was $3000 when it closed on Tuesday, the amount should not be different when the store opens on Wednesday. If a customer's title is *Ms.*, the customer's gender should be *F*. Each of these examples involves comparing two data items for reasonableness or consistency. You should consider making as many such comparisons as possible when writing your own programs.

Frequently, testing for reasonableness and consistency involves using additional data files. For example, to check that a user has entered a valid county of residence for a state, you might use a file that contains every county name within every state in the United States, and check the user's county against those contained in the file.

Good defensive programs try to foresee all possible inconsistencies and errors. The more accurate your data, the more useful information you will produce as output from your programs.

 When you become a professional programmer, you want your programs to work correctly as a source of professional pride. On a more basic level, you do not want to be called in to work at 3:00 a.m. when the overnight run of your program fails because of errors you created.

TWO TRUTHS & A LIE

Common Loop Applications

1. An accumulator is a variable that you use to gather or accumulate values.

2. An accumulator typically is initialized to 0.

3. An accumulator is typically reset to 0 after it is output.

The false statement is #3. There is typically no need to reset an accumulator after it is output.

Comparing Selections and Loops

New programmers sometimes struggle when determining whether to use a selection or a loop to solve some programming problems. Much of the confusion occurs because decisions and loops both start by testing conditions and continue by taking action based on the outcome of the test.

However, an important difference between a selection and a loop is that in the selection structure, the two logical paths that emerge from the decision join together following their actions. In the loop structure, the paths that emerge from the decision do not join together. Instead, with a loop, one of the logical branches that emerges from the structure-controlling decision eventually returns to the same decision. Figure 5-22 compares flowcharts for a selection structure and a loop structure.

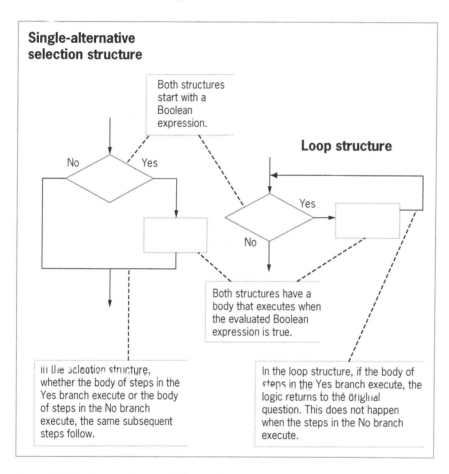

Figure 5-22   Comparing a selection and a loop
© 2015 Cengage Learning

When a client describes a programming need, you can listen for certain words to help you decide whether to use a selection or a loop structure. For example, when program requirements contain words like *if, else, unless,* and *otherwise,* the necessary logic might be a selection structure. On the other hand, when program requirements contain words like *while, until, as long as, during, for each, repeat,* and *continue,* the necessary logic might include a loop. However, as you learned with AND and OR logic in the previous chapter, clients do not always use language as precisely as computers, so listening for such keywords is only a guideline.

When you find yourself repeating selection structures that are very similar, you should consider using a loop. For example, suppose your supervisor says, "If you don't reach the end of the file when you are reading an employee record, display the record and read another one.

Keep doing this until you run out of records." Because the supervisor used the word *if* to start the request, your first inclination might be to create logic that looks like Figure 5-23.

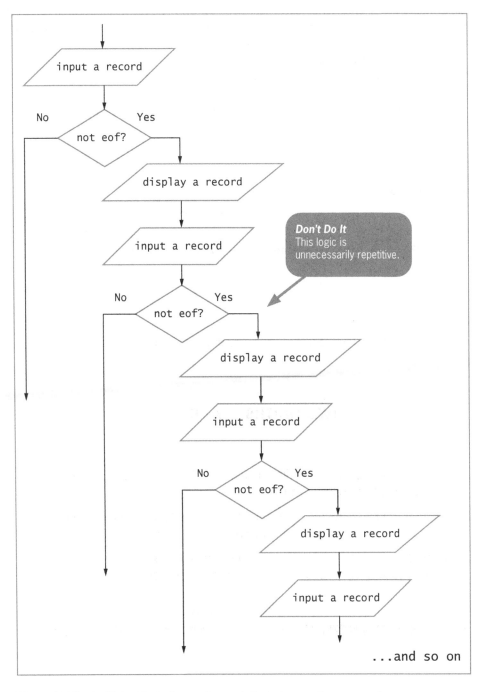

Figure 5-23   Inefficient logic for reading and displaying employee records

The logic in Figure 5-23 works—each time an employee record is input and the **eof** condition is not met, the data is displayed and another record is input. However, the logic in Figure 5-23 is flawed. First, if you do not know how many input records there are, the logic might never end. After each record is input, it is always necessary to check again for the **eof** condition. Second, even if you do know the number of input records, the logic becomes very unwieldy after three or four records. When you examine Figure 5-23, you see that the same set of steps is repeated. Actions that are repeated are best handled in a loop. Figure 5-24 shows a better solution to the problem. In Figure 5-24, the first employee record is input, and as long as the **eof** condition is not met, the program continuously displays and reads additional records.

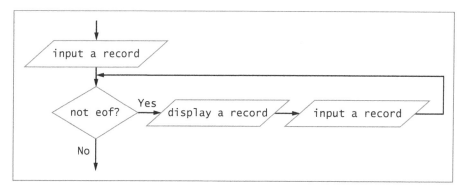

Figure 5-24   Efficient and structured logic for getting and displaying employee records

TWO TRUTHS & A LIE

Comparing Selections and Loops

1. Selection and loop structures differ in that selection structures only take action when a test condition is true.

2. Selection and loop structures are similar in that the tested condition that begins either structure always has two possible outcomes.

3. One difference between selection and loop structures is that the structure-controlling question is repeated in a loop structure.

The false statement is #1. Selection structures can take different actions when a test condition is true and when it is false.

Chapter Summary

- A loop contains one set of instructions that operates on multiple, separate sets of data.

- Three actions are taken with a loop control variable in every `while` loop: You must initialize a loop control variable, compare the variable to some value that controls whether the loop continues or stops, and alter the variable that controls the loop.

- Nested loops are loops that execute within the confines of other loops. When nesting loops, you maintain two separate loop control variables and alter each at the appropriate time.

- Common mistakes that programmers make when writing loops include failing to initialize the loop control variable, neglecting to alter the loop control variable, using the wrong comparison expression with the loop control variable, and including statements inside the loop that belong outside the loop.

- Most computer languages support a `for` statement or `for` loop that you can use with definite loops when you know how many times a loop will repeat. The `for` statement uses a loop control variable that it automatically initializes, tests, and alters.

- Loops are used in many applications—for example, to accumulate totals in business reports. Loops also are used to ensure that user data entries are valid by repeatedly reprompting the user.

- In the selection structure, the two logical paths that emerge from a test join together following their actions. In the loop structure, the paths that emerge from the test do not join together; instead, one of the paths eventually returns to the same test.

Key Terms

A **loop control variable** is a variable that determines whether a loop will continue.

A **definite loop** is one for which the number of repetitions is a predetermined value.

A **counted loop**, or **counter-controlled loop**, is a loop whose repetitions are managed by a counter.

To **increment** a variable is to add a constant value to it, frequently 1.

To **decrement** a variable is to decrease it by a constant value, frequently 1.

A **counter** is any numeric variable you use to count the number of times an event has occurred.

An **indefinite loop** is one for which you cannot predetermine the number of executions.

Nested loops occur when a loop structure exists within another loop structure.

An **outer loop** contains another loop when loops are nested.

An **inner loop** is contained within another loop when loops are nested.

A **for statement**, or **for loop**, can be used to code definite loops and has a loop control variable that it automatically initializes, tests, and alters.

A **step value** is a number by which a loop control variable is altered on each pass through a loop.

A **pretest loop** tests its controlling condition before each iteration, meaning that the loop body might never execute.

A **posttest loop** tests its controlling condition after each iteration, meaning that the loop body executes at least one time.

An **accumulator** is a variable that you use to gather or accumulate values, such as a running total.

A **summary report** lists only totals, without individual detail records.

Defensive programming is a technique with which you try to prepare for all possible errors before they occur.

To **validate data** is to ensure that data items are meaningful and useful—for example, by ensuring that values are the correct data type, fall within an acceptable range, or are reasonable.

GIGO (garbage in, garbage out) means that if your input is incorrect, your output is worthless.

Forcing a data item means you override incorrect data by setting it to a specific, default value.

Exercises

Review Questions

1. The structure that allows you to write one set of instructions that operates on multiple, separate sets of data is the _____.

    a. sequence   c. selection

    b. loop   d. case

2. The loop that frequently appears in a program's mainline logic _____.

    a. always depends on whether a variable equals 0

    b. is an example of an infinite loop

    c. is an unstructured loop

    d. works correctly based on the same logic as other loops

3. Which of the following is *not* a step that must occur with every correctly working loop?

   a. Initialize a loop control variable before the loop starts.

   b. Compare the loop control value to a sentinel during each iteration.

   c. Set the loop control value equal to a sentinel during each iteration.

   d. Alter the loop control variable during each iteration.

4. The statements executed within a loop are known collectively as the _____ .

   a. loop body   c. sequences

   b. loop controls   d. sentinels

5. A counter keeps track of _____ .

   a. the number of times an event has occurred

   b. the number of machine cycles required by a segment of a program

   c. the number of loop structures within a program

   d. the number of times software has been revised

6. Adding 1 to a variable is also called _____ it.

   a. digesting   c. decrementing

   b. resetting   d. incrementing

7. Which of the following is a definite loop?

   a. a loop that executes as long as a user continues to enter valid data

   b. a loop that executes 1000 times

   c. both of the above

   d. none of the above

8. Which of the following is an indefinite loop?

   a. a loop that executes exactly 10 times

   b. a loop that follows a prompt that asks a user how many repetitions to make and uses the value to control the loop

   c. both of the above

   d. none of the above

9. When you decrement a variable, you _____ .

   a. set it to 0   c. subtract a value from it

   b. reduce it by one-tenth   d. remove it from a program

10. When two loops are nested, the loop that is contained by the other is the _____ loop.

   a. captive   c. inner

   b. unstructured   d. outer

11. When loops are nested, _____ .

    a. they typically share a loop control variable

    b. one must end before the other begins

    c. both must be the same type—definite or indefinite

    d. none of the above

12. Most programmers use a for loop _____ .

    a. for every loop they write

    b. when they know the exact number of times a loop will repeat

    c. when a loop must repeat many times

    d. when a loop will not repeat

13. A report that lists only totals, with no details about individual records, is a(n) _____ report.

    a. accumulator   c. group

    b. final   d. summary

14. Typically, the value added to a counter variable is _____ .

    a. 0   c. the same for each iteration

    b. 1   d. different in each iteration

15. Typically, the value added to an accumulator variable is _____ .

    a. 0   c. the same for each iteration

    b. 1   d. different in each iteration

16. After an accumulator or counter variable is displayed at the end of a program, it is best to _____ .

    a. delete the variable from the program

    b. reset the variable to 0

    c. subtract 1 from the variable

    d. none of the above

17. When you _____ , you make sure data items are the correct type and fall within the correct range.

    a. validate data   c. use object orientation

    b. employ offensive programming   d. count loop iterations

18. Overriding a user's entered value by setting it to a predetermined value is known as _____ .

    a. forcing   c. validating

    b. accumulating   d. pushing

19. To ensure that a user's entry is the correct data type, frequently you _____ .

    a. prompt the user to verify that the type is correct

    b. use a method built into the programming language

    c. include a statement at the beginning of the program that lists the data types allowed

    d. all of the above

20. A variable might hold an incorrect value even when it is _____ .

    a. the correct data type

    b. within a required range

    c. a constant coded by the programmer

    d. all of the above

Programming Exercises

1. What is output by each of the pseudocode segments in Figure 5-25?

a.
```
a = 1
b = 2
c = 5
while a < c
    a = a + 1
    b = b + c
endwhile
output a, b, c
```

b.
```
d = 4
e = 6
f = 7
while d > f
    d = d + 1
    e = e - 1
endwhile
output d, e, f
```

c.
```
g = 4
h = 6
while g < h
    g = g + 1
endwhile
output g, h
```

d.
```
j = 2
k = 5
n = 9
while j < k
    m = 6
    while m < n
        output "Goodbye"
        m = m + 1
    endwhile
    j = j + 1
endwhile
```

e.
```
j = 2
k = 5
m = 6
n = 9
while j < k
    while m < n
        output "Hello"
        m = m + 1
    endwhile
    j = j + 1
endwhile
```

f.
```
p = 2
q = 4
while p < q
    output "Adios"
    r = 1
    while r < q
        output "Adios"
        r = r + 1
    endwhile
    p = p + 1
endwhile
```

Figure 5-25   Pseudocode segments for Exercise 1

2. Design the logic for a program that outputs every number from 1 through 20.

3. Design the logic for a program that outputs every number from 1 through 20 along with its value doubled and tripled.

4. Design the logic for a program that outputs every even number from 2 through 100.

5. Design the logic for a program that outputs numbers in reverse order from 25 down to 0.

6. Design the logic for a program that allows a user to enter a number. Display the sum of every number from 1 through the entered number.

7. Design the logic for a program that allows a user to continuously enter numbers until the user enters *0*. Display the sum of the numbers entered.

8. Design a program that allows a user to enter any quantity of numbers until a negative number is entered. Then display the highest number and the lowest number.

9. a. Design an application for the Homestead Furniture Store that gets sales transaction data, including an account number, customer name, and purchase price. Output the account number and name, then output the customer's payment each month for the next 12 months. Assume that there is no finance charge, that the customer makes no new purchases, and that the customer pays off the balance with equal monthly payments.

   b. Modify the Homestead Furniture Store application so it executes continuously for any number of customers until a sentinel value is supplied for the account number.

10. a. Design an application for Domicile Designs that gets sales transaction data, including an account number, customor name, and purchase price. The store charges 1.25 percent interest on the balance due each month. Output the account number and name, then output the customer's projected balance each month for the next 12 months. Assume that when the balance reaches $25 or less, the customer can pay off the account. At the beginning of every month, 1.25 percent interest is added to the balance, and then the customer makes a payment equal to 7 percent of the current balance. Assume that the customer makes no new purchases.

   b. Modify the Domicile Designs application so it executes continuously for any number of customers until a sentinel value is supplied for the account number.

11. a. Design a program for Hunterville College. The current tuition is $15,000 per year, and tuition is expected to increase by 4 percent each year. Display the tuition each year for the next 10 years.

   b. Modify the Hunterville College program so that the user enters the rate of tuition increase instead of having it fixed at 4 percent.

   c. Modify the Hunterville College program so that the user enters the rate of tuition increase for the first year. The rate then increases by 0.5 percent each subsequent year.

12. Yabe Online Auctions requires its sellers to post items for sale for a six-week period during which the price of any unsold item drops 12 percent each week. For example, an item that costs $10.00 during the first week costs 12 percent less, or $8.80, during the second week. During the third week, the same item is 12 percent less than $8.80, or $7.74. Design an application that allows a user to input prices until an appropriate sentinel value is entered. Program output is the price of each item during each week, one through six.

13. Design a retirement planning calculator for Skulling Financial Services. Allow a user to enter a number of working years remaining in the user's career and the annual amount of money the user can save. Assume that the user earns three percent simple interest on savings annually. Program output is a schedule that lists each year number in retirement starting with year 0 and the user's savings at the start of that year. Assume that the user spends $50,000 per year in retirement and then earns three percent interest on the remaining balance. End the list after 40 years, or when the user's balance is 0 or less, whichever comes first.

14. Ellison Private Elementary School has three classrooms in each of nine grades, kindergarten (grade 0) through grade 8, and allows parents to pay tuition over the nine-month school year. Design the application that outputs nine tuition payment coupons for each of the 27 classrooms. Each coupon should contain the grade number (0 through 8), the classroom number (1 through 3), the month (1 through 9), and the amount of tuition due. Tuition for kindergarten is $80 per month. Tuition for the other grades is $60 per month times the grade level.

15. a. Design a program for the Hollywood Movie Rating Guide, which can be installed in a kiosk in theaters. Each theater patron enters a value from 0 to 4 indicating the number of stars that the patron awards to the Guide's featured movie of the week. If a user enters a star value that does not fall in the correct range, reprompt the user continuously until a correct value is entered. The program executes continuously until the theater manager enters a negative number to quit. At the end of the program, display the average star rating for the movie.

    b. Modify the movie-rating program so that a user gets three tries to enter a valid rating. After three incorrect entries, the program issues an appropriate message and continues with a new user.

16. Design a program for the Café Noir Coffee Shop to provide some customer market research data. When a customer places an order, a clerk asks for the customer's zip code and age. The clerk enters that data as well as the number of items the customer orders. The program operates continuously until the clerk enters a 0 for zip code at the end of the day. When the clerk enters an invalid zip code (more than 5 digits) or an invalid age (defined as less than 10 or more than 110), the program reprompts the clerk continuously. When the clerk enters fewer than 1 or more than 12 items, the program reprompts the clerk two more times. If the clerk enters a high value on the third attempt, the program accepts the high value, but if the clerk enters a negative value on the third attempt, an error message is displayed

and the order is not counted. At the end of the program, display a count of the number of items ordered by customers from the same zip code as the coffee shop (54984), and a count from other zip codes. Also display the average customer age as well as counts of the number of items ordered by customers under 30 and by customers 30 and older.

Performing Maintenance

1. A file named MAINTENANCE05-01.txt is included with your downloadable student files. Assume that this program is a working program in your organization and that it needs modifications as described in the comments (lines that begin with two slashes) at the beginning of the file. Your job is to alter the program to meet the new specifications.

Find the Bugs

1. Your downloadable files for Chapter 5 include DEBUG05-01.txt, DEBUG05-02.txt, and DEBUG05-03.txt. Each file starts with some comments that describe the problem. Comments are lines that begin with two slashes (//). Following the comments, each file contains pseudocode that has one or more bugs you must find and correct.

2. Your downloadable files for Chapter 5 include a file named DEBUG05-04.jpg that contains a flowchart with syntax and/or logical errors. Examine the flowchart and then find and correct all the bugs.

Game Zone

1. In Chapter 2, you learned that in many programming languages you can generate a random number between 1 and a limiting value named LIMIT by using a statement similar to randomNumber = random(LIMIT). In Chapter 4, you created the logic for a guessing game in which the application generates a random number and the player tries to guess it. Now, create the guessing game itself. After each guess, display a message indicating whether the player's guess was correct, too high, or too low. When the player eventually guesses the correct number, display a count of the number of guesses that were required.

2. Create the logic for a game that simulates rolling two dice by generating two random numbers between 1 and 6 inclusive. The player chooses a number between 2 and 12 (the lowest and highest totals possible for two dice). The player then "rolls" two dice up to three times. If the number chosen by the user comes up, the user wins and the game ends. If the number does not come up within three rolls, the computer wins.

3. Create the logic for the dice game Pig, in which a player can compete with the computer. The object of the game is to be the first to score 100 points. The user and computer take turns "rolling" a pair of dice following these rules:

    - On a turn, each player rolls two dice. If no 1 appears, the dice values are added to a running total for the turn, and the player can choose whether to roll again or pass the turn to the other player. When a player passes, the accumulated turn total is added to the player's game total.

    - If a 1 appears on one of the dice, the player's turn total becomes 0; in other words, nothing more is added to the player's game total for that turn, and it becomes the other player's turn.

    - If a 1 appears on both of the dice, not only is the player's turn over, but the player's entire accumulated total is reset to 0.

    - When the computer does not roll a 1 and can choose whether to roll again, generate a random value from 1 to 2. The computer will then decide to continue when the value is 1 and decide to quit and pass the turn to the player when the value is not 1.

 ## Up for Discussion

1. Suppose you wrote a program that you suspect contains an infinite loop because it keeps running for several minutes with no output and without ending. What would you add to your program to help you discover the origin of the problem?

2. Suppose you know that every employee in your organization has a seven-digit ID number used for logging on to the computer system. A loop would be useful to guess every combination of seven digits in an ID. Are there any circumstances in which you should try to guess another employee's ID number?

3. If every employee in an organization had a seven-digit ID number, guessing all the possible combinations would be a relatively easy programming task. Describe how you would write a program that guesses all the combinations, and then discuss how you could alter the format of employee IDs to make them more difficult to guess.

Arrays

In this chapter, you will learn about:

◎ Storing data in arrays

◎ How an array can replace nested decisions

◎ Using constants with arrays

◎ Searching an array for an exact match

◎ Using parallel arrays

◎ Searching an array for a range match

◎ Remaining within array bounds

◎ Using a **for** loop to process an array

Storing Data in Arrays

An **array** is a series or list of values in computer memory. All the values must be the same data type. Usually, all the values in an array have something in common; for example, they might represent a list of employee ID numbers or prices for items sold in a store.

Whenever you require multiple storage locations for objects, you can use a real-life counterpart of a programming array. If you store important papers in a series of file folders and label each folder with a consecutive letter of the alphabet, then you are using the equivalent of an array. If you keep receipts in a stack of shoe boxes and label each box with a month, you are also using the equivalent of an array. Similarly, when you plan courses for the next semester at your school by looking down a list of course offerings, you are using an array.

 The arrays discussed in this chapter are single-dimensional arrays, which are similar to lists. Arrays with multiple dimensions are covered in Chapter 8 of the Comprehensive version of this book.

Each of these real-life arrays helps you organize objects or information. You *could* store all your papers or receipts in one huge cardboard box, or find courses if they were printed randomly in one large book. However, using an organized storage and display system makes your life easier in each case. Similarly, an array provides an organized storage and display system for a program's data.

How Arrays Occupy Computer Memory

When you declare an array, you declare a structure that contains multiple data items; each data item is one **element** of the array. Each element has the same data type, and each element occupies an area in memory next to, or contiguous to, the others. You can indicate the number of elements an array will hold—the **size of the array**—when you declare the array along with your other variables and constants. For example, you might declare an uninitialized, three-element numeric array named prices and an uninitialized string array of 10 employee names as follows:

```
num prices[3]
```

```
string employeeNames[10]
```

When naming arrays, programmers follow the same rules as when naming variables. That is, array names must start with a letter and contain no embedded spaces. Additionally, many programmers observe one of the following conventions when naming arrays to make it more obvious that the name represents a group of items:

- Arrays are often named using a plural noun such as prices or employeeNames.

- Arrays are often named by adding a final word that implies a group, such as priceList, priceTable, or priceArray.

Each array element is differentiated from the others with a unique **subscript**, also called an **index**, which is a number that indicates the position of a particular item within an array. All array elements have the same group name, but each individual element also has a unique subscript indicating how far away it is from the first element. For example, a five-element array uses subscripts 0 through 4, and a ten-element array uses subscripts 0 through 9. In all languages, subscript values must be sequential integers (whole numbers). In most modern languages, such as Visual Basic, Java, C++, and C#, the first array element is accessed using subscript 0, and this book follows that convention.

To use an array element, you place its subscript within square brackets or parentheses (depending on the programming language) after the group name. This book will use square brackets to hold array subscripts so that you don't mistake array names for method names. Many newer programming languages such as C++, Java, and C# also use the square bracket notation.

After you declare an array, you can assign values to some or all of the elements individually. Providing array values sometimes is called **populating the array**. The following code shows a three-element array declaration, followed by three separate statements that populate the array:

```
Declarations
    num prices[3]
prices[0] = 25.00
prices[1] = 36.50
prices[2] = 47.99
```

Figure 6-1 shows an array named prices that contains three elements, so the elements are prices[0], prices[1], and prices[2]. The array elements have been assigned the values 25.00, 36.50, and 47.99, respectively. The element prices[0] is zero numbers away from the beginning of the array. The element prices[1] is one number away from the beginning of the array and prices[2] is two numbers away.

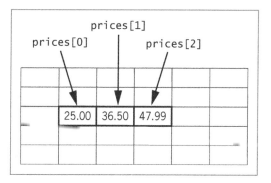

 When programmers refer to array element prices[0], they say "prices sub 0" or simply "prices zero."

Figure 6-1   Appearance of a three-element array in computer memory
© 2015 Cengage Learning

If appropriate, you can declare and initialize array elements in one statement. Most programming languages use a statement similar to the following to declare a three-element array and assign a list of values to it:

```
num prices[3] = 25.00, 36.50, 47.99
```

You have learned that you can declare multiple variables of the same data type in a single statement, such as the following:

```
num testScore = 0, age
```

If you want to declare single variables and an array of the same data type in the same statement, you can achieve better clarity by using notation such as curly braces to set off array element values, as in the following:

```
num prices[3] = { 25.00, 36.50, 47.99 }, testScore = 0, age
```

When you use a list of values to initialize an array, the first value you list is assigned to the first array element (element 0), and the subsequent values are assigned to the remaining elements in order. Many programming languages allow you to initialize an array with fewer starting values than there are array elements declared, but no language allows you to initialize an array using more starting values than positions available. When starting values are supplied for an array in this book, each element will be provided with a value.

After an array has been declared and appropriate values have been assigned to specific elements, you can use an individual element in the same way you would use any other data item of the same type. For example, you can input values to array elements and you can output the values, and if the elements are numeric, you can perform arithmetic with them. Quick Reference 6-1 summarizes the characteristics of arrays.

QUICK REFERENCE 6-1 Characteristics of Arrays

- An array is a list of data items in contiguous memory locations.
- Each data item in an array is an *element*.
- Each array element is the same data type; by default, this means that each element is the same size.
- Each element is differentiated from the others by a subscript, which is a whole number.
- Usable subscripts for an array range from 0 to one less than the number of elements in an array.
- Each array element can be used in the same way as a single item of the same data type.

Watch the video *Understanding Arrays*.

TWO TRUTHS & A LIE

Storing Data in Arrays

1. In an array, each element has the same data type.

2. Each array element is accessed using a subscript, which can be a number or a string.

3. Array elements always occupy adjacent memory locations.

The false statement is #2. An array subscript must be a whole number. It can be a named constant, an unnamed constant, or a variable.

How an Array Can Replace Nested Decisions

Consider an application requested by a company's human resources department to produce statistics on employees' claimed dependents. The department wants a report that lists the number of employees who have claimed 0, 1, 2, 3, 4, or 5 dependents. (Assume that you know that no employees have more than five dependents.) For example, Figure 6-2 shows a typical report.

Dependents	Count
0	43
1	35
2	24
3	11
4	5
5	1

Figure 6-2   Typical Dependents report
© 2015 Cengage Learning

Without using an array, you could write the application that produces counts for the six categories of dependents (0 through 5) by using a series of decisions. Figure 6-3 shows the pseudocode and flowchart for the decision-making part of such an application. Although this logic works, its length and complexity are unnecessary once you understand how to use an array.

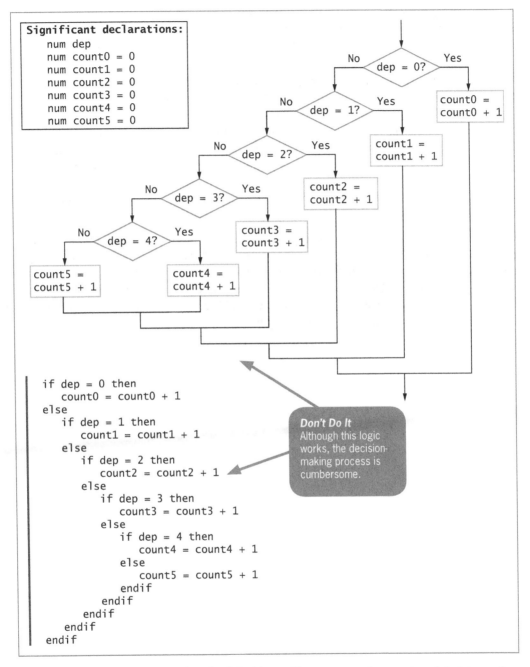

Significant declarations:
```
num dep
num count0 = 0
num count1 = 0
num count2 = 0
num count3 = 0
num count4 = 0
num count5 = 0
```

```
if dep = 0 then
    count0 = count0 + 1
else
    if dep = 1 then
        count1 = count1 + 1
    else
        if dep = 2 then
            count2 = count2 + 1
        else
            if dep = 3 then
                count3 = count3 + 1
            else
                if dep = 4 then
                    count4 = count4 + 1
                else
                    count5 = count5 + 1
                endif
            endif
        endif
    endif
endif
```

Don't Do It
Although this logic works, the decision-making process is cumbersome.

Figure 6-3   Flowchart and pseudocode of decision-making process using a series of decisions—the hard way

© 2015 Cengage Learning

The decision-making process in Figure 6-3 accomplishes its purpose, and the logic is correct, but the process is cumbersome and certainly not recommended. Follow the logic here so that you understand how the application works. In the next pages, you will see how to make the application more elegant.

In Figure 6-3, the variable dep is compared to 0. If it is 0, 1 is added to count0. If it is not 0, then dep is compared to 1. Based on the result, 1 is added to count1 or dep is compared to 2, and so on. Each time the application executes this decision-making process, 1 ultimately is added to one of the six variables that acts as a counter. The dependent-counting logic in Figure 6-3 works, but even with only six categories of dependents, the decision-making process is unwieldy. What if the number of dependents might be any value from 0 to 10, or 0 to 20? With either of these scenarios, the basic logic of the program would remain the same; however, you would need to declare many additional variables to hold the counts, and you would need many additional decisions.

Using an array provides an alternate approach to this programming problem and greatly reduces the number of statements you need. When you declare an array, you provide a group name for a number of associated variables in memory. For example, the six dependent count accumulators can be redefined as a single array named counts. The individual elements become counts[0], counts[1], counts[2], counts[3], counts[4], and counts[5], as shown in the revised decision-making process in Figure 6-4.

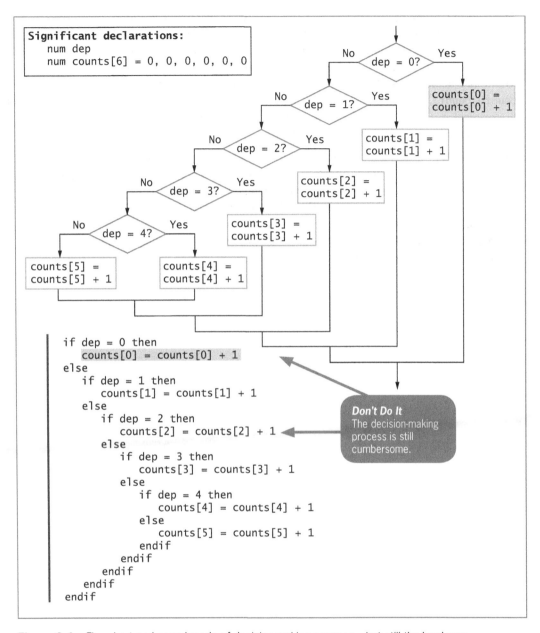

```
Significant declarations:
  num dep
  num counts[6] = 0, 0, 0, 0, 0, 0
```

                                          No   Yes
                                              dep = 0?

                              No   Yes   counts[0] =
                                  dep = 1?   counts[0] + 1

                    No   Yes   counts[1] =
                        dep = 2?   counts[1] + 1

              No   Yes   counts[2] =
                  dep = 3?   counts[2] + 1

        No   Yes   counts[3] =
            dep = 4? counts[3] + 1

counts[5] =   counts[4] =
counts[5] + 1   counts[4] + 1

```
        if dep = 0 then
           counts[0] = counts[0] + 1
        else
           if dep = 1 then
              counts[1] = counts[1] + 1
           else
              if dep = 2 then
                 counts[2] = counts[2] + 1
              else
                 if dep = 3 then
                    counts[3] = counts[3] + 1
                 else
                    if dep = 4 then
                       counts[4] = counts[4] + 1
                    else
                       counts[5] = counts[5] + 1
                    endif
                 endif
              endif
           endif
        endif
```

Don't Do It
The decision-making
process is still
cumbersome.

233

Figure 6-4   Flowchart and pseudocode of decision-making process—but still the hard way

The shaded statement in Figure 6-4 shows that when **dep** is 0, 1 is added to `counts[0]`. You can see similar statements for the rest of the `counts` array elements; when **dep** is 1, 1 is added to `counts[1]`, when **dep** is 2, 1 is added to `counts[2]`, and so on. When the **dep** value is 5, this means it was not 1, 2, 3, or 4, so 1 is added to `counts[5]`. In other words, 1 is added to one of the elements of the `counts` array instead of to an individual variable named `count0`, `count1`, `count2`, `count3`, `count4`, or `count5`. Is this version a big improvement over the original in Figure 6-3? Of course it isn't. You still have not taken advantage of the benefits of using the array in this application.

The true benefit of using an array lies in your ability to use a variable as a subscript to the array, instead of using a literal constant such as 0 or 5. Notice in the logic in Figure 6-4 that within each decision, the value compared to **dep** and the constant that is the subscript in the resulting *Yes* process are always identical. That is, when **dep** is 0, the subscript used to add 1 to the `counts` array is 0; when **dep** is 1, the subscript used for the `counts` array is 1, and so on. Therefore, you can just use **dep** as a subscript to the array. You can rewrite the decision-making process as shown in Figure 6-5.

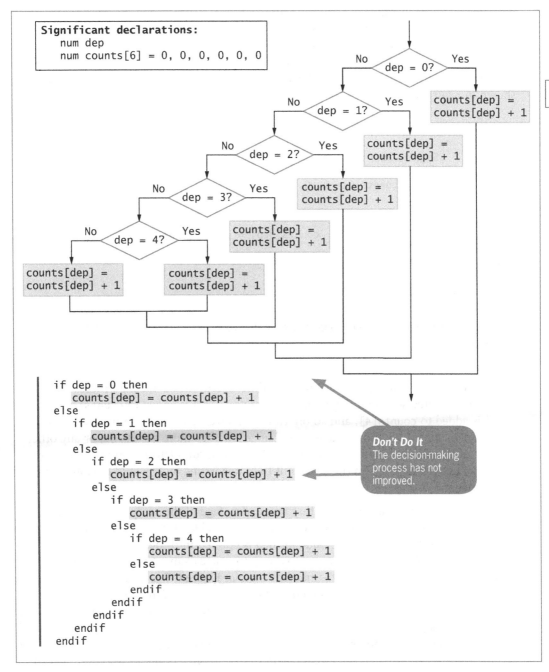

Figure 6-5 Flowchart and pseudocode of decision-making process using an array—but still a hard way

© 2015 Cengage Learning

The code segment in Figure 6-5 looks no more efficient than the one in Figure 6-4. However, notice the shaded statements in Figure 6-5—the process that occurs after each decision is exactly the same. In each case, no matter what the value of dep is, you always add 1 to counts [dep]. If you always will take the same action no matter what the answer to a question is, there is no need to ask the question. Instead, you can rewrite the decision-making process as shown in Figure 6-6.

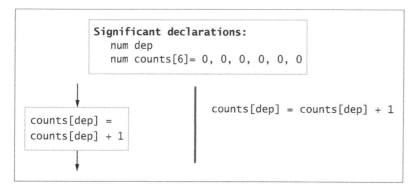

Figure 6-6   Flowchart and pseudocode of efficient decision-making process using an array
© 2015 Cengage Learning

The single statement in Figure 6-6 eliminates the *entire* decision-making process that was the original highlighted section in Figure 6-5! When dep is 2, 1 is added to counts[2]; when dep is 4, 1 is added to counts[4], and so on. *Now* you have significantly improved the original logic. What's more, this process does not change whether there are 20, 30, or any other number of possible categories. To use more than five accumulators, you would declare additional counts elements in the array, but the categorizing logic would remain the same as it is in Figure 6-6.

Figure 6-7 shows an entire program that takes advantage of the array to produce the report that shows counts for dependent categories. Variables and constants are declared and, in the getReady() module, a first value for dep is entered into the program. In the countDependents() module, 1 is added to the appropriate element of the count array and the next value is input. The loop in the mainline logic in Figure 6-7 is an indefinite loop; it continues as long as the user does not enter the sentinel value. When data entry is complete, the finishUp() module displays the report. First, the heading is output, then dep is reset to 0, and then each dep and counts[dep] are output in a loop. The first output statement contains 0 (as the number of dependents) and the value stored in counts[0]. Then, 1 is added to dep and the same set of instructions is used again to display the counts for each number of dependents. The loop in the finishUp() module is a definite loop; it executes precisely six times.

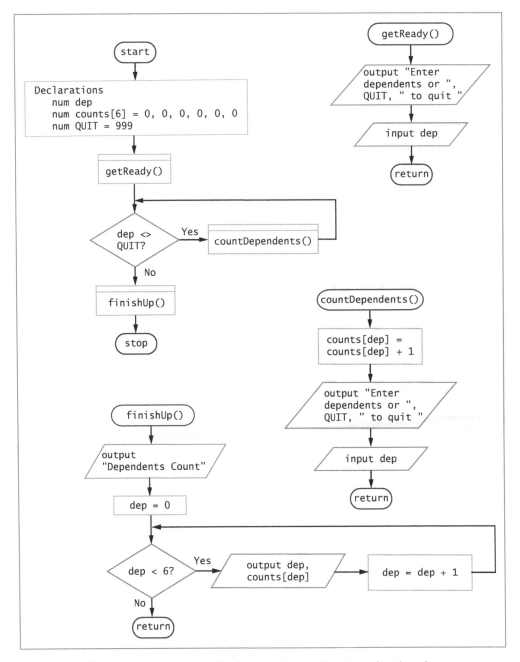

Figure 6-7 Flowchart and pseudocode for Dependents report program *(continues)*

(continued)

```
start
   Declarations
      num dep
      num counts[6] = 0, 0, 0, 0, 0, 0
      num QUIT = 999
   getReady()
   while dep <> QUIT
      countDependents()
   endwhile
   finishUp()
stop

getReady()
   output "Enter dependents or ", QUIT, " to quit "
   input dep
return

countDependents()
   counts[dep] = counts[dep] + 1
   output "Enter dependents or ", QUIT, " to quit "
   input dep
return

finishUp()
   output "Dependents Count"
   dep = 0
   while dep < 6
      output dep, counts[dep]
      dep = dep + 1
   endwhile
return
```

Figure 6-7   Flowchart and pseudocode for Dependents report program
© 2015 Cengage Learning

The program in Figure 6-7 could be improved by making sure that the value of the subscript dep is within range before adding 1 to counts[dep]. Later in this chapter, you learn more about ensuring that a subscript falls within the valid range for an array.

The dependent-counting program would have *worked* if it contained a long series of decisions and output statements, but the program is easier to write when you use an array and access its values using the number of dependents as a subscript. Additionally, the new program is more efficient, easier for other programmers to understand, and easier to maintain. Arrays are never mandatory, but often they can drastically cut down on your programming time and make your logic easier to understand.

Learning to use arrays properly can make many programming tasks far more efficient and professional. When you understand how to use arrays, you will be able to provide elegant solutions to problems that otherwise would require tedious programming steps.

Watch the video *Accumulating Values in an Array.*

TWO TRUTHS & A LIE

How an Array Can Replace Nested Decisions

1. You can use an array to replace a long series of decisions.

2. You experience a major benefit of arrays when you use an unnamed numeric constant as a subscript as opposed to using a variable.

3. The process of displaying every element in a 10-element array is basically no different from displaying every element in a 100-element array.

The false statement is #2. You experience a major benefit of arrays when you use a variable as a subscript as opposed to using a constant.

Using Constants with Arrays

In Chapter 2, you learned that named constants hold values that do not change during a program's execution. When working with arrays, you can use constants in several ways:

- To hold the size of an array
- As the array values
- As subscripts

Using a Constant as the Size of an Array

The program in Figure 6-7 still contains one minor flaw. Throughout this book you have learned to avoid *magic numbers*—that is, unnamed constants. As the totals are output in the loop at the end of the program in Figure 6-7, the array subscript is compared to the constant 6. The program can be improved if you use a named constant instead. Using a named constant makes your code easier to modify and understand. In most programming languages you can take one of two approaches:

- You can declare a named numeric constant such as ARRAY_SIZE = 6. Then you can use this constant every time you access the array, always making sure any subscript you use remains less than the constant value.

- In many languages, a value that represents the array size is automatically provided for each array you create. For example, in Java, after you declare an array named counts, its size is stored in a field named counts.length. In both C# and Visual Basic, the array size is counts.Length, with an uppercase *L*. No automatically created value exists in C or C++.

Using Constants as Array Element Values

Sometimes the values stored in arrays should be constants because they are not changed during program execution. For example, suppose that you create an array that holds names for the months of the year. When declaring an array of named constants, programmers conventionally use all uppercase letters with underscores separating words. Don't confuse the array identifier with its contents—the convention in this book is to use all uppercase letters in constant identifiers, but not necessarily in array values. An array named MONTHS that holds constant values might be declared as follows:

```
string MONTHS[12] = "January", "February", "March", "April",
    "May", "June", "July", "August", "September", "October",
    "November", "December"
```

Using a Constant as an Array Subscript

Occasionally you will want to use an unnamed numeric constant as a subscript to an array. For example, to display the first value in an array named salesArray, you might write a statement that uses an unnamed literal constant as a subscript, as follows:

```
output salesArray[0]
```

You might also have occasion to use a named constant as a subscript. For example, if salesArray holds sales values for each of 20 states covered by your company, and Indiana is state 5, you could output the value for Indiana using an unnamed constant as follows:

```
output salesArray[5]
```

However, if you declare a named constant as num INDIANA = 5, then you can display the same value using this statement:

```
output salesArray[INDIANA]
```

An advantage to using a named constant in this case is that the statement becomes self-documenting—anyone who reads your statement more easily understands that your intention is to display the sales value for Indiana.

TWO TRUTHS & A LIE

Using Constants with Arrays

1. If you create a named constant equal to an array size, you can use it as a subscript to the array.

2. If you create a named constant equal to an array size, you can use it as a limit against which to compare subscript values.

3. When you declare an array in Java, C#, or Visual Basic, a constant that represents the array size is automatically provided.

The false statement is #1. If the constant is equal to the array size, then it is larger than any valid array subscript.

Searching an Array for an Exact Match

In the dependent-counting application in this chapter, the array's subscript variable conveniently held small whole numbers—the number of dependents allowed was 0 through 5—and the **dep** variable directly accessed the array. Unfortunately, real life doesn't always happen in small integers. Sometimes you don't have a variable that conveniently holds an array position; sometimes you have to search through an array to find a value you need.

Consider a mail-order business in which customers place orders that contain a name, address, item number, and quantity ordered. Assume that the item numbers from which a customer can choose are three-digit numbers, but perhaps they are not consecutively numbered 001 through 999. For example, let's say that you offer six items: 106, 108, 307, 405, 457, and 688, as shown in the shaded VALID_ITEMS array declaration in Figure 6-8. The array is declared as constant because the item numbers do not change during program execution. When a customer orders an item, a clerical worker can tell whether the order is valid by looking down the list and manually verifying that the ordered item number is on it. In a similar fashion, a computer program can use a loop to test the ordered item number against each VALID_ITEMS element, looking for an exact match. When you search through a list from one end to the other, you are performing a **linear search**.

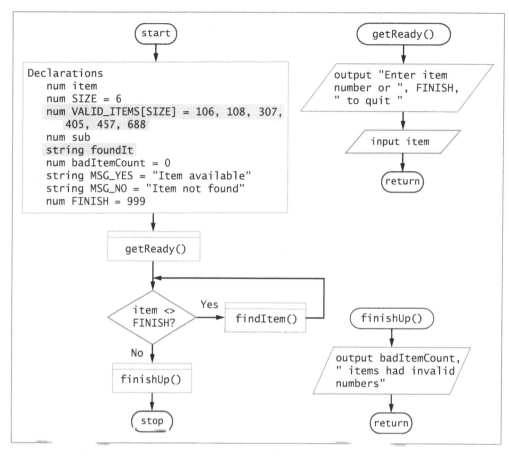

Figure 6-8   Flowchart and pseudocode for program that verifies item availability (continues)

(continued)

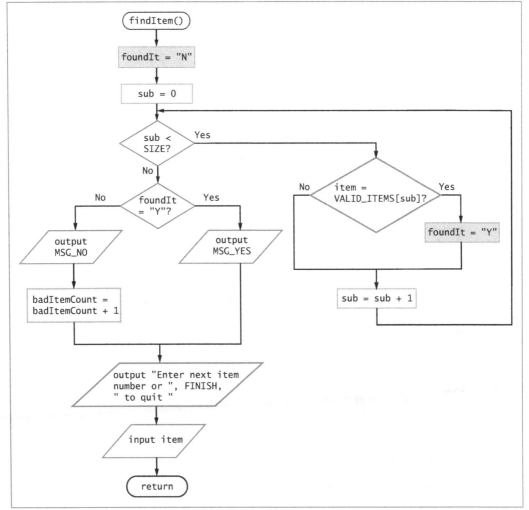

Figure 6-8   Flowchart and pseudocode for program that verifies item availability *(continues)*

(continued)

244

```
start
   Declarations
      num item
      num SIZE = 6
      num VALID_ITEMS[SIZE] = 106, 108, 307,
         405, 457, 688
      num sub
      string foundIt
      num badItemCount = 0
      string MSG_YES = "Item available"
      string MSG_NO = "Item not found"
      num FINISH = 999
   getReady()
   while item <> FINISH
      findItem()
   endwhile
   finishUp()
stop

getReady()
   output "Enter item number or ", FINISH, " to quit "
   input item
return

findItem()
   foundIt = "N"
   sub = 0
   while sub < SIZE
      if item = VALID_ITEMS[sub] then
         foundIt = "Y"
      endif
      sub = sub + 1
   endwhile
   if foundIt = "Y" then
      output MSG_YES
   else
      output MSG_NO
      badItemCount = badItemCount + 1
   endif
   output "Enter next item number or ", FINISH, " to quit "
   input item
return

finishUp()
   output badItemCount, " items had invalid numbers"
return
```

Figure 6-8   Flowchart and pseudocode for program that verifies item availability
© 2015 Cengage Learning

To determine if an ordered item number is valid, you could use a series of six decisions to compare the number to each of the six allowed values. However, the superior approach shown in Figure 6-8 is to create an array that holds the list of valid item numbers and then to search through the array for an exact match to the ordered item. If you search through the entire array without finding a match for the item the customer ordered, it means the ordered item number is not valid.

The findItem() module in Figure 6-8 takes the following steps to verify that an item number exists:

- A flag variable named foundIt is set to "N". A **flag** is a variable that is set to indicate whether some event has occurred. In this example, N indicates that the item number has not yet been found in the list. (See the first shaded statement in the findItem() method in Figure 6-8.)

- A subscript, sub, is set to 0. This subscript will be used to access each VALID_ITEMS element.

- A loop executes, varying sub from 0 through one less than the size of the array. Within the loop, the customer's ordered item number is compared to each item number in the array. If the customer-ordered item matches any item in the array, the flag variable is assigned "Y". (See the last shaded statement in the findItem() method in Figure 6-8.) After all six valid item numbers have been compared to the ordered item, if the customer item matches none of them, then the flag variable foundIt will still hold the value "N".

- If the flag variable's value is "Y" after the entire list has been searched, it means that the item is valid and an appropriate message is displayed, but if the flag has not been assigned "Y", the item was not found in the array of valid items. In this case, an error message is output and 1 is added to a count of bad item numbers.

 As an alternative to using the string foundIt variable in the method in Figure 6-8, you might prefer to use a numeric variable that you set to 1 or 0. Most programming languages also support a Boolean data type that you can use for foundIt; when you declare a variable to be Boolean, you can set its value to true or false.

TWO TRUTHS & A LIE

Searching an Array for an Exact Match

1. Only whole numbers can be stored in arrays.
2. Only whole numbers can be used as array subscripts.
3. A flag is a variable that indicates whether some event has occurred.

The false statement is #1. Whole numbers can be stored in arrays, but so can many other objects, including strings and numbers with decimal places.

Using Parallel Arrays

When you accept an item number into a mail-order company program, you usually want to accomplish more than simply verifying the item's existence. For example, you might want to determine the name, price, or available quantity of the ordered item. Tasks like these can be completed efficiently using parallel arrays. **Parallel arrays** are two or more arrays in which each element in one array is associated with the element in the same relative position in the other array. Although any array can contain just one data type, each array in a set of parallel arrays might be a different type.

Suppose that you have a list of item numbers and their associated prices. One array named VALID_ITEMS contains six elements; each element is a valid item number. Its parallel array also has six elements. The array is named VALID_PRICES; each element is a price of an item. Each price in the VALID_PRICES array is conveniently and purposely stored in the same position as the corresponding item number in the VALID_ITEMS array. Figure 6-9 shows how the parallel arrays might look in computer memory.

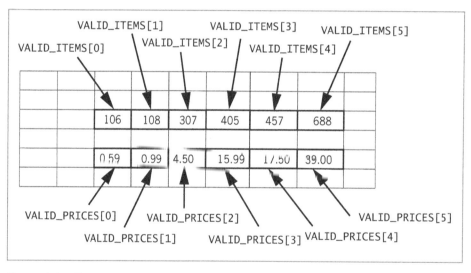

Figure 6-9   Parallel arrays in memory
© 2015 Cengage Learning

When you use parallel arrays:

- Two or more arrays contain related data.

- A subscript relates the arrays. That is, elements at the same position in each array are logically related.

Figure 6-10 shows a program that declares parallel arrays. The VALID_PRICES array is shaded; each element in it corresponds to a valid item number.

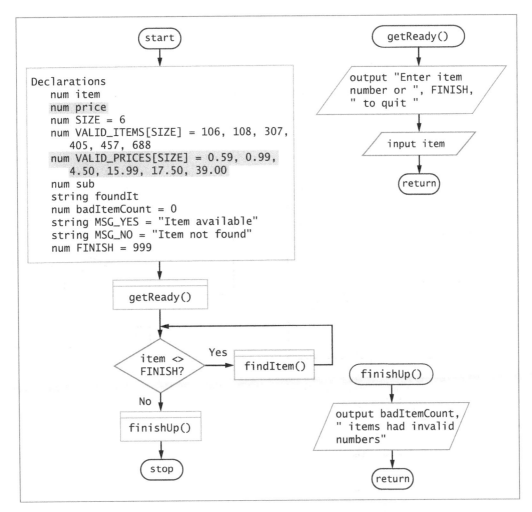

Figure 6-10 Flowchart and pseudocode of program that finds an item price using parallel arrays *(continues)*

(continued)

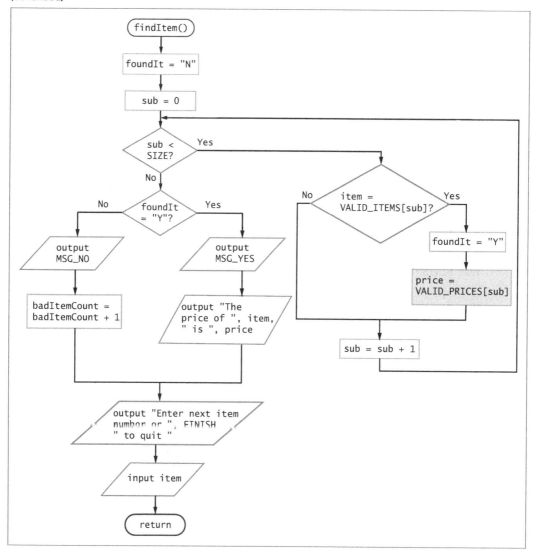

Figure 6-10   Flowchart and pseudocode of program that finds an item price using parallel arrays *(continues)*

(continued)

```
start
   Declarations
      num item
      num price
      num SIZE = 6
      num VALID_ITEMS[SIZE] = 106, 108, 307,
         405, 457, 688
      num VALID_PRICES[SIZE] = 0.59, 0.99,
         4.50, 15.99, 17.50, 39.00
      num sub
      string foundIt
      num badItemCount = 0
      string MSG_YES = "Item available"
      string MSG_NO = "Item not found"
      num FINISH = 999
   getReady()
   while item <> FINISH
      findItem()
   endwhile
   finishUp()
stop

getReady()
   output "Enter item number or ", FINISH, " to quit "
   input item
return

findItem()
   foundIt = "N"
   sub = 0
   while sub < SIZE
      if item = VALID_ITEMS[sub] then
         foundIt = "Y"
         price = VALID_PRICES[sub]
      endif
      sub = sub + 1
   endwhile
   if foundIt = "Y" then
      output MSG_YES
      output "The price of ", item, " is ", price
   else
      output MSG_NO
      badItemCount = badItemCount + 1
   endif
   output "Enter next item number or ", FINISH, " to quit "
   input item
return

finishUp()
   output badItemCount, " items had invalid numbers"
return
```

Figure 6-10   Flowchart and pseudocode of program that finds an item price using parallel arrays
© 2015 Cengage Learning

Some programmers object to using a cryptic variable name for a subscript, such as sub in Figure 6-10, because such names are not descriptive. These programmers would prefer a name like priceIndex. Others approve of short names when the variable is used only in a limited area of a program, as it is used here, to step through an array. Programmers disagree on many style issues like this one. As a programmer, it is your responsibility to find out what conventions are used among your peers in an organization.

As the program in Figure 6-10 receives a customer's order, it looks through each of the VALID_ITEMS values separately by varying the subscript sub from 0 to the number of items available. When a match for the item number is found, the program pulls the corresponding parallel price out of the list of VALID_PRICES values and stores it in the price variable. (See shaded statements in Figure 6-10.)

The relationship between an item's number and its price is an **indirect relationship**. That means you don't access a price directly by knowing the item number. Instead, you determine the price by knowing an item number's array position. Once you find a match for the ordered item number in the VALID_ITEMS array, you know that the price of the item is in the same position in the other array, VALID_PRICES. When VALID_ITEMS[sub] is the correct item, VALID_PRICES[sub] must be the correct price, so sub links the parallel arrays.

Parallel arrays are most useful when value pairs have an indirect relationship. If values in your program have a direct relationship, you probably don't need parallel arrays. For example, if items were numbered 0, 1, 2, 3, and so on consecutively, you could use the item number as a subscript to the price array instead of using a parallel array to hold item numbers. Even if the items were numbered 200, 201, 202, and so on consecutively, you could subtract a constant value (200) from each and use that as a subscript instead of using a parallel array.

Suppose that a customer orders item 457. Walk through the logic yourself to see if you come up with the correct price per item, $17.50. Then, suppose that a customer orders item 458. Walk through the logic and see whether the appropriate *Item not found* message is displayed.

Improving Search Efficiency

The mail-order program in Figure 6-10 is still a little inefficient. When a customer orders item 106 or 108, a match is found on the first or second pass through the loop, and continuing to search provides no further benefit. However, even after a match is made, the program in Figure 6-10 continues searching through the item array until sub reaches the value SIZE. One way to stop the search when the item has been found and foundIt is set to "Y" is to change the loop-controlling question. Instead of simply continuing the loop while the number of comparisons does not exceed the highest allowed array subscript, you should continue the loop while the searched item is not found *and* the number of comparisons has not exceeded the maximum. Leaving the loop as soon as a match is found improves the program's efficiency. The larger the array, the more beneficial it becomes to exit the searching loop as soon as you find the desired value.

Figure 6-11 shows the improved version of the findItem() module with the altered loop-controlling question shaded.

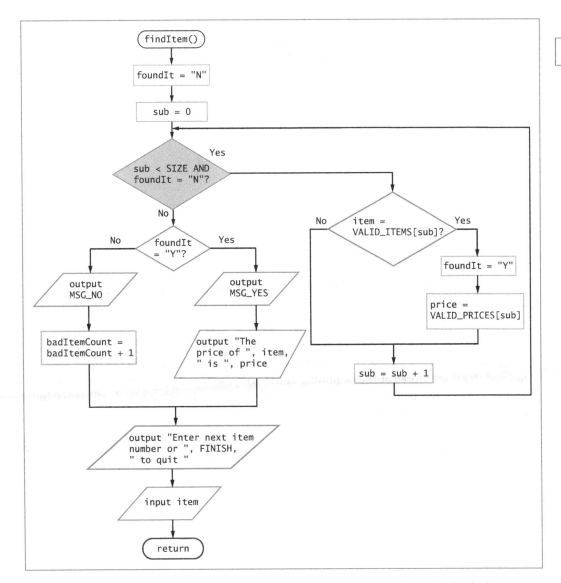

Figure 6-11 Flowchart and pseudocode of the module that finds an item price and exits the loop as soon as it is found *(continues)*

(continued)

```
findItem()
    foundIt = "N"
    sub = 0
    while sub < SIZE AND foundIt = "N"
        if item = VALID_ITEMS[sub] then
            foundIt = "Y"
            price = VALID_PRICES[sub]
        endif
        sub = sub + 1
    endwhile
    if foundIt = "Y" then
        output MSG_YES
        output "The price of ", item, " is ", price
    else
        output MSG_NO
        badItemCount = badItemCount + 1
    endif
    output "Enter next item number or ", FINISH, " to quit "
    input item
return
```

Figure 6-11   Flowchart and pseudocode of the module that finds an item price and exits the loop as soon as it is found
© 2015 Cengage Learning

Notice that the price-finding program offers the greatest efficiency when the most frequently ordered items are stored at the beginning of the array, so that only the seldom-ordered items require many loops before finding a match. Often, you can improve search efficiency by rearranging array elements.

As you study programming, you will learn other search techniques. For example, a **binary search** starts looking in the middle of a sorted list, and then determines whether it should continue higher or lower.

Watch the video *Using Parallel Arrays.*

Searching an Array for a Range Match

Customer order item numbers need to match available item numbers exactly to determine the correct price of an item. Sometimes, however, programmers want to work with ranges of values in arrays. In Chapter 4, you learned that a range of values is any series of values—for example, 1 through 5 or 20 through 30.

Suppose that a company decides to offer quantity discounts when a customer orders multiple items, as shown in Figure 6-12.

You want to be able to read in customer order data and determine a discount percentage based on the quantity ordered. For example, if a customer has ordered 20 items, you want to be able to output *Your discount is 15 percent*. One ill-advised approach might be to set up an array with as many elements as any customer might ever order, and store the appropriate discount

Quantity	Discount %
0–8	0
9–12	10
13–25	15
26 or more	20

Figure 6-12 Discounts on orders by quantity
© 2015 Cengage Learning

for each possible number, as shown in Figure 6-13. This array is set up to contain the discount for 0 items, 1 item, 2 items, and so on. This approach has at least three drawbacks:

- It requires a very large array that uses a lot of memory.

- You must store the same value repeatedly. For example, each of the first nine elements receives the same value, 0, and each of the next four elements receives the same value, 10.

- How do you know you have enough array elements? Is a customer order quantity of 75 items enough? What if a customer orders 100 or 1000 items? No matter how many elements you place in the array, there's always a chance that a customer will order more.

```
num DISCOUNTS[76]
 = 0, 0, 0, 0, 0, 0, 0, 0, 0,
   0.10, 0.10, 0.10, 0.10,
   0.15, 0.15, 0.15, 0.15, 0.15,
   0.15, 0.15, 0.15, 0.15, 0.15,
   0.15, 0.15, 0.15,
   0.20, 0.20, 0.20, 0.20, 0.20,
   0.20, 0.20, 0.20, 0.20, 0.20,
   0.20, 0.20, 0.20, 0.20, 0.20,
   0.20, 0.20, 0.20, 0.20, 0.20,
   0.20, 0.20, 0.20, 0.20, 0.20,
   0.20, 0.20, 0.20, 0.20, 0.20,
   0.20, 0.20, 0.20, 0.20, 0.20,
   0.20, 0.20, 0.20, 0.20, 0.20,
   0.20, 0.20, 0.20, 0.20, 0.20
```

> **Don't Do It**
> Although this array is usable, it is repetitious, prone to error, and difficult to use.

Figure 6-13   Usable—but inefficient—discount array
© 2015 Cengage Learning

A better approach is to create two parallel arrays, each with four elements, as shown in Figure 6-14. Each discount rate is listed once in the DISCOUNTS array, and the low end of each quantity range is listed in the QUAN_LIMITS array.

```
num DISCOUNTS[4]    =   0, 0.10, 0.15, 0.20
num QUAN_LIMITS[4] = 0,    9,   13,   26
```

Figure 6-14   Parallel arrays to use for determining discount
© 2015 Cengage Learning

To find the correct discount for any customer's ordered quantity, you can start with the *last* quantity range limit (QUAN_LIMITS[3]). If the quantity ordered is at least that value, 26, the loop is never entered and the customer gets the highest discount rate (DISCOUNTS[3], or 20 percent). If the quantity ordered is not at least QUAN_LIMITS[3]—that is, if it is less than 26—then you reduce the subscript and check to see if the quantity is at least QUAN_LIMITS[2], or 13. If so, the customer receives DISCOUNTS[2], or 15 percent, and so on. Figure 6-15 shows a program that accepts a customer's quantity ordered and determines the appropriate discount rate.

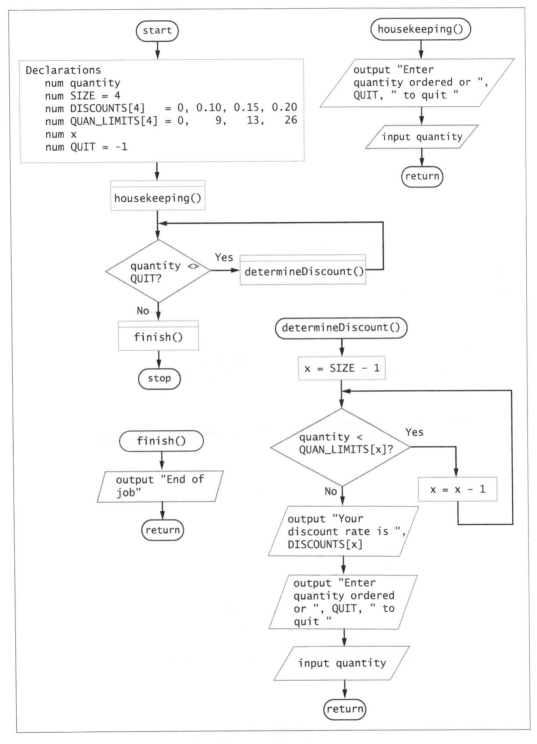

Figure 6-15 Program that determines discount rate (*continues*)

(continued)

```
start
   Declarations
      num quantity
      num SIZE = 4
      num DISCOUNTS[4] =   0, 0.10, 0.15, 0.20
      num QUAN_LIMITS[4] = 0,    9,   13,   26
      num x
      num QUIT = -1
   housekeeping()
   while quantity <> QUIT
      determineDiscount()
   endwhile
   finish()
stop

housekeeping()
   output "Enter quantity ordered or ", QUIT, " to quit "
   input quantity
return

determineDiscount()
   x = SIZE - 1
   while quantity < QUAN_LIMITS[x]
      x = x - 1
   endwhile
   output "Your discount rate is ", DISCOUNTS[x]
   output "Enter quantity ordered or ", QUIT, " to quit "
   input quantity
return

finish()
   output "End of job"
return
```

Figure 6-15   Program that determines discount rate
© 2015 Cengage Learning

An alternate approach to the one taken in Figure 6-15 is to store the high end of every range in an array. Then you start with the *lowest* element and check for values *less than or equal to* each array element value.

When using an array to store range limits, you use a loop to make a series of comparisons that would otherwise require many separate decisions. The program that determines customer discount rates in Figure 6-15 requires fewer instructions than one that does not use an array, and modifications to the program will be easier to make in the future.

Remaining within Array Bounds

To ensure that valid subscripts are used with an array, you must understand two related concepts:

- The array's size
- The bounds of usable subscripts

Understanding Array Size

Every array has a finite size. You can think of an array's size in one of two ways—either by the number of elements in the array or by the number of bytes in the array. Arrays are always composed of elements of the same data type, and elements of the same data type always occupy the same number of bytes of memory, so the number of bytes in an array is always a multiple of the number of elements in an array. For example, in Java, integers occupy 4 bytes of memory, so an array of 10 integers occupies exactly 40 bytes.

 For a complete discussion of bytes and how they measure computer memory, read Appendix A.

Understanding Subscript Bounds

In every programming language, when you access data stored in an array you must use a subscript containing a value that accesses memory occupied by the array. If you do, your subscript is **in bounds**; if you do not, your subscript is **out of bounds**.

A subscript accesses an array element using arithmetic. An array name is a memory address and a subscript indicates the value that should be multiplied by the data type size to calculate the subscript's element address. For example, assume that a `prices` array is stored at memory location 4000, as shown in Figure 6-16, and assume that your computer stores numeric variables using four bytes each. As the figure shows, element 0 is at memory location 4000 + 0 * 4, or 4000, element 1 is at memory location 4000 + 1 * 4, or 4004, and element 2 is at memory location 4000 + 2 * 4, or 4008. If you use a subscript that is out of bounds, your program will attempt to access an address that is not part of the array's space.

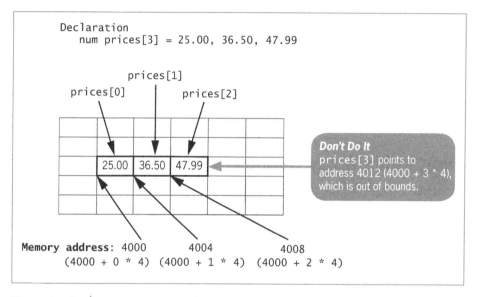

Figure 6-16   An array and its associated memory addresses
© 2015 Cengage Learning

A common error by beginning programmers is to forget that array subscripts start with 0. If you assume that an array's first subscript is 1, you will always be "off by one" in your array manipulation. For example, if you try to manipulate a 10-element array using subscripts 1 through 10, you will commit two errors: You will fail to access the first element that uses subscript 0, and you will attempt to access an extra element at position 10 when the highest usable subscript is 9.

For example, examine the program in Figure 6-17. The program accepts a numeric value for `monthNum` and displays the name associated with that month. The logic in Figure 6-17 makes a questionable assumption: that every number entered by the user is a valid month number.

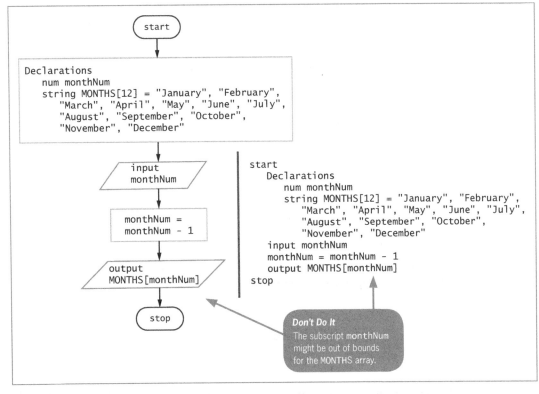

Figure 6-17 Determining the month string from a user's numeric entry
© 2015 Cengage Learning

In the program in Figure 6-17, notice that 1 is subtracted from monthNum before it is used as a subscript. Although January is the first month in the year, its name occupies the location in the array with the 0 subscript. With values that seem naturally to start with 1, like month numbers, some programmers would prefer to create a 13-element array and simply never use the zero-position element. That way, each "natural" month number would be the correct value to access its data without subtracting. Other programmers dislike wasting memory by creating an extra, unused array element. Although workable programs can be created with or without the extra array element, professional programmers should follow the conventions and preferences of their colleagues and managers.

In Figure 6-17, if the user enters a number that is too small or too large, one of two things will happen depending on the programming language you use. When you use a subscript value that is negative or higher than the highest allowed subscript:

- Some programming languages will stop execution of the program and issue an error message.

- Other programming languages will not issue an error message but will access a value in a memory location that is outside the area occupied by the array. That area might contain garbage, or worse, it accidentally might contain the name of an incorrect month.

Either way, a logical error occurs. Users enter incorrect data frequently; a good program should be able to handle the mistake and not allow the subscript to be out of bounds.

 A user might enter an invalid number or might not enter a number at all. In Chapter 5, you learned that many languages have a built-in method with a name like isNumeric() that can test for such mistakes.

You can improve the program in Figure 6-17 by adding a test that ensures the subscript used to access the array is within the array bounds. If you find that the input value is not between 1 and 12 inclusive, you might take one of the following approaches:

- Display an error message and end the program.

- Use a default value for the month. For example, when an entered month is invalid, you might want to assume that it is December.

- Continuously reprompt the user for a new value until it is valid.

The way you handle an invalid month depends on the requirements of your program as spelled out by your user, supervisor, or company policy.

TWO TRUTHS & A LIE

Remaining within Array Bounds

1. Elements in an array frequently are different data types, so calculating the amount of memory the array occupies is difficult.

2. If you attompt to access an array with a subscript that is too small, some programming languages will stop execution of the program and issue an error message.

3. If you attempt to access an array with a subscript that is too large, some programming languages access an incorrect memory location outside the array bounds.

The false statement is #1. Array elements are always the same data type, and elements of the same data type always occupy the same number of bytes of memory, so the number of bytes in an array is always a multiple of the number of elements in an array.

Using a for Loop to Process an Array

In Chapter 5, you learned about the for loop—a loop that, in a single statement, initializes a loop control variable, compares it to a limit, and alters it. The for loop is a particularly convenient tool when working with arrays because you frequently need to process every element of an array from beginning to end. As with a while loop, when you use a for loop, you must be careful to stay within array bounds, remembering that the highest usable array subscript is one less than the size of the array. Figure 6-18 shows a for loop that correctly displays all of a company's department names that are stored in an array declared as DEPTS. Notice that dep is incremented through one less than the number of departments because with a five-item array, the subscripts you can use are 0 through 4.

```
start
   Declarations
      num dep
      num SIZE = 5
      string DEPTS[SIZE] = "Accounting", "Personnel",
         "Technical", "Customer Service", "Marketing"
   for dep = 0 to SIZE - 1 step 1
      output DEPTS[dep]
   endfor
stop
```

Figure 6-18 Pseudocode that uses a for loop to display an array of department names
© 2015 Cengage Learning

The loop in Figure 6-18 is slightly inefficient because, as it executes five times, the subtraction operation that deducts 1 from SIZE occurs each time. Five subtraction operations do not consume much computer power or time, but in a loop that processes thousands or millions of array elements, the program's efficiency would be compromised. Figure 6-19 shows a superior solution. A new constant called ARRAY_LIMIT is calculated once, then used repeatedly in the comparison operation to determine when to stop cycling through the array.

```
start
   Declarations
      num dep
      num SIZE = 5
      num ARRAY_LIMIT = SIZE - 1
      string DEPTS[SIZE] = "Accounting", "Personnel",
         "Technical", "Customer Service", "Marketing"
   for dep = 0 to ARRAY_LIMIT step 1
      output DEPTS[dep]
   endfor
stop
```

Figure 6-19 Pseudocode that uses a more efficient for loop to output department names
© 2015 Cengage Learning

TWO TRUTHS & A LIE

Using a `for` Loop to Process an Array

1. The `for` loop is a particularly convenient tool when working with arrays because initializing, testing, and altering a loop control variable are coded together.

2. You frequently need to process every element of an array from beginning to end in a linear fashion.

3. One advantage to using a `for` loop to process array elements is that you need not be concerned with array bounds.

The false statement is #3. As with a `while` loop, when you use a `for` loop, you must be careful to stay within array bounds.

Chapter Summary

- An array is a named series or list of values in computer memory, all of which have the same data type but are differentiated with subscripts. Each array element occupies an area in memory next to, or contiguous to, the others.

- You often can use a variable as a subscript to an array, which allows you to replace multiple nested decisions with many fewer statements.

- Constants can be used to hold an array's size, to represent its values, or as subscripts. Using named constants can make programs easier to understand and maintain.

- Searching through an array to find a value you need involves initializing a subscript, using a loop to test each array element, and setting a flag when a match is found.

- With parallel arrays, each element in one array is associated with the element in the same relative position in the other array.

- When you need to compare a value to a range of values in an array, you can store either the low- or high-end value of each range for comparison.

- When you access data stored in an array, it is important to use a subscript containing a value that accesses memory within the array bounds.

- The `for` loop is a particularly convenient tool when processing every element of an array sequentially.

Key Terms

An **array** is a series or list of values in computer memory, all of which have the same name but are differentiated with special numbers called subscripts.

An **element** is a single data item in an array.

The **size of the array** is the number of elements it can hold.

A **subscript**, also called an **index**, is a number that indicates the position of a particular item within an array.

Populating an array is the act of assigning values to the array elements.

A **linear search** is a search through a list from one end to the other.

A **flag** is a variable that indicates whether some event has occurred.

In **parallel arrays**, each element in one array is associated with the element in the same relative position in the other array(s).

An **indirect relationship** describes the relationship between parallel arrays in which an element in the first array does not directly access its corresponding value in the second array.

A **binary search** is one that starts in the middle of a sorted list, and then determines whether it should continue higher or lower to find a target value.

In bounds describes an array subscript that is within the range of acceptable subscripts for its array.

Out of bounds describes an array subscript that is not within the range of acceptable subscripts for its array.

Exercises

Review Questions

1. A subscript is a(n) _____ .

   a. element in an array

   b. alternate name for an array

   c. number that represents the highest value stored within an array

   d. number that indicates the position of an array element

2. Each element in an array must have the same _____ as the others.

 a. data type

 b. subscript

 c. value

 d. memory location

3. Suppose that you have declared a numeric array named `values` that has 13 elements. Which of the following must be true?

 a. `values[0]` is smaller than `values[1]`

 b. `values[2]` is stored adjacent to `values[4]`

 c. `values[13]` is out of bounds

 d. `values[12]` is the largest value in the array

4. The subscripts of any array are always _____.

 a. integers

 b. fractions

 c. characters

 d. strings of characters

5. Suppose that you have declared a numeric array named `numbers`, and two of its elements are `numbers[1]` and `numbers[4]`. You know that _____.

 a. the two elements hold the same value

 b. the array holds exactly four elements

 c. there are exactly two elements between those two elements

 d. the two elements are at the same memory location

6. Suppose that you have declared a numeric array named `numbers`, and two of its elements are `numbers[1]` and `numbers[4]`. You know that _____.

 a. `numbers[4]` is larger than `numbers[1]`

 b. the array has at least five elements

 c. the array has been initialized

 d. the two elements are three bytes apart in memory

7. Suppose that you want to write a program that inputs customer data and displays a summary of the number of customers who owe more than $1000 each, in each of 12 sales regions. Customer data variables include `name`, `zipCode`, `balanceDue`, and `regionNumber`. At some point during record processing, you would add 1 to an array element whose subscript would be represented by _____.

 a. `name`

 b. `zipCode`

 c. `balanceDue`

 d. `regionNumber`

8. A program contains a seven-element array that holds the names of the days of the week. At the start of the program, you display the day names using a subscript named dayNum. You display the same array values again at the end of the program, where you _____ as a subscript to the array.

   a. must use dayNum

   b. can use dayNum, but can also use another variable

   c. must not use dayNum

   d. must use a numeric constant instead of a variable

9. Suppose that you have declared an array as follows: num values[4] = 0, 0, 0, 0. Which of the following is an allowed operation?

   a. values[2] = 17

   b. input values[0]

   c. values[3] = values[0] + 10

   d. all of the above

10. Suppose that you have declared an array as follows: num values[4] = 0, 0, 0, 0. Which of the following is an allowed operation?

    a. values[4] = 80

    b. values[2] = values[4] - values[0]

    c. output values[3]

    d. all of the above

11. Filling an array with values during a program's execution is known as _____ the array.

    a. executing

    b. colonizing

    c. populating

    d. declaring

12. A _____ is a variable that can be set to indicate whether some event has occurred.

    a. subscript

    b. banner

    c. counter

    d. flag

13. What do you call two arrays in which each element in one array is associated with the element in the same relative position in the other array?

    a. cohesive arrays

    b. parallel arrays

    c. hidden arrays

    d. perpendicular arrays

14. In most modern programming languages, the highest subscript you should use with a 12-element array is _____.

    a. 10

    b. 11

    c. 12

    d. 13

15. Parallel arrays _____.

   a. frequently have an indirect relationship
   b. never have an indirect relationship
   c. must be the same data type

   d. must not be the same data type

16. Each element in a seven-element array can hold _____ value(s).

   a. one   c. at least seven
   b. seven   d. an unlimited number of

17. After the annual dog show in which the Barkley Dog Training Academy awards points to each participant, the academy assigns a status to each dog based on the criteria in Table 6-1.

Points Earned	Level of Achievement
0–5	Good
6–7	Excellent
8–9	Superior
10	Unbelievable

Table 6-1   Barkley Dog Training Academy achievement levels

The academy needs a program that compares a dog's points earned with the grading scale, so that each dog can receive a certificate acknowledging the appropriate level of achievement. Of the following, which set of values would be most useful for the contents of an array used in the program?

   a. 0, 6, 9, 10   c. 5, 7, 9, 10
   b. 5, 7, 8, 10   d. any of the above

18. When you use a subscript value that is negative or higher than the number of elements in an array, _____.

   a. execution of the program stops and an error message is issued
   b. a value in a memory location that is outside the area occupied by the array will be accessed
   c. a value in a memory location that is outside the area occupied by the array will be accessed, but only if the value is the correct data type
   d. the resulting action depends on the programming language used

19. In every array, a subscript is out of bounds when it is _____ .

    a. negative   c. 1
    b. 0   d. 999

20. You can access every element of an array using a _____ .

    a. `while` loop   c. both of the above
    b. `for` loop   d. none of the above

Programming Exercises

1. a. Design the logic for a program that allows a user to enter 12 numbers, then displays them in the reverse order of entry.

   b. Modify the reverse-display program so that the user can enter any amount of numbers up to 12 until a sentinel value is entered.

2. a. Design the logic for a program that allows a user to enter 12 numbers, then displays each number and its difference from the numeric average of the numbers entered.

   b. Modify the program in Exercise 2a so that the user can enter any amount of numbers up to 12 until a sentinel value is entered.

3. a. Design the logic for a program that allows a user to enter 12 numbers, then displays all of the numbers, the largest number, and the smallest.

   b. Modify the program in Exercise 3a so that the user can enter any amount of numbers up to 12 until a sentinel value is entered.

4. a. Registration workers at a conference for authors of children's books have collected data about conference participants, including the number of books each author has written and the target age of their readers. The participants have written from 1 to 40 books each, and target readers' ages range from 0 through 16. Design a program that continuously accepts an author's name, number of books written, and target reader age until a sentinel value is entered. Then display a list of how many participants have written each number of books (1 through 40).

   b. Modify the author registration program so that the output is a list of how many participants have written 1 to 5 books, 6 to 12 books, and 13 or more books.

   c. Modify the author registration program so that the output is a count of the number of books written for each of the following age groups: under 3, 3 through 7, 8 through 10, 11 through 13, and 14 and older.

5. a. The Downdog Yoga Studio offers five types of classes, as shown in Table 6-2. Design a program that accepts a number representing a class and then displays the name of the class.

   b. Modify the Downdog Yoga Studio program so that numeric class requests can be entered continuously until a sentinel value is entered. Then display each class number, name, and a count of the number of requests for each class.

Class Number	Class Name
1	Yoga 1
2	Yoga 2
3	Children's Yoga
4	Prenatal Yoga
5	Senior Yoga

Table 6-2   Downdog Yoga Studio classes

6. a. Watson Elementary School contains 30 classrooms numbered 1 through 30. Each classroom can contain any number of students up to 35. Each student takes an achievement test at the end of the school year and receives a score from 0 through 100. Write a program that accepts data for each student in the school—student ID, classroom number, and score on the achievement test. Design a program that lists the total points scored for each of the 30 classrooms.

   b. Modify the Watson Elementary School program so that the average of the test scores is output for each classroom, rather than total scores for each classroom.

7. The Jumpin' Jive coffee shop charges $2.00 for a cup of coffee and offers the add-ins shown in Table 6-3.

   Design the logic for an application that allows a user to enter ordered add-ins continuously until a sentinel value is entered. After each item, display its price or the message *Sorry, we do not carry that* as output. After all items have been entered, display the total price for the order.

Product	Price ($)
Whipped cream	0.89
Cinnamon	0.25
Chocolate sauce	0.59
Amaretto	1.50
Irish whiskey	1.75

Table 6-3   Add-in list for Jumpin' Jive coffee shop

8. Design the application logic for a company that wants a report containing a breakdown of payroll by department. Input includes each employee's department number, hourly salary, and number of hours worked. The output is a list of the seven departments in the company and the total gross payroll (rate

Department Number	Department Name
1	Personnel
2	Marketing
3	Manufacturing
4	Computer Services
5	Sales
6	Accounting
7	Shipping

Table 6-4   Department numbers and names

times hours) for each department. The department names are shown in Table 6-4.

Weekly Gross Pay ($)	Withholding Percentage (%)
0.00–300.00	10
300.01–550.00	13
550.01–800.00	16
800.01 and up	20

Table 6-5 Withholding percentage based on gross pay

9. Design a program that computes pay for employees. Allow a user to continuously input employees' names until an appropriate sentinel value is entered. Also input each employee's hourly wage and hours worked. Compute each employee's gross pay (hours times rate), withholding tax percentage (based on Table 6-5), withholding tax amount, and net pay (gross pay minus withholding tax). Display all the results for each employee. After the last employee has been entered, display the sum of all the hours worked, the total gross payroll, the total withholding for all employees, and the total net payroll.

10. Countrywide Tours conducts sightseeing trips for groups from its home base in Iowa. Create an application that continuously accepts tour data, including a three-digit tour number; the numeric month, day, and year values representing the tour start date; the number of travelers taking the tour; and a numeric code that represents the destination. As data is entered for each tour, verify that the month, day, year, and destination code are valid; if any of these is not valid, continue to prompt the user until valid data is entered. The valid destination codes are shown in Table 6-6.

Code	Destination	Price per Person ($)
1	Chicago	300.00
2	Boston	480.00
3	Miami	1050.00
4	San Francisco	1300.00

Table 6-6 Countrywide Tours codes and prices

Number of Tourists	Discount per Tourist ($)
1–5	0
6–12	75
13–20	125
21–50	200
51 and over	300

Table 6-7 Countrywide Tours discounts

Design the logic for an application that outputs each tour number, validated start date, destination code, destination name, number of travelers, gross total price for the tour, and price for the tour after discount. The gross total price is the tour price per guest times the number of travelers. The final price includes a discount for each person in larger tour groups, based on Table 6-7.

11.   a. *Daily Life Magazine* wants an analysis of the demographic characteristics of its readers. The marketing department has collected reader survey records containing the age, gender, marital status, and annual income of readers. Design an application that allows a user to enter reader data and, when data entry is complete, produces a count of readers by age groups as follows: under 20, 20–29, 30–39, 40–49, and 50 and older.

      b. Modify the *Daily Life Magazine* program so that it produces a count of readers by gender within age group—that is, under-20 females, under-20 males, and so on.

      c. Modify the *Daily Life Magazine* program so that it produces a count of readers by income groups as follows: under $30,000, $30,000–$49,999, $50,000–$69,999, and $70,000 and up.

12.   Glen Ross Vacation Property Sales employs seven salespeople, as shown in Table 6-8.

When a salesperson makes a sale, a record is created, including the date, time, and dollar amount of the sale. The time is expressed in hours and minutes, based on a 24-hour clock. The sale amount is expressed in whole dollars. Salespeople earn a commission that differs for each sale, based on the rate schedule in Table 6-9.

Design an application that produces each of the following:

a. A list of each salesperson number, name, total sales, and total commissions

b. A list of each month of the year as both a number and a word (for example, *01 January*), and the total sales for the month for all salespeople

c. A list of total sales as well as total commissions earned by all salespeople for each of the following time frames, based on hour of the day: 00–05, 06–12, 13–18, and 19–23

ID Number	Salesperson Name
103	Darwin
104	Kratz
201	Shulstad
319	Fortune
367	Wickert
388	Miller
435	Vick

Table 6-8   Glen Ross salespeople

Sale Amount ($)	Commission Rate (%)
0–50,999	4
51,000–125,999	5
126,000–200,999	6
201,000 and up	7

Table 6-9   Glen Ross commission schedule

13. a. Design an application in which the number of days for each month in the year is stored in an array. (For example, January has 31 days, February has 28, and so on. Assume that the year is not a leap year.) Display 12 sentences in the same format for each month; for example, the sentence displayed for January is *Month 1 has 31 days*.

   b. Modify the months and days program to contain a parallel array that stores month names. Display 12 sentences in the same format; for example, the first sentence is *January has 31 days*.

   c. Modify the months and days program to prompt the user for a month number and display the corresponding sentence in the same format as in Exercise 13b.

   d. Prompt a user to enter a birth month and day, and continue to prompt until the day entered is in range for the month. Compute the day's numeric position in the year. (For example, February 2 is day 33.) Then, using parallel arrays, find and display the traditional Zodiac sign for the date. For example, the sign for February 2 is Aquarius.

Performing Maintenance

1. A file named MAINTENANCE06-01.txt is included with your downloadable student files. Assume that this program is a working program in your organization and that it needs modifications as described in the comments (lines that begin with two slashes) at the beginning of the file. Your job is to alter the program to meet the new specifications.

Find the Bugs

1. Your downloadable files for Chapter 6 include DEBUG06-01.txt, DEBUG06-02.txt, and DEBUG06-03.txt. Each file starts with some comments that describe the problem. Comments are lines that begin with two slashes (//). Following the comments, each file contains pseudocode that has one or more bugs you must find and correct.

2. Your downloadable files for Chapter 6 include a file named DEBUG06-04.jpg that contains a flowchart with syntax and/or logical errors. Examine the flowchart and then find and correct all the bugs.

Game Zone

1. Create the logic for a Magic 8 Ball game in which the user enters a question such as *What does my future hold?* The computer randomly selects one of eight possible vague answers, such as *It remains to be seen*.

2. Create the logic for an application that contains an array of 10 multiple-choice questions related to your favorite hobby. Each question contains three answer

choices. Also create a parallel array that holds the correct answer to each question—A, B, or C. Display each question and verify that the user enters only A, B, or C as the answer—if not, keep prompting the user until a valid response is entered. If the user responds to a question correctly, display *Correct!*; otherwise, display *The correct answer is* and the letter of the correct answer. After the user answers all the questions, display the number of correct and incorrect answers.

3. a. Create the logic for a dice game. The application randomly "throws" five dice for the computer and five dice for the player. After each random throw, store the results in an array. The application displays all the values, which can be from 1 to 6 inclusive for each die. Decide the winner based on the following hierarchy of die values. Any higher combination beats a lower one; for example, five of a kind beats four of a kind.

   - Five of a kind

   - Four of a kind

   - Three of a kind

   - A pair

For this game, the numeric dice values do not count. For example, if both players have three of a kind, it's a tie, no matter what the values of the three dice are. Additionally, the game does not recognize a full house (three of a kind plus two of a kind). Figure 6-20 shows how the game might be played in a command-line environment.

Figure 6-20 Typical execution of the dice game

   b. Improve the dice game so that when both players have the same number of matching dice, the higher value wins. For example, two 6s beats two 5s.

4. Design the logic for the game Hangman, in which the user guesses letters in a hidden word. Store the letters of a word in an array of characters. Display a dash for each missing letter. Allow the user to continuously guess a letter until all the letters in the word are guessed correctly. As the user enters each guess, display the word again, filling in the guessed letter if it was correct. For example, if the hidden word

is *computer*, first display a series of eight dashes: - - - - - - - -. After the user guesses *p*, the display becomes - - -*p*- - - -. Make sure that when a user makes a correct guess, all the matching letters are filled in. For example, if the word is *banana* and the user guesses *a*, all three *a* characters should be filled in.

5. Create two parallel arrays that represent a standard deck of 52 playing cards. One array is numeric and holds the values 1 through 13 (representing Ace, 2 through 10, Jack, Queen, and King). The other array is a string array that holds suits (Clubs, Diamonds, Hearts, and Spades). Create the arrays so that all 52 cards are represented. Then, create a War card game that randomly selects two cards (one for the player and one for the computer) and declares a winner or a tie based on the numeric value of the two cards. The game should last for 26 rounds and use a full deck with no repeated cards. For this game, assume that the lowest card is the Ace. Display the values of the player's and computer's cards, compare their values, and determine the winner. When all the cards in the deck are exhausted, display a count of the number of times the player wins, the number of times the computer wins, and the number of ties.

Here are some hints:

- Start by creating an array of all 52 playing cards.

- Select a random number for the deck position of the player's first card and assign the card at that array position to the player.

- Move every higher-positioned card in the deck "down" one to fill in the gap. In other words, if the player's first random number is 49, select the card at position 49 (both the numeric value and the string), move the card that was in position 50 to position 49, and move the card that was in position 51 to position 50. Only 51 cards remain in the deck after the player's first card is dealt, so the available-card array is smaller by one.

- In the same way, randomly select a card for the computer and "remove" the card from the deck.

Up for Discussion

1. A train schedule is an everyday, real-life example of an array. Identify at least four more.

2. Every element in an array always has the same data type. Why is this necessary?

Advanced Modularization Techniques

In this chapter, you will learn about:

- ◎ The parts of a method
- ◎ Methods with no parameters
- ◎ Methods that require parameters
- ◎ Methods that return a value
- ◎ Passing arrays to methods
- ◎ Overloading methods
- ◎ Using predefined methods
- ◎ Method design issues, including implementation hiding, cohesion, and coupling
- ◎ Recursion

The Parts of a Method

In object-oriented programming languages such as Java and C#, modules are most often called *methods*. In Chapter 2, you learned about many features of methods and much of the vocabulary associated with them. For example:

- A **method** is a program module that contains a series of statements that carry out a task; you can invoke or call a method from another program or method. The calling program or method is the called method's **client**.

- Any program can contain an unlimited number of methods, and each method can be called an unlimited number of times.

- The rules for naming methods are different in every programming language, but they often are similar to the language's rules for variable names. In this text, method names are followed by a set of parentheses.

- A method must include a **method header** (sometimes also called the *method declaration*), which contains identifying information about the method.

- A method includes a **method body**. The body contains the method's **implementation**—the statements that carry out the method's tasks.

- A **method return statement** returns control to the calling method after a method executes. Although methods with multiple `return` statements are allowed in many programming languages, that practice is not recommended. Structured programming requires that a method must contain a single entry point and a single exit point. Therefore, a method should have only one `return` statement, and it should be the last statement.

- Variables and constants can be declared within a method. A data item declared in a method is **local** to that method, meaning it is in scope, or recognized only within that method.

- The opposite of local is global. When a data item is known to all of a program's methods or modules, it is a **global** data item. In general, programmers prefer local data items because when data is contained within the method that uses it, the method is more portable and less prone to error. In Chapter 2, you learned that when a method is described as *portable*, it can easily be moved to another application and used there.

- Methods can have parameter lists that provide details about data passed into methods. These lists are not required.

- Methods have return types that provide information about data the method returns. In some languages, like C++, a default return type is implied if no return type is listed.

Quick Reference 9-1 shows important parts of a method. You learn more about these parts in the rest of this chapter.

QUICK REFERENCE 9-1 The Anatomy of a Method

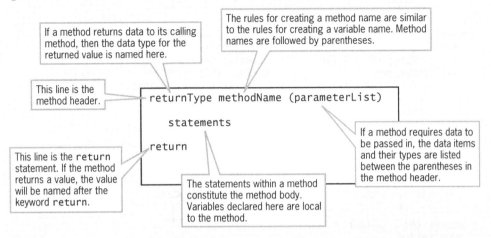

If a method returns data to its calling method, then the data type for the returned value is named here.

The rules for creating a method name are similar to the rules for creating a variable name. Method names are followed by parentheses.

This line is the method header.

```
returnType methodName (parameterList)

    statements

    return
```

If a method requires data to be passed in, the data items and their types are listed between the parentheses in the method header.

This line is the `return` statement. If the method returns a value, the value will be named after the keyword `return`.

The statements within a method constitute the method body. Variables declared here are local to the method.

TWO TRUTHS & A LIE

The Parts of a Method

1. A program can contain an unlimited number of methods, but each method can be called only once.

2. A method includes a header and a body.

3. Variables and constants are in scope within, or local to, only the method in which they are declared.

The false statement is #1. Each method can be called an unlimited number of times.

Using Methods with no Parameters

Figure 9-1 shows a program that allows a user to enter a preferred language (English or Spanish) and then, using the chosen language, asks the user to enter his or her weight. The program then calculates the user's weight on the moon as 16.6 percent of the user's weight on Earth. The main program contains declarations for two variables and a constant. The program calls the displayInstructions() method, which contains its own local variable and constants that are invisible (and therefore not available) to the main program. The method prompts the user for a language indicator and displays a prompt in the selected language. Figure 9-2 shows a typical program execution in a command-line environment.

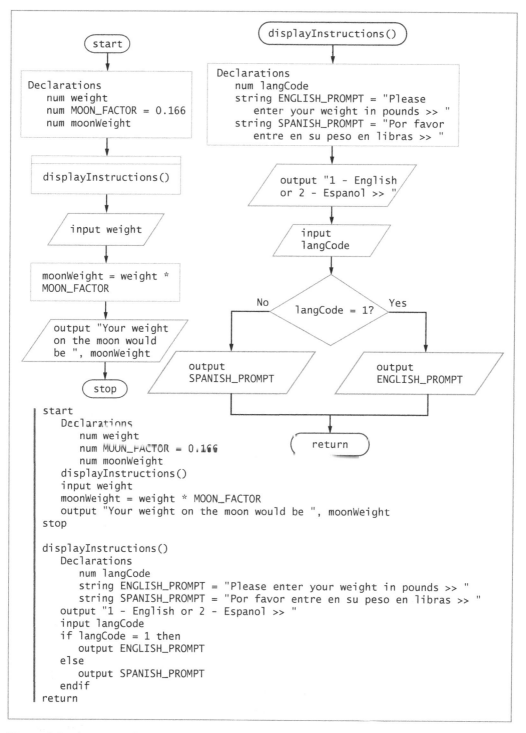

Figure 9-1   A program that calculates the user's weight on the moon
© 2015 Cengage Learning

In Chapter 2, you learned that this book uses a rectangle with a horizontal stripe across the top to represent a method call statement in a flowchart. Some programmers prefer to use a rectangle with two vertical stripes at the sides, and you should use that convention if your organization prefers it. This book reserves the shape with two vertical stripes to represent a method from a library that is external to the program.

Figure 9-2   Output of moon weight calculator program in Figure 9-1
© 2015 Cengage Learning

In Figure 9-1, the main program and the called method each contain only data items that are needed at the local level. The main program does not know about or have access to the variables and constants langCode, ENGLISH_PROMPT, and SPANISH_PROMPT declared locally within the method. Similarly, in modern programming languages, the displayInstructions() method does not have knowledge of or access to weight, MOON_FACTOR, or moonWeight, which are declared in the main program. In this program, there is no need for either method to know about the data in the other. However, sometimes two or more parts of a program require access to the same data. When methods must share data, you can pass the data into methods and return data out of them.

In this chapter, you learn how to pass data into and receive data from called methods. When you call a method from a program or other method, you should know four things:

- What the method does in general—in other words, you should know why you are calling the method

- The name of the called method

- What type of information to send to the method, if any

- What type of return data to expect from the method, if any

TWO TRUTHS & A LIE

Using Methods with no Parameters

1. When a method contains variable declarations, those variables are local to the method.

2. The values of variables declared locally within a method can be used by a calling method, but not by other methods.

3. In modern languages, the usual methodology is to declare variables locally in their methods and pass their values to other methods as needed.

The false statement is #2. When a variable is declared locally within a method, its value cannot be used by other methods. If its value is needed by a calling method, the value must be returned from the method.

Creating Methods that Require Parameters

Some methods require information to be sent in from the outside. When a program passes a data item to a method, the data item is an **argument to the method**, or more simply, an argument. When the method receives the data item, it is a **parameter to the method**, or more simply, a parameter. *Parameter* and *argument* are closely related terms. A calling method sends an argument to a called method. A called method accepts the value as its parameter.

If a method could not receive parameters, you would have to use global variables or write an infinite number of methods to cover every possible situation. As a real-life example, when you make a restaurant reservation, you do not need to employ a different method for every date of the year at every possible time of day. Rather, you can supply the date and time as information to the person who carries out the method. The method that records the reservation is carried out in the same manner, no matter what date and time are supplied.

As a programming example, if you design a square() method that multiplies a numeric value by itself, you should supply the method with a parameter that represents the value to be squared, rather than developing a square1() method that squares the value 1, a square2() method that squares the value 2, and so on. To call a square() method that accepts a parameter, you might write a statement that uses a constant, like square(17) or square(86), or one that uses a variable, like square(inputValue), and let the method use whatever argument you send.

When you write the declaration for a method that can receive a parameter, you must provide a **parameter list** that includes the following items for the parameter within the method declaration's parentheses:

- The type of the parameter

- A local name for the parameter

Later in this chapter, you learn to create parameter lists with more than one parameter. A method's name and parameter list constitute the method's **signature**.

For example, suppose that you decide to improve the moon weight program in Figure 9-1 by making the final output more user-friendly and adding the explanatory text in the chosen language. It makes sense that if the user can request a prompt in a specific language, the user would want to see the output explanation in the same language. However, in Figure 9-1, the `langCode` variable is local to the `displayInstructions()` method and therefore cannot be used in the main program. You could rewrite the program by taking several approaches:

- You could rewrite the program without including any methods. That way, you could prompt the user for a language preference and display the prompt and the result in the appropriate language. This approach works, but you would not be taking advantage of the benefits provided by modularization. Those benefits include making the main program more streamlined and abstract, and making the `displayInstructions()` method a self-contained unit that can easily be transported to other programs—for example, applications that might determine a user's weight on Saturn or Mars.

- You could retain the `displayInstructions()` method, but make at least the `langCode` variable global by declaring it outside of any methods. If you took this approach, you would lose some of the portability of the `displayInstructions()` method because everything it used would no longer be contained within the method.

- You could retain the `displayInstructions()` method as is with its own local declarations, but add a section to the main program that also asks the user for a preferred language to display the result. The disadvantage to this approach is that the user must answer the same question twice during one execution of the program.

- You could store the variable that holds the language code in the main program so that it could be used to determine the result language. You could also retain the `displayInstructions()` method, but pass the language code to it so the prompt would appear in the appropriate language. This is the best choice because it employs modularity, which keeps the main program simpler and creates a portable method. A program that uses the method is shown in Figure 9-3, and a typical execution appears in Figure 9-4.

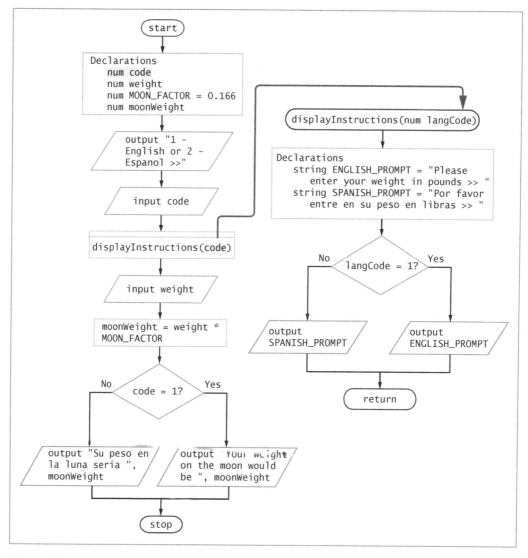

Figure 9-3   Moon weight program that passes an argument to a method *(continues)*

(continued)

```
start
   Declarations
      num code
      num weight
      num MOON_FACTOR = 0.166
      num moonWeight
   output "1 - English or 2 - Espanol >>"
   input code
   displayInstructions(code) ─────────────────┐
   input weight                                │
   moonWeight = weight * MOON_FACTOR           │
   if code = 1 then                            │
      output "Your weight on the moon would be ", moonWeight
   else                                        │
      output "Su peso en la luna sería ", moonWeight
   endif                                       │
stop                                           │
                                               │
displayInstructions(num langCode)◄─────────────┘
   Declarations
      string ENGLISH_PROMPT = "Please enter your weight in pounds >> "
      string SPANISH_PROMPT = "Por favor entre en su peso en libras >> "
   if langCode = 1 then
      output ENGLISH_PROMPT
   else
      output SPANISH_PROMPT
   endif
return
```

Figure 9-3   Moon weight program that passes an argument to a method
© 2015 Cengage Learning

Figure 9-4   Typical execution of moon weight program in Figure 9-3
© 2015 Cengage Learning

In the main program in Figure 9-3, a numeric variable named **code** is declared and the user is prompted for a value. The value then is passed to the **displayInstructions()** method. The value of the language code is stored in two places in memory:

- The main method stores the code in the variable **code** and passes it to **displayInstructions()** as an argument.

- The **displayInstructions()** method accepts the value of the argument **code** as the value of the parameter **langCode**. In other words, within the method, **langCode** takes on the value that **code** had in the main program.

You can think of the parentheses in a method declaration as a funnel into the method; parameters listed there hold values that are "dropped in" to the method.

A variable passed into a method is **passed by value**; that is, a copy of its value is sent to the method and stored in a new memory location accessible to the method. The displayInstructions() method could be called using any numeric value as an argument, whether it is a variable, a named constant, or a literal constant. In other words, suppose that the main program contains the following declarations:

```
num x = 2
num langCode = 2
num SPANISH = 2
```

Then any of the following statements would work to call the displayInstructions() method:

- displayInstructions(x), using a variable

- displayInstructions(langCode), using a different variable

- displayInstructions(SPANISH), using a named constant

- displayInstructions(2), using a literal constant

If the value used as an argument in the method call is a variable or named constant, it might possess the same identifier as the parameter declared in the method header, or it might possess a different identifier. Within a method, the passed variable or named constant is simply a temporary placeholder; it makes no difference what name the variable or constant "goes by" in the calling program.

Each time a method executes, any parameters listed in the method header are redeclared—that is, new memory locations are reserved and named. When the method ends at the return statement, the locally declared parameter variables ceaoo to exist For example, Figure 9-5 shows a program that declares a variable, assigns a value to it, displays it, and sends it to a method. Within the method, the parameter is displayed, altered, and displayed again. When control returns to the main program, the original variable is displayed one last time. As the execution in Figure 9-6 shows, even though the variable in the method was altered, the original variable in the main program retains its starting value because it never was altered; it occupies a different memory address from the variable in the method.

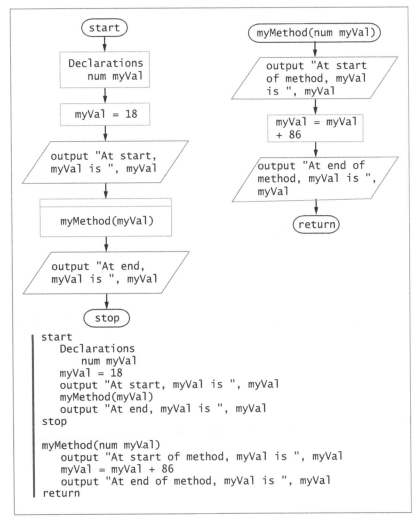

```
start
    Declarations
        num myVal
    myVal = 18
    output "At start, myVal is ", myVal
    myMethod(myVal)
    output "At end, myVal is ", myVal
stop

myMethod(num myVal)
    output "At start of method, myVal is ", myVal
    myVal = myVal + 86
    output "At end of method, myVal is ", myVal
return
```

Figure 9-5 A program that calls a method in which the argument and parameter have the same identifier

© 2015 Cengage Learning

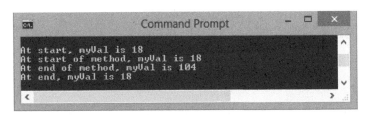

Figure 9-6 Execution of the program in Figure 9-5

© 2015 Cengage Learning

Watch the video *Methods with a Parameter*.

Creating Methods that Require Multiple Parameters

You create and use a method with multiple parameters by doing the following:

- You list the arguments within the method call, separated by commas.

- You list a data type and local identifier for each parameter within the method header's parentheses, separating each declaration with a comma. Even if multiple parameters are the same data type, the type must be repeated with each parameter.

The arguments sent to a method in a method call are its **actual parameters**. The variables in the method declaration that accept the values from the actual parameters are **formal parameters**.

For example, suppose that you want to create a `computeTax()` method that calculates a tax on any value passed into it. You can create a method to which you pass two values—the amount to be taxed as well as a rate by which to tax it. Figure 9-7 shows a method that accepts two such parameters.

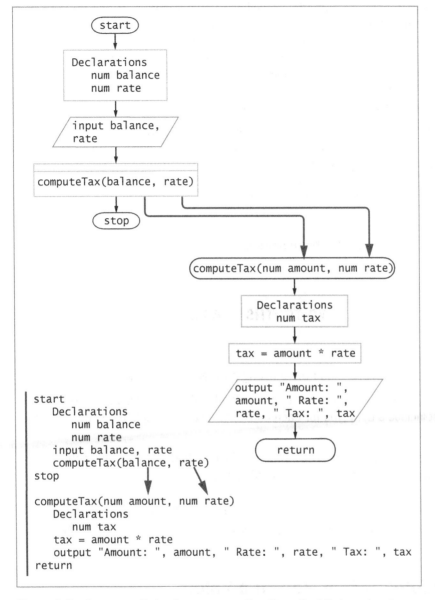

Figure 9-7 A program that calls a `computeTax()` method that requires two parameters
© 2015 Cengage Learning

 In Figure 9-7, notice that one of the arguments to the method has the same name as the corresponding method parameter, and the other has a different name from its corresponding parameter. Each could have the same identifier as its counterpart, or all could be different. Each identifier is local to its own method.

In Figure 9-7, two parameters (num amount and num rate) appear within the parentheses in the method header. A comma separates each parameter, and each requires its own declared data type (in this case, both are numeric) as well as its own identifier. When multiple values are passed to a method, they are accepted into the parameters in the order in which they are passed. You can write a method so that it takes any number of parameters in any order. However, when you call a method, the arguments you send to the method must match in order—both in number and in type—the parameters listed in the method declaration. A call of computeTax(rate, balance) instead of computeTax(balance, rate) would result in incorrect values being displayed in the output statement.

If method arguments are the same type—for example, two numeric arguments—passing them to a method in the wrong order results in a logical error. The program will compile and execute, but will produce incorrect results in most cases. If a method expects arguments of diverse types—for example, a number and a string—then passing arguments in the wrong order is a syntax error, and the program will not compile.

  Watch the video *Methods with Multiple Parameters.*

TWO TRUTHS & A LIE

Creating Methods that Require Parameters

1. A value sent to a method from a calling program is a parameter.

2. When you write the declaration for a method that can receive parameters, you must include a data type for each parameter even if multiple parameters are the same type.

3. When a variable is used as an argument in a method call, it can have the same identifier as the parameter in the method header.

The false statement is #1. A calling method sends an argument; when the method receives the value, it is a parameter.

Creating Methods that Return a Value

A variable declared within a method ceases to exist when the method ends—it goes out of scope. When you want to retain a value that exists when a method ends, you can return the value from the method to the calling method. When a method returns a value, the method must have a **return type** that matches the data type of the returned value. A return type can be any type, which includes num and string, as well as other types specific to the programming language you are using. A method can also return nothing, in which case the return type is void, and the method is a **void method**. (The term *void* means "nothing" or "empty.") A method's return type is known more succinctly as a **method's type**, and it is listed in front of the method name when the method is defined. Previously, this book has not included return types for methods because all the methods have been void. From this point forward, a return type is included with every method header.

 Along with an identifier and parameter list, a return type is part of a method's declaration. A method's return type is not part of its signature, although you might hear some programmers claim that it is. Only the method name and parameter list constitute the signature.

For example, a method that returns the number of hours an employee has worked might have the following header:

```
num getHoursWorked()
```

This method returns a numeric value, so its type is num.

When a method returns a value, you usually want to use the returned value in the calling method, although this is not required. For example, Figure 9-8 shows how a program might use the value returned by the getHoursWorked() method. A variable named hours is declared in the main program. The getHoursWorked() method call is part of an assignment statement. When the method is called, the logical control is transferred to the getHoursWorked() method, which contains a variable named workHours. A value is obtained for this variable, which is returned to the main program where it is assigned to hours. After logical control returns to the main program from the getHoursWorked() method, the method's local variable workHours no longer exists. However, its value has been stored in the main program where, as hours, it can be displayed and used in a calculation.

 As an example of when you might call a method but not use its returned value, consider a method that gets a character from the keyboard and returns its value to the calling program. In some applications, you would want to use the value of the returned characters. However, in other applications, you might want to tell the user to press any key. Then, you could call the method to accept the character from the keyboard, but you would not care which key was pressed or which key value was returned.

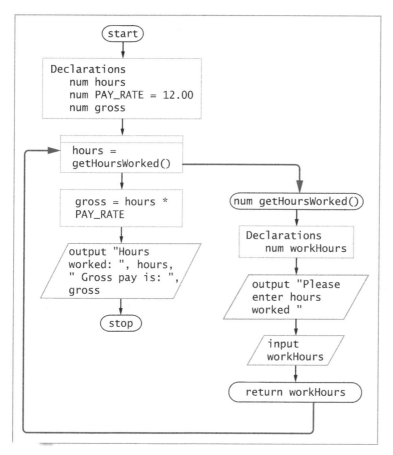

Figure 9-8   A payroll program that calls a method that returns a value
© 2015 Cengage Learning

In Figure 9-8, notice the return type num that precedes the method name in the getHoursWorked() method header. A method's declared return type must match the type of the value used in the return statement; if it does not, the program will not compile. A numeric value is correctly included in the return statement—the last statement in the getHoursWorked() method. When you place a value in a return statement, the value is sent from the called method back to the calling method.

A method's return statement can return one value at most. The returned value can be a variable or a constant. The value can be a simple data type or a complex data type. For example, in Chapter 10 you will learn to create objects, which are more complex data types.

You are not required to assign a method's return value to a variable to use the value. Instead, you can use a method's returned value directly, without storing it. You use a method's value in the same way you would use any variable of the same type. For example, you can output a return value in a statement such as the following:

```
output "Hours worked is ", getHoursWorked()
```

Because getHoursWorked() returns a numeric value, you can use the method call getHoursWorked() in the same way that you would use any simple numeric value. Figure 9-9 shows an example of a program that uses a method's return value directly without storing it. The value of the shaded workHours variable returned from the method is used directly in the calculation of gross in the main program.

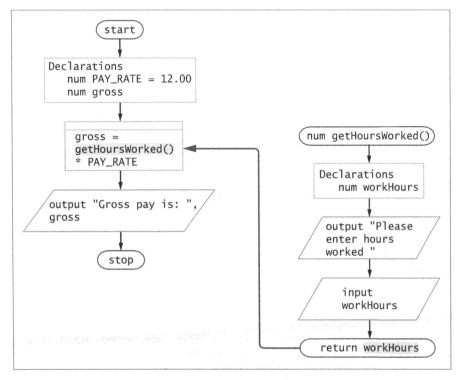

Figure 9-9 A program that uses a method's returned value without storing it
© 2015 Cengage Learning

 When a program needs to use a method's returned value in more than one place, it makes sense to store the returned value in a variable instead of calling the method multiple times. A program statement that calls a method requires more computer time and resources than a statement that does not call any outside methods. Programmers use the term **overhead** to describe any extra time and resources required by an operation.

As mentioned earlier, in most programming languages you technically are allowed to include multiple return statements in a method, but this book does not recommend the practice for most business programs. For example, consider the findLargest() method in Figure 9-10. The method accepts three parameters and returns the largest of the values. Although this method works correctly and you might see this technique used, its style is awkward and not structured. In Chapter 3, you learned that structured logic requires each structure to contain one entry point and one exit point. The return statements in Figure 9-10 violate this convention by leaving decision structures before they are complete. Figure 9-11 shows the

superior and recommended way to handle the problem. In Figure 9-11, the largest value is
stored in a variable. Then, when the nested decision structure is complete, the stored value is
returned in the last method statement.

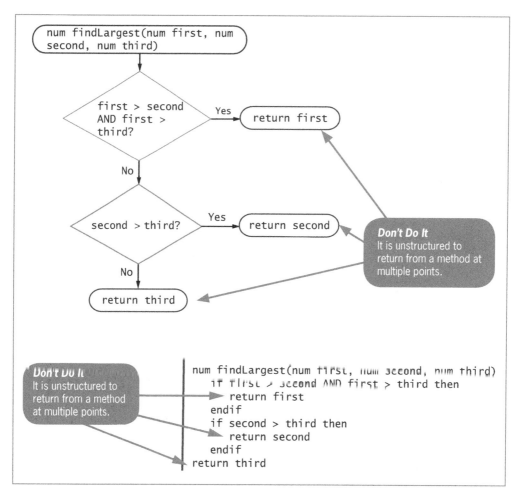

Figure 9-10   Unstructured approach to returning one of several values
© 2015 Cengage Learning

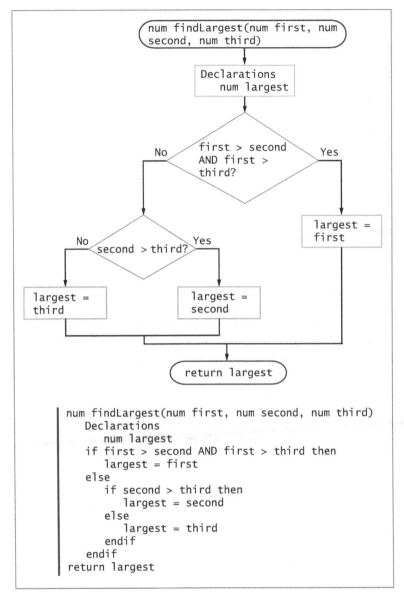

```
num findLargest(num first, num second, num third)
   Declarations
      num largest
   if first > second AND first > third then
      largest = first
   else
      if second > third then
         largest = second
      else
         largest = third
      endif
   endif
return largest
```

Figure 9-11   Recommended, structured approach to returning one of several values
© 2015 Cengage Learning

Using an IPO Chart

When designing methods to use within larger programs, some programmers find it helpful to use an **IPO chart**, a tool that identifies and categorizes each item needed within the method as pertaining to input, processing, or output. For example, consider a method that finds the smallest of three numeric values. When you think about designing this method, you can start by placing each of its components in one of the three processing categories, as shown in Figure 9-12.

Input	Processing	Output
First value Second value Third value	If the first value is smaller than each of the other two, save it as the smallest value; otherwise, if the second value is smaller than the third, save it as the smallest value; otherwise, save the third value as the smallest value	Smallest value

Figure 9-12   IPO chart for the method that finds the smallest of three numeric values
© 2015 Cengage Learning

The IPO chart in Figure 9-12 provides an overview of the processing steps involved in the method. Like a flowchart or pseudocode, an IPO chart is just another tool to help you plan the logic of your programs. Many programmers create an IPO chart only for specific methods in their programs and as an alternative to flowcharting or writing pseudocode. IPO charts provide an overview of input to the method, the processing steps that must occur, and the resulting output. This book emphasizes creating flowcharts and pseudocode, but you can find many more examples of IPO charts on the Web.

TWO TRUTHS & A LIE

Creating Methods that Return a Value

1. The return type for a method can be any type, which includes numeric, character, and string, as well as other more specific types that exist in the programming language you are using.

2. A method's return type must be the same type as one of the method's parameters.

3. You are not required to use a method's returned value.

The false statement is #2. The return type of a method can be any type. The return type must match the type of value in the method's return statement. A method's return type is not required to match any of the method's parameters.

Passing an Array to a Method

In Chapter 6, you learned that you can declare an array to create a list of elements, and that you can use any individual array element in the same manner you would use any single variable of the same type. For example, suppose that you declare a numeric array as follows:

```
num someNums[12]
```

You can subsequently output someNums[0] or perform arithmetic with someNums[11], just as you would for any simple variable that is not part of an array. Similarly, you can pass a single array element to a method in exactly the same manner you would pass a variable or constant.

Consider the program shown in Figure 9-13. This program creates an array of four numeric values and then outputs them. Next, the program calls a method named tripleTheValue() four times, passing each of the array elements in turn. The method outputs the passed value, multiplies it by 3, and outputs it again. Finally, back in the calling program, the four numbers are output again. Figure 9-14 shows an execution of this program in a command-line environment.

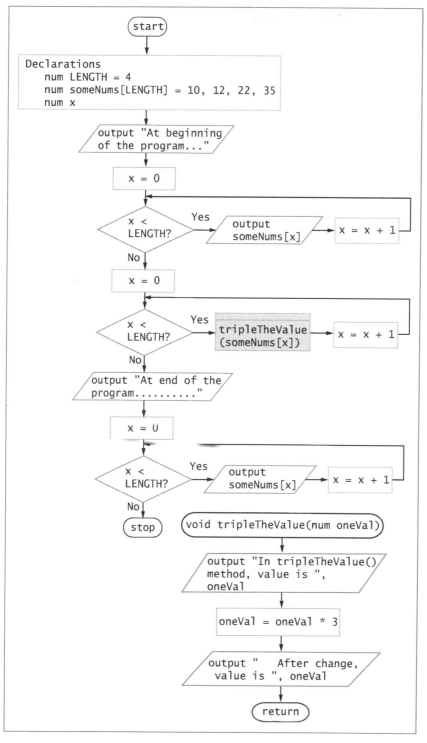

Figure 9-13   PassArrayElement program *(continues)*

(continued)

```
start
   Declarations
      num LENGTH = 4
      num someNums[LENGTH] = 10, 12, 22, 35
      num x
   output "At beginning of the program..."
   x = 0
   while x < LENGTH
      output someNums[x]
      x = x + 1
   endwhile
   x = 0
   while x < LENGTH
      tripleTheValue(someNums[x])
      x = x + 1
   endwhile
   output "At end of the program.........."
   x = 0
   while x < LENGTH
      output someNums[x]
      x = x + 1
   endwhile
stop

void tripleTheValue(num oneVal)
   output "In tripleTheValue() method, value is ", oneVal
   oneVal = oneVal * 3
   output "     After change, value is ", oneVal
return
```

Figure 9-13   PassArrayElement program
© 2015 Cengage Learning

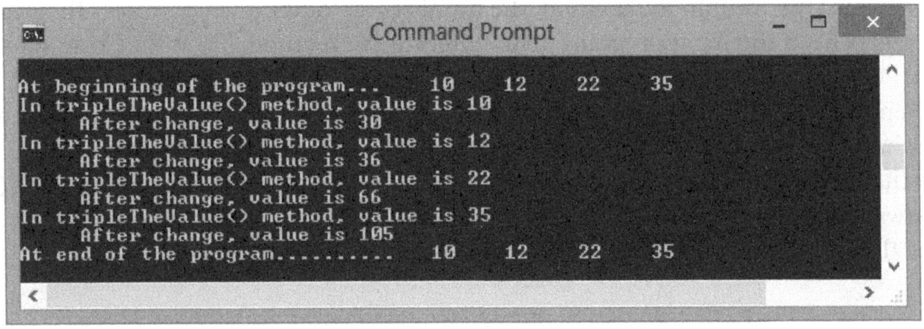

Figure 9-14   Output of the PassArrayElement program
© 2015 Cengage Learning

As you can see in Figure 9-14, the program displays the four original values, then passes each value to the tripleTheValue() method, where it is displayed, multiplied by 3, and displayed again. After the method executes four times, the logic returns to the main program where the four values are displayed again, showing that they are unchanged by the new assignments within `tripleTheValue()`. The `oneVal` variable is local to the `tripleTheValue()` method; therefore, any changes to it are not permanent and are not reflected in the array declared in the main program. Each `oneVal` variable in the `tripleTheValue()` method holds only a copy of the array element passed into the method, and the `oneVal` variable that holds each newly assigned, larger value exists only while the `tripleTheValue()` method is executing. In all respects, a single array element acts just like any single variable of the same type would.

Instead of passing a single array element to a method, you can pass an entire array as an argument. You can indicate that a method parameter must be an array by using the convention of placing square brackets after the data type in the method's parameter list. When you pass an array to a method, changes you make to array elements within the method are permanent; that is, they are reflected in the original array that was sent to the method. Arrays, unlike simple built-in types, are **passed by reference**; the method receives the actual memory address of the array and has access to the actual values in the array elements. The name of an array represents a memory address, and the subscript used with an array name represents an offset from that address.

Some languages, such as Visual Basic, use parentheses after an identifier to indicate an array as a parameter to a method. Many other languages, including Java, C++, and C#, use square brackets after the data type. Because this book uses parentheses following method names, it uses brackets to indicate arrays.

Simple nonarray variables usually are passed to methods by value. Many programming languages provide the means to pass variables by reference as well as by value. The syntax to accomplish this differs among the languages that allow it; you will learn more about this concept when you study a specific language.

The program shown in Figure 9-15 creates an array of four numeric values. After the numbers are output, the entire array is passed to a method named `quadrupleTheValues()`. Within the method header, the parameter is declared as an array by using square brackets after the parameter type. Within the method, the numbers are output, which shows that they retain their values from the main program upon entering the method. Then the array values are multiplied by 4. Even though `quadrupleTheValues()` returns nothing to the calling program, when the program displays the array for the last time within the mainline logic, all of the values have been changed to their new quadrupled values. Figure 9-16 shows an execution of the program. Because arrays are passed by reference, the `quadrupleTheValues()` method "knows" the address of the array declared in the calling program and makes its changes directly to the original array that was declared in the calling program.

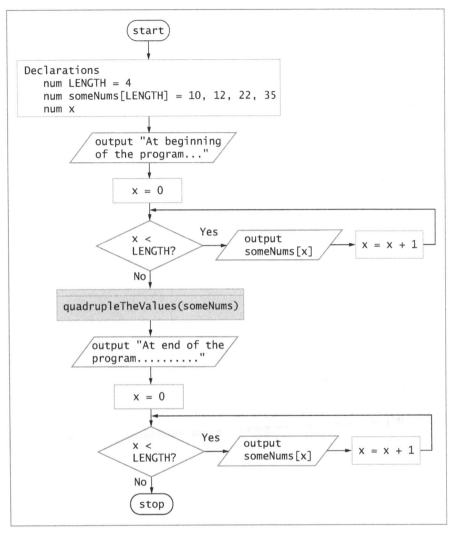

Figure 9-15   PassEntireArray program *(continues)*

(continued)

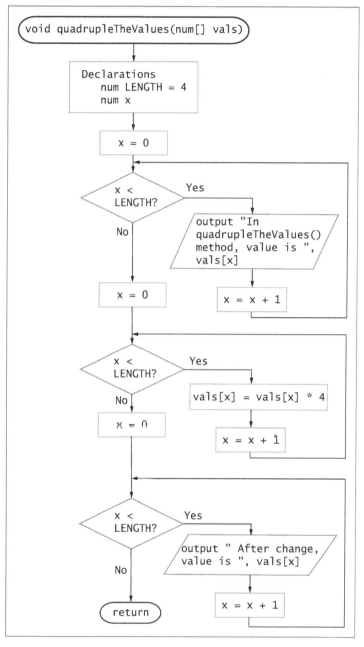

Figure 9-15   `PassEntireArray` program *(continues)*

(continued)

```
start
   Declarations
      num LENGTH = 4
      num someNums[LENGTH] = 10, 12, 22, 35
      num x
   output "At beginning of the program..."
   x = 0
   while x < LENGTH
      output someNums[x]
      x = x + 1
   endwhile
   quadrupleTheValues(someNums)
   output "At end of the program........."
   x = 0
   while x < LENGTH
      output someNums[x]
      x = x + 1
   endwhile
stop

void quadrupleTheValues(num[] vals)
   Declarations
      num LENGTH = 4
      num x
   x = 0
   while x < LENGTH
      output "In quadrupleTheValues() method, value is ", vals[x]
      x = x + 1
   endwhile
   x = 0
   while x < LENGTH
      vals[x] = vals[x] * 4
      x = x + 1
   endwhile
   x = 0
   while x < LENGTH
      output "     After change, value is ", vals[x]
      x = x + 1
   endwhile
return
```

Figure 9-15   PassEntireArray program
© 2015 Cengage Learning

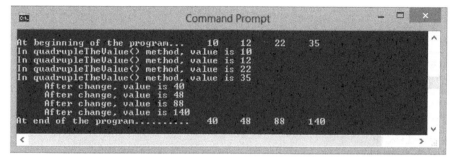

Figure 9-16   Output of the PassEntireArray program
© 2015 Cengage Learning

When an array is a method parameter, the square brackets in the method header remain empty and do not hold a size. The array name that is passed is a memory address that indicates the start of the array. Depending on the language you are working in, you can control the values you use for a subscript to the array in different ways. In some languages, you might also want to pass a constant that indicates the array size to the method. In other languages, you can access the automatically created length field for the array. Either way, the array size itself is never implied when you use the array name. The array name only indicates the starting point from which subscripts will be used.

TWO TRUTHS & A LIE

Passing an Array to a Method

1. You can pass an entire array as a method's argument.

2. You can indicate that a method parameter must be an array by placing square brackets after the data type in the method's parameter list.

3. Arrays, unlike simple built-in types, are passed by value; the method receives a copy of the original array.

The false statement is #3. Arrays, unlike simple built-in types, are passed by reference; the method receives the actual memory address of the array and has access to the actual values in the array elements.

Overloading Methods

In programming, **overloading** involves supplying diverse meanings for a single identifier. When you use the English language, you frequently overload words. When you say *break a window, break bread, break the bank,* and *take a break,* you describe four very different actions that use different methods and produce different results. However, anyone who speaks English well comprehends your meaning because *break* is understood in the context of the discussion.

 In most programming languages, some operators are overloaded. For example, a + between two values indicates addition, but a single + to the left of a value means the value is positive. The + sign has different meanings based on the arguments used with it.

 Overloading a method is an example of **polymorphism**—the ability of a method to act appropriately according to the context. Literally, *polymorphism* means "many forms."

When you **overload a method**, you write multiple methods with a shared name but different parameter lists. When you call an overloaded method, the language translator understands which version of the method to use based on the arguments used. For example, suppose that you create a method to output a message and the amount due on a customer bill, as shown in Figure 9-17. The method receives a numeric parameter that represents the customer's balance and produces two lines of output. Assume that you also need a method that is similar to printBill(), except the new method applies a discount to the customer bill. One solution to this problem would be to write a new method with a different name—for example, printBillWithDiscount(). A downside to this approach is that a programmer who uses your methods must remember the names of each slightly different version. It is more natural for your methods' clients to use a single well-designed method name for the task of printing bills, but to be able to provide different arguments as appropriate. In this case, you can overload the printBill() method so that, in addition to the version that takes a single numeric argument, you can create a version that takes two numeric arguments—one that represents the balance and one that represents the discount rate. Figure 9-17 shows the two versions of the printBill() method.

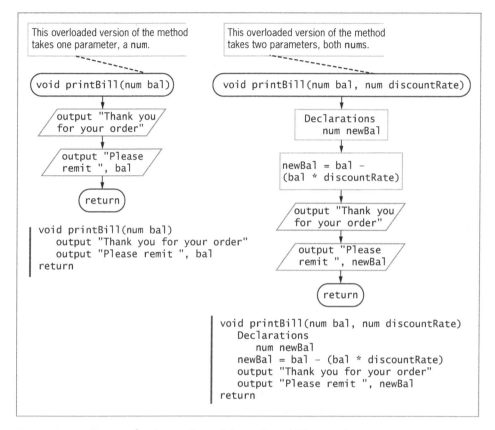

Figure 9-17 Two overloaded versions of the printBill() method
© 2015 Cengage Learning

If both versions of printBill() are included in a program and you call the method using a single numeric argument, as in printBill(custBalance), the first version of the method in Figure 9-17 executes. If you use two numeric arguments in the call, as in printBill (custBalance, rate), the second version of the method executes.

If it suited your needs, you could provide more versions of the printBill() method, as shown in Figure 9-18. The first version accepts a numeric parameter that holds the customer's balance, and a string parameter that holds an additional message that can be customized for the bill recipient and displayed on the bill. For example, if a program makes a method call such as the following, this version of printBill() will execute:

printBill(custBal, "Due in 10 days")

The second version of the method in Figure 9-18 accepts three parameters, providing a balance, discount rate, and customized message. For example, the following method call would use this version of the method:

printBill(balanceDue, discountRate, specialMessage)

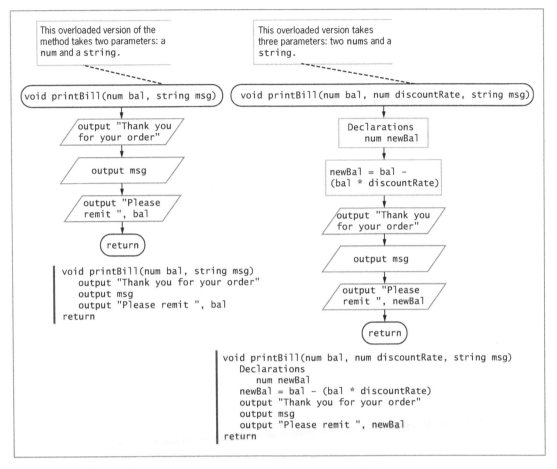

Figure 9-18 Two additional overloaded versions of the `printBill()` method
© 2015 Cengage Learning

Overloading methods is never required in a program. Instead, you could create multiple methods with unique identifiers such as `printBill()` and `printBillWithDiscountAndMessage()`. Overloading methods does not reduce your work when creating a program; you need to write each method individually. The advantage is provided to your method's clients; those who use your methods need to remember just one appropriate name for all related tasks.

 In many programming languages, the `output` statement is actually an overloaded method that you call. Using a single name such as `output`, whether you want to output a number, a `string`, or any combination of the two, is convenient.

Even if you write two or more overloaded versions of a method, many program clients will use just one version. For example, suppose that you develop a bill-creating program that contains all four versions of the `printBill()` method just discussed, and then sell it to different companies. An organization that adopts your program and its methods might only want to use one or two versions of the method. You probably own many devices for which only some of the features are meaningful to you; for example, some people who own microwave ovens only use the *Popcorn* button or never use *Defrost*.

Avoiding Ambiguous Methods

When you overload a method, you run the risk of creating **ambiguous methods**—a situation in which the compiler cannot determine which method to use. Every time you call a method, the compiler decides whether a suitable method exists; if so, the method executes, and if not, you receive an error message. For example, suppose that you write two versions of a `printBill()` method, as shown in the program in Figure 9-19. One version of the method is intended to accept a customer balance and a discount rate, and the other is intended to accept a customer balance and a discount amount expressed in dollars.

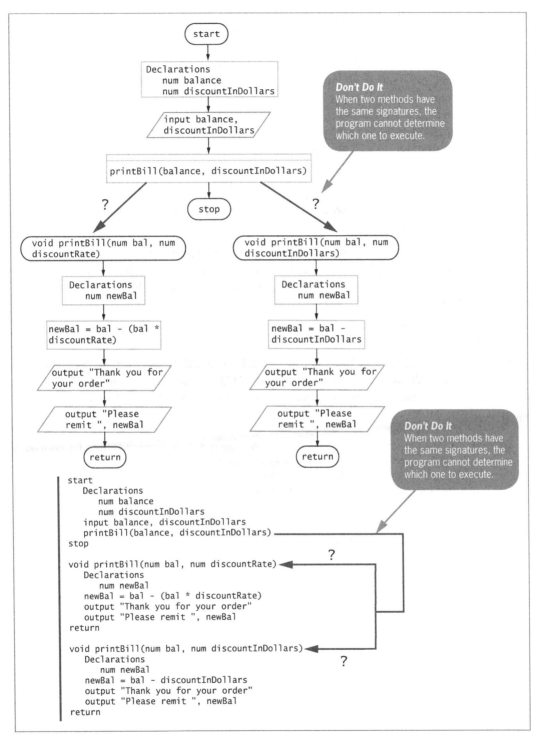

Each of the two versions of printBill() in Figure 9-19 is a valid method on its own. However, when the two versions exist in the same program, a problem arises. When the main program calls printBill() using two numeric arguments, the compiler cannot determine which version to call. You might think that the version of the method with a parameter named discountInDollars would execute, because the method call uses the identifier discountInDollars. However, the compiler determines which version of a method to call based on argument data types only, not their identifiers. Because both versions of the printBill() method could accept two numeric parameters, the compiler cannot determine which version to execute, so an error occurs and program compilation stops.

 An overloaded method is not ambiguous on its own—it becomes ambiguous only if you make a method call that matches multiple method signatures. In many languages, a program with potentially ambiguous methods will run without problems if you don't make any method calls that match more than one method.

Methods can be overloaded correctly by providing different parameter lists for methods with the same name. Methods with identical names that have identical parameter lists but different return types are not overloaded—they are ambiguous. For example, the following two method headers create ambiguity:

```
string aMethod(num x)
num aMethod(num y)
```

The compiler determines which version of a method to call based on parameter lists, not return types. When the method call aMethod(17) is made, the compiler will not know which of the two methods to execute because both possible choices take a numeric argument.

 All the popular object-oriented programming languages support multiple numeric data types. For example, Java, C#, C++, and Visual Basic all support integer (whole number) data types that are different from floating-point (decimal place) data types. Many languages have even more specialized numeric types, such as signed and unsigned. Methods that accept different specific types are correctly overloaded.

 Watch the video *Overloading Methods*.

TWO TRUTHS & A LIE

Overloading Methods

1. In programming, overloading involves supplying diverse meanings for a single identifier.

2. When you overload a method, you write multiple methods with different names but identical parameter lists.

3. Methods can be overloaded correctly by providing different parameter lists for methods with the same name.

The false statement is #2. When you overload a method, you write methods with a shared name but different parameter lists.

Using Predefined Methods

All modern programming languages contain many methods that have already been written for programmers. Predefined methods might originate from several sources:

- Some prewritten methods are built into a language. For example, methods that perform input and output are usually predefined.

- When you work on a program in a team, each programmer might be assigned specific methods to create, and your methods will interact with methods written by others.

- If you work for a company, many standard methods may already have been written and you will be required to use them. For example, the company might have a standard method that displays its logo.

Predefined methods save you time and effort. For example, in most languages, displaying a message on the screen involves using a built-in method. When you want to display *Hello* on the command prompt screen in C#, you write the following:

```
Console.WriteLine("Hello");
```

In Java, you write:

```
System.out.println("Hello");
```

In these statements, you can recognize `WriteLine()` and `println()` as method names because they are followed by parentheses; the parentheses hold an argument that represents the message to display. If these methods were not prewritten, you would have to know the low-level details of how to manipulate pixels on a screen to display the characters. Instead, by using the prewritten methods, you can concentrate on the higher-level task of displaying a useful and appropriate message.

In C#, the convention is to begin method names with an uppercase letter. In Java, method names conventionally begin with a lowercase letter. The `WriteLine()` and `println()` methods follow their respective language's convention. The `WriteLine()` and `println()` methods are both overloaded in their respective languages. For example, if you pass a string to either method, the version of the method that accepts a string parameter executes, but if you pass a number, another version that accepts a numeric parameter executes.

Most programming languages also contain a variety of mathematical methods, such as those that compute the square root or absolute value of a number. Other methods retrieve the current date and time from the operating system or select a random number to use in a game application. These methods were written as a convenience for you—computing a square root and generating random numbers are complicated tasks, so it is convenient to have methods already written, tested, and available when you need them. The names of the methods that perform these functions differ among programming languages, so you need to research the language's documentation to use them. For example, many of a language's methods are described in introductory programming language textbooks, and you can also find language documentation online.

Whether you want to use a predefined method or any other method, you should know the following four details:

- What the method does in general—for example, compute a square root.

- The method's name—for example, it might be `sqrt()`.

- The method's required parameters—for example, a square root method might require a single numeric parameter. There might be multiple overloaded versions of the method from which you can choose. For example, one method version might accept an integer and another version might accept a floating-point number.

- The method's return type—for example, a square root method most likely returns a numeric value that is the square root of the argument passed to the method.

You do not need to know how the method is implemented—that is, how the instruction statements are written within it. Like all methods, you can use built-in methods without worrying about their low-level implementation details.

TWO TRUTHS & A LIE

Using Predefined Methods

1. The name of a method that performs a specific function (such as generating a random number) is likely to be the same in various programming languages.

2. When you want to use a predefined method, you should know what the method does in general, along with its name, required parameters, and return type.

3. When you want to use a predefined method, you do not need to know how the method works internally to be able to use the method effectively.

The false statement is #1. Methods that perform standard functions are likely to have different names in various languages.

Method Design Issues: Implementation Hiding, Cohesion, and Coupling

To design effective methods, you should consider several program qualities:

- You should employ implementation hiding; that is, a method's client should not need to understand a method's internal mechanisms.

- You should strive to increase cohesion.

- You should strive to reduce coupling.

Understanding Implementation Hiding

An important principle of modularization is the notion of **implementation hiding**, the encapsulation of method details. That is, when a program makes a request to a method, it doesn't know the details of how the method is executed. For example, when you make a restaurant reservation, you do not need to know how the reservation is actually recorded at the restaurant—perhaps it is written in a book, marked on a large chalkboard, or entered into a computerized database. The implementation details don't concern you as a patron, and if the restaurant changes its methods from one year to the next, the change does not affect your use of the reservation method—you still call and provide your name, a date, and a time. With well-written methods, using implementation hiding means that a method that calls another must know only the following:

- The name of the called method

- What type of information to send to the method

- What type of return data to expect from the method

In other words, the calling method needs to understand only the **interface to the method** that is called. The interface is the only part of a method with which the method's client (or method's caller) interacts. The program does *not* need to know how the method works internally. Additionally, if you substitute a new, improved method implementation but the interface to the method does not change, you won't need to make changes in any methods that call the altered method.

Programmers refer to hidden implementation details as existing in a **black box**—you can examine what goes in and what comes out, but not the details of how the method works inside.

Increasing Cohesion

When you begin to design computer programs, it is difficult to decide how much to put into a method. For example, a process that requires 40 instructions can be contained in a single 40-instruction method, two 20-instruction methods, five 8-instruction methods, or many other combinations. In most programming languages, any of these combinations is allowed; you can write a program that executes and produces correct results no matter how you divide the individual steps into methods. However, placing too many or too few instructions in a single method makes a program harder to follow and reduces flexibility.

To help determine the appropriate division of tasks among methods, you want to analyze each method's **cohesion**, which refers to how the internal statements of a method serve to accomplish the method's purpose. In highly cohesive methods, all the operations are related, or "go together." Such methods are **functionally cohesive**—all their operations contribute to the performance of a single task. Functionally cohesive methods usually are more reliable than those that have low cohesion; they are considered stronger, and they make programs easier to write, read, and maintain.

For example, consider a method that calculates gross pay. The method receives parameters that define a worker's pay rate and number of hours worked. The method computes gross pay and displays it. The cohesion of this method is high because each of its instructions contributes to one task—computing gross pay. If you can write a sentence describing what a method does using only two words—for example, *Compute gross, Cube value,* or *Display record*—the method is probably functionally cohesive.

You might work in a programming environment that has a rule such as *No method will be longer than can be printed on one page* or *No method will have more than 30 lines of code*. The rule maker is trying to achieve more cohesion, but such rules are arbitrary. A two-line method could have low cohesion and a 40-line method might have high cohesion. Because good, functionally cohesive methods perform only one task, they tend to be short. However, the issue is not size. If it takes 20 statements to perform one task within a method, the method is still cohesive.

Most programmers do not consciously make decisions about cohesiveness for each method they write. Rather, they develop a "feel" for what types of tasks belong together, and for which subsets of tasks should be diverted to their own methods.

Reducing Coupling

Coupling is a measure of the strength of the connection between two program methods; it expresses the extent to which information is exchanged by methods. Coupling is either tight or loose, depending on how much one method relies on information from another. **Tight coupling**, which occurs when methods depend on each other excessively, makes programs more prone to errors. With tight coupling, you have many data paths to keep track of, many chances for bad data to pass from one method to another, and many chances for one method to alter information needed by another method. **Loose coupling** occurs when methods do not depend on others. In general, you want to reduce coupling as much as possible because connections between methods make them more difficult to write, maintain, and reuse.

Imagine four cooks wandering in and out of a kitchen while preparing a stew. If each is allowed to add seasonings at will without the knowledge of the other cooks, you could end up with a culinary disaster. Similarly, if four payroll program methods can alter your gross pay without the "knowledge" of the other methods, you could end up with a financial disaster. A program in which several methods have access to your gross pay figure has methods that are tightly coupled. A superior program would control access to the payroll value by passing it only to methods that need it.

You can evaluate whether coupling between methods is loose or tight by examining how methods share data.

- Tight coupling occurs when methods have access to the same globally defined variables. When one method changes the value stored in a variable, other methods are affected. You should avoid tight coupling, but be aware that you might see it in programs written by others.

- Loose coupling occurs when a copy of data that must be shared is passed from one method to another. That way, the sharing of data is always purposeful—variables must be explicitly passed to and from methods that use them. The loosest (best) methods pass single arguments if possible, rather than many variables or entire records.

Additionally, there is a time and a place for shortcuts. If a memo must go out in five minutes, you don't have time to change fonts or add clip art with your word processor. Similarly, if you need a quick programming result, you might very well use cryptic variable names, tight coupling, and minimal cohesion. When you create a professional application, however, you should keep professional guidelines in mind.

TWO TRUTHS & A LIE

Method Design Issues: Implementation Hiding, Cohesion, and Coupling

1. A calling method must know the interface to any method it calls.

2. You should try to avoid loose coupling, which occurs when methods do not depend on others.

3. Functional cohesion occurs when all operations in a method contribute to the performance of only one task.

The false statement is #2. You should aim for loose coupling so that methods are independent.

Understanding Recursion

Recursion occurs when a method is defined in terms of itself. A method that calls itself is a **recursive method**. Some programming languages do not allow a method to call itself, but those that do can be used to create recursive methods that produce interesting effects.

Figure 9-20 shows a simple example of recursion. The program calls an `infinity()` method, which displays *Help!* and calls itself again (see the shaded statement). The second call to `infinity()` displays *Help!* and generates a third call. The result is a large number of repetitions of the `infinity()` method. The output is shown in Figure 9-21.

```
start
    infinity()
stop

infinity()
    output "Help! "
    infinity()
return
```

Figure 9-20   A program that calls a recursive method
© 2015 Cengage Learning

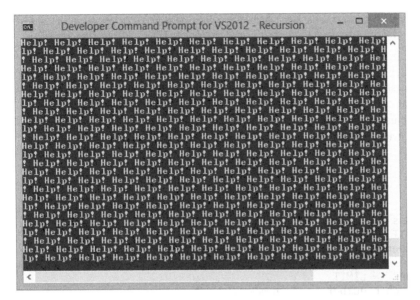

Figure 9-21 Output of the program in Figure 9-20
© 2015 Cengage Learning

Every time you call a method, the address to which the program should return at the completion of the method is stored in a memory location called the **stack**. When a method ends, the address is retrieved from the stack and the program returns to the location where the method call was made, then proceeds to the next instruction. For example, suppose that a program calls methodA() and that methodA() calls methodB(). When the program calls methodA(), a return address is stored in the stack, and then methodA() begins execution. When methodA() calls methodB(), a return address in methodA() is stored in the stack and methodB() begins execution. When methodB() ends, the last entered address is retrieved from the stack and program control returns to complete methodA(). When methodA() ends, the remaining address is retrieved from the stack and program control returns to the main program method to continue execution.

Like all computer memory, the stack has a finite size. When the program in Figure 9-20 calls the infinity() method, the stack receives so many return addresses that it eventually overflows. The recursive calls will end after an excessive number of repetitions and the program issues an error message.

Of course, there is no practical use for an infinitely recursive program. Just as you must be careful not to create endless loops, when you write useful recursive methods you must provide a way for the recursion to stop eventually. The input values that cause a method to recur are called the **recursive cases**, and the input value that makes the recursion stop is called the **base case** or **terminating case**.

Using recursion successfully is easier if you thoroughly understand looping. You learned about loops in Chapter 5. An everyday example of recursion is printed on shampoo bottles: *Lather, rinse, repeat.*

Figure 9-22 shows an application that uses recursion productively. The program calls a recursive method that computes the sum of every integer from 1 up to and including the method's argument value. For example, the sum of every integer up to and including 3 is 1+2+3, or 6, and the sum of every integer up to and including 4 is 1+2+3+4, or 10.

```
start
    Declarations
        num LIMIT = 10
        num number
    number = 1
    while number <= LIMIT
        output "When number is ", number,
            " then cumulativeSum(number) is ",
            cumulativeSum(number)
        number = number + 1
    endwhile
return

num cumulativeSum(num number)
    Declarations
        num returnVal
    if number = 1 then
        returnVal = number
    else
        returnVal = number + cumulativeSum(number - 1)
    endif
return returnVal
```

Figure 9-22   Program that uses a recursive cumulativeSum() method
© 2015 Cengage Learning

When thinking about cumulative summing relationships, remember that the sum of all the integers up to and including any number is that number plus the sum of the integers for the next lower number. In other words, consider the following:

- The sum of the digits from 1, up to and including 1, is simply 1.

- The sum of the digits from 1 through 2 is the previous sum, plus 2.

- The sum of the digits from 1 through 3 is the previous sum, plus 3.

- The sum of the digits from 1 through 4 is the previous sum, plus 4.

- And so on.

The recursive cumulativeSum() method in Figure 9-22 uses this knowledge. For each number, its cumulative sum consists of the value of the number itself plus the cumulative sum of all the previous lesser numbers. The program in Figure 9-22 calls the cumulativeSum() method 10 times in a loop to show the cumulative sum of every integer from 1 through 10. Figure 9-23 shows the output.

```
Developer Command Prompt for VS2012 - CumulativeSum

When number is 1 then cumulativeSum(number) is 1
When number is 2 then cumulativeSum(number) is 3
When number is 3 then cumulativeSum(number) is 6
When number is 4 then cumulativeSum(number) is 10
When number is 5 then cumulativeSum(number) is 15
When number is 6 then cumulativeSum(number) is 21
When number is 7 then cumulativeSum(number) is 28
When number is 8 then cumulativeSum(number) is 36
When number is 9 then cumulativeSum(number) is 45
When number is 10 then cumulativeSum(number) is 55
```

Figure 9-23   Output of the program in Figure 9-22
© 2015 Cengage Learning

If you examine Figures 9-22 and 9-23 together, you can see the following:

- When 1 is passed to the cumulativeSum() method, the if statement within the method determines that the argument is equal to 1, returnVal becomes 1, and 1 is returned for output. (The input value 1 is the base case or terminating case.)

- On the next pass through the loop, 2 is passed to the cumulativeSum() method. When the method receives 2 as an argument, the if statement within the method is false, and returnVal is set to 2 plus the value of cumulativeSum(1). (The input value 2 is a recursive case.) This second call to cumulativeSum() using 1 as an argument returns a 1, so when the method ends, it returns 2+1, or 3.

- On the third pass through the loop within the calling program, 3 is passed to the cumulativeSum() method. When the method receives 3 as an argument, the if statement within the method is false and the method returns 3 plus the value of cumulativeSum(2). (The input value 3, like 2, is a recursive case.) The value of this call is 2 plus cumulativeSum(1). The value of cumulativeSum(1) is 1. Ultimately, cumulativeSum(3) is 3+2+1.

Many sophisticated programs that operate on lists of items use recursive processing. However, following the logic of a recursive method can be difficult, and programs that use recursion are sometimes error-prone and hard to debug. Because such programs also can be hard for others to maintain, some business organizations forbid their programmers from using recursive logic in company programs. Many of the problems solved by recursive methods can be solved using loops. For example, examine the program in Figure 9-24. This program produces the same result as the previous recursive program, but in a more straightforward fashion.

```
start
   Declarations
      num number
      num total
      num LIMIT = 10
   total = 0
   number = 1
   while number <= LIMIT
      total = total + number
      output "When number is ", number,
         " then the cumulative sum of 1 through",
         number, " is ", total
      number = number + 1
   endwhile
stop
```

Figure 9-24   Nonrecursive program that computes cumulative sums
© 2015 Cengage Learning

A humorous illustration of recursion is found in this sentence: "In order to understand recursion, you must first understand recursion." A humorous dictionary entry is "Recursion: See Recursion." These examples contain an element of truth, but useful recursive algorithms always have a point at which the infinite loop is exited. In other words, the base case or terminating case is always reached at some point.

Watch the video *Recursion*.

TWO TRUTHS & A LIE

Understanding Recursion

1. A method that calls itself is a recursive method.

2. Every time you call a method, the address to which the program should return at the completion of the method is stored in a memory location called the stack.

3. Following the logic of a recursive method is usually much easier than following the logic of an ordinary program, so recursion makes debugging easier.

The false statement is #3. Following the logic of a recursive method is difficult, and programs that use recursion are sometimes error-prone and hard to debug.

Chapter Summary

- A method is a program module that contains a series of statements that carry out a task. Any program can contain an unlimited number of methods, and each method can be called an unlimited number of times. A method must include a header, a body, and a `return` statement that marks the end of the method.

- Variables and constants are in scope within, or local to, only the method within which they are declared.

- When you pass a data item into a method, it is an argument to the method. When the method receives the data item, it is called a parameter. When you write the declaration for a method that can receive parameters, you must include the data type and a local name for each parameter within the method declaration's parentheses. You can pass multiple arguments to a called method by listing the arguments within the method call and separating them with commas. When you call a method, the arguments you send to the method must match in order—both in number and in type—the parameters listed in the method declaration.

- A method's return type indicates the data type of the value that the method will send back to the location where the method call was made. The return type also is known as a method's type, and is placed in front of the method name when the method is defined. When a method returns a value, you usually want to use the returned value in the calling method, although this is not required.

- You can pass a single array element to a method in exactly the same manner you would pass a variable or constant. You can indicate that a method parameter is an array by placing square brackets after the data type in the method's parameter list. When you pass an array to a method, it is passed by reference; that is, the method receives the actual memory address of the array and has access to the actual values in the array elements.

- When you overload a method, you write multiple methods with a shared name but different parameter lists. The compiler understands your meaning based on the arguments you use when calling the method. Overloading a method introduces the risk of creating ambiguous methods—a situation in which the compiler cannot determine which version of a method to use.

- All modern programming languages contain many built-in, prewritten methods to save you time and effort.

- With well-written methods, the implementation is hidden. To call a method, you need only know the name of the method, what type of information to send to the method, and what type of return data to expect from the method. When writing methods, you should strive to achieve high cohesion and loose coupling.

- Recursion occurs when a method is defined in terms of itself. Following the logic of a recursive method can be difficult, and programs that use recursion are sometimes error-prone and hard to debug.

Key Terms

A **method** is a program module that contains a series of statements that carry out a task.

A method's **client** is a program or other method that uses the method.

A **method header** precedes a method body; the header includes the method identifier and possibly other necessary identifying information, such as a return type and parameter list.

A **method body** contains all the statements in the method.

Implementation describes the body of a method or the statements that carry out the tasks of a method.

A **method** `return` **statement** marks the end of a method and identifies the point at which control returns to the calling method.

Local describes data items that are only known to the method in which they are declared.

Global describes data items that are known to all the methods in a program.

An **argument to a method** is a value passed to a method in the call to the method.

A **parameter to a method** is a data item defined in a method header that accepts data passed into the method from the outside.

A **parameter list** is all the data types and parameter names that appear in a method header.

A method's **signature** includes its name and parameter list.

A variable passed into a method is **passed by value**; that is, a copy of its value is sent to the method and stored in a new memory location accessible to the method.

Actual parameters are the arguments in a method call.

Formal parameters are the variables in the method declaration that accept the values from the actual parameters.

A method's **return type** indicates the data type of the value that the method will send back to the location where the method call was made.

A **void method** returns no value.

A **method's type** is the type of its return value.

Overhead refers to all the resources and time required by an operation.

An **IPO chart** identifies and categorizes each item needed within the method as pertaining to input, processing, or output.

Passed by reference describes how values are accepted into a method when the method receives the actual memory address item. Arrays are passed by reference.

Overloading involves supplying diverse meanings for a single identifier.

Polymorphism is the ability of a method to act appropriately according to the context.

To **overload a method** is to create multiple versions with the same name but different parameter lists.

Ambiguous methods are those methods that the compiler cannot distinguish between because they have the same name and parameter types.

Implementation hiding is a programming principle that describes the encapsulation of method details.

The **interface to a method** includes the method's return type, name, and arguments. It is the part that a client sees and uses.

A **black box** is the analogy programmers use to refer to hidden method implementation details.

Cohesion is a measure of how the internal statements of a method serve to accomplish the method's purpose.

Functional cohesion occurs when all operations in a method contribute to the performance of only one task. Functional cohesion is the highest level of cohesion; you should strive for it in all methods you write.

Coupling is a measure of the strength of the connection between two program methods.

Tight coupling occurs when methods excessively depend on each other; it makes programs more prone to errors.

Loose coupling occurs when methods do not depend on others.

Recursion occurs when a method is defined in terms of itself.

A **recursive method** is a method that calls itself.

The **stack** is a memory area that holds addresses to which methods should return.

Recursive cases describe the input values that cause a recursive method to execute again.

The **base case** or **terminating case** of a recursive method describes the value that ends the repetition.

Exercises

Review Questions

1. Which of the following is true?

   a. A program can call one method at most.

   b. A method can contain one or more other methods.

   c. A program can contain a method that calls another method.

   d. All of the above are true.

2. Which of the following must every method have?

   a. a parameter list   c. a return value

   b. a header   d. all of the above

3. Which of the following is most closely related to the concept of *local*?

   a. abstract   c. program level

   b. object-oriented   d. in scope

4. Although the terms *parameter* and *argument* are closely related, the difference is that *argument* refers to _____ .

   a. a value in a method call   c. a formal parameter

   b. a passed constant   d. a variable that is local to a method

5. A method's interface is its _____ .

   a. parameter list   c. identifier

   b. return type   d. all of the above

6. When you write the declaration for a method that can receive a parameter, which of the following must be included in the method declaration?

   a. the name of the argument that will be used to call the method

   b. a local name for the parameter

   c. the data type of the parameter

   d. two of the above

7. When you use a variable name in a method call, it _____ as the variable in the method header.

   a. can have the same name   c. must have the same name

   b. cannot have the same name   d. cannot have the same data type

8. Assume that you have written a method with the header void myMethod(num a, string b). Which of the following is a correct method call?

   a. myMethod(12)   c. myMethod("Goodbye")

   b. myMethod(12, "Hello")   d. It is impossible to tell.

9. Assume that you have written a method with the header num yourMethod(string name, num code). The method's type is _____ .

   a. num   c. num and string

   b. string   d. void

10. Assume that you have written a method with the header string myMethod(num score, string grade). Also assume that you have declared a numeric variable named test. Which of the following is a correct method call?

   a. myMethod()   c. myMethod(test, test)

   b. myMethod(test)   d. myMethod(test,"A")

11. The value used in a method's return statement must _____ .

   a. be numeric

   b. be a variable

   c. match the data type used before the method name in the header

   d. two of the above

12. When a method receives a copy of the value stored in an argument used in the method call, it means the variable was _____ .

   a. unnamed

   b. passed by value

   c. passed by reference

   d. assigned its original value when it was declared

13. A void method _____ .

   a. contains no statements   c. returns nothing

   b. requires no parameters   d. has no name

14. When an array is passed to a method, it is _____ .

   a. passed by reference   c. unnamed in the method

   b. passed by value   d. unalterable in the method

15. When you overload a method, you write multiple methods with the same _____ .

   a. name   c. number of parameters

   b. parameter list   d. return type

16.   A program contains a method with the header num calculateTaxes(num amount, string name). Which of the following methods can coexist in the same program with no possible ambiguity?

   a.   num calculateTaxes(string name, num amount)

   b.   string calculateTaxes(num money, string taxpayer)

   c.   num calculateTaxes(num annualPay, string taxpayerId)

   d.   All of these can coexist without ambiguity.

17.   Methods in the same program with identical names and identical parameter lists are _____ .

   a.   overloaded   c.   overwhelmed

   b.   overworked   d.   ambiguous

18.   Methods in different programs with identical names and identical parameter lists are _____ .

   a.   overloaded   c.   both of the above

   b.   illegal   d.   none of the above

19.   The notion of _____ most closely describes the way a calling method is not aware of the statements within a called method.

   a.   abstraction   c.   implementation hiding

   b.   object-oriented   d.   encapsulation

20.   Programmers should strive to _____ .

   a.   increase coupling

   b.   increase cohesion

   c.   both of the above

   d.   neither a nor b

 Programming Exercises

1.   Create an IPO chart for each of the following methods:

   a.   The method that calculates the amount owed on a restaurant check, including tip

   b.   The method that calculates your yearly education-related expenses

   c.   The method that calculates your annual housing expenses, including rent or mortgage payment and utilities

2. Create the logic for a program that continuously prompts the user for a number of dollars until the user enters 0. Pass each entered amount to a conversion method that displays a breakdown of the passed amount into the fewest bills; in other words, the method calculates the number of 20s, 10s, 5s, and 1s needed.

3. a. Create the logic for a program that calculates and displays the amount of money you would have if you invested $5000 at 2 percent simple interest for one year. Create a separate method to do the calculation and return the result to be displayed.

   b. Modify the program in Exercise 3a so that the main program prompts the user for the amount of money and passes it to the interest-calculating method.

   c. Modify the program in Exercise 3b so that the main program also prompts the user for the interest rate and passes both the amount of money and the interest rate to the interest-calculating method.

4. Create the logic for a program that accepts an annual salary as input. Pass the salary to a method that calculates the highest monthly housing payment the user can afford, assuming that the year's total payment is no more than 25 percent of the annual salary.

5. a. Create the logic for a program that performs arithmetic functions. Design the program to contain two numeric variables, and prompt the user for values for the variables. Pass both variables to methods named sum() and difference(). Create the logic for the methods sum() and difference(); they compute the sum of and difference between the values of two arguments, respectively. Each method should perform the appropriate computation and display the results.

   b. Modify the program in Exercise 5a so that the two entered values are passed to a method named getChoice(). The getChoice() method asks the user whether addition or subtraction should be performed and then passes the two values to the appropriate method, where the result is displayed.

6. Create the logic for a program that continuously prompts a user for a numeric value until the user enters 0. The application passes the value in turn to the following methods:

   - A method that displays all whole numbers from 1 up to and including the entered number

   - A method that computes the sum of all the whole numbers from 1 up to and including the entered number

   - A method that computes the product of all the whole numbers from 1 up to and including the entered number

7. Create the logic for a program that calls a method that computes the final price for a sales transaction. The program contains variables that hold the price of an item, the salesperson's commission expressed as a percentage, and the customer discount expressed as a percentage. Create a calculatePrice() method that determines the

final price and returns the value to the calling method. The `calculatePrice()` method requires three arguments: product price, salesperson commission rate, and customer discount rate. A product's final price is the original price plus the commission amount minus the discount amount. The customer discount is taken as a percentage of the total price after the salesperson commission has been added to the original price.

8. Create the logic for a program that continuously prompts the user for two numeric values that represent the dimensions of a room in feet. Include two overloaded methods that compute the room's area. One method takes two numeric parameters and calculates the area by multiplying the parameters. The other takes a single numeric parameter, which is squared to calculate area. Each method displays its calculated result. Accept input and respond as follows:

- When the user enters zero for the first value, end the program.

- If the user enters a negative number for either value, continue to reprompt the user until the value is not negative.

- If both numbers entered are greater than 0, call the method version that accepts two parameters and pass it both values.

- If the second value is zero, call the version of the method that accepts just one parameter and pass it the nonzero value.

9. a. Plan the logic for an insurance company program to determine policy premiums. The program continuously prompts the user for an insurance policy number. When the user enters an appropriate sentinel value, end the program. Call a method that prompts each user for the type of policy needed—health or auto. While the user's response does not indicate health or auto, continue to prompt the user. When the value is valid, return it from the method. Pass the user's response to a new method where the premium is set and returned $550 for a health policy or $225 for an auto policy. Display the results for each policy.

   b. Modify Exercise 9a so that the premium-setting method calls one of two additional methods—one that determines the health premium or one that determines the auto premium. The health insurance method asks users whether they smoke; the premium is $550 for smokers and $345 for nonsmokers. The auto insurance method asks users to enter the number of traffic tickets they have received in the last three years. The premium is $225 for drivers with three or more tickets, $190 for those with one or two tickets, and $110 for those with no tickets. Each of these two methods returns the premium amount to the calling method, which returns the amount to be displayed.

10. Create the logic for a program that prompts the user for numeric values for a month, day, and year. Then pass the three variables to the following methods:

   a. A method that displays the date with dashes in month-day-year order, as it is often represented in the United States—for example, *6-24-2015*

   b. A method that displays the date with dashes in day-month-year order, as it is often represented in the United Kingdom—for example, *24-6-2015*

   c. A method that displays the date with dashes in year-month-day order, as it is represented in the International Standard—for example, *2015-6-24*

   d. A method that prompts the user for the desired format ("US", "UK", or "IS") and then passes the three values to one of the methods described in parts a, b, and c of this exercise

11. Create the logic for a program that computes hotel guest rates at Cornwall's Country Inn. Include two overloaded methods named `computeRate()`. One version accepts a number of days and calculates the rate at $99.99 per day. The other accepts a number of days and a code for a meal plan. If the code is *A*, three meals per day are included, and the price is $169.00 per day. If the code is *C*, breakfast is included, and the price is $112.00 per day. All other codes are invalid. Each method returns the rate to the calling program where it is displayed. The main program asks the user for the number of days in a stay and whether meals should be included; then, based on the user's response, the program either calls the first method or prompts for a meal plan code and calls the second method.

12. Create the logic for a program that prompts a user for 10 numbers and stores them in an array. Pass the array to a method that reverses the order of the numbers. Display the reversed numbers in the main program.

13. Create the logic for a program that prompts a user for six numbers and stores them in an array. Pass the array to a method that calculates the arithmetic average of the numbers and returns the value to the calling program. Display each number and how far it is from the arithmetic average. Continue to prompt the user for additional sets of six numbers until the user wants to quit.

14. The Information Services Department at the Springfield Library has created methods with the following signatures:

Signature	Description
num getNumber(num high, num low)	Prompts the user for a number, and continues to prompt until the number falls between designated high and low limits; returns a valid number
string getCharacter()	Prompts the user for a character string and returns the entered string
num lookUpISBN(string title)	Accepts the title of a book and returns the ISBN; returns a 0 if the book cannot be found
string lookUpTitle(num isbn)	Accepts the ISBN of a book and returns a title; returns a space character if the book cannot be found
string isBookAvailable(num isbn)	Accepts an ISBN, searches the library database, and returns "Y" or "N" indicating whether the book is currently available

Table 9-1   Library methods

a. Design an interactive program that does the following, using the prewritten methods whenever they are appropriate.

  ♦ Prompt the user for and read a library card number, which must be between 1000 and 9999.

  ♦ Prompt the user for and read a search option—1 to search for a book by ISBN, 2 to search for a book by title, and 3 to quit. If the entry is invalid, repeat the request.

  ♦ While the user does not enter 3, prompt for an ISBN or title based on the user's previous selection. If the user enters an ISBN, get and display the book's title and ask the user to enter a "Y" or "N" to confirm whether the title is correct.

  ♦ If the user has entered a valid ISBN or a title that matches a valid ISBN, check whether the book is available, and display an appropriate message for the user.

  ♦ The user can continue to search for books until he or she enters 3 as the search option.

b. Develop the logic that implements each of the methods in Exercise 14a.

15. Each of the programs in Figure 9-25 uses a recursive method. Try to determine the output in each case.

a.
```
start
   output recursiveA(0)
stop
num recursiveA(num x)
   num result
   if x = 0 then
      result = x
   else
      result = x *
            (recursiveA(x - 1))
   endif
return result
```

b.
```
start
   output recursiveB(2)
stop
num recursiveB(num x)
   num result
   if x = 0 then
      result = x
   else
      result = x *
            (recursiveB(x - 1))
   endif
return result
```

c.
```
start
   output recursiveC(2)
stop
num recursiveC(num x)
   num result
   if x = 1 then
      result = x
   else
      result = x *
            (recursiveC(x - 1))
   endif
return result
```

Figure 9-25 Problems for Exercise 15
© 2015 Cengage Learning

Performing Maintenance

1. A file named MAINTENANCE09-01.txt is included with your downloadable student files. Assume that this program is a working program in your organization and that it needs modifications as described in the comments (lines that begin with two slashes) at the beginning of the file. Your job is to alter the program to meet the new specifications.

Find the Bugs

1. Your downloadable files for Chapter 9 include DEBUG09-01.txt, DEBUG09-02.txt, and DEBUG09-03.txt. Each file starts with some comments that describe the problem. Comments are lines that begin with two slashes (//). Following the comments, each file contains pseudocode that has one or more bugs you must find and correct.

2. Your downloadable files for Chapter 9 include a file named DEBUG09-04.jpg that contains a flowchart with syntax and/or logical errors. Examine the flowchart and then find and correct all the bugs.

Game Zone

1. In the Game Zone sections of Chapters 6 and 8, you designed the logic for a quiz that contains questions about a topic of your choice. Now, modify the program so it contains an array of five multiple-choice quiz questions related to the topic of your choice. Each question contains four answer choices. Also, create a parallel

array that holds the correct answer to each question—A, B, C, or D. In turn, pass each question to a method that displays the question and accepts the player's answer. If the player does not enter a valid answer choice, force the player to reenter the choice. Return the user's valid (but not necessarily correct) answer to the main program. After the user's answer is returned to the main program, pass it and the correct answer to a method that determines whether the values are equal and displays an appropriate message. After the user answers all five questions, display the number of correct and incorrect answers that the user chose.

2. In the Game Zone section of Chapter 6, you designed the logic for the game Hangman, in which the user guesses letters in a hidden word. Improve the game to store an array of 10 words. One at a time, pass each word to a method that allows the user to guess letters continuously until the game is solved. The method returns the number of guesses it took to complete the word. Store the number in an array before returning to the method for the next word. After all 10 words have been guessed, display a summary of the number of guesses required for each word as well as the average number of guesses per word.

Up for Discussion

1. One advantage to writing a program that is subdivided into methods is that such a structure allows different programmers to write separate methods, thus dividing the work. Would you prefer to write a large program by yourself, or to work on a team in which each programmer produces one or more methods? Why?

2. In this chapter, you learned that hidden implementations are often said to exist in a black box. What are the advantages and disadvantages to this approach in both programming and real life?

Object-Oriented Programming

In this chapter, you will learn about:

- ◎ The principles of object-oriented programming
- ◎ Classes
- ◎ Public and private access
- ◎ Ways to organize classes
- ◎ Instance methods
- ◎ Static methods
- ◎ Using objects

Principles of Object-Oriented Programming

Object-oriented programming (OOP) is a programming model that focuses on an application's components and data and the methods you need to manipulate them. With OOP, you consider the items that a program will manipulate—for example, a customer invoice, a loan application, a button that a user clicks, or a menu from which a user selects an option. These items are called *objects*, and when you program, you define their characteristics, functions, and capabilities.

OOP uses all of the familiar concepts of modular procedural programming, such as variables, methods, and passing arguments. Methods in object-oriented programs continue to use sequence, selection, and looping structures and make use of arrays. However, OOP adds several new concepts to programming and involves a different way of thinking. A considerable amount of new vocabulary is involved as well. First, you will read about OOP concepts in general, and then you will learn the specific terminology.

Five important features of object-oriented languages are:

- Classes
- Objects
- Polymorphism
- Inheritance
- Encapsulation

Classes and Objects

In object-oriented terminology, a **class** describes a group or collection of objects with common attributes. An **object** is one **instance** of a class. Object-oriented programmers sometimes say an object is one **instantiation** of a class; when a program creates an object, it **instantiates** the object. The words in boldface in the previous sentence both derive from *instance*. For example, your redChevroletAutomobileWithTheDent is an instance of the class that describes all automobiles, and your goldenRetrieverDogNamedGinger is an instance of the class that describes all dogs. A class is like a blueprint from which many houses might be built, or like a recipe from which many meals can be prepared. One house and one meal are each an instance of their class; countless instances might be created eventually. For example, Figure 10-1 depicts a Dog class and two instances of it.

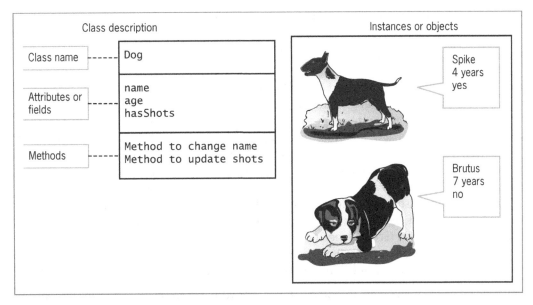

Figure 10-1   A **Dog** class and two instances

Objects both in the real world and in object-oriented programming may contain attributes and methods. **Attributes** are the characteristics of an object. For example, some of your automobile's attributes are its make, model, year, and purchase price. These attributes don't change during the car's life. Examples of attributes that change frequently include whether the automobile is currently running, its gear, its speed, and whether it is dirty. All automobiles possess the same attributes, but not the same values for those attributes. Similarly, your dog has the attributes of its breed, name, age, and whether its shots are current. Methods are the actions that can be taken on an object; often they alter, use, or retrieve the attributes. For example, an automobile has methods for changing and viewing its speed, and a dog has methods for setting and finding out its shot status.

Thinking of items as instances of a class allows you to apply your general knowledge of the class to the individual objects created from it. You know what attributes an object has when you know what class defines it. For example, if your friend purchases an `Automobile`, you know it has a model name, and if your friend gets a `Dog`, you know the dog has a breed. You might not know the current status of your friend's `Automobile`, such as its current speed, or the status of her `Dog`'s shots, but you do know what attributes exist for the `Automobile` and `Dog` classes, which allows you to imagine these objects reasonably well before you see them. You know enough to ask the `Automobile`'s model and not its breed; you know enough to ask the `Dog`'s name and not its engine size. As another example, when you use a new application on your computer, you expect each component to have specific, consistent attributes, such as a button being clickable or a window being closable. Each component gains these attributes as an instance of the general class of GUI (graphical user interface) components.

Most programmers employ a naming convention in which class names begin with an uppercase letter and multiple-word identifiers are run together, such as `SavingsAccount` or `TemporaryWorker`. Each new word within the identifier starts with an uppercase letter. In Chapter 2, you learned that this convention is known as *Pascal casing*.

Much of your understanding of the world comes from your ability to categorize objects and events into classes. As a young child, you learned the concept of *animal* long before you knew the word. Your first encounter with an animal might have been with the family dog, a neighbor's cat, or a goat at a petting zoo. As you developed speech, you might have used the same term for all of these creatures, gleefully shouting "Doggie!" as your parents pointed out cows, horses, and sheep in picture books or along the roadside on drives in the country. As you grew more sophisticated, you learned to distinguish dogs from cows; still later, you learned to distinguish breeds. Your understanding of the class `Animal` helps you see the similarities between dogs and cows, and your understanding of the class `Dog` helps you see the similarities between a Great Dane and a Chihuahua. Understanding classes gives you a framework for categorizing new experiences. You might not know the term *okapi*, but when you learn it's an animal, you begin to develop a concept of what an okapi might be like.

When you think in an object-oriented manner, everything is an object. You can think of any inanimate physical item as an object—your desk, your computer, and your house are all called *objects* in everyday conversation. You can think of living things as objects, too—your houseplant, your pet goldfish, and your sister are objects. Events also are objects—the stock purchase you made, the mortgage closing you attended, and your graduation party are all objects.

Everything is an object, and every object is an instance of a more general class. Your desk is an instance of the class that includes all desks, and your pet goldfish is an instance of the class that contains all fish. These statements represent **is-a relationships** because you can say, "My oak desk with the scratch on top *is a* `Desk` and my goldfish named Moby *is a* `Fish`." Your goldfish, my guppy, and the zoo's shark each constitute one instance of the `Fish` class.

Object-oriented programmers also use the term *is-a* when describing inheritance. You will learn about inheritance later in this chapter and in Chapter 11.

The concept of a class is useful because of its reusability. For example, if you invite me to a graduation party, I automatically know many things about the party object. I assume that there will be attributes such as a starting time, a number of guests, some quantity of food, and gifts. I understand parties because of my previous knowledge of the `Party` class, of which all parties are tangible examples or instances. I don't know the number of guests or the date or time of this particular party, but I understand that because all parties have a date and time, then this one must as well. Similarly, even though every stock purchase is unique, each must have a dollar amount and a number of shares. All objects have predictable attributes because they are instantiated from specific classes.

The data components of a class that belong to every instantiated object are the class's **instance variables**. Instance variables often are called **fields** to help distinguish them from other variables you might use. The set of all the values or contents of an object's instance variables is known as its **state**. For example, the current state of a particular party might be 8 p.m. and Friday; the state of a particular stock purchase might be $10 and five shares.

In addition to their attributes, classes have methods associated with them, and every object instantiated from a given class possesses the same methods. For example, at some point you might want to issue invitations for a party. You might name the method issueInvitations(), and it might display some text as well as the values of the party's date and time fields. Your graduation party, then, might be named myGraduationParty. As an object of the Party class, it might have data members for the date and time, like all parties, and it might have a method to issue invitations. When you use the method, you might want to be able to send an argument to issueInvitations() that indicates how many copies to print. When you think of an object and its methods, it's as though you can send a message to the object to direct it to accomplish a particular task—you can tell the party object named myGraduationParty to print the number of invitations you request. Even though yourAnniversaryParty also is an instance of the Party class, and even though it also has access to the issueInvitations() method, you will send a different argument value to yourAnniversaryParty's issueInvitations() method than I send to myGraduationParty's corresponding method. Within an object-oriented program, you continuously make requests to an object's methods, often including arguments as part of those requests.

In grammar, a noun is equivalent to an object and the values of a class's attributes are adjectives—they describe the characteristics of the objects. An object also can have methods, which are equivalent to verbs.

When you program in object-oriented languages, you frequently create classes from which objects will be instantiated. You also write applications to use the objects, along with their data and methods. Often, you will write programs that use classes created by others; at other times, you might create a class that other programmers will use to instantiate objects within their own programs. A program or class that instantiates objects of another prewritten class is a **class client** or **class user**. For example, your organization might already have a class named Customer that contains attributes such as name, address, and phoneNumber, and you might create clients that include arrays of thousands of Customers. Similarly, in a GUI operating environment, you might write applications that include prewritten components from classes with names like Window and Button.

Polymorphism

The real world is full of objects. Consider a door. A door needs to be opened and closed. You open a door with an easy-to-use interface known as a doorknob. Object-oriented programmers would say you are *passing a message* to the door when you tell it to open by turning its knob. The same message (turning a knob) has a different result when applied to your radio than when applied to a door. As depicted in Figure 10-2, the procedure you use to open something—call it the "open" procedure—works differently on a door than it does on a desk drawer, a bank account, a computer file, or your eyes. However, even though these procedures operate differently using the various objects, you can call each of these procedures "open."

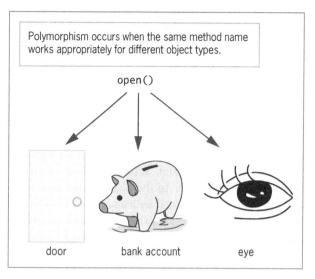

Polymorphism occurs when the same method name works appropriately for different object types.

open()

door   bank account   eye

Figure 10-2   Examples of polymorphism
© 2015 Cengage Learning

Within classes in object-oriented programs, you can create multiple methods with the same name, which will act differently and appropriately when used with different types of objects. In Chapter 9, you learned that this concept is called *polymorphism*, and you learned to overload methods. For example, you might use a method named print() to print a customer invoice, loan application, or envelope. Because you use the same method name to describe the different actions needed to print these diverse objects, you can write statements in object-oriented programming languages that are more like English; you can use the same method name to describe the same type of action, no matter what type of object is being acted upon. Using the method name print() is easier than remembering printInvoice(), printLoanApplication(), and so on. Object-oriented languages understand verbs in context, just as people do.

As another example of the advantages to using one name for a variety of objects, consider a screen you might design for a user to enter data into an application you are writing. Suppose that the screen contains a variety of objects—some forms, buttons, scroll bars, dialog boxes, and so on. Suppose also that you decide to make all the objects blue. Instead of having to memorize the method names that these objects use to change color—perhaps changeFormColor(), changeButtonColor(), and so on—your job would be easier if the creators of all those objects had developed a setColor() method that works appropriately with each type of object.

Purists find a subtle difference between overloading and polymorphism. Some reserve the term *polymorphism* (or **pure polymorphism**) for situations in which one method body is used with a variety of arguments. For example, a single method that can be used with any type of object is polymorphic. The term *overloading* is applied to situations in which you define multiple methods with a single name—for example, three methods, all named display(), that display a number, an employee, and a student, respectively. Certainly, the two terms are related; both refer to the ability to use a single name to communicate multiple meanings. For now, think of overloading as a primitive type of polymorphism.

Inheritance

Another important concept in object-oriented programming is **inheritance**, which is the process of acquiring the traits of one's predecessors. In the real world, a new door with a stained glass window inherits most of its traits from a standard door. It has the same purpose, it opens and closes in the same way, and it has the same knob and hinges. As Figure 10-3 shows, the door with the stained glass window simply has one additional trait—its window. Even if you have never seen a door with a stained glass window, you know what it is and how to use it because you understand the characteristics of all doors. With object-oriented programming, once you create an object, you can develop new objects that possess all the traits of the original object plus any new traits you desire. If you develop a CustomerBill class of objects, there is no need to develop an OverdueCustomerBill class from scratch. You can create the new class to contain all the characteristics of the already developed one, and simply add necessary new characteristics. This not only reduces the work involved in creating new objects, it makes them easier to understand because they possess most of the characteristics of already developed objects.

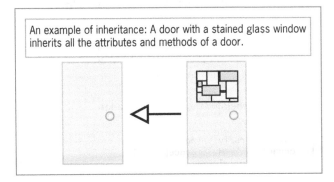

An example of inheritance: A door with a stained glass window inherits all the attributes and methods of a door.

Figure 10-3 An example of inheritance

© 2015 Cengage Learning

 Watch the video *An Introduction to Object-Oriented Programming*.

Encapsulation

Real-world objects often employ encapsulation and information hiding. **Encapsulation** is the process of combining all of an object's attributes and methods into a single package; the package includes data that is frequently hidden from outside classes as well as methods that are available to outside classes to access and alter the data. **Information hiding** is the concept that other classes should not alter an object's attributes—only the methods of an object's own class should have that privilege. (The concept is also called **data hiding**.) Outside classes should only be allowed to make a request that an attribute be altered; then it is up to the class's methods to determine whether the request is appropriate. When using a door, you usually are unconcerned with the latch or hinge construction, and you don't have access to

433

the interior workings of the knob. You care only about the functionality and the interface, the user-friendly boundary between the user and internal mechanisms of the device. When you turn a door's knob, you are interacting appropriately with the interface. Banging on the knob would be an inappropriate interaction, so the door would not respond. Similarly, the detailed workings of objects you create within object-oriented programs can be hidden from outside programs and modules if necessary, and the methods you write can control how the objects operate. When the details are hidden, programmers can focus on the functionality and the interface, as people do with real-life objects.

In summary, understanding object-oriented programming means that you must consider five of its integral components: classes, objects, polymorphism, inheritance, and encapsulation. Quick Reference 10-1 illustrates these components.

QUICK REFERENCE 10-1 Components of Object-Oriented Programming

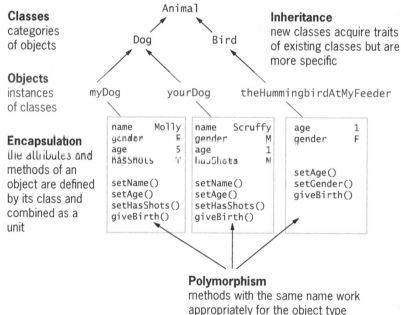

TWO TRUTHS & A LIE

Principles of Object-Oriented Programming

1. Learning about object-oriented programming is difficult because it does not use the concepts you already know, such as declaring variables and using modules.

2. In object-oriented terminology, a class describes a group or collection of objects with common attributes; an instance of a class is an existing object of a class.

3. A program or class that instantiates objects of another prewritten class is a class client or class user.

The false statement is #1. Object-oriented programming uses many features of procedural programming, including declaring variables and using modules.

Defining Classes and Creating Class Diagrams

A class is a category of things; an object is a specific instance of a class. A **class definition** is a set of program statements that lists the characteristics of each object and the methods each object can use.

A class definition can contain three parts:

- Every class has a name.
- Most classes contain data, although this is not required.
- Most classes contain methods, although this is not required.

For example, you can create a class named Employee. Each Employee object will represent one employee who works for an organization. Data fields, or attributes of the Employee class, include fields such as lastName, hourlyWage, and weeklyPay.

The methods of a class include all the actions you want to perform with the class. Appropriate methods for an Employee class might include setHourlyWage(), getHourlyWage(), and calculateWeeklyPay(). The job of setHourlyWage() is to provide values for an Employee's wage data field, the purpose of getHourlyWage() is to retrieve the wage value, and the purpose of calculateWeeklyPay() is to multiply the Employee's hourlyWage by the number of hours in a workweek to calculate a weekly salary. With object-oriented languages, you think of the class name, data, and methods as a single encapsulated unit.

Declaring a class does not create actual objects. A class is just an abstract description of what an object will be if any objects are actually instantiated. Just as you might understand all the characteristics of an item you intend to manufacture before the first item rolls off the assembly line, you can create a class with fields and methods long before you instantiate objects from it.

When you declare a simple variable that is a built-in data type, you write a statement such as one of the following:

```
num money
string name
```

When you write a program that declares an object that is a class data type, you write a statement such as the following:

```
Employee myAssistant
```

In some object-oriented programming languages, you need to add more to the declaration statement to actually create an Employee object. For example, in Java you would write:

```
Employee myAssistant = new Employee();
```

You will understand more about the format of this statement when you learn about constructors in Chapter 11.

When you declare the myAssistant object, it contains all the data fields and has access to all the methods contained within its class. In other words, a larger section of memory is set aside than when you declare a simple variable, because an Employee contains several fields. You can use any of an Employee's methods with the myAssistant object. The usual syntax is to provide an object name, a dot (period), and a method name with parentheses and a possible argument list. For example, you can write a program that contains statements such as those shown in Figure 10-4.

```
start
    Declarations
        Employee myAssistant
    myAssistant.setLastName("Reynolds")
    myAssistant.setHourlyWage(16.75)
    output "My assistant makes ",
        myAssistant.getHourlyWage(), " per hour"
stop
```

Figure 10-4   Application that declares and uses an Employee object
© 2015 Cengage Learning

The program segment in Figure 10-4 is very short. In a more useful real-life program, you might read employee data from a data file before assigning it to the object's fields, each Employee might contain dozens of fields, and your application might create hundreds or thousands of objects.

Besides referring to Employee as a class, many programmers would refer to it as a **user-defined type**, but a more accurate term is **programmer-defined type**. A class from which objects are instantiated is the data type of its objects. Object-oriented programmers typically refer to a class like Employee as an **abstract data type** (ADT); this term implies that the type's data is private and can be accessed only through methods. You learn about private data later in this chapter.

When you write a statement such as `myAssistant.setHourlyWage(16.75)`, you are making a call to a method that is contained within the `Employee` class. Because `myAssistant` is an `Employee` object, it is allowed to use the `setHourlyWage()` method that is part of its class. You can tell from the method call that `setHourlyWage()` must accept a numeric parameter.

When you write the application in Figure 10-4, you do not need to know what statements are written within the `Employee` class methods, although you could make an educated guess based on the method names. Before you could execute the application in Figure 10-4, someone would have to write appropriate statements within the `Employee` class methods. If you wrote the methods, of course you would know their contents, but if another programmer has already written the methods, you could use the application without knowing the details contained in the methods. To use the methods, you only need to know their names, parameter lists, and return types.

In Chapter 9, you learned that the ability to use methods as a black box without knowing their contents is a feature of encapsulation. The real world is full of many black-box devices. For example, you can use your television and microwave oven without knowing how they work internally—all you need to understand is the interface. Similarly, with well-written methods that belong to classes you use, you need not understand how they work internally to be able to use them; you need only understand the ultimate result when you use them.

In the client program segment in Figure 10-4, the focus is on the object—the `Employee` named `myAssistant`—and the methods you can use with that object. This is the essence of object-oriented programming.

 In older object-oriented programming languages, simple numbers and characters are said to be **primitive data types**; this distinguishes them from objects that are class types. In the newest programming languages, every item you name, even one that is a numeric or string type, is an object created from a class that defines both data and methods.

 When you instantiate objects, their data fields are stored at separate memory locations. However, all objects of the same class share one copy of the class's methods. You will learn more about this concept later in this chapter.

Creating Class Diagrams

A **class diagram** consists of a rectangle divided into three sections, as shown in Figure 10-5. The top section contains the name of the class, the middle section contains the names and data types of the attributes, and the bottom section contains the methods. This generic class diagram shows two attributes and three methods, but a given class might have any number of attributes or methods, including none. Programmers often use a class diagram to plan or illustrate class features. Class diagrams also are useful for describing a class to nonprogrammers.

Figure 10-6 shows the class diagram for the `Employee` class. By convention, a class diagram lists the names of the data items first; each name is followed by a colon and the data type. Method names are listed next, and each is followed by its data type (return type). Listing the names first and the data types last emphasizes the purposes of the fields and methods.

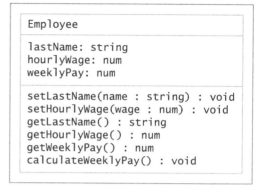

ClassName

Attribute1 : dataType
Attribute2 : dataType

Method1() : dataType
Method2() : dataType
Method3() : dataType

Figure 10-5 Generic class diagram
© 2015 Cengage Learning

Employee

lastName: string
hourlyWage: num
weeklyPay: num

setLastName(name : string) : void
setHourlyWage(wage : num) : void
getLastName() : string
getHourlyWage() : num
getWeeklyPay() : num
calculateWeeklyPay() : void

Figure 10-6 Employee class diagram
© 2015 Cengage Learning

Class diagrams are a type of Unified Modeling Language (UML) diagram. Chapter 13 covers the UML.

Some developers prefer to insert the word void within the parentheses of methods listed in class diagrams when the methods do not have parameter lists. For example, void could be inserted between the parentheses in getLastName() in the class diagram in Figure 10-6. Inserting void shows that a parameter list was not inadvertently omitted. You should follow the conventions of your organization.

Figures 10-5 and 10-6 both show that a class diagram is intended to be only an overview of class attributes and methods. A class diagram shows *what* data items and methods the class will use, not the details of the methods nor *when* they will be used. It is a design tool that helps you see the big picture in terms of class requirements. Figure 10-6 shows the Employee class containing three data fields that represent an employee's name, hourly pay rate, and weekly pay amount. Every Employee object created in a program that uses this class will contain these three data fields. In other words, when you declare an Employee object, the single declaration statement allocates enough memory to hold all three fields.

Figure 10-6 also shows that the Employee class contains six methods. For example, the first method is defined as follows:

```
setLastName(name : string) : void
```

This notation means that the method name is setLastName(), that it takes a single string parameter named name, and that it returns nothing.

Various books, Web sites, and organizations use class diagrams that describe methods in different ways. For example, some developers use the method name only, and others omit parameter lists. This book will take the approach of being as complete as possible, so the class diagrams you see here will contain each method's identifier, parameter list with types, and return type.

The `Employee` class diagram shows that two of the six methods take parameters (`setLastName()` and `setHourlyWage()`). The diagram also shows the return type for each method—three void methods, two numeric methods, and one string method. The class diagram does not indicate what takes place inside the method, although you might be able to make an educated guess. Later, when you write the code that actually creates the `Employee` class, you include method implementation details. For example, Figure 10-7 shows some pseudocode you can use to list the details for the methods in the `Employee` class.

```
class Employee
    Declarations
        string lastName
        num hourlyWage
        num weeklyPay

    void setLastName(string name)
        lastName = name
    return

    void setHourlyWage(num wage)
        hourlyWage = wage
        calculateWeeklyPay()
    return

    string getLastName()
    return lastName

    num getHourlyWage()
    return hourlyWage

    num getWeeklyPay()
    return weeklyPay

    void calculateWeeklyPay()
        Declarations
            num WORK_WEEK_HOURS = 40
        weeklyPay = hourlyWage * WORK_WEEK_HOURS
    return
endClass
```

Figure 10-7 Pseudocode for `Employee` class described in the class diagram in Figure 10-6
© 2015 Cengage Learning

In Figure 10-7, the `Employee` class attributes are identified with a data type and a field name. In addition to listing the required data fields, the figure shows the complete methods for the `Employee` class. The purposes of the methods can be divided into three categories:

- Two of the methods accept values from the outside world; these methods, by convention, have the prefix *set*. These methods are used to set the data fields in the class.

- Three of the methods send data to the outside world; these methods, by convention, have the prefix *get*. These methods return field values to a client program.

- One method performs work within the class; this method is named calculateWeeklyPay(). This method does not communicate with the outside; its purpose is to multiply hourlyWage by the number of hours in a week.

The Set Methods

In Figure 10-7, two methods begin with the word *set*; they are setLastName() and setHourlyWage(). The purpose of a **set method** or **mutator method** is to set or change the values of data fields defined within the class. There is no requirement that such methods start with *set*; the prefix is merely conventional and clarifies the intention of the methods. The method setLastName() is implemented as follows:

```
void setLastName(string name)
    lastName = name
return
```

In this method, a string name is passed in as a parameter and assigned to the field lastName. Because lastName is contained in the same class as this method, the method has access to the field and can alter it.

Similarly, the method setHourlyWage() accepts a numeric parameter and assigns it to the class field hourlyWage. This method also calls the calculateWeeklyPay() method, which sets weeklyPay based on hourlyWage. By writing the setHourlyWage() method to call the calculateWeeklyPay() method automatically, you guarantee that the weeklyPay field is updated any time hourlyWage changes.

When you create an Employee object with a statement such as Employee mySecretary, you can use statements such as the following:

```
mySecretary.setLastName("Johnson")
mySecretary.setHourlyWage(15.00)
```

Instead of literal constants, you could pass variables or named constants to the methods as long as they were the correct data type. For example, if you write a program in which you make the following declaration, then the assignment in the next statement is valid.

```
Declarations
    num PAY_RATE_TO_START = 8.00
mySecretary.setHourlyWage(PAY_RATE_TO_START)
```

In some languages—for example, Visual Basic and C#—you can create a **property** instead of creating a set method. Using a property provides a way to set a field value using a simpler syntax. By convention, if a class field is hourlyWage, its property would be HourlyWage, and in a program you could make a statement similar to mySecretary.HourlyWage = PAY_RATE_TO_START. The implementation of the property HourlyWage (with an uppercase initial letter) would be written in a format very similar to that of the setHourlyWage() method.

Like other methods, the methods that manipulate fields within a class can contain any statements you need. For example, a more complicated setHourlyWage() method that validates input might be written, as in Figure 10-8. In this version, the wage passed to the method is tested against minimum and maximum values, and is assigned to the class field hourlyWage only if it falls within the prescribed limits. If the wage is too low, the MINWAGE value is substituted, and if the wage is too high, the MAXWAGE value is substituted.

```
void setHourlyWage(num wage)
    Declarations
        num MINWAGE = 6.00
        num MAXWAGE = 70.00
    if wage < MINWAGE then
        hourlyWage = MINWAGE
    else
        if wage > MAXWAGE then
            hourlyWage = MAXWAGE
        else
            hourlyWage = wage
        endif
    endif
    calculateWeeklyPay()
return
```

Figure 10-8 setHourlyWage() method including validation
© 2015 Cengage Learning

Similarly, if the set methods in a class required them, the methods could contain output statements, loops, array declarations, or any other legal programming statements. However, if the main purpose of a method is not to set a field value, then for clarity the method should not be named with the *set* prefix.

The Get Methods

The purpose of a **get method** or **accessor method** is to return a value to the world outside the class. In the Employee class in Figure 10-7, the three get methods have the prefix *get*: getLastName(), getHourlyWage(), and getWeeklyPay(). The methods are implemented as follows:

```
string getLastName()
return lastName
```

```
num getHourlyWage()
return hourlyWage
```

```
num getWeeklyPay()
return weeklyPay
```

Each of these methods simply returns the value in the field associated with the method name. Like set methods, any of these get methods could also contain more complex statements as needed. For example, in a more complicated class, you might return the hourly wage of an employee only if the user had also passed an appropriate access code to the method, or you might return the weekly pay value as a string with a dollar sign attached instead of as a numeric value. When you declare an Employee object such as Employee mySecretary, you can then make statements in a program similar to the following:

```
Declarations
    string employeeName
employeeName = mySecretary.getLastName()
output "Wage is ", mySecretary.getHourlyWage()
output "Pay for half a week is ", mySecretary.getWeeklyPay() * 0.5
```

In other words, the value returned from a get method can be used as any other variable of its type would be used. You can assign the value to another variable, display it, perform arithmetic with it, or make any other statement that works correctly with the returned data type.

In some languages—for example, Visual Basic and C#—instead of creating a get method, you can add statements to the property to return a value using simpler syntax. For example, if you created an HourlyWage property, you could write a program that contains the statement output mySecretary. HourlyWage.

Work Methods

The Employee class in Figure 10-7 contains one method that is neither a get nor a set method. This method, calculateWeeklyPay(), is a **work method** within the class. A work method is also known as a **help method** or **facilitator**. It contains a locally named constant that represents the hours in a standard workweek, and it computes the weeklyPay field value by multiplying hourlyWage by the named constant. The method is written as follows:

```
void calculateWeeklyPay()
    Declarations
        num WORK_WEEK_HOURS = 40
    weeklyPay = hourlyWage * WORK_WEEK_HOURS
return
```

No values need to be passed into this method, and no value is returned from it because the method does not communicate with the outside world. Instead, this method is called only from another method in the same class (the setHourlyWage() method), and that method is called from the outside world. Each time a program uses the setHourlyWage() method to alter an Employee's hourlyWage field, calculateWeeklyPay() is called to recalculate the weeklyPay field. No setWeeklyPay() method is included in this Employee class because the intention is that weeklyPay is set only inside the calculateWeeklyPay() method each time the setHourlyWage() method calls it. If you wanted programs to be able to set the weeklyPay field directly, you would have to write a method to allow it.

Programmers who are new to class creation often want to pass the hourlyWage value into the calculateWeeklyPay() method so that it can use the value in its calculation. Although this technique would work, it is not required. The calculateWeeklyPay() method has direct access to the hourlyWage field by virtue of being a member of the same class.

For example, Figure 10-9 shows a program that declares an Employee object and sets the hourly wage value. The program displays the weeklyPay value. Then a new value is assigned to hourlyWage, and weeklyPay is displayed again. As you can see from the output in Figure 10-10, the weeklyPay value has been recalculated even though it was never set directly by the client program.

```
start
   Declarations
      num LOW = 9.00
      num HIGH = 14.65
      Employee myGardener
   myGardener.setLastName("Greene")
   myGardener.setHourlyWage(LOW)
   output "My gardener makes ",
      myGardener.getWeeklyPay(), " per week"
   myGardener.setHourlyWage(HIGH)
   output "My gardener makes ",
      myGardener.getWeeklyPay(), " per week"
stop
```

Figure 10-9 Program that sets and displays Employee data two times
© 2015 Cengage Learning

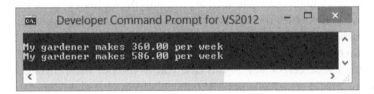

Figure 10-10 Execution of program in Figure 10-9
© 2015 Cengage Learning

TWO TRUTHS & A LIE

Defining Classes and Creating Class Diagrams

1. Every class has a name, data, and methods.

2. After an object has been instantiated, its methods can be accessed using the object's identifier, a dot, and a method call.

3. A class diagram consists of a rectangle divided into three sections; the top section contains the name of the class, the middle section contains the names and data types of the attributes, and the bottom section contains the methods.

The false statement is #1. Most classes contain data and methods, although neither is required.

Understanding Public and Private Access

When you buy a new product, one of the usual conditions of its warranty is that the manufacturer must perform all repair work. For example, if your computer has a warranty and something goes wrong with its operation, you cannot open the system unit yourself, remove and replace parts, and then expect to get your money back for a device that does not work properly. Instead, when something goes wrong, you must take the computer to an approved technician. The manufacturer guarantees that your machine will work properly only if the manufacturer can control how the computer's internal mechanisms are modified.

Similarly, in object-oriented design, you do not want outside programs or methods to alter your class's data fields unless you have control over the process. For example, you might design a class that performs complicated statistical analysis on some data, and you would not want others to be able to alter your carefully crafted result. Or, you might design a class from which others can create an innovative and useful GUI screen object. In this case you would not want anyone altering the dimensions of your artistic design. To prevent outsiders from changing your data fields in ways you do not endorse, you force other programs and methods to use a method that is part of your class to alter data. (Earlier in this chapter, you learned that the principle of keeping data private and inaccessible to outside classes is called *information hiding* or *data hiding*.)

To prevent unauthorized field modifications, object-oriented programmers usually specify that their data fields will have **private access**—the data cannot be accessed by any method that is not part of the class. The methods themselves, like setHourlyWage() in the Employee class, support public access. When methods have **public access**, other programs and methods may use the methods to get access to the private data.

Figure 10-11 shows a complete Employee class to which access specifiers have been added to describe each attribute and method. An **access specifier** is the adjective that defines the type of access (public or private) outside classes will have to the attribute or method. In the figure, each access specifier is shaded.

```
class Employee
   Declarations
      private string lastName
      private num hourlyWage
      private num weeklyPay

   public void setLastName(string name)
      lastName = name
   return

   public void setHourlyWage(num wage)
      hourlyWage = wage
      calculateWeeklyPay()
   return

   public string getLastName()
   return lastName

   public num getHourlyWage()
   return hourlyWage

   public num getWeeklyPay()
   return weeklyPay

   private void calculateWeeklyPay()
      Declarations
         num WORK_WEEK_HOURS = 40
      weeklyPay = hourlyWage * WORK_WEEK_HOURS
   return
endClass
```

Figure 10-11   Employee class including public and private access specifiers
© 2015 Cengage Learning

 In many object-oriented programming languages, if you do not declare an access specifier for a data field or method, then it is private by default. This book will follow the convention of explicitly specifying access for every class member.

In Figure 10-11, each of the data fields is private, which means each field is inaccessible to an object declared in a program. In other words, if a program declares an Employee object, such as Employee myAssistant, then the following statement is illegal:

Don't Do It
You cannot directly assign a value to a private data field from outside its class.

myAssistant.hourlyWage = 15.00

Instead, hourlyWage can be assigned only through a public method as follows:

myAssistant.setHourlyWage(15.00)

If you made hourlyWage public instead of private, then a direct assignment statement would work, but you would violate the important OOP principle of data hiding using encapsulation. Data fields should usually be private, and a client application should be able to access them only through the public interfaces—in other words, through the class's public methods. That way, if you have restrictions on the value of hourlyWage, those restrictions will be enforced by the public method that acts as an interface to the private data field. Similarly, a public get method might control how a private value is retrieved. Perhaps you do not want clients to have access to an Employee's hourlyWage if it is more than a specific value, or maybe you want to return the wage to the client as a string with a dollar sign attached. Even when a field has no data value requirements or restrictions, making data private and providing public set and get methods establishes a framework that makes such modifications easier in the future.

In the Employee class in Figure 10-11, all of the methods are public except one—the calculateWeeklyPay() method is private. That means if you write a program and declare an Employee object such as Employee myAssistant, then the following statement is not permitted:

myAssistant.calculateWeeklyPay() ◄——

> **Don't Do It**
> The calculateWeeklyPay() method is not accessible outside the class.

Because it is private, the only way to call the calculateWeeklyPay() method is from another method that already belongs to the class. In this example, it is called from the setHourlyWage() method. This prevents a client program from setting hourlyWage to one value while setting weeklyPay to an incompatible value. By making the calculateWeeklyPay() method private, you ensure that the class retains full control over when and how it is used.

Classes usually contain private data and public methods, but as you have just seen, they can contain private methods. Classes can contain public data items as well. For example, an Employee class might contain a public constant data field named MINIMUM_WAGE; outside programs then would be able to access that value without using a method. Public data fields are not required to be named constants, but they frequently are.

In some object-oriented programming languages, such as C++, you can label a set of data fields or methods as public or private using the access specifier name just once, then follow it with a list of the items in that category. In other languages, such as Java, you use the specifier *public* or *private* with each field or method. For clarity, this book will label each field and method as public or private.

Many programmers like to specify in class diagrams whether each component in a class is public or private. Figure 10-12 shows the conventions that are typically used. A minus sign (−) precedes the items that are private (less accessible); a plus sign (+) precedes those that are public (more accessible).

```
Employee

-lastName : string
-hourlyWage : num
-weeklyPay : num

+setLastName(name : string) : void
+setHourlyWage(wage : num) : void
+getLastName() : string
+getHourlyWage() : num
+getWeeklyPay() : num
-calculateWeeklyPay() : void
```

447

Figure 10-12   Employee class diagram with public and private access specifiers
© 2015 Cengage Learning

 When you learn more about inheritance in Chapter 11, you will learn about an additional access specifier—the protected access specifier. In a class diagram, you use an octothorpe, also called a pound sign or number sign (#), to indicate protected access.

 In object-oriented programming languages, the main program is most often written as a method named main() or Main(), and that method is virtually always defined as public.

 Watch the video Creating a Class.

TWO TRUTHS & A LIE

Understanding Public and Private Access

1. Object-oriented programmers usually specify that their data fields will have private access.

2. Object-oriented programmers usually specify that their methods will have private access.

3. In a class diagram, a minus sign (–) precedes the items that are private; a plus sign (+) precedes those that are public.

The false statement is #2. Object-oriented programmers usually specify that their methods will have public access.

Organizing Classes

The `Employee` class in Figure 10-12 contains just three data fields and six methods; most classes you create for professional applications will have many more. For example, in addition to a last name and pay information, real employees require an employee number, a first name, address, phone number, hire date, and so on, as well as methods to set and get those fields. As classes grow in complexity, deciding how to organize them becomes increasingly important.

Although it is not required, most programmers place data fields in some logical order at the beginning of a class. For example, an ID number is most likely used as a unique identifier for each employee, so it makes sense to list the employee ID number first in the class. An employee's last name and first name "go together," so it makes sense to store the two components adjacently. Despite these common-sense rules, in most languages you have considerable flexibility when positioning your data fields within a class. For example, depending on the class, you might choose to store the data fields alphabetically, or you might group together all the fields that are the same data type. Alternatively, you might choose to store all public data items first, followed by private ones, or vice versa.

In some languages, you can organize data fields and methods in any order within a class. For example, you could place all the methods first, followed by all the data fields, or you could organize the class so that data fields are followed by methods that use them. This book will follow the convention of placing all data fields first so that you can see their names and data types before reading the methods that use them. This format also echoes the way data and methods appear in standard class diagrams.

For ease in locating a class's methods, some programmers store them in alphabetical order. Other programmers arrange them in pairs of get and set methods, in the same order as the data fields are defined. Another option is to list all accessor (get) methods together and all mutator (set) methods together. Depending on the class, you might decide to create other logically functional groupings. Of course, if your company distributes guidelines for organizing class components, you must follow those rules.

TWO TRUTHS & A LIE

Organizing Classes

1. As classes grow in complexity, deciding how to organize them becomes increasingly important.

2. You have a considerable amount of flexibility in how you organize data fields within a class.

3. In a class, methods must be stored in the order in which they are used.

The false statement is #3. Methods can be stored in alphabetical order, in pairs of get and set methods, in the same order as the data fields are defined, or in any other logically functional groupings.

Understanding Instance Methods

Classes contain data and methods, and every instance of a class possesses the same data and has access to the same methods. For example, Figure 10-13 shows a class diagram for a simple Student class that contains just one private data field for a student's grade point average. The class also contains get and set methods for the field. Figure 10-14 shows the pseudocode for the Student class. This class becomes the model for a new data type named Student; when Student objects are created eventually, each will have its own gradePointAverage field and have access to methods to get and set it.

```
Student

-gradePointAverage : num

+setGradePointAverage(gpa: num) : void
+getGradePointAverage() : num
```

Figure 10-13   Class diagram for Student class
© 2015 Cengage Learning

```
class Student
    Declarations
        private num gradePointAverage

    public void setGradePointAverage(num gpa)
        gradePointAverage = gpa
    return

    public num getGradePointAverage()
    return gradePointAverage
endClass
```

Figure 10-14   Pseudocode for the Student class
© 2015 Cengage Learning

If you create multiple Student objects using the class in Figure 10-14, you need a separate storage location in computer memory to store each Student's unique grade point average. For example, Figure 10-15 shows a client program that creates three Student objects and assigns values to their gradePointAverage fields. It also shows how the Student objects look in memory after the values have been assigned.

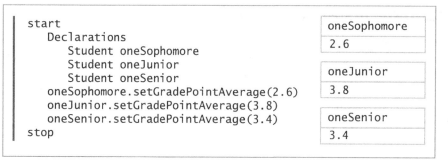

Figure 10-15   StudentDemo program and how Student objects look in memory
© 2015 Cengage Learning

It makes sense for each Student object in Figure 10-15 to have its own gradePointAverage field, but it does not make sense for each Student to have its own copy of the methods that get and set gradePointAverage. Creating identical copies of a method for each instance would be inefficient. Instead, even though every Student has its own gradePointAverage field, only one copy of each of the methods getGradePointAverage() and setGradePointAverage() is stored in memory; however, each instantiated object of the class can use the single method copy. A method that works appropriately with different objects is an **instance method**.

Although the Student class contains only one copy of the get and set methods, they work correctly for any number of instances. Therefore, methods like getGradePointAverage() and setGradePointAverage() are instance methods. Because only one copy of each instance method is stored, the computer needs a way to determine which gradePointAverage is being set or retrieved when one of the methods is called. The mechanism that handles this problem is illustrated in Figure 10-16. When a method call such as oneSophomore. setGradePointAverage(2.6) is made, the true method call, which is invisible and automatically constructed, includes the memory address of the oneSophomore object. (These method calls are represented by the three narrow boxes in the center of Figure 10-16.)

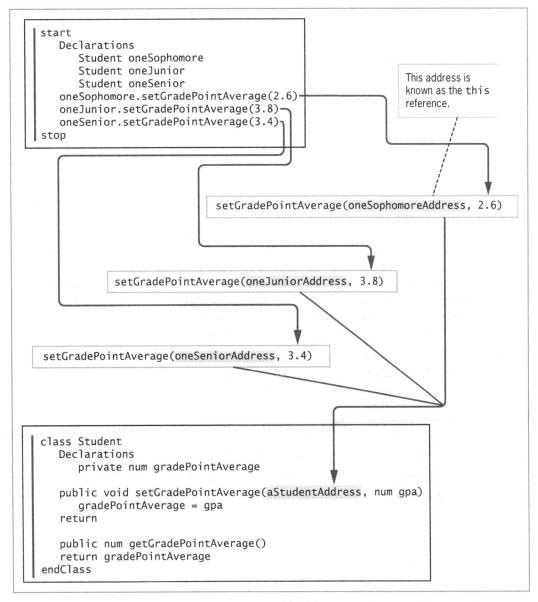

Figure 10-16 How **Student** object memory addresses are passed from an application to an instance method of the **Student** class

Within the **setGradePointAverage()** method in the **Student** class, an invisible and automatically created parameter is added to the list. (For illustration purposes, this parameter is named **aStudentAddress** and is shaded in the **Student** class definition in Figure 10-16. In fact, no parameter is created with that name.) This parameter accepts the address of a **Student** object because the instance method belongs to the **Student** class; if this method belonged to another class—Employee, for example—then the method would accept an address for that type of object. The shaded addresses are not written as code in any program—they are "secretly" sent and received behind the scenes. The address variable in Figure 10-16 is called a this reference. A **this reference** is an automatically created variable that holds the address of an object and passes it to an instance method whenever the method is called. It is called a this reference because it refers to "this particular object" that is using the method at the moment. In other words, an instance method receives a this reference to a specific class instance. In the application in Figure 10-16, when oneSophomore uses the setGradePointAverage() method, the address of the oneSophomore object is contained in the this reference. Later in the program, when the oneJunior object uses the setGradePointAverage() method, the this reference will hold the address of that Student object.

Figure 10-16 shows each place the this reference is used in the Student class. It is implicitly passed as a parameter to each instance method. You never explicitly refer to the this reference when you write the method header for an instance method; Figure 10-16 just shows where it implicitly exists. Within each instance method, the this reference is implied any time you refer to one of the class data fields. For example, when you call setGradePointAverage() using a oneSophomore object, the gradePointAverage assigned within the method is the "*this* gradePointAverage", or the one that belongs to the oneSophomore object. The phrase "this gradePointAverage" usually is written as this, followed by a dot, followed by the field name—this.gradePointAverage.

The this reference exists throughout every instance method. You can explicitly use the this reference with data fields, but it is not required. Figure 10-17 shows two locations where the this reference can be used implicitly, or where you can (but do not have to) use it explicitly. Within an instance method, the following two identifiers mean exactly the same thing:

- any field name defined in the class

- this, followed by a dot, followed by the same field name

For example, within the setGradePointAverage() method, gradePointAverage and this. gradePointAverage refer to exactly the same memory location.

```
class Student
   Declarations
      private num gradePointAverage

   public void setGradePointAverage(num gpa)
      this.gradePointAverage = gpa
   return

   public num getGradePointAverage()
      return this.gradePointAverage
endClass
```

You can write this as a reference in these locations.

Figure 10-17   Explicitly using this in the Student class

The `this` reference can be used only with identifiers that are part of the class definition—that is, field names or instance methods. You cannot use it with local variables that are parameters to instance methods or declared within the method bodies. For example, in Figure 10-17 you can refer to `this.gradePointAverage`, but you cannot refer to `this.gpa` because gpa is not a class field—it is only a local variable.

 The syntax for using `this` differs among programming languages. For example, within a class in C++, you can refer to the `Student` class `gradePointAverage` value as `this->gradePointAverage` or `(*this).gradePointAverage`, but in Java you refer to it as `this.gradePointAverage`. In Visual Basic, the `this` reference is named Me, so the variable would be `Me.gradePointAverage`.

Usually you do not need to use the `this` reference explicitly within the methods you write, but the `this` reference is always there, working behind the scenes, accessing the data field for the correct object.

 Your organization might prefer that you explicitly use the `this` reference for clarity even though it is not required to create a workable program. It is the programmer's responsibility to follow the conventions established at work or by clients.

As an example of when you might use the `this` reference explicitly, consider the following `setGradePointAverage()` method and compare it to the version in the `Student` class in Figure 10-17.

```
public void setGradePointAverage(num gradePointAverage)
   this.gradePointAverage = gradePointAverage
return
```

In this version of the method, the programmer has used the identifier `gradePointAverage` both as the parameter to the method and as the instance field within the class. Therefore, `gradePointAverage` is the name of a local variable within the method whose value is received by passing; it also is the name of a class field. To differentiate the two, you explicitly use the `this` reference with the copy of `gradePointAverage` that is a member of the class. Omitting the `this` reference in this case would result in the local parameter `gradePointAverage` being assigned to itself, and the class's instance variable would not be set. Any time a local variable in a method has the same identifier as a field, the field is hidden; you must use a `this` reference to distinguish the field from the local variable.

 Watch the video *The this Reference.*

TWO TRUTHS & A LIE

Understanding Instance Methods

1. An instance method operates correctly yet differently for each separate instance of a class.

2. A this reference is a variable you must explicitly declare with each class you create.

3. When you write an instance method in a class, the following two identifiers within the method always mean exactly the same thing: any field name or this followed by a dot, followed by the same field name.

The false statement is #2. A this reference is an automatically created variable that holds the address of an object and passes it to an instance method whenever the method is called. You do not declare it explicitly.

Understanding Static Methods

Some methods do not require a this reference because it makes no sense for them either implicitly or explicitly. For example, the displayStudentMotto() method in Figure 10-18 could be added to the Student class. Its purpose is to display a motto that all Student objects use in the same way. The method does not use any data fields from the Student class, so it does not matter which Student object calls it. If you write a program in which you declare 100 Student objects, the displayStudentMotto() method executes in exactly the same way for each of them; it does not need to know whose motto is displayed and it does not need to access any specific object addresses. As a matter of fact, you might want to display the Student motto without instantiating *any* Student objects. Therefore, the displayStudentMotto() method can be written as a static method instead of an instance method.

```
public static void displayStudentMotto()
   output "Every student is an individual"
   output "in the pursuit of knowledge."
   output "Every student strives to be"
   output "a literate, responsible citizen."
return
```

Figure 10-18   Student class displayStudentMotto() method
© 2015 Cengage Learning

When you write a class, you can indicate two types of methods:

- **Static methods**, also called **class methods**, are those for which no object needs to exist, like the displayStudentMotto() method in Figure 10-18. Static methods do not receive a this reference as an implicit parameter. Typically, static methods include the word static in the method header, as shown shaded in Figure 10-18. (Java, C#, and C++ use the keyword static. In Visual Basic, the keyword Shared is used in place of static.)

- **Nonstatic methods** are methods that exist to be used with an object. These instance methods receive a this reference to a specific object. In most programming languages, you use the word static when you want to declare a static class member, but you do not use a special word when you want a class member to be nonstatic. In other words, methods in a class are nonstatic instance methods by default.

 In everyday language, the word *static* means "stationary"; it is the opposite of *dynamic*, which means "changing." In other words, static methods are always the same for every instance of a class, whereas nonstatic methods act differently depending on the object used to call them.

In most programming languages, you use a static method with the class name (but not an object name), as in the following:

Student.displayStudentMotto()

In other words, no object is necessary with a static method.

 In some languages, notably C++, besides using a static method with the class name, you also can use a static method with any object of the class, as in oneSophomore.displayStudentMotto().

TWO TRUTHS & A LIE

Understanding Static Methods

1. Class methods do not receive a this reference.
2. Static methods do not receive a this reference.
3. Nonstatic methods do not receive a this reference.

The false statement is #3. Nonstatic methods receive a this reference automatically.

Using Objects

A class is a complex data type defined by a programmer, but in many ways you can use its instances as you use items of simpler data types. For example, you can pass an object to a method, return an object from a method, or use arrays of objects.

Consider the InventoryItem class in Figure 10-19. The class represents items that a company manufactures and holds in inventory. Each item has a number, description, and price. The class contains a get and set method for each of the three fields.

```
class InventoryItem
    Declarations
        private string inventoryNumber
        private string description
        private num price

    public void setInventoryNumber(string number)
        inventoryNumber = number
    return

    public void setDescription(string description)
        this.description = description
    return

    public void setPrice(num price)
        if(price < 0)
            this.price = 0
        else
            this.price = price
        endif
    return

    public string getInventoryNumber()
    return inventoryNumber

    public string getDescription()
    return description

    public num getPrice()
    return price

endClass
```

Notice the uses of the this reference to differentiate between the method parameter and the class field.

Figure 10-19   InventoryItem class
© 2015 Cengage Learning

Passing an Object to a Method

You can pass an object to a method in the same way you can pass a simple numeric or string variable. For example, Figure 10-20 shows a program that declares an InventoryItem object and passes it to a method for display. The InventoryItem is declared in the main program and assigned values. Then the completed item is passed to a method, where it is displayed. Figure 10-21 shows the execution of the program.

```
start
   Declarations
      InventoryItem oneItem
   oneItem.setInventoryNumber("1276")
   oneItem.setDescription("Mahogany chest")
   oneItem.setPrice(450.00)
   displayItem(oneItem)
stop

public static void displayItem(InventoryItem item)
   Declarations
      num TAX_RATE = 0.06
      num tax
      num pr
      num total
   output "Item #", item.getInventoryNumber()
   output item.getDescription()
   pr = item.getPrice()
   tax = pr * TAX_RATE
   total = pr + tax
   output "Price is $", pr, " plus $", tax, " tax"
   output "Total is $", total
return
```

Figure 10-20 Application that declares and uses an `InventoryItem` object
© 2015 Cengage Learning

Figure 10-21 Execution of application in Figure 10-20
© 2015 Cengage Learning

The `InventoryItem` declared in the main program in Figure 10-20 is passed to the `displayItem()` method in much the same way a numeric or string variable would be. The method receives a copy of the `InventoryItem` that is known locally by the identifier `item`. Within the method, the field values of the local item can be retrieved, displayed, and used in arithmetic statements in the same way they could have been in the main program where the `InventoryItem` was originally declared.

Returning an Object from a Method

Figure 10-22 shows a more realistic application that uses `InventoryItem` objects. In the main program, an `InventoryItem` is declared and the user is prompted for a number. As long as the user does not enter the `QUIT` value, a loop is executed in which the entered inventory item number is passed to the `getItemValues()` method. Within that method, a local `InventoryItem` object is declared. This local object gathers and holds the user's input values. The user is prompted for a description and price, and then the passed item number and newly obtained description and price are assigned to the local `InventoryItem` object via its set methods. The completed object is returned to the program, where it is assigned to the `InventoryItem` object. That item is then passed to the `displayItem()` method. As in the previous example, the method calculates tax and displays results. Figure 10-23 shows a typical execution.

```
start
    Declarations
        InventoryItem oneItem
        string itemNum
        string QUIT = "0"
    output "Enter item number or ", QUIT, " to quit... "
    input itemNum
    while itemNum <> QUIT
        oneItem = getItemValues(itemNum)
        displayItem(oneItem)
        output "Enter next item number or ", QUIT, " to quit... "
        input itemNum
    endwhile
stop

public static InventoryItem getItemValues(string number)
    Declarations
        InventoryItem inItem
        string desc
        num price
    output "Enter description... "
    input desc
    output "Enter price... "
    input price
    inItem.setInventoryNumber(number)
    inItem.setDescription(desc)
    inItem.setPrice(price)
return inItem

public static void displayItem(InventoryItem item)
    Declarations
        num TAX_RATE = 0.06
        num tax
        num pr
        num total
    output "Item #", item.getInventoryNumber()
    output item.getDescription()
    pr = item.getPrice()
    tax = pr * TAX_RATE
    total = pr + tax
    output "Price is $", pr, " plus $", tax, " tax"
    output "Total is $", total
return
```

Figure 10-22   Application that uses `InventoryItem` objects

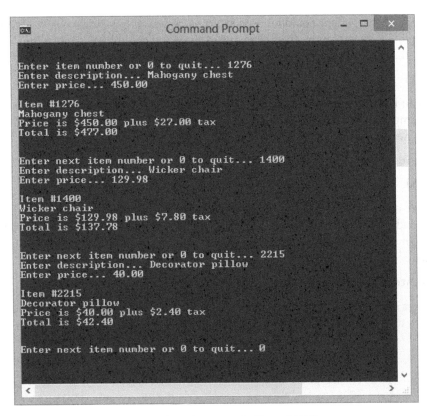

Figure 10-23   Typical execution of program in Figure 10-22
© 2015 Cengage Learning

In Figure 10-22, notice that the return type for the `getItemValues()` method is
`InventoryItem`. A method can return only a single value. Therefore, it is convenient that the
`getItemValues()` method can encapsulate two strings and a number in a single
`InventoryItem` object that it returns to the main program.

Using Arrays of Objects

In Chapter 6, you learned that when you declare an array, you use the data type, an identifier,
and a size contained in brackets. For example, the following statements declare `num` and
`string` arrays, respectively:

```
num scores[10]
string names[5]
```

You can use the same syntax to declare object arrays: a data type (class), an identifier, and a
size in brackets. For example, you could declare an array of seven `InventoryItem` objects as
follows:

```
InventoryItem items[7]
```

Any individual items array element could be used in the same way as any single object of the InventoryItem type. For example, the third element in the array could be passed to the displayItem() method in Figure 10-22 using the following statement:

```
display(items[2])
```

The entire array can be passed to a method that defines an array of the correct type as a parameter. For example, the statement displayArray(items) can be used to call a method with the following header:

```
public static void displayArray(InventoryItem[] list)
```

Within this method, the array would be known as list.

Any public member of the InventoryItem class can be used with any object in the array by using a subscript to identify the element. For example, the xth element in the items array can use the public setInventoryNumber() method of the InventoryItem class by using the following statement:

```
items[x].setInventoryNumber(34);
```

Figure 10-24 shows a complete program that declares seven InventoryItem objects, sets their values, and displays them.

```
start
   Declarations
      num SIZE = 7
      InventoryItem items[SIZE]
      num sub
   sub = 0
   while sub < SIZE
      items[sub] = getItemValues()
      sub = sub + 1
   endwhile
   displayItems(items, SIZE)
stop

public static InventoryItem getItemValues()
   Declarations
      InventoryItem item
      num itemNum
      string desc
      num price
   output "Enter item number … "
   input itemNum
   output "Enter description… "
   input desc
   output "Enter price… "
   input price
   item.setInventoryNumber(number)
   item.setDescription(desc)
   item.setPrice(price)
return item

public static void displayItems(InventoryItem[] items, num SIZE)
   Declarations
      num TAX_RATE = 0.06
      num tax
      num pr
      num total
      int x
   x = 0
   while x < SIZE
      output "Item number #", items[x].getInventoryNumber()
      output items[x].getDescription()
      pr = items[x].getPrice()
      tax = pr * TAX_RATE
      total = pr + tax
      output "Price is $", pr, " plus $", tax, " tax"
      output "Total is $", total
      x = x + 1
   endwhile
return
```

Figure 10-24   Application that uses an array of InventoryItem objects

© 2015 Cengage Learning

In the program in Figure 10-24, a constant is declared for the size of the array, and then the array is declared. The program uses a `while` loop to call a method named `getItemValues()` seven times. The method accepts no parameters. It declares an `InventoryItem` object, and then it prompts the user for an item number, description, and price. Those values are assigned to the `InventoryItem` object using its public methods. The completed object is then returned to the main program, which passes the array and its size to a method named `displayItems()` that displays data for all the items.

The program in Figure 10-24 could have been written so that the entire array was passed to a method to get the data, and then a loop could have been used within the method. The program also could have been written so that the display method accepted only one `InventoryItem` object instead of the entire array, and then it would have been necessary to call the method seven times in a loop. As you have learned throughout this book, there are often multiple ways to accomplish the same goal. A mixture of methods was used for the program in Figure 10-24 to demonstrate how both approaches work.

TWO TRUTHS & A LIE

Using Objects

1. You can pass an object to a method.

2. Because only one value can be returned from a method, you cannot return an object that holds more than one field.

3. You can declare an object locally within a method.

The false statement is #2. An object can be returned from a method.

Chapter Summary

- Classes are the basic building blocks of object-oriented programming. A class describes a collection of objects; each object is an instance of a class. A class's fields, or instance variables, hold its data, and every object that is an instance of a class has access to the same methods. A program or class that instantiates objects of another prewritten class is a class client or class user. In addition to classes and objects, three important features of object-oriented languages are polymorphism, inheritance, and encapsulation.

- A class definition is a set of program statements that list the fields and methods each object can use. A class definition can contain a name, data, and methods. Programmers often use a class diagram to illustrate class features. Many methods contained in a class can be divided into three categories: set methods, get methods, and work methods.

- Object-oriented programmers usually specify that their data fields will have private access—that is, the data cannot be accessed by any method that is not part of the class. The methods frequently support public access, which means that other programs and methods may use the methods that control access to the private data. In a class diagram, a minus sign (–) precedes each item that is private; a plus sign (+) precedes each item that is public.

- As classes grow in complexity, deciding how to organize them becomes increasingly important. Depending on the class, you might choose to store the data fields by listing a key field first. You also might list fields alphabetically, by data type, or by accessibility. Methods might be stored in alphabetical order or in pairs of get and set methods.

- An instance method operates correctly yet differently for every object instantiated from a class. When an instance method is called, a `this` reference that holds the object's memory address is automatically and implicitly passed to the method.

- A class may contain two types of methods: static methods, which are also known as class methods and do not receive a `this` reference as an implicit parameter; and nonstatic methods, which are instance methods and do receive a `this` reference implicitly.

- You can use objects in many of the same ways you use items of simpler data types, such as passing them to and from methods and creating arrays.

463

Key Terms

Object-oriented programming (OOP) is a programming model that focuses on an application's components and data and the methods you need to manipulate them.

A **class** describes a group or collection of objects with common attributes.

An **object** is one tangible example of a class; it is an instance of a class.

An **instance** is one tangible example of a class; it is an object.

An **instantiation** of a class is an instance or object.

To **instantiate** an object is to create it.

Attributes are the characteristics that define an object.

An **is-a relationship** exists between an object and its class.

A class's **instance variables** are the data components that belong to every instantiated object.

Fields are object attributes or data.

The **state** of an object is the set of all the values or contents of its instance variables.

A **class client** or **class user** is a program or class that instantiates objects of another prewritten class.

Pure polymorphism describes situations in which one method is used with a variety of arguments.

Inheritance is the process of acquiring the traits of one's predecessors.

Encapsulation is the process of combining all of an object's attributes and methods into a single package.

Information hiding (or **data hiding**) is the concept that other classes should not alter an object's attributes—only the methods of an object's own class should have that privilege.

A **class definition** is a set of program statements that define the fields and methods for a class.

A **user-defined type**, or **programmer-defined type**, is a type that is not built into a language but is created by an application's programmer.

An **abstract data type** (ADT) is a programmer-defined type, such as a class.

Primitive data types are simple numbers and characters that are not class types.

A **class diagram** consists of a rectangle divided into three sections that show the name, data, and methods of a class.

A **set method** is an instance method that sets or changes the value of a data field defined in a class.

A **mutator method** is an instance method that sets or changes the value of a data field defined in a class.

A **property** provides methods that allow you to get and set a class field value using a simple syntax.

A **get method** is an instance method that returns a value from a field defined in a class.

An **accessor method** is an instance method that returns a value from a field defined in a class.

A **work method** performs tasks within a class.

A **help method** or **facilitator** is a work method.

Private access specifies that data or methods cannot be used by any method that is not part of the same class.

Public access specifies that other programs and methods may use the specified data or methods within a class.

An **access specifier** is the adjective that defines the type of access outside classes will have to the attribute or method.

An **instance method** operates correctly yet differently for each object. An instance method is nonstatic and implicitly receives a `this` reference.

A **`this` reference** is an automatically created variable that holds the address of an object and passes it to an instance method whenever the method is called.

Static methods are those for which no object needs to exist; they are not instance methods and they do not receive a `this` reference.

A **class method** is a static method; it is not an instance method and it does not receive a `this` reference.

Nonstatic methods are methods that exist to be used with an object; they are instance methods and receive a `this` reference.

Exercises

 Review Questions

1. Which of the following means the same as *object*?

   a. class
   b. instance
   c. field
   d. category

2. Which of the following means the same as *instance variable*?

   a. class
   b. instance
   c. category
   d. field

3. A program that instantiates objects of another prewritten class is a(n) _____ .

   a. client
   b. object
   c. instance
   d. GUI

4. The relationship between an instance and a class is a(n) _____ relationship.

   a. has-a
   b. is-a
   c. polymorphic
   d. hostile

5. Which of these does not belong with the others?

   a. instance variable
   b. attribute
   c. field
   d. object

6. The process of acquiring the traits of one's predecessors is _____ .

   a. polymorphism
   b. encapsulation
   c. inheritance
   d. orientation

7. When discussing classes and objects, *encapsulation* means that _____ .

   a. all the fields belong to the same object
   b. all the fields are private
   c. all the fields and methods are grouped together
   d. all the methods are public

8.   Every class definition must contain _____ .

    a.   a name   c.   methods

    b.   data   d.   all of the above

9.   Assume that a working program contains the following statement:
`myDog.setName("Bowser")`

Which of the following do you know?

    a.   `setName()` is a public method.

    b.   `setName()` accepts a string parameter.

    c.   both of the above

    d.   none of the above

10.   Assume that a working program contains the following statement:
`name = myDog.getName()`

Which of the following do you know?

    a.   `getName()` returns a string.

    b.   `getName()` returns a value that is the same data type as `name`.

    c.   both of the above

    d.   none of the above

11.   A class diagram _____ .

    a.   provides an overview of a class's data and methods

    b.   provides method implementation details

    c.   is never used by nonprogrammers because it is too technical

    d.   all of the above

12.   Which of the following is the most likely scenario for a specific class?

    a.   Its data is private and its methods are public.

    b.   Its data is public and its methods are private.

    c.   Its data and methods are both public.

    d.   Its data and methods are both private.

13.   An instance method _____ .

    a.   is static   c.   both of the above

    b.   receives a `this` reference   d.   none of the above

14.   Assume that you have created a class named `Dog` that contains a data field named `weight` and an instance method named `setWeight()`. Further assume that the `setWeight()` method accepts a numeric parameter named `weight`. Which of the following statements correctly sets a `Dog`'s weight within the `setWeight()` method?

    a.   `weight = weight`   c.   `weight = this.weight`

    b.   `this.weight = this.weight`   d.   `this.weight = weight`

15. A static method is also known as a(n) _____ method.

    a. instance   c. private
    b. public   d. class

16. By default, methods contained in a class are _____ methods.

    a. static   c. class
    b. nonstatic   d. public

17. Assume that you have created a class named MyClass, and that a working program contains the following statement:

    output MyClass.number

    Which of the following do you know?

    a. number is a numeric field.   c. number is an instance variable.
    b. number is a static field.   d. all of the above

18. Assume that you have created an object named myObject and that a working program contains the following statement:

    output myObject.getSize()

    Which of the following do you know?

    a. getSize() is a static method.
    b. getSize() returns a number.
    c. getSize() receives a this reference.
    d. all of the above

19. Assume that you have created a class that contains a private field named myField and a nonstatic public method named myMethod(). Which of the following is true?

    a. myMethod() has access to myField and can use it.
    b. myMethod() does not have access to myField and cannot use it.
    c. myMethod() can use myField but cannot pass it to other methods.
    d. myMethod() can use myField only if it is passed to myMethod() as a parameter.

20. An object can be _____ .

    a. stored in an array   c. returned from a method
    b. passed to a method   d. all of the above

Programming Exercises

1. Identify three objects that might belong to each of the following classes:

    a. Building
    b. Artist
    c. BankLoan

2. Identify three different classes that might contain each of these objects:

   a. William Shakespeare

   b. My favorite red sweater

   c. Public School 23 in New York City

3. Design a class named TermPaper that holds an author's name, the subject of the paper, and an assigned letter grade. Include methods to set the values for each data field and display the values for each data field. Create the class diagram and write the pseudocode that defines the class.

4. Design a class named Automobile that holds the vehicle identification number, make, model, and color of an automobile. Include methods to set the values for each data field, and include a method that displays all the values for each field. Create the class diagram and write the pseudocode that defines the class.

5. Complete the following tasks:

   a. Design a class named CheckingAccount that holds a checking account number, name of account holder, and balance. Include methods to set values for each data field and a method that displays all the account information. Create the class diagram and write the pseudocode that defines the class.

   b. Design an application that declares two CheckingAccount objects and sets and displays their values.

   c. Design an application that declares an array of five CheckingAccount objects. Prompt the user for data for each object, and then display all the values.

   d. Design an application that declares an array of five CheckingAccount objects. Prompt the user for data for each object, and then pass the array to a method that determines the sum of the balances.

6. Complete the following tasks:

   a. Design a class named StockTransaction that holds a stock symbol (typically one to four characters), stock name, and price per share. Include methods to set and get the values for each data field. Create the class diagram and write the pseudocode that defines the class.

   b. Design an application that declares two StockTransaction objects and sets and displays their values.

   c. Design an application that declares an array of 10 StockTransaction objects. Prompt the user for data for each object, and then display all the values.

   d. Design an application that declares an array of 10 StockTransaction objects. Prompt the user for data for each object, and then pass the array to a method that determines and displays the two stocks with the highest and lowest price per share.

7. Complete the following tasks:

   a. Design a class named `Pizza`. Data fields include a string field for a topping (such as pepperoni) and numeric fields for diameter in inches (such as 12) and price (such as 13.99). Include methods to get and set values for each of these fields. Create the class diagram and write the pseudocode that defines the class.

   b. Design an application that declares two `Pizza` objects and sets and displays their values.

   c. Design an application that declares an array of 10 `Pizza` objects. Prompt the user for data for each `Pizza`, then display all the values.

   d. Design an application that declares an array of 10 `Pizza` objects. Prompt the user for a topping and diameter for each `Pizza`, and pass each object to a method that computes the price and returns the complete `Pizza` object to the main program. Then display all the `Pizza` values. A 12–inch pizza is $13.99, a 14–inch pizza is $16.99, and a 15–inch pizza is $19.99. Any other entered size is invalid and should cause the price to be set to 0.

8. Complete the following tasks:

   a. Design a class named `BaseballGame` that has fields for two team names and a final score for each team. Include methods to set and get the values for each data field. Create the class diagram and write the pseudocode that defines the class.

   b. Design an application that declares three `BaseballGame` objects and sets and displays their values.

   c. Design an application that declares an array of 12 `BaseballGame` objects. Prompt the user for data for each object, and display all the values. Then pass each object to a method that displays the name of the winning team or "Tie" if the score is a tie.

 Performing Maintenance

1. A file named MAINTENANCE10-01.txt is included with your downloadable student files. Assume that this program is a working program in your organization and that it needs modifications as described in the comments (lines that begin with two slashes) at the beginning of the file. Your job is to alter the program to meet the new specifications.

Find the Bugs

1. Your downloadable student files for Chapter 10 include DEBUG10-01.txt, DEBUG10-02.txt, and DEBUG10-03.txt. Each file starts with some comments that describe the problem. Comments are lines that begin with two slashes (//). Following the comments, each file contains pseudocode that has one or more bugs you must find and correct.

2. Your downloadable files for Chapter 10 include a file named DEBUG10-04.jpg that contains a class diagram with syntax and/or logical errors. Examine the class diagram and then find and correct all the bugs.

Game Zone

1. a. Playing cards are used in many computer games, including versions of such classics as Solitaire, Hearts, and Poker. Design a Card class that contains a string data field to hold a suit (spades, hearts, diamonds, or clubs) and a numeric data field for a value from 1 to 13. Include get and set methods for each field. Write an application that randomly selects two playing cards and displays their values.

   b. Using two Card objects, design an application that plays a simple version of the card game War. Deal two Cards—one for the computer and one for the player. Determine the higher card, then display a message indicating whether the cards are equal, the computer won, or the player won. (Playing cards are considered equal when they have the same value, no matter what their suit is.) For this game, assume that the Ace (value 1) is low. Make sure that the two Cards dealt are not the same Card. For example, a deck cannot contain more than one Queen of Spades.

Up for Discussion

1. In this chapter, you learned that instance data and methods belong to objects, but that static data and methods belong to a class as a whole. Consider the real-life class named StateInTheUnitedStates. Name some real-life attributes of this class that are static attributes and instance attributes. Create another example of a real-life class and discuss what its static and instance members might be.

2. Some programmers use a convention called *Hungarian notation* when naming their variables and class fields. What is Hungarian notation, and why do many object-oriented programmers feel it is not a valuable convention to use?

Understanding Numbering Systems and Computer Codes

The numbering system you know best is the **decimal numbering system**—the system based on 10 digits, 0 through 9. Mathematicians call decimal-system numbers **base 10** numbers. When you use the decimal system, only the value symbols 0 through 9 are available; if you want to express a value larger than 9, you must use multiple digits from the same pool of 10, placing them in columns.

When you use the decimal system, you analyze a multicolumn number by mentally assigning place values to each column. The value of the far right column is 1, the value of the next column to the left is 10, the next column is 100, and so on; the column values are multiplied by 10 as you move to the left. There is no limit to the number of columns you can use; you simply keep adding columns to the left as you need to express higher values. For example, Figure A-1 shows how the value 305 is represented in the decimal system. You simply sum the value of the digit in each column after it has been multiplied by the value of its column.

```
  Column value
  100   10    1
 +----+----+----+
 |  3 |  0 |  5 |
 +----+----+----+

 3 * 100  = 300
 0 * 10   =   0
 5 * 1    =   5
            ---
            305
```

Figure A-1   Representing 305 in the decimal system

© 2015 Cengage Learning

The **binary numbering system** works in the same way as the decimal numbering system, except that it uses only two digits, 0 and 1. Mathematicians call these numbers **base 2** numbers. When you use the binary system, you must use multiple columns if you want to express a value greater than 1 because no single symbol is available that represents any value other than 0 or 1. However, instead of each new column to the left being 10 times greater than the previous column, each new column in the binary system is only two times the value of the previous column. For example, Figure A-2 shows how the numbers 9 and 305 are represented in the binary system. Notice that in both the binary system and the decimal system, it is perfectly acceptable—and often necessary—to create numbers with 0 in one or more columns. As with the decimal system, there is no limit to the number of columns used in a binary number—you can use as many as it takes to express a value.

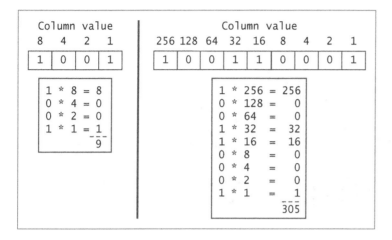

Figure A-2 Representing decimal values 9 and 305 in the binary system

© 2015 Cengage Learning

A computer stores every piece of data it uses as a set of 0s and 1s. Each 0 or 1 is known as a **bit**, which is short for *binary digit*. Every computer uses 0s and 1s because all values in a computer are stored as electronic signals that are either on or off. This two-state system is most easily represented using just two digits.

Computers use a set of binary digits to represent stored characters. If computers used only one binary digit to represent characters, then only two different characters could be represented, because the single bit could be only 0 or 1. If computers used only two digits to represent characters, then only four characters could be represented—the four codes 00, 01, 10, and 11, which in decimal values are 0, 1, 2, and 3, respectively. Many computers use sets of eight binary digits to represent each character they store, because using eight binary digits provides 256 different combinations. A set of eight bits is a **byte**. One byte combination can represent an *A*, another a *B*, still others *a* and *b*, and so on. Two hundred fifty-six combinations are enough so that each capital letter, lowercase letter, digit, and punctuation mark used in English has its own code; even a space has a code. For example, in the system named the **American Standard Code for Information Interchange (ASCII)**, 01000001 represents the character *A*. The binary number 01000001 has a decimal value of 65, but this numeric value is not important to ordinary computer users; it is simply a code that stands for *A*.

The ASCII code is not the only computer code, but it is typical, and is the one used in most personal computers. The **Extended Binary Coded Decimal Interchange Code**, or **EBCDIC**, is an eight-bit code that is used in IBM mainframe computers. In these computers, the principle is the same— every character is stored in a byte as a series of binary digits. However, the actual values used are different. For example, in EBCDIC, an *A* is 11000001, or 193. Another code used by languages such as Java and C# is **Unicode**; with this code, 16 bits are used to represent each character. The character *A* in Unicode has the same decimal value as the ASCII *A*, 65, but it is stored as 0000000001000001.

Using two bytes provides many more possible combinations than using only eight bits—65,536 to be exact. With Unicode, enough codes are available to represent all English letters and digits, as well as characters from many international alphabets.

Ordinary computer users seldom think about the numeric codes behind the letters, numbers, and punctuation marks they enter from their keyboards or see displayed on a monitor. However, they see the consequence of the values behind letters when they see data sorted in alphabetical order. When you sort a list of names, *Andrea* comes before *Brian*, and *Caroline* comes after *Brian* because the numeric code for *A* is lower than the code for *B*, and the numeric code for *C* is higher than the code for *B*, no matter whether you use ASCII, EBCDIC, or Unicode.

Table A-1 shows the decimal and binary values behind the most commonly used characters in the ASCII character set—the letters, numbers, and punctuation marks you can enter from your keyboard using a single key press. (Other values not shown in Table A-1 also have specific purposes. For example, when you display the character that holds the decimal value 7, nothing appears on the screen, but a bell sounds. Programmers often use this character when they want to alert a user to an error or some other unusual condition.)

 Each binary number in Table A-1 is shown containing two sets of four digits; this convention makes the eight-digit numbers easier to read. Four digits, or a half byte, is a **nibble**.

Decimal Number	Binary Number	ASCII Character	Decimal Number	Binary Number	ASCII Character
32	0010 0000	Space	43	0010 1011	+ Plus sign
33	0010 0001	! Exclamation point	44	0010 1100	, Comma
34	0010 0010	" Quotation mark, or double quote	45	0010 1101	- Hyphen or minus sign
35	0010 0011	# Number sign, also called an octothorpe or a pound sign	46	0010 1110	. Period or decimal point
			47	0010 1111	/ Slash or front slash
36	0010 0100	$ Dollar sign	48	0011 0000	0
37	0010 0101	% Percent	49	0011 0001	1
38	0010 0110	& Ampersand	50	0011 0010	2
39	0010 0111	' Apostrophe, single quote	51	0011 0011	3
40	0010 1000	(Left parenthesis	52	0011 0100	4
41	0010 1001	) Right parenthesis	53	0011 0101	5
42	0010 1010	* Asterisk	54	0011 0110	6

Table A-1   Decimal and binary values for common ASCII characters (*continues*)

(continued)

Decimal Number	Binary Number	ASCII Character		Decimal Number	Binary Number	ASCII Character	
55	0011 0111	7		83	0101 0011	S	
56	0011 1000	8		84	0101 0100	T	
57	0011 1001	9		85	0101 0101	U	
58	0011 1010	:	Colon	86	0101 0110	V	
59	0011 1011	;	Semicolon	87	0101 0111	W	
60	0011 1100	<	Less-than sign	88	0101 1000	X	
61	0011 1101	=	Equal sign	89	0101 1001	Y	
62	0011 1110	>	Greater-than sign	90	0101 1010	Z	
63	0011 1111	?	Question mark	91	0101 1011	[	Opening or left bracket
64	0100 0000	@	At sign	92	0101 1100	\	Backslash
65	0100 0001	A		93	0101 1101	]	Closing or right bracket
66	0100 0010	B		94	0101 1110	^	Caret
67	0100 0011	C		95	0101 1111	_	Underline or underscore
68	0100 0100	D		96	0110 0000	`	Grave accent
69	0100 0101	E		97	0110 0001	a	
70	0100 0110	F		98	0110 0010	b	
71	0100 0111	G		99	0110 0011	c	
72	0100 1000	H		100	0110 0100	d	
73	0100 1001	I		101	0110 0101	e	
74	0100 1010	J		102	0110 0110	f	
75	0100 1011	K		103	0110 0111	g	
76	0100 1100	L		104	0110 1000	h	
77	0100 1101	M		105	0110 1001	i	
78	0100 1110	N		106	0110 1010	j	
79	0100 1111	O		107	0110 1011	k	
80	0101 0000	P		108	0110 1100	l	
81	0101 0001	Q					
82	0101 0010	R					

Table A-1   Decimal and binary values for common ASCII characters (*continues*)

(continued)

Decimal Number	Binary Number	ASCII Character	Decimal Number	Binary Number	ASCII Character
109	0110 1101	m	118	0111 0110	v
110	0110 1110	n	119	0111 0111	w
111	0110 1111	o	120	0111 1000	x
112	0111 0000	p	121	0111 1001	y
113	0111 0001	q	122	0111 1010	z
114	0111 0010	r	123	0111 1011	{ Opening or left brace
115	0111 0011	s	124	0111 1100	| Vertical line or pipe
116	0111 0100	t	125	0111 1101	} Closing or right brace
117	0111 0101	u	126	0111 1110	~ Tilde

Table A-1 Decimal and binary values for common ASCII characters

The Hexadecimal System

The **hexadecimal numbering system** is the **base 16** system; it uses 16 digits. As shown in Table A-2, the digits are 0 through 9 and A through F. Computer professionals often use the hexadecimal system to express addresses and instructions as they are stored in computer memory because hexadecimal provides convenient shorthand expressions for groups of binary values. In Table A-2, each hexadecimal value represents one of the 16 possible combinations of four-digit binary values. Therefore, instead of referencing memory contents as a 16-digit binary value, for example, programmers can use a 4-digit hexadecimal value.

Decimal Value	Hexadecimal Value	Binary Value (shown using four digits)	Decimal Value	Hexadecimal Value	Binary Value (shown using four digits)
0	0	0000	8	8	1000
1	1	0001	9	9	1001
2	2	0010	10	A	1010
3	3	0011	11	B	1011
4	4	0100	12	C	1100
5	5	0101	13	D	1101
6	6	0110	14	E	1110
7	7	0111	15	F	1111

Table A-2 Values in the decimal and hexadecimal systems

In the hexadecimal system, each column is 16 times the value of the column to its right. Therefore, column values from right to left are 1, 16, 256, 4096, and so on. Figure A-3 shows how 78, 171, and 305 are expressed in hexadecimal.

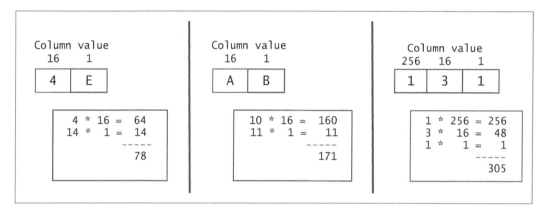

Figure A-3   Representing decimal values 78, 171, and 305 in the hexadecimal system

© 2015 Cengage Learning

Measuring Storage

In computer systems, both internal memory and external storage are measured in bits and bytes. Eight bits make a byte, and a byte frequently holds a single character (in ASCII or EBCDIC) or half a character (in Unicode). Because a byte is such a small unit of storage, the size of memory and files is often expressed in thousands or millions of bytes. Table A-3 describes some commonly used terms for storage measurement.

Term	Abbreviation	Number of Bytes Using Binary System	Number of Bytes Using Decimal System	Example
Kilobyte	KB or kB	1024	one thousand	In Microsoft Word, this appendix occupies about 70 kB on a hard disk.
Megabyte	MB	1,048,576 (1024 × 1024 kilobytes)	one million	One megabyte can hold an average book in text format.
Gigabyte	GB	1,073,741,824 (1,024 megabytes)	one billion	A gigabyte can hold a symphony recording in high fidelity or a movie at TV quality.

Table A-3   Commonly used terms for computer storage (*continues*)

(continued)

Term	Abbreviation	Number of Bytes Using Binary System	Number of Bytes Using Decimal System	Example
Terabyte	TB	1024 gigabytes	one trillion	Some hard drives are 1 terabyte. The Web archive data of the Library of Congress occupied about 500 terabytes when this book was published.
Petabyte	PB	1024 terabytes	one quadrillion	The Google Web site processes about 24 petabytes per day.
Exabyte	EB	1024 petabytes	one quintillion	A popular expression claims that all words ever spoken by humans could be stored in text form in 5 exabytes.
Zettabyte	ZB	1024 exabytes	one sextillion	A popular expression claims that all words ever spoken by humans could be stored in audio form in 42 zettabytes.
Yottabyte	YB	1024 zettabytes	one septillion (a 1 followed by 24 zeros)	The combined space on all hard drives in the world is less than 1 yottabyte.

Table A-3   Commonly used terms for computer storage

In the metric system, *kilo* means 1000. However, in Table A-3, notice that a kilobyte is 1024 bytes. The discrepancy occurs because everything stored in a computer is based on the binary system, so multiples of two are used in most measurements. If you multiply 2 by itself 10 times, the result is 1024, which is a little over 1000. Similarly, a gigabyte is 1,073,741,824 bytes, which is more than a billion.

Confusion arises because many hard-drive manufacturers use the decimal system instead of the binary system to describe storage. For example, if you buy a hard drive that holds 10 gigabytes, it holds exactly 10 billion bytes. However, in the binary system, 10 GB is 10,737,418,240 bytes, so when you check your hard drive's capacity, your computer will report that you don't quite have 10 GB, but only 9.31 GB.

Key Terms

The **decimal numbering system** is the numbering system based on 10 digits and in which column values are multiples of 10.

Base 10 describes numbers created using the decimal numbering system.

The **binary numbering system** is the numbering system based on 2 digits and in which column values are multiples of 2.

Base 2 describes numbers created using the binary numbering system.

A **bit** is a binary digit; it is a unit of storage equal to one-eighth of a byte.

A **byte** is a storage measurement equal to eight bits.

American Standard Code for Information Interchange (**ASCII**) is an eight-bit character coding scheme used on many personal computers.

Extended Binary Coded Decimal Interchange Code (**EBCDIC**) is an eight-bit character coding scheme used on many larger computers.

Unicode is a 16-bit character coding scheme.

A **nibble** is a storage measurement equal to four bits, or a half byte.

The **hexadecimal numbering system** is the numbering system based on 16 digits and in which column values are multiples of 16.

Base 16 describes numbers created using the hexadecimal numbering system.

Solving Difficult Structuring Problems

In Chapter 3, you learned that you can solve any logical problem using only the three standard structures—sequence, selection, and loop. Modifying an unstructured program to make it adhere to structured rules often is a simple matter. Sometimes, however, structuring a more complicated program can be challenging. Still, no matter how complicated, large, or poorly structured a problem is, the same tasks can *always* be accomplished in a structured manner.

Consider the flowchart segment in Figure B-1. Is it structured?

No, it is not structured. To straighten out the flowchart segment, making it structured, you can use the "spaghetti" method. Untangle each path of the flowchart as if you were attempting to untangle strands of spaghetti in a bowl. The objective is to create a new flowchart segment that performs exactly the same tasks as the first, but using only the three structures—sequence, selection, and loop.

To begin to untangle the unstructured flowchart segment, you start at the beginning with the decision labeled A, shown in Figure B-2. This step must represent

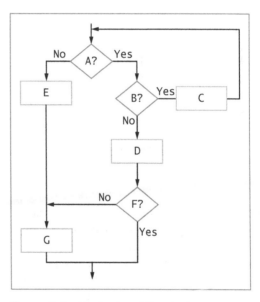

Figure B-1   Unstructured flowchart segment
© 2015 Cengage Learning

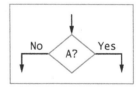

Figure B-2   Structuring, Step 1
© 2015 Cengage Learning

the beginning of either a selection or a loop, because a sequence would not contain a decision.

If you follow the logic on the *No*, or left, side of the question in the original flowchart, you can pull up on the left branch of the decision. You encounter process E, followed by G, followed by the end, as shown in Figure B-3. Compare the *No* actions after Decision A in the first flowchart (Figure B-1) with the actions after Decision A in Figure B-3; they are identical.

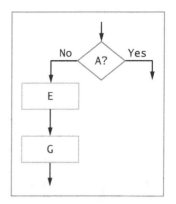

Figure B-3 Structuring, Step 2
© 2015 Cengage Learning

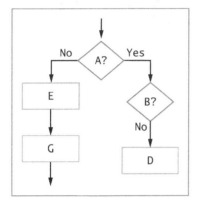

Figure B-4 Structuring, Step 3
© 2015 Cengage Learning

Now continue on the right, or *Yes*, side of Decision A in Figure B-1. When you follow the flowline, you encounter a decision symbol labeled B. Pull on B's left side, and a process, D, comes up next. See Figure B-4.

After Step D in the original diagram, a decision labeled F comes up. Pull on its left, or *No*, side and you get a process, G, and then the end. When you pull on F's right, or *Yes*, side in the original flowchart, you simply reach the end, as shown in Figure B-5. Notice in Figure B-5 that the G process now appears in two locations. When you improve unstructured flowcharts so that they become structured, you often must repeat steps to eliminate crossed lines and spaghetti logic that is difficult to follow.

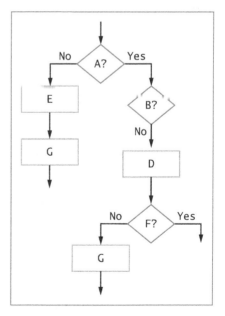

Figure B-5 Structuring, Step 4
© 2015 Cengage Learning

The biggest problem in structuring the original flowchart segment from Figure B-1 follows the right, or *Yes*, side of the B decision. When the answer to B is *Yes*, you encounter process C, as shown in Figures B-1 and B-6. The structure that begins with Decision C looks like a loop because it doubles back, up to Decision A. However, a structured loop must have the appearance shown in Figure B-7: a question followed by a structure, returning right back to the question. In Figure B-1, if the path coming from C returned directly to B, there would be no problem; it would be a simple, structured loop. However, as it is, Question A must be repeated. The spaghetti technique requires that if lines of logic are tangled up, start repeating the steps in question. So, you repeat an A decision after C, as Figure B-6 shows.

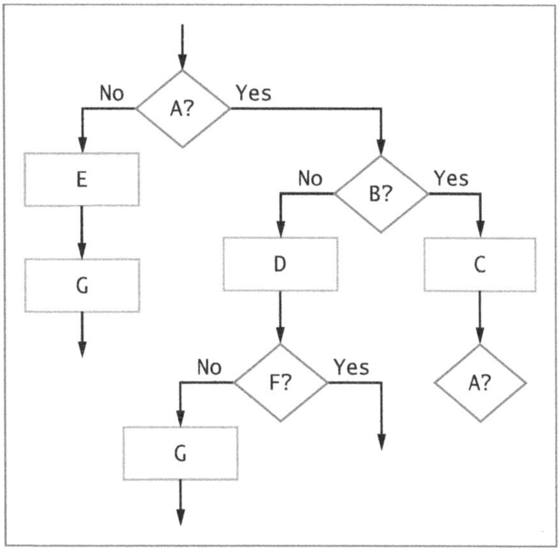

Figure B-6 Structuring, Step 5
© 2015 Cengage Learning

In the original flowchart segment in Figure B-1, when A is *Yes*, Question B always follows. So, in Figure B-8, after A is *Yes* and B is *Yes*, Step C executes, and A is asked again; when A is *Yes*, B repeats. In the original, when B is *Yes*, C executes, so in Figure B-8, on the right side of B, C repeats. After C, A occurs. On the right side of A, B occurs. On the right side of B, C occurs. After C, A should occur again, and so on. Soon you should realize that, to follow the steps in the same order as in the original flowchart segment, you will repeat these same steps forever.

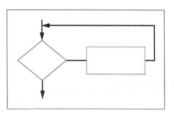

Figure B-7 A structured loop
© 2015 Cengage Learning

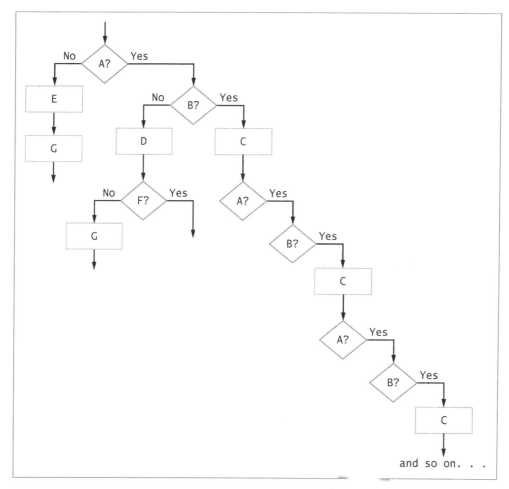

Figure B-8   Structuring, Step 6
© 2015 Cengage Learning

If you continue with Figure B-8, you will never be able to finish the flowchart; every C is always followed by another A, B, and C. Sometimes, to make a program segment structured, you have to add an extra flag variable to get out of an infinite mess. A flag is a variable that you set to indicate a true or false state. Typically, a variable is called a flag when its only purpose is to tell you whether some event has occurred. You can create a flag variable named shouldRepeat and set its value to *Yes* or *No*, depending on whether it is appropriate to repeat Decision A. When A is *No*, the shouldRepeat flag should be set to *No* because, in this situation, you never want to repeat Question A again. See Figure B-9.

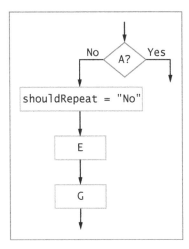

Figure B-9 Adding a flag to the flowchart
© 2015 Cengage Learning

Similarly, after A is *Yes*, but when B is *No*, you never want to repeat Question A again. Figure B-10 shows that you set **shouldRepeat** to *No* when the answer to B is *No*. Then you continue with D and the F decision that executes G when F is *No*.

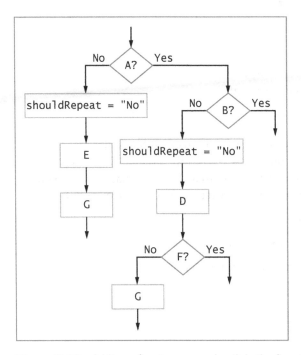

Figure B-10 Adding a flag to a second path in the flowchart
© 2015 Cengage Learning

However, in the original flowchart segment in Figure B-1, when the B decision result is *Yes*, you *do* want to repeat A. So, when B is *Yes*, perform the process for C and set the shouldRepeat flag equal to *Yes*, as shown in Figure B-11.

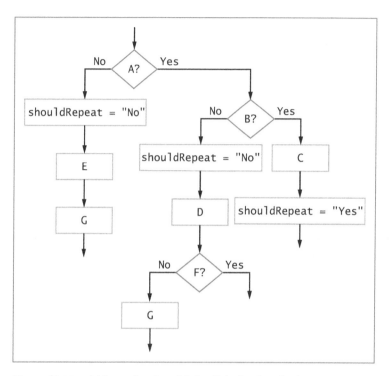

Figure B-11   Adding a flag to a third path in the flowchart
© 2015 Cengage Learning

Now all paths of the flowchart can join together at the bottom with one final question: Is shouldRepeat equal to *Yes*? If it isn't, exit; but if it is, extend the flowline to go back to repeat Question A. See Figure B-12. Take a moment to verify that the steps that would execute following Figure B-12 are the same steps that would execute following Figure B-1.

- When A is *No*, E and G always execute.

- When A is *Yes* and B is *No*, D and decision F always execute.

- When A is *Yes* and B is *Yes*, C always executes and A repeats.

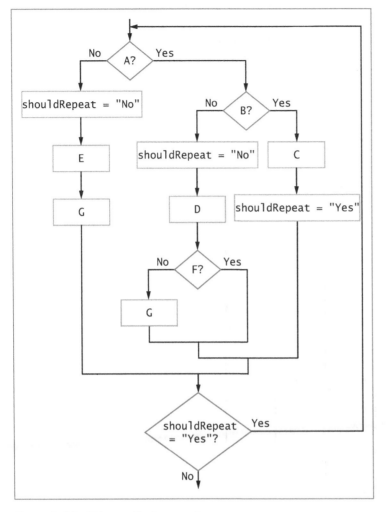

Figure B-12 Tying up the loose ends

Figure B-12 contains three nested selection structures. Notice how the F decision begins a complete selection structure whose *Yes* and *No* paths join together when the structure ends. This F selection structure is within one path of the B decision structure; the B decision begins a complete selection structure whose *Yes* and *No* paths join at the bottom. Likewise, the B selection structure resides entirely within one path of the A selection structure.

The flowchart segment in Figure B-12 performs identically to the original spaghetti version in Figure B-1. However, is this new flowchart segment structured? There are so many steps in the diagram, it is hard to tell. You may be able to see the structure more clearly if you create a module named aThroughG(). If you create the module shown in Figure B-13, then the original flowchart segment can be drawn as in Figure B-14.

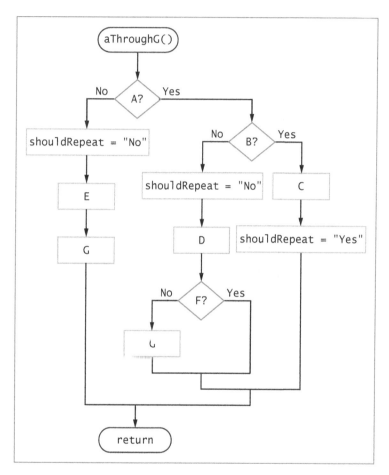

Figure B-13   The aThroughG() module

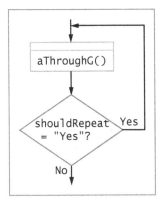

Figure B-14 Logic in Figure B-12, substituting a module for steps A through G
© 2015 Cengage Learning

Now you can see that the completed flowchart segment in Figure B-14 is a do-until loop. If you prefer to use a while loop, you can redraw Figure B-14 to perform a sequence followed by a while loop, as shown in Figure B-15.

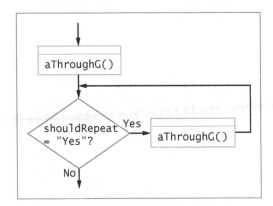

Figure B-15 Logic in Figure B-14, substituting a sequence and while loop for the do-until loop
© 2015 Cengage Learning

It has taken some extra effort, including repeating specific steps and using some flag variables, but every logical problem can be solved and made to conform to structured rules by using the three structures: sequence, selection, and loop.

Creating Print Charts

A printed report is a very common type of output. You can design a printed report on a printer spacing chart, which also is called a print chart or a print layout. Many modern-day programmers use various software tools to design their output, but you also can create a print chart by hand. This appendix provides some of the details for creating a traditional handwritten print chart. Even if you never design output on your own, you might see print charts in the documentation of existing programs.

Figure C-1 shows a printer spacing chart, which basically looks like graph paper. The chart has many boxes, and in each box the designer places one character that will be printed. The rows and columns in the chart usually are numbered for reference.

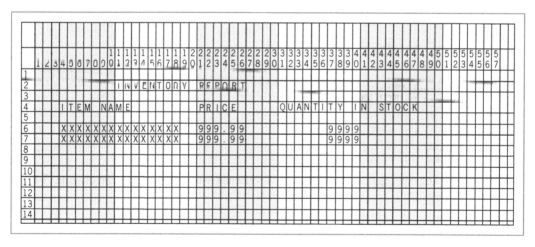

Figure C-1 A printer spacing chart

For example, suppose that you want to create a printed report with the following features:

- A printed title, INVENTORY REPORT, that begins 11 spaces from the left edge of the page and one line down

- Column headings for ITEM NAME, PRICE, and QUANTITY IN STOCK, two lines below the title and placed over the actual data items that are displayed

- Variable data appearing below each of the column headings

The exact spacing and the use of uppercase or lowercase characters in the print chart make a difference. Notice that the constant data in the output—the items that remain the same in every execution of the report—do not need to follow the same rules as variable names in the program. Within a report, constants like INVENTORY REPORT and ITEM NAME can contain spaces. These headings exist to help readers understand the information presented in the report, not for a computer to interpret; there is no need to run the names together, as you do when choosing identifiers for variables.

A print layout typically shows how the variable data will appear on the report. Of course, the data will probably be different every time the program is executed. Thus, instead of writing in actual item names and prices, the users and programmers usually use Xs to represent generic variable characters, and 9s to represent generic variable numeric data. (Some programmers use Xs for both character and numeric data.) Each line containing Xs and 9s is a detail line, or a line that displays the data details. Detail lines typically appear many times per page, as opposed to heading lines, which contain the title and any column headings, and usually appear only once per page.

Even though an actual inventory report might eventually go on for hundreds or thousands of detail lines, writing two or three rows of Xs and 9s is sufficient to show how the data will appear. For example, if a report contains employee names and salaries, those data items will occupy the same print positions on output for line after line, whether the output eventually contains 10 employees or 10,000. A few rows of identically positioned Xs and 9s are sufficient to establish the pattern.

Two Variations on the Basic Structures—case and do-while

You can solve any logic problem you might encounter using only the three structures: sequence, selection, and loop. However, many programming languages allow two more structures: the case structure and the do-while loop. These structures are never *needed* to solve a problem—you can always use a series of selections instead of the case structure, and you can always use a sequence plus a while loop in place of the do-while loop. However, sometimes these additional structures are convenient. Programmers consider them all to be acceptable, legal structures.

The case Structure

You can use the **case structure** when there are several distinct possible values for a single variable, and each value requires a different subsequent action. Suppose that you work at a school at which tuition varies per credit hour, depending on whether a student is a freshman, sophomore, junior, or senior. The structured flowchart and pseudocode in Figure D-1 show a series of decisions that assigns different tuition values depending on the value of year.

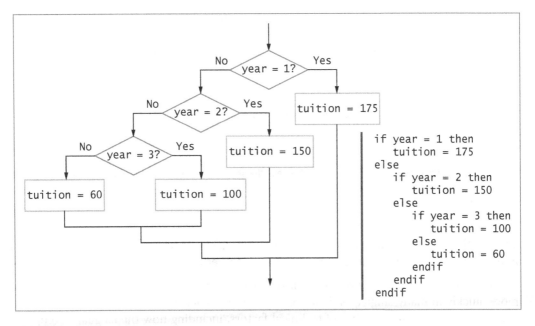

Figure D-1   Flowchart and pseudocode of tuition decisions
© 2015 Cengage Learning

The logic shown in Figure D-1 is correct and completely structured. The year = 3? selection structure is contained within the year = 2? structure, which is contained within the year = 1? structure. (This example assumes that if year is not 1, 2, or 3, the student receives the senior tuition rate.)

Even though the program segments in Figure D-1 are correct and structured, many programming languages permit using a case structure, as shown in Figure D-2. When using the case structure, you test a variable against a series of values, taking appropriate action based on the variable's value. Many people feel programs that contain the case structure are easier to read than a program with a long series of decisions, and the case structure is allowed because the same results *could* be achieved with a series of structured selections (thus making the program structured). That is, if the first program is structured and the second one reflects the first one point by point, then the second one must be structured as well.

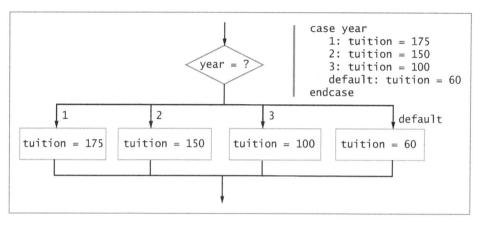

Figure D-2 Flowchart and pseudocode of case structure that determines tuition
© 2015 Cengage Learning

  The term *default* in Figure D-2 means *if none of the other cases is true.* Various programming languages use different syntaxes for the default case.

You use the case structure only when a series of decisions is based on a single expression. If multiple expressions are tested, then you must use a series of decisions.

Besides being easier to read and possibly less prone to error, the case structure often executes more quickly in many languages than the series of decisions it represents. The speed of execution depends on a number of technical factors, including how the language compiler was written and how many clauses appear in the case statement. The case structure appears in this appendix instead of the main text for two major reasons:

- The syntax used in the case structure varies widely among languages.
- Logically, the case structure is "extra." All logical problems can be solved using the structures sequence, selection, and loop. When you write your own programs, it is always acceptable to express a complicated decision-making process as a series of individual selections.

The do-while Loop

Recall that a structured loop (often called a while loop) looks like Figure D-3. A special-case loop called a do-while loop looks like Figure D-4.

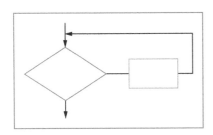

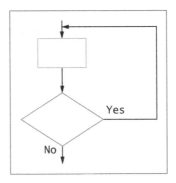

Figure D-4   Structure of a
do-while loop, which is a posttest
loop
© 2015 Cengage Learning

Figure D-3   The while loop, which
is a pretest loop
© 2015 Cengage Learning

An important difference exists between these two structures. In a while loop, you ask a question and, depending on the answer, you might or might not enter the loop to execute the loop's procedure. Conversely, in a **do-while loop**, you ensure that the procedure executes at least once; then, depending on the answer to the controlling question, the loop may or may not execute additional times.

Notice that the word *do* begins the name of the do-while loop. This should remind you that the action you "do" precedes testing the condition.

In a while loop, the tested condition that controls a loop comes at the beginning, or "top," of the loop body. A while loop is a pretest loop because a condition is tested before entering the loop even once. In a do-while loop, the tested condition that controls the loop comes at the end, or "bottom," of the loop body. Do-while loops are posttest loops because a condition is tested after the loop body has executed.

You encounter examples of do-while looping every day. For example:

```
do
    pay a bill
while more bills remain to be paid
```

As another example:

```
do
    wash a dish
while more dishes remain to be washed
```

In these examples, the activity (paying bills or washing dishes) must occur at least one time. With a do-while loop, you ask the question that determines whether you continue only after the activity has been executed at least once.

You never are required to use a posttest loop; you can duplicate the same series of actions by creating a sequence followed by a standard, pretest while loop. Consider the flowcharts and pseudocode in Figure D-5.

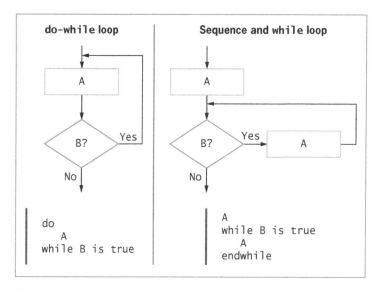

Figure D-5   Flowchart and pseudocode for do-while loop and while loop that do the same thing
© 2015 Cengage Learning

On the left side of Figure D-5, A executes, and then B is asked. If B is yes, then A executes and B is asked again. On the right side of the figure, A executes, and then B is asked. If B is yes, then A executes and B is asked again. In other words, both sets of flowchart and pseudocode segments do exactly the same thing.

Because programmers understand that any posttest loop (do-while) can be expressed with a sequence followed by a while loop, most languages allow at least one version of the posttest loop for convenience.

Recognizing the Characteristics Shared By All Structured Loops

As you examine Figures D-3 and D-4, notice that in the while loop, the loop-controlling question is placed at the beginning of the steps that repeat. In the do-while loop, the loop-controlling question is placed at the end of the sequence of steps that repeat.

All structured loops, both pretest and posttest, share these two characteristics:

- The loop-controlling question must provide either the entry to or exit from the repeating structure.

- The loop-controlling question provides the *only* entry to or exit from the repeating structure.

In other words, there is exactly one loop-controlling value, and it provides either the only entrance to or the only exit from the loop.

Some languages support a **do-until loop**, which is a posttest loop that iterates until the loop-controlling question is false. The `do-until` loop follows structured loop rules.

Recognizing Unstructured Loops

Figure D-6 shows an unstructured loop. It is not a `while` loop, which begins with a decision and, after an action, returns to the decision. It is also not a `do-while` loop, which begins with an action and ends with a decision that might repeat the action. Instead, it begins like a posttest loop (a `do-while` loop), with a process followed by a decision, but one branch of the decision does not repeat the initial process. Instead, it performs an additional new action before repeating the initial process.

If you need to use the logic shown in Figure D-6—performing a task, asking a question, and perhaps performing an additional task before looping back to the first process—then the way to make the logic structured is to repeat the initial process within the loop at the end of the loop. Figure D-7 shows the same logic as Figure D-6, but now it is structured logic, with a sequence of two actions occurring within the loop.

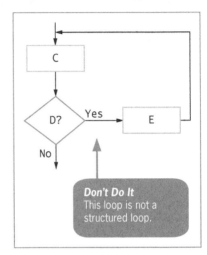

Figure D-6   Unstructured loop
© 2015 Cengage Learning

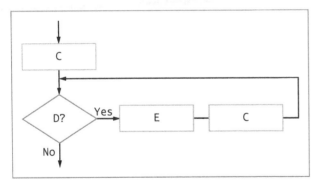

Figure D-7   Sequence and structured loop that accomplish the same tasks as Figure D-6
© 2015 Cengage Learning

 Especially when you are first mastering structured logic, you might prefer to use only the three basic structures—sequence, selection, and `while` loop. Every logical problem can be solved using only these three structures, and you can understand all of the examples in this book using only these three structures.

Key Terms

A **case structure** tests a single variable against multiple values, providing separate actions for each logical path.

A **do-while loop** is a posttest loop in which the body executes before the loop-controlling condition is tested.

A **do-until loop** is a posttest loop that iterates until the loop-controlling condition is false.

Glossary

A

abstract class—A class from which concrete objects cannot be instantiated, but which can serve as a basis for inheritance.

abstract data type (ADT)—A programmer-defined type, such as a class.

abstraction—The process of paying attention to important properties while ignoring nonessential details.

access specifier—The adjective that defines the type of access outside classes will have to an attribute or method.

accessibility—Describes screen design issues that make programs easier to use for people with physical limitations.

accessor method—An instance method that returns a value from a field defined in a class. See also *get method*.

accumulator—A variable used to gather or accumulate values.

activity diagram—A UML diagram that shows the flow of actions of a system, including branches that occur when decisions affect the outcome.

actual parameters—The arguments in a method call.

addresses—Numbers that identify computer memory and storage locations.

aggregation—A whole-part relationship, specifically when the part can exist without the whole.

algorithm—The sequence of steps necessary to solve any problem.

alphanumeric values—The set of values that include alphabetic characters, numbers, and punctuation.

alternate keys—In a database, the remaining candidate keys after a primary key is chosen.

ambiguous methods—Methods that the compiler cannot distinguish because they have the same name and parameter types.

American Standard Code for Information Interchange (ASCII)—An eight-bit character coding scheme used on many personal computers.

ancestors—The entire list of parent classes from which a class is derived.

AND decision—A decision in which two conditions must both be true for an action to take place.

animation—The rapid display of still images, each slightly different from the previous one, that produces the illusion of movement.

annotation symbol—A flowchart symbol used to hold comments; it is most often represented by a three-sided box connected with a dashed line to the step it explains.

anomaly—An irregularity in a database's design that causes problems and inconveniences.

app—A piece of application software; the term is frequently used for applications on mobile devices.

application software—All the programs that help users with tasks (for example, accounting or word processing), in contrast to *system software*.

argument to a method—A value passed to a method in the method call.

array—A series or list of variables in computer memory, all of which have the same name but are differentiated with subscripts.

ascending order—Describes the arrangement of data items from lowest to highest.

assignment operator—The equal sign; it always requires the name of a memory location on its left side.

assignment statement—A statement that stores a value on its right side to the named location on its left side.

association relationship—Describes the connection or link between objects in a UML diagram.

atomic attributes—In a database, describes columns that are as small as possible so that they contain undividable pieces of data.

atomic transactions—A series of transactions that execute completely or not at all, avoiding partial completion of a task.

attribute—One field in a database table or an object. In a database, an attribute is a column; in an object, an attribute is an instance variable.

authentication techniques—Security techniques that include storing and verifying passwords and using physical characteristics, such as fingerprints or voice recognition, before users can be authorized to view data.

B

backup file—A copy that is kept in case values need to be restored to their original state.

base 2—Describes numbers created using the binary numbering system.

base 10—Describes numbers created using the decimal numbering system.

base 16—Describes numbers created using the hexadecimal numbering system.

base case—Describes the input that halts a recursive method; also called a *terminating case*.

base class—A class that is used as a basis for inheritance.

base table—The "one" table in a one-to-many relationship in a database.

batch—A group of transactions applied all at once.

batch processing—Processing that performs the same tasks with many records in sequence.

behavior diagrams—UML diagrams that emphasize what happens in a system.

binary decision—A yes-or-no decision; so called because there are two possible outcomes.

binary files—Files that contain data that has not been encoded as text.

binary language—A computer language represented using a series of 0s and 1s.

binary numbering system—The numbering system based on two digits; column values are multiples of 2.

binary operator—An operator that requires two operands—one on each side.

binary search—A search that starts in the middle of a sorted list, and then determines whether it should continue higher or lower to find a target value.

bit—A binary digit; a unit of storage equal to one-eighth of a byte.

black box—The analogy that programmers use to refer to the details of hidden methods.

blob—A binary large object, or BLOb, which is a collection of binary data such as an image, video, or audio clip stored in a database system.

block—A group of statements that execute as a single unit.

Boolean expression—An expression that represents only one of two states, usually expressed as true or false.

bubble sort—A sorting algorithm in which list elements are arranged in ascending or descending order by comparing items in pairs and swapping them when they are out of order.

byte—A unit of computer storage equal to eight bits.

C

call a module—To use a module's name to invoke it, causing it to execute.

camel casing—A naming convention in which the initial letter is lowercase, multiple-word names are run together, and each new word within the name begins with an uppercase letter.

candidate keys—Columns or attributes that could serve as a primary key in a table.

cardinality—Describes an arithmetic relationship between objects.

cascading `if` statement—A series of nested `if` statements.

case structure—A structure that tests a single variable against multiple values, providing separate actions for each logical path.

catch an exception—To receive an exception from a throw so it can be handled.

`catch` block—A segment of code written to handle an exception that might be thrown by the `try` block that precedes it.

central processing unit (CPU)—The computer hardware component that processes data.

character—A letter, number, or special symbol such as *A*, *7*, or *$*.

child class—A derived class.

child file—A copy of a file after revision.

class—A group or collection of objects with common attributes.

class client or **class user**—A program or class that instantiates objects of another prewritten class.

class definition—A set of program statements that define the fields and methods of a class.

class diagram—A tool for describing a class that consists of a rectangle divided into three sections that show the name, data, and methods of a class.

class method—A static method; class methods are not instance methods and they do not receive a `this` reference.

client—A program or other method that uses a method.

closing a file—An action that makes a file no longer available to an application.

coding the program—The act of writing the statements of a program in a programming language.

cohesion—A measure of how a method's internal statements are focused to accomplish the method's purpose.

command line—The location on a computer screen where entries are typed to communicate with the computer's operating system.

communication diagram—A UML diagram that emphasizes the organization of objects that participate in a system.

compiler—Software that translates a high-level language into machine language and identifies syntax errors. A compiler is similar to an interpreter; however, a compiler translates all the statements in a program prior to executing them.

component diagram—A UML diagram that emphasizes the files, database tables, documents, and other components used by a system's software.

composition—The technique of placing an object within an object of another class.

compound condition—A condition constructed when multiple decisions are required before determining an outcome.

compound key or **composite key**—In a database, a key constructed from multiple columns. See also *concatenated key*.

computer file—A collection of data stored on a nonvolatile device in a computer system.

computer memory—The temporary, internal storage within a computer.

653

654

computer system—A combination of all the components required to process and store data using a computer.

concatenate columns—To combine database table columns to produce a compound key.

concatenated key—In a database, a key constructed from multiple columns. See also *compound key*.

concurrent update problem—A problem that can occur when two database users revise the same record at the same time.

conditional AND operator—A symbol used to combine decisions so that two or more conditions must be true for an action to occur. Also called an *AND* operator.

conditional OR operator—A symbol used to combine decisions when any one condition can be true for an action to occur. Also called an *OR* operator.

constructor—An automatically called method that instantiates an object.

container—One of a class of objects whose main purpose is to hold other elements—for example, a window.

control break—A temporary detour in the logic of a program for special group processing.

control break field—A variable that holds the value that signals a special processing break in a program.

control break program—A program in which a change in the value of a variable initiates special actions or processing.

control break report—A report that lists items in groups. Frequently, each group is followed by a subtotal.

conversion—The set of actions an organization must take to switch over to using a new program or system.

counter—Any numeric variable used to count the number of times an event has occurred.

coupling—A measure of the strength of the connection between two program methods.

D

data dictionary—A list of every variable name used in a program, along with its type, size, and description.

data hierarchy—Represents the relationship of databases, files, records, fields, and characters.

data integrity—Describes a database that follows a set of rules to make its data accurate and consistent.

data redundancy—The unnecessary repetition of data.

data type—The characteristic of a variable that describes the kind of values the variable can hold and the types of operations that can be performed with it.

database—A logical container that holds a group of files, often called tables, that together serve the information needs of an organization.

database management software—A set of programs that allows users to create and manage data.

dead path—A logical path that can never be traveled.

deadlock—A flaw in multithreaded programs in which two or more threads wait for each other to execute.

debugging—The process of finding and correcting program errors.

decimal numbering system—The numbering system based on 10 digits; column values are multiples of 10.

decision structure—A program structure in which a question is asked, and, depending on the answer, one of two courses of action is taken. Then, no matter which path is followed, the paths join and the next task executes.

decision symbol—A symbol that represents a decision in a flowchart; it is shaped like a diamond.

declaration—A statement that names a variable and its data type.

declaring variables—The process of naming program variables and assigning a type to them.

decrement—To change a variable by decreasing it by a constant value, frequently 1.

default constructor—A constructor that requires no arguments.

default input and output devices—Hardware devices that do not require opening; usually they are the keyboard and monitor, respectively.

defensive programming—A technique in which programmers try to prepare for all possible errors before they occur.

definite loop—A loop for which the number of repetitions is a predetermined value.

delete anomaly—A problem that occurs when a row is deleted from a database table; the result is loss of related data.

denormalize—To place a database table in a lower normal form by repeating information.

deployment diagram—A UML diagram that focuses on a system's hardware.

derived class—An extended class.

descending order—Describes the arrangement of data items from highest to lowest.

desk-checking—The process of walking through a program solution on paper.

destructor—An automatically called method that contains the actions required when an instance of a class is destroyed.

detail loop tasks—The steps that are repeated for each set of input data.

direct access files—Random access files.

directories—Organization units on storage devices; each can contain multiple files as well as additional directories. In a graphical interface system, directories are often called *folders*.

documentation—All of the supporting material that goes with a program.

DOS prompt—The command line in the DOS operating system.

do-until loop—A posttest loop that iterates until its controlling condition is false.

do-while loop—A posttest loop in which the body executes before the loop control variable is tested.

dual-alternative if or **dual-alternative selection**—A selection structure that defines one action to be taken when the tested condition is true, and another action to be taken when it is false.

dummy value—A preselected value that stops the execution of a program.

E

echoing input—The act of repeating input back to a user either in a subsequent prompt or in output.

element—A separate array variable.

elided—Describes the omitted parts of UML diagrams that are edited for clarity.

else clause—A part of a decision that holds the action or actions that execute only when the Boolean expression in the decision is false.

encapsulation—The act of containing a task's instructions and data in the same method.

encryption—The process of coding data into a format that human beings cannot read.

end-of-job task—A step at the end of a program to finish the application.

end-structure statement—A statement that designates the end of a pseudocode structure.

entity—One record or row in a database table.

eof—An end-of-data file marker, short for *end of file*.

event—An occurrence that generates a message sent to an object.

event-driven or **event-based**—Describes programs and actions that occur in response to user-initiated events such as clicking a mouse button.

exception—The generic term used for an error in object-oriented languages.

exception-handling techniques—The object-oriented techniques for managing errors.

655

executing—To have a computer use a written and compiled program; also called *running*.

extend variation—A UML use case variation that shows functions beyond those found in a base case.

Extended Binary Coded Decimal Interchange Code (EBCDIC)—An eight-bit character coding scheme used on many larger computers.

extended class—A derived class.

external documentation—All the external material that programmers develop to support a program; contrast with *program comments*, which are internal program documentation.

F

facilitator—A work method.

field—A single data item, such as `lastName`, `streetAddress`, or `annualSalary`.

file—A group of records that go together for some logical reason.

first normal form, or **1NF**—The normalization form in which repeating groups are eliminated from a database.

flag—A variable that indicates whether some event has occurred.

floating-point value—A fractional, numeric variable that contains a decimal point.

flowchart—A pictorial representation of the logical steps it takes to solve a problem.

flowline—An arrow that connects the steps in a flowchart.

folders—Organization units on storage devices; each can contain multiple files as well as additional folders. Folders are graphic directories.

for statement—A statement that can be used to code definite loops; also called a *for loop*. The statement contains a loop control variable that it automatically initializes, evaluates, and alters.

foreign key—A column that is not a key in a table but contains an attribute that is a key in a related table.

fork—A feature of a UML activity diagram that defines a logical branch in which all paths are followed simultaneously.

formal parameters—The variables in a method declaration that accept values from the actual parameters.

fragile—Describes classes that depend on field names from parent classes and are prone to errors.

functional cohesion—The extent to which all operations in a method contribute to the performance of only one task.

functional dependence—A relationship in which an attribute can be determined by another.

G

garbage—Describes the unknown value stored in an unassigned variable.

generalization variation—A variation used in a UML diagram when a use case is less specific than others and the more specific case should be substituted for a general one.

get method—An instance method that returns a value from a field defined in a class. See also *accessor method*.

gigabyte—A billion bytes.

GIGO—Acronym for *garbage in, garbage out*; it means that if input is incorrect, output is worthless.

global—Describes variables that are known to an entire program.

goto-less programming—A name to describe structured programming, because structured programmers do not use a "go to" statement.

graphical user interface (GUI)—A program interface that uses screens to display program output and allows users to interact with a program in a graphical environment.

H

hardware—The equipment of a computer system.

has-a relationship—A whole-part relationship; the type of relationship that exists when using composition.

help method—A work method.

hexadecimal numbering system—The numbering system based on 16 digits; column values are multiples of 16.

hierarchy chart—A diagram that illustrates modules' relationships to each other.

high-level programming language—A programming language that is English-like, as opposed to a low-level programming language.

housekeeping tasks—Tasks that must be performed at the beginning of a program to prepare for the rest of the program.

Hungarian notation—A naming convention in which a data type or other information is stored as part of a name.

I

I/O symbol—An input/output symbol.

icons—Small pictures on a screen that help a user navigate a system.

identifier—A program component's name.

IDE—The acronym for Integrated Development Environment, which is the visual development environment in some programming languages.

if-then—A structure similar to an if-then-else, but no alternative or "else" action is necessary.

if-then clause—The part of a decision that holds the resulting action when the Boolean expression in the decision is true.

if-then-else—Another name for a selection structure.

immutable—Not changing during normal operation.

implementation—The body of a method; the statements that carry out the tasks of a method.

implementation hiding—A programming principle that describes the encapsulation of method details.

in bounds—Describes an array subscript that is within the range of acceptable subscripts for its array.

in scope—The characteristic of variables and constants declared within a method that apply only within that method.

inaccessible—Describes any field or method that cannot be reached.

include variation—A UML use case variation in which a case can be part of multiple use cases.

increment—To change a variable by adding a constant value to it, frequently 1.

indefinite loop—A loop for which the number of executions cannot be predicted when the program is written.

index—A list of key fields paired with the storage address for the corresponding data record.

indirect relationship—Describes the relationship between parallel arrays in which an element in the first array does not directly access its corresponding value in the second array.

infinite loop—A repeating flow of logic without an ending.

information—Processed data.

information hiding or **data hiding**—The concept that other classes should not alter an object's attributes—only the methods of an object's own class should have that privilege.

inheritance—The process of acquiring the traits of one's predecessors.

initializing a variable—The act of assigning the first value to a variable, often at the same time the variable is created.

inner loop—When loops are nested, the loop that is contained within the other loop.

input—Describes the entry of data items into computer memory using hardware devices such as keyboards and mice.

input symbol—A symbol that indicates an input operation and is represented in flowcharts as a parallelogram.

input/output symbol—A parallelogram in flowcharts.

insert anomaly—A problem that can occur in a database when new rows are added to a table; the result is incomplete rows.

657

insertion sort—A sorting algorithm in which each list element is examined one at a time; if an element is out of order relative to any of the items earlier in the list, each earlier item is moved down one position and then the tested element is inserted.

instance—An existing object or tangible example of a class.

instance method—A method that operates correctly yet differently for each class object; an instance method is nonstatic and receives a `this` reference.

instance variables—The data components that belong to every instantiated object.

instant access files—Random access files in which records must be accessed immediately.

instantiate—To create an object.

instantiation—An instance of a class.

integer—A whole number.

integrated development environment (IDE)—A software package that provides an editor, compiler, and other programming tools.

integrity constraints—Rules that help to ensure data in a database is consistent and within range.

interaction diagrams—UML diagrams that emphasize the flow of control and data among the system elements being modeled.

interactive program—A program in which a user makes direct requests or provides input while a program executes.

interactivity diagram—A diagram that shows the relationship between screens in an interactive GUI program.

interface to a method—A method's return type, name, and arguments; the part of a method that a client sees and uses.

internal documentation—Documentation within a program. See also *program comments*.

IPO chart—A program development tool that delineates input, processing, and output tasks.

is-a relationship—The relationship between an object and each of the classes in its ancestry.

iteration—The action of repeating.

J

join—A feature of a UML activity diagram that reunites the flow of control after a fork.

join column—The column on which two tables are connected in a database.

join operation, or **join**—The operation that connects two tables based on the values in one or more common columns.

K

kebob case—A term sometimes used to describe the naming convention in which dashes separate parts of a name.

key—A field or column that uniquely identifies a record.

key field—The field whose contents make a record unique among all records in a file.

keywords—The limited word set that is reserved in a language.

kilobyte—Approximately 1000 bytes.

L

left-to-right associativity—Describes operators that evaluate the expression to the left first.

libraries—Stored collections of classes that serve related purposes.

linear search—A search through a list from one end to the other.

linked list—A list that contains an extra field in every record that holds the physical address of the next logical record.

listener—In object-oriented programming, an object that is interested in an event and responds to it.

local—Describes variables that are declared within the method that uses them.

lock—A mechanism that prevents changes to a database for a period of time.

logic—The complete sequence of instructions that lead to a problem solution.

logical error—An error that occurs when incorrect instructions are performed, or when instructions are performed in the wrong order.

logical NOT operator—A symbol that reverses the meaning of a Boolean expression.

logical order—The order in which a list is used, even though it is not necessarily stored in that physical order.

loop—A structure that repeats actions while a condition continues.

loop body—The set of actions that occur within a loop.

loop control variable—A variable that determines whether a loop will continue.

loop structure—A structure that repeats actions while a test condition remains true.

loose coupling—A relationship that occurs when methods do not depend on others.

low-level language—A programming language not far removed from machine language, as opposed to a high-level programming language.

lower camel casing—Another name for the camel casing naming convention.

lvalue—The memory address identifier to the left of an assignment operator.

M

machine language—A computer's on/off circuitry language; the low-level language made up of 1s and 0s that the computer understands.

magic number—An unnamed numeric constant.

main program—A program that runs from start to stop and calls other modules; also called a *main program method*.

mainline logic—The overall logic of the main program from beginning to end.

maintenance—All the improvements and corrections made to a program after it is in production.

making a decision—Testing a value to determine a logical path.

making declarations—The process of naming program variables and assigning a type to them.

many-to-many relationship—A relationship in which multiple rows in a database table can correspond to multiple rows in another table.

master file—A file that holds complete and relatively permanent data.

matrix—A term sometimes used by mathematicians to describe a two-dimensional array.

mean—The arithmetic average.

median—The value in the middle position of a list when the values are sorted.

megabyte—A million bytes.

merging files—The act of combining two or more files while maintaining the sequential order.

method—A series of statements that carry out a task.

method body—The set of all the statements in a method.

method header—A program component that precedes a method's body; the header includes the method identifier and possibly other necessary information, such as a return type and parameter list.

method return statement—A statement that marks the end of the method and identifies the point at which control returns to the calling method.

method type—The data type of a method's return value.

Microsoft Visual Studio IDE—A software package that contains useful tools for creating programs in Visual Basic, C++, and C#.

mixed case with underscores—A naming convention similar to snake casing, in which words are separated with underscores, but new words start with an uppercase letter.

modeling—The process of designing an application before writing code.

modularization—The process of breaking down a program into modules.

module—A small program unit used with other modules to make a program. Programmers also refer to modules as subroutines, procedures, functions, and methods.

module's body—The part of a module that contains all the statements in the module.

module's header—The part of a module that includes the module identifier and possibly other necessary identifying information.

module's `return` statement—The part of a module that marks its end and identifies the point at which control returns to the program or module that called the module.

multidimensional arrays—Lists with more than one dimension.

multiple inheritance—The ability to inherit from more than one class.

multiplicity—An arithmetic relationship between objects.

multithreading—Using multiple threads of execution.

mutator method—An instance method that sets or changes the values of a data field within a class object. See also *set method*.

N

named constant—A named memory location, similar to a variable, except its value never changes during the execution of a program. Conventionally, constants are named using all capital letters.

nested decision—A decision within the `if then` or `else` clause of another decision; also called a *nested `if`*.

nested loop—A loop structure within another loop structure; nesting loops are loops within loops.

nesting structures—Placing a structure within another structure.

nibble—A storage measurement equal to four bits, or a half byte.

nondefault constructor—A constructor that requires at least one argument. See also *parameterized constructor*.

nonkey attribute—Any column in a database table that is not a key.

nonstatic methods—Methods that exist to be used with an object; they are instance methods and they receive a `this` reference.

nonvolatile—Describes storage whose contents are retained when power is lost.

normal forms—Rules for constructing a well-designed database.

normalization—The process of designing and creating a set of database tables that satisfies the users' needs and avoids redundancies and anomalies.

null case—The branch of a decision in which no action is taken.

nulls—Empty columns in a database.

numeric—Describes data that consists of numbers.

numeric constant—A specific numeric value.

numeric variable—A variable that holds numeric values.

O

object—One tangible example of a class; an instance of a class.

object code—Code that has been translated to machine language.

object diagrams—UML diagrams that are similar to class diagrams, but that model specific instances of classes.

object dictionary—A list of the objects used in a program, including which screens they are used on and whether any code, or script, is associated with them.

object-oriented programming (OOP)—A programming model that focuses on components and data items (objects) and describes their attributes and behaviors.

one-dimensional array—A list accessed using a single subscript.

one-to-many relationship—The relationship in which one row in a table can be related to many rows in another table. It is the most common type of relationship among tables.

one-to-one relationship—The relationship in which a row in one table corresponds to exactly one row in another table.

opening a file—The process of locating a file on a storage device, physically preparing it for reading, and associating it with an identifier inside a program.

operating system—The software that runs a computer and manages its resources.

OR decision—A decision that contains two or more conditions; if at least one condition is met, the resulting action takes place.

order of operations—Describes the rules of precedence.

out of bounds—Describes an array subscript that is not within the range of acceptable subscripts.

outer loop—The loop that contains a nested loop.

output—Describes the operation of retrieving information from memory and sending it to a device, such as a monitor or printer, so people can view, interpret, and work with the results.

output symbol—A symbol that indicates an output operation and is represented as a parallelogram in flowcharts.

overhead—All the resources and time required by an operation.

overload a method—To create multiple methods with the same name but different parameter lists.

overloading—Supplying diverse meanings for a single identifier.

overriding—The mechanism by which a child class method is used by default when a parent class contains a method with the same signature.

P

packages—Another name for libraries in some languages.

page schematic—A wireframe.

parallel arrays—Two or more arrays in which each element in one array is associated with the element in the same relative position in the other array or arrays.

parameter list—All the data types and parameter names that appear in a method header.

parameter to a method—A data item defined in a method header that accepts data passed into the method from the outside.

parameterized constructor—A constructor that requires at least one argument. See also *nondefault constructor*.

parent class—A base class.

parent file—A copy of a file before revision.

partial key dependency—The condition that occurs when a column in a database table depends on only part of the table's key.

Pascal casing—A naming convention in which the initial letter is uppercase, multiple-word names are run together, and each new word within the name begins with an uppercase letter.

passed by reference—Describes a method parameter that represents the item's memory address.

passed by value—Describes a variable that has a copy of its value sent to a method and stored in a new memory location accessible to the method.

path—The combination of a file's disk drive and the complete hierarchy of directories in which the file resides.

permanent storage device—A hardware device that holds nonvolatile data; examples include hard disks, DVDs, Zip disks, USB drives, and reels of magnetic tape.

permissions—Attributes assigned to a user to indicate which parts of a database the user can view, change, or delete.

persistent lock—A long-term database lock required when users want to maintain a consistent view of their data while making modifications over a long transaction.

physical order—The order in which a list is actually stored even though it might be accessed in a different logical order.

pixel—A picture element; one of the tiny dots of light that form a grid on a monitor.

polymorphism—The ability of a method to act appropriately depending on the context.

populating an array—To assign values to array elements.

portable—Describes a module that can more easily be reused in multiple programs.

posttest loop—A loop that tests its controlling condition after each iteration, meaning that the loop body executes at least one time.

precedence—The quality of an operation that determines the order in which it is evaluated.

pretest loop—A loop that tests its controlling condition before each iteration, meaning that the loop body might never execute.

primary key—A field or column that uniquely identifies a record or database object.

priming input or **priming read**—The statement that reads the first input data record prior to starting a structured loop.

primitive data types—In a programming language, simple number and character types that are not class types.

private access—A privilege of class members in which data or methods cannot be used by any method that is not part of the same class.

procedural programming—A programming technique that focuses on the procedures that programmers create.

processing—To organize data items, check them for accuracy, or perform mathematical operations on them.

processing symbol—A symbol represented as a rectangle in flowcharts.

program—Sets of instructions for a computer.

program code—The set of instructions a programmer writes in a programming language.

program comment—A nonexecuting statement that programmers place within code to explain program statements in English. See also *internal documentation*.

program development cycle—The steps that occur during a program's lifetime, including planning, coding, translating, testing, producing, and maintaining the program.

program level—The level at which global variables are declared.

programming—The act of developing and writing programs.

programming language—A language such as Visual Basic, C#, C++, Java, or COBOL, used to write programs.

prompt—A message that is displayed on a monitor, asking the user for a response.

property—A method that gets and sets a field value using simple syntax.

protected access specifier—A specifier used when outside classes should not be able to use a data field unless they are children of the original class.

protected node—The UML diagram name for an exception-throwing `try` block.

pseudocode—An English-like representation of the logical steps it takes to solve a problem.

public access—A privilege of class members in which other programs and methods may use the specified data or methods within a class.

pure polymorphism—The situation in which one method implementation can be used with a variety of arguments in object-oriented programming.

Q

query—A question used to access values in a database; its purpose is often to display a subset of data.

query by example—The process of creating a database query by filling in blanks.

R

random access files—Files that contain records that can be located in any physical order and accessed directly.

random access memory (RAM)—Temporary, internal computer storage.

random-access storage device—A storage device, such as a disk, from which records can be accessed in any order.

range check—The comparison of a variable to a series of values that mark the limiting ends of ranges.

reading from a file—The act of copying data from a file on a storage device into RAM.

real numbers—Floating-point numbers.

real-time—Describes applications that require a record to be accessed immediately while a client is waiting.

record—A group of fields stored together as a unit because they hold data about a single entity.

recovery—The process of returning a database to a correct form that existed before an error occurred.

recursion—A programming event that occurs when a method is defined in terms of itself.

recursive cases—Describe the input values that cause a recursive method to execute again.

recursive method—A method that calls itself.

registering components—The act of signing up components so they can react to events initiated by other components.

related table—The "many" table in a one-to-many relationship in a database.

relational comparison operator—A symbol that expresses Boolean comparisons. Examples include =, >, <, >=, <=, and <>.

relational database—A group of tables from which connections can be made to produce virtual tables.

relationship—A connection between two tables in a database.

reliability—The feature of modular programs that ensures a module has been tested and proven to function correctly.

remainder operator—An arithmetic operator used in some programming languages that results in the remainder left when its operands are divided.

repeating group—A subset of rows in a database table that all depend on the same key.

repetition—Another name for a loop structure.

return type—The data type for any value a method returns.

reusability—The feature of modular programs that allows individual modules to be used in a variety of applications.

reverse engineering—The process of creating an improved model of an existing system.

right-associativity and **right-to-left associativity**—Descriptions of operators that evaluate the expression to the right first.

running—To have a computer use a written and compiled program. Also called *executing*.

S

scenario—A variation in the sequence of actions required in a UML use case diagram.

screen blueprint—A wireframe.

script—A procedural module that depends on user-initiated events in object-oriented programs.

scripting language—A language such as Python, Lua, Perl, or PHP used to write programs that are typed directly from a keyboard and are stored as text rather than as binary executable files. Also called *scripting programming languages* or *script languages*.

second normal form, or **2NF**—The normalization form in which partial key dependencies are eliminated from a database.

SELECT-FROM-WHERE—An SQL statement that selects fields to view from a table where one or more conditions are met.

selection structure—A program structure that contains a question and takes one of two courses of action depending on the answer. Then, no matter which path is followed, program logic continues with the next task.

self-documenting—Describes programs that contain meaningful and descriptive data, method, and class names.

semantic error—An error that occurs when a correct word is used in an incorrect context.

sentinel value—A value that represents an entry or exit point.

sequence diagram—A UML diagram that shows the timing of events in a single use case.

sequence structure—A program structure that contains steps that execute in order. A sequence can contain any number of tasks, but there is no chance to branch off and skip any of the tasks.

664

sequential file—A file in which records are stored one after another in some order.

sequential order—The arrangement of records when they are stored one after another on the basis of the value in a particular field.

set method—An instance method that sets or changes the values of a data field within an object. See also *mutator method*.

short-circuit evaluation—A logical feature in which each part of a larger expression is evaluated only as far as necessary to determine the final outcome.

signature—A method's name and parameter list.

single-alternative if or **single-alternative selection**—A selection structure in which action is required for only one branch of the decision. This form of the selection structure is also called an if-then, because no "else" action is necessary.

single-dimensional array—A list accessed using a single subscript.

single-level control break—A break in the logic of a program based on the value of a single variable.

sinking sort—A bubble sort.

size of the array—The number of elements an array can hold.

snake casing—A naming convention in which parts of a name are separated by underscores.

software—Programs that tell the computer what to do.

sorting—The process of placing records in order by the value in a specific field or fields.

source code—The readable statements of a program, written in a programming language.

source of an event—The component from which an event is generated.

spaghetti code—Snarled, unstructured program logic.

stack—A memory location that holds the memory addresses to which method calls should return.

stacking structures—To attach program structures end to end.

starvation—A flaw in multithreaded programs in which a thread is abandoned because other threads occupy all the computer's resources.

state—The set of all the values or contents of a class's instance variables.

state machine diagram—A UML diagram that shows the different statuses of a class or object at different points in time.

static methods—Methods for which no object needs to exist; static methods are not instance methods and they do not receive a this reference.

step value—A number used to increase a loop control variable on each pass through a loop.

stereotype—A feature that adds to the UML vocabulary of shapes to make them more meaningful for the reader.

storage device—A hardware apparatus that holds information for later retrieval.

storyboard—A picture or sketch of screens the user will see when running a program.

string—Describes data that is nonnumeric.

string constant or **literal string constant**—A specific group of characters enclosed within quotation marks.

string variable—A variable that can hold text that includes letters, digits, and special characters such as punctuation marks.

structure—A basic unit of programming logic; each structure is a sequence, selection, or loop.

structure diagrams—UML diagrams that emphasize the "things" in a system.

structured programs—Programs that follow the rules of structured logic.

Structured Query Language (SQL)—A commonly used language for accessing data in database tables.

subclass—A derived class.

subscript—A number that indicates the position of an element within an array.

summary report—A report that lists only totals, without individual detail records.

sunny day case—A program execution in which nothing goes wrong.

superclass—A base class.

swap values—To exchange the values of two variables.

syntax—The rules of a language.

syntax error—An error in language or grammar.

system design—The detailed specification of how all the parts of a system will be implemented and coordinated.

system software—The programs that manage a computer, in contrast to *application software*.

T

table—A database file that contains data in rows and columns; also, a term sometimes used by mathematicians to describe a two-dimensional array.

temporary variable—A working variable that holds intermediate results during a program's execution.

terminal symbol—A symbol used at each end of a flowchart; its shape is a lozenge. Also called a *start/stop symbol*.

terminating case—Describes the input that halts a recursive method; also called the *base case*.

text editor—A program used to create simple text files; it is similar to a word processor, but without as many features.

text files—Files that contain data that can be read in a text editor.

third normal form, or **3NF**—The normalization form in which transitive dependencies are eliminated from a database.

this reference—An automatically created variable that holds the address of an object and passes it to an instance method whenever the method is called.

thread—The flow of execution of one set of program statements.

thread synchronization—A set of techniques that coordinates threads of execution to help avoid potential multithreading problems.

three-dimensional arrays—Arrays in which each element is accessed using three subscripts.

throw an exception—To pass an exception out of a block where it occurs, usually to a block that can handle it.

throw statement—An object-oriented programming statement that sends an Exception object out of a method or code block to be handled elsewhere.

tight coupling—A problem that occurs when methods excessively depend on each other; it makes programs more prone to errors.

time signal—A UML diagram symbol that indicates a specific amount of time has passed before an action is started.

TOE chart—A program development tool that lists tasks, objects, and events.

transaction file—A file that holds temporary data used to update a master file.

transitive dependency—A database condition in which the value of a nonkey attribute determines or predicts the value of another nonkey attribute.

trivial expression—An expression that always evaluates to the same value.

truth table—A diagram used in mathematics and logic to help describe the truth of an entire expression based on the truth of its parts.

try—To execute code that might throw an exception.

try block—A block of code that attempts to execute while acknowledging that an exception might occur.

two-dimensional arrays—Arrays that have rows and columns of values accessed using two subscripts.

type-safety—The feature of programming languages that prevents assigning values of an incorrect data type.

U

unary operator—An operator that uses only one operand.

Unicode—A 16-bit character coding scheme.

Unified Modeling Language (UML)—A standard way to specify, construct, and document systems that use object-oriented methods.

unnamed constant—A literal numeric or string value.

unnormalized—Describes a database table that contains repeating groups.

unstructured programs—Programs that do *not* follow the rules of structured logic.

update a master file—To modify the values in a master file based on transaction records.

update anomaly—A problem that occurs when the data in a database table needs to be altered; the result is repeated data.

upper camel casing—Another name for the Pascal casing naming convention.

use case diagrams—UML diagrams that show how a business works from the perspective of those who actually interact with the business.

user-defined type or **programmer-defined type**—A type that is not built into a language but is created by an application's programmer.

users or **end users**—People who work with and benefit from computer programs.

V

validating data—Ensuring that data falls within an acceptable range.

variable—A named memory location of a specific data type, whose contents can vary or differ over time.

view—A way of looking at a database.

visible—A characteristic of data items that means they "can be seen" only within the method in which they are declared.

visual development environment—A programming environment in which programs are created by dragging components such as buttons and labels onto a screen and arranging them visually.

void method—A method that returns no value.

volatile—A characteristic of internal memory in which its contents are lost every time the computer loses power.

W

while loop or **while...do loop**—A loop in which a process continues while some condition continues to be true.

whole-part relationship—An association in which an object of one class is part of an object of a larger whole class.

wildcard—A symbol that means *any* or *all*.

wireframe—A picture or sketch of a screen the user will see when running a program.

work method—A method that performs tasks within a class.

writing to a file—The act of copying data from RAM to persistent storage.

X

x-axis—An imaginary line that represents horizontal positions in a screen window.

x-coordinate—A position value that increases from left to right across a screen window.

Y

y-axis—An imaginary line that represents vertical positions in a screen window.

y-coordinate—A position value that increases from top to bottom across a screen window.

Index

Note: Page numbers in **boldface** type indicate where key terms are defined.

Special Characters

> (greater than operator), 132
< (less than operator), 132
~ (tilde), 479
() (parentheses), 55
<> (not-equal-to operator), 132
{} (curly braces), 202
! (exclamation point), 157
% (percent sign), 50
* (asterisk), 47, 49
+ (plus sign), 47, 49, 452
- (minus sign), 47, 49, 452
/ (slash), 47, 49
= (equal sign), 49, 132
>= (greater-than-or-equal-to operator), 132–133, 134
<= (less-than-or-equal-to operator), 132
[] (square brackets), 357, 400
; (semicolon), 202

A

abbreviations, caution about use, 69
abstract classes, **492**
abstract data types (ADTs), **442**
abstraction, **52**, 52–53
access, private and public, **450**, 450–453
access specifiers, **450**, 452–453
    protected, **489**, 489–491
accessibility, **523**

accessor methods, **447**, 447–448
accumulators, 203–207, **204**
actions, user-initiated, 518
activity diagrams, **564**, 564–566
actual parameters, **388**
addition operator (+), 47, 49
addresses, **363**
ADTs (abstract data types), **442**
aggregations, **560**
algorithms, **9**, **330**
    bubble sort. See bubble sort
alphabetic sorts, 329
alphanumeric values, **39**
alternate keys, **585**
ambiguous methods, **408**
    avoiding, 408–411
American Standard Code for Information Interchange (ASCII), **626**, 627–629
ancestors, **486**
AND decisions, **135**, 135–145
    avoiding common errors, 143–144
    nested, 135, 138–140, 143–144
AND operator, **140**, 140–142
    combining with OR operator, precedence, 163–166
animation, **535**, 535–538
    free images, 538
annotation symbol, **67**
anomalies, **601**
    relational databases, 601
app(s), **2**

679